Table of Contents

Introduction

The Commentary on the Lectionary for Sundays and Feast Days

Volume 3

Almost exactly two years ago, volume one of this commentary on the lectionary was first published as a Kindle book. I produced it with no idea how well – if at all – it would be received. One year on, I believe I can claim a modest success. Verbal reaction was very positive, and at one point, for a couple of weeks, Volume 1 reached number one in the sales list for its Kindle category 'New Testament Mediations' though it must be admitted the category is a small one! It seemed a good idea therefore to continue the series, and so Volume 2 came into being. Now, volume 3 joins its companions

This commentary and its predecessors were written with a practical application in mind – Primarily for those engaged in the areas of preaching and catechesis, but also for anyone who would like to explore more fully the riches of lectionary gospel texts. Not everyone has the time or opportunity to consult the vast array of commentaries on the gospels, so this commentary arose because I wanted to share with others the fruits of my own studies in the gospels, with liturgical and catechetical purposes in mind. In 2006, I gained a Ph.D. from the University of Glasgow, and have since written articles and given talks and short courses on the Sunday lectionary gospel texts. I first produced notes on the Sunday gospels of the three year cycle for the "Priests for Scotland" website in July 2007. The series of postings came to their natural end in November 2010 once the three year cycle had been covered in full. Since then, I have been revising the notes, correcting anomalies and typing and other errors, and so they have emerged updated, edited and corrected, and hopefully more systematically developed throughout the liturgical year span. I know of a number of people – priests, deacons, catechists, readers of the gospels – who have found those notes useful, and so, encouraged by the fact that they were resourcing people in their earlier form, I decided to collate them into this book, starting with Year A, and following this with second and third volumes for years B and C. All of the notes in each of the volumes have been used as the basis of actual homilies and actual RCIA and other catechetical sessions.

The question which remains perhaps is, why did I bother to add yet another 'commentary' to the huge list that already exists? There are two main reasons for this. The first is that to the best of my knowledge, this kind of commentary doesn't exist elsewhere in print. There are many books and periodicals that provide sermon notes, ideas for sermons, stories for preachers and even complete short homilies. There are also excellent commentaries on each of the gospels. This book does not aim to add to these. This is a commentary dedicated exclusively to the gospel passages for Sundays of each of the three liturgical years in the Lectionary in use in the Roman Catholic Church (and to some extent, it will cover most of the Sunday gospel texts of the Common Lectionary). It aims to provide a distillation of up to date biblical scholarship which is relevant to the texts laid out for liturgical use. It therefore links passes according to the organisational principles of liturgical seasons, and the semi-continuous arrangement of gospel texts rather than according to the structure of the gospel itself. It most certainly does not aim to set out 'sermon notes' or themes for sermons. That having been said, the notes for each liturgical celebration are prefaced by some questions which I hope will prompt preachers, catechists and those who wish to reflect prayerfully and deeply on these gospels to a consideration of some profound issues raised by these gospel texts.

The notes concentrate almost entirely on the Sunday gospels; only occasionally there may be a reference to the other two readings. They are offered as a resource for preachers and anyone who makes use of the lectionary for personal or catechetical purposes and who wishes to understand a bit more fully the liturgical scriptural texts. They provide commentary on the lectionary readings: they are not 'sermon notes' and will not provide ready-made homilies or suggestions on themes for homilies. They offer a distillation of up-to-date biblical scholarship on the gospels, edited in order to provide useful exegetical information and scholarly opinion which may make life easier for preachers and catechists, leaders of scripture study groups, and those who desire to know more about the background not only to each passage, but to the gospels themselves as a whole. There are no footnotes or references, but there is at the end of the text a list of books and articles which were consulted in compiling this work, and which readers may find helpful for further reading. In the reflections for each Sunday, attempts are made to link to previous Sundays where appropriate (especially in Ordinary time), and pointers are given as to where themes have already been, or will subsequently be encountered. One of the biggest problems in the understanding of the gospels for preaching is, it seems to me, a lack of awareness of the way in which a given evangelist places individual episodes within a larger context. These notes may help to keep track of on-going themes developed through shorter episodes, and running over a series of weeks. Hence, the notes are arranged in 'chapters' which are governed by units from within the gospel.

An Introduction to Luke's Gospel

Some Important Characteristics of Luke's Gospel as found in The Lectionary for Sundays and Feast Days

If Mark's gospel was the first to be written, and we can with some justification credit its author with inventing the canonical gospel. So influential was this author (whose name and identity we do not know, despite the tradition of calling him Mark) that three other books, to a greater or lesser follow the pattern set by Mark. John, the name used for the author or authors of the fourth gospel, wrote a document which is quite different from Mark's prototype, but even this gospel shares some material with Mark (especially the feeding of the five thousand and Jesus walking on water, Mark 6:31-51; John 6:1-21). John apparently presupposes that his readers are familiar with the other gospels because he occasionally refers to things done by Jesus, but which he did not mention. There's an example of this in John 6:26 where Jesus appears to refer to signs he has worked, and the people saw. Famously, John only lists seven signs worked by Jesus during his life.

The dependence of Matthew and to a lesser extent Luke on Mark is if extreme importance. Not only have Matthew and Luke followed closely the order of events as Mark relates them, they also use large quantities of the prototype gospel almost entirely unchanged. Matthew uses around 90% of Matthew unchanged, and Luke a more modest 50%! Matthew and Luke occasionally share the material they have added to Mark's basic narrative, but they rarely, if ever, do so in exactly the same way. Thus, Matthew presents a major episode of Jesus teaching, which we know as the Sermon on the Mount. In Luke, a similar but much shorter sentence is known as the Sermon on the Plain, because Luke states that Jesus came down from the mountain after a night of prayer and proceeded to teach. Probably the the greatest difference we notice between Mark, and the two evangelists Matthew and Luke is the additional material these later writers add to both the beginning and the end of their gospels – the infancy narratives and passion and resurrection stories. Interestingly, the material that Matthew and Luke add at the beginning and the end of their gospels is unique to their gospels. Thus, there is no overlap between the infancy narratives of these two writers: there are no wise men in Luke, and no shepherds in Matthew! Likewise, Matthew's account of the soldiers on duty guarding Jesus' tomb is not found in Luke; and the famous incident of the two disciples and the unrecognised risen Jesus on the road to Emmaus is unique to Luke. What is interesting however is that Luke's post-resurrection stories bear a similarity to those found in John! Many of these features will be returned to in the main body of the commentary when the appropriate passages occur in the liturgical cycle.

Before we leave this introduction to the gospel of Luke, it is worth giving some consideration to the shape of this gospel, and the theological of its writer. There was a time when this gospel was recognised for the exquisite writing of its author, but the prevailing view was that although the evangelist could construct a wonderfully moving narrative, the gospel as a whole was short on theology. This view is thankfully no longer held by the majority of writers. Luke's literary skill is such that he is the only New Testament writer to have deliberately set out to construct a two volume work – the gospel, and the book we call the Acts of the Apostles. This may not sound like the most interesting piece of information on Luke the author you will be likely to encounter, but it does have significance for the way both the gospel and Acts are laid out. Although the books are placed apart in the New Testament as we know it – the Gospel of John comes between them, it is crucial that we consider these two as volumes of a single work. Possibly the reason that Luke wrote them separately was a very practical one: each 'book' is long enough to take up the whole of the maximum size of papyrus scroll which existed in his day. The gospel of Luke and the Acts of the Apostles are of comparable size, close to the maximum practical size for such documents, which suggests they were intended as two volumes of a single work.

When we consider Luke-Acts as a single, two-volume work, there are important consequences which we then must take into account. A two-volume work gives Luke freedom to arrange material in a way other evangelists can't. A good example is found in the way Luke handles the thorny issue of how Jesus was dealt with by the religious authorities. There is a strong body of opinion that Luke was a Gentile convert, but one who had a great respect for Jewish traditions. He may well have belonged to the category of 'God Fearer'; a Gentile who supported Jewish institutions financially, but who never converted to Judaism. Interestingly, Luke mentions two of these: the centurion who financed the synagogue in Capernaum (c.f. Luke 7:1-10), and Roman centurion Cornelius (c.f. Acts 10). Luke's respect for the Jewish religious system is such that in the Pasion Narrative, he avoids quoting the High Priest as accusing the Son of God of blasphemy! He does not dodge the issue entirely: he transfers the accusation to the trial of Stephen in Acts 7. This may sound a bit devious, but one of Luke's great themes in Acts is that disciples replicate details of Jesus' life and death in their own circumstances.

An important turning-point in Luke occurs at 9:51. Until then, Luke closely follows the structure of Mark, and then at this verse largely parts company with the earlier gospel structure. In a short phrase, Luke says "As the time drew near for him to be taken up to heaven, Jesus resolutely took the road for Jerusalem…" (Luke 9:51). This decision will overshadow the rest of Jesus' ministry. At times he will be preoccupied with his goal and speak of a baptism with which he must yet be baptised (Luke 12:50); at other times he will tell the most remarkable parables about the love and mercy of God (e.g. the three parables of the lost sheep, coin and son, Luke 15); he will reach out to outcasts like the Samaritans in parables (Luke 10:30-37); and he will seek out and save what was lost (Zacchaeus; Luke 19:1-11). There will be surprises too: Pharisees who give Jesus useful information that Herod is out to get him (Luke 13:31-32) and Jesus will frequently dine in the houses of Pharisees with the self-styled great and good, although it has to be acknowledged that these tales of dinner-gatherings tend not to end well! Consistently, Jesus is cast by Luke as the Prophet, the fulfilment of the one promised by Moses in Deuteronomy 18:15; "Your God will raise up for you a prophet like myself, from among yourselves… to him you must listen" (Deuteronomy 18:15).

There is a consistency throughout Luke, even when the narrative appears to roam freely; Luke has the ability as a writer to draw us back to the central theme of Jesus, the Saviour, the Prophet, the one whose destiny is to die in Jerusalem. This is realised by disciples after the resurrection when they wander away from Jerusalem, but meet the Risen Christ whom they do not recognise. As he explains the scriptures which say the Christ MUST suffer and die and rise again, as he breaks bread with them, they recognise his presence among them, even though he has vanished from sight. As we listen to the words of the Risen Christ through the medium of the gospel of Luke, as we break the bread of the Eucharist today, we too may be drawn into the mystery of the saving acts of God brought to us through the saviour, born of the virgin Mary, first acknowledged by shepherds, and finally recognised in the breaking of bread.

The Lectionary for Sundays and Feast Days, Volume 3
Year C

The layout of this Commentary.

The commentary notes for each Sunday or Feast can be accessed individually, although for easier navigation, they are grouped under chapter headings as well.

The Four Major Seasons of the Year (Advent, Christmas, Lent and Easter) are set out in Chapters 1 – 4. Each Sunday and Feast Day has a separate title which can be 'clicked on' to access the commentary on the gospel for that particular day.

The Sundays of Ordinary Time are presented in units from Chapters 5 – 9

Chapter 10 is an appendix containing notes for Feasts which when they fall on a Sunday, take preference over that Sunday – unless these already exist among the seasons (e.g. The Epiphany during Christmas, or The Ascension during Easter).

Chapter 1.
Advent and Christmas Year C

Introduction

Can one of the four gospels be described as 'better' than the others? I don't think we would ever think in those terms, although we may each have our own favourite. I believe it is important however to leave aside preferences when we consider each gospel as it appears in its own liturgical year. Each gospel has its own special characteristics, and because of this, each is capable of shedding light on the mystery and ministry of Jesus of Nazareth in a way which might not be just as obvious in the other gospels. Our task is to consider as widely and as fully as possible the particular features of Jesus of Nazareth which are brought out in each evangelist's portrait of him. Then, over the three year liturgical cycle, we will be much better equipped to recognise more completely the Jesus depicted in all of the gospels, and the God he reveals to us as His Father and our Father.

Each gospel has its own particular theological stamp. Mark, particularly in the second half of his gospel, focuses on the Jesus who is revealed as the Son of God precisely in the manner of his death. During his lifetime however,

Jesus goes unrecognised by human beings, and especially by his disciples to whom he gives intensive teaching throughout the journey narrative of chapters 8 – 10. Matthew depicts Jesus as the one who fulfils the scriptures – from Moses, to the Law itself, and who constantly reminds us that Jesus' actions were carried out 'in order to fulfil the scriptures'. John's gospel is of course the most theological of the four, from the profound concept of the Word Made Flesh, through Jesus, the One sent by the Father, to Jesus, the one who fulfils the true meaning of the major Jewish Feasts, not to mention the Temple itself, and finally Jesus, the One who gives glory to God in his Hour, when he, the Son of Man, is lifted up so that all who see him might be saved. Powerful stuff!

This brings us to Luke, the gospel we will read on almost all of the Sundays of the coming year. There was a time, and not so long ago, when it was thought that although the gospel of Luke was written with consummate artistry, it was rather short on theological content. Thankfully, those days are past. What we do find is that Luke's theology tends to be spread widely throughout the gospel, rather than laid out in major sections or organised into individual units. In the course of the year, we will become very aware of Luke's use of important and recurrent themes. These will include the proclamation of the Good News, a view of a salvation which is worked out in the here and now and not just in a time to come, and that Jesus is the Prophet who will fulfil his destiny through his death in Jerusalem. We will find that Jerusalem and the Temple are important and recurring motifs, and there will be a strong emphasis on prayer, especially in the life of Jesus, but also particularly in the Acts of the Apostles. Although Acts is the second volume of Luke's two-volume work, will not often figure in this commentary, which is primarily concerned with the gospel passages for Sundays and Feast Days. Of course, resurrection is the major theme because, as Luke stresses, it was ordained (or written) that the Christ would suffer, die, and so enter into his glory. The Holy Spirit is prominent from the very beginning of the gospel in the annunciation stories, the conception and birth of Jesus. The Spirit is present at his baptism and throughout his ministry. When Jesus acts, the Spirit is upon him and has anointed him, and of course the role of the Spirit from Pentecost onward is the major theme in Acts. Luke's gospel is always associated with the preferential option for the poor, and this will be a recurring, but not entirely dominating theme in the course of the year ahead. Most, if not all of these themes are to be found in Advent and Christmas liturgical gospel texts. The Spirit will come upon several people even before Jesus is born; the first humans to hear of his birth will be the marginalised shepherds, ensuring that the good news of his birth is proclaimed to the poor. Prophecy will abound, and an important and recurring motif will be that all of the events which are being recounted here, while being presented as details of the unfolding divine plan, will also be firmly rooted in human history. Salvation is of divine origin, but it unfolds in the here and now of human existence. This last point is a good place to begin our Advent reflections.

1st Sunday of Advent Year C; Luke 21:25-28. 34-36

Stand up straight, hold your heads up, because your liberation is at hand.

Questions to ponder

☐   How do you react to the thought of the return of the son of Man?
☐   Does it come as a surprise to hear that we should stand up straight in the presence of the Son of Man?
☐   How are we supposed to maintain readiness and alertness at all times?

Of the four major liturgical seasons, Advent is the most at risk of being swamped by its neighbour! It's not hard to see why: we're all too familiar with the annual commercial onset of all things Christmas related weeks before Advent gets underway. As a result, Advent can disappear into little more than a prelude to Christmas. This is a great pity, because Advent is such a rich season in its own right. Admittedly, it can be difficult to keep track of the multiple themes that are part of the season – the second coming of Christ for the first two to three weeks, and then the series of Infancy Narrative gospel passages that we read from 17 December onwards, passages which are all too often called Christmas stories, but which are very much Old Testament-oriented, and therefore Advent-oriented. It should, however, be easier to do justice to the four Sundays of Advent, since each year these follow the same theme from Sunday to Sunday. The pattern of gospel readings each year during Advent is always the same: 1st Sunday, a focus on the day when the Son of Man will return. Without any variation, this is the way the Church begins its new year – every year! John the Baptist always makes his first appearance on the 2nd Sunday of Advent, looking very much like the prophet Elijah in appearance (animal skins, strange diet, wilderness dwelling), and as a voice in the wilderness, proclaiming the need to prepare a way for the Lord. John returns on the 3rd Sunday of Advent, and the focus is on his baptism for forgiveness of sins, and his message about true repentance. Finally, on the 4th Sunday of Advent, the gospel is always an Annunciation story. This is clear enough for Years A and B, but in year C, the 4th Sunday of Advent gospel is the one we usually call the Visitation. I will be suggesting, however, that in the Advent context we should consider this one as an Annunciation story as well.

We could do worse than begin by paying close attention to the opening words of the gospel for today (not the introductory, "Jesus said to his disciples", because these are inserted into the text for liturgical purposes so that we know to whom the passage is addressed). Jesus' first words to be read on the first day of the new liturgical year are: "There will be signs". The final verse of this passage begins "stay awake" or, in other translations, 'stay alert'. Between these verses, the tone is set for the year ahead – remaining alert to recognise the signs which will be there for us to see. So far so good, but what are these signs? For what are we to remain alert? The first verse puts us in the picture. The signs to which Jesus refers will be in the sun, moon and stars. This scene was also described for us in Mark's gospel for Sunday 33 of year B. In both gospels this is the time for the return of the Son of Man, and both gospels are insistent that the signs are not to be confused with portents of earthly disasters. The one thing we do not learn in either gospel though is when these things will happen. Gospel signs like these have captivated readers for two millennia.. Jesus' opponents had asked him, as a test, for a sign from heaven (Luke 11:16); just before the present episode, disciples had asked what signs there would be after Jesus had prophesied that the Jerusalem Temple would be so thoroughly destroyed that not one stone would be left standing upon another (Luke 21:7). What Jesus now speaks about, however, neither has to do with the Temple and its destruction, nor with the suffering to be undergone by people when it happens. Instead, Jesus states that there will be confusion among all nations when the signs in the sun and moon are seen; people will die in fear as the very heavens will be shaken. It must be noted however that these signs are not in the least related to floods, earthquakes, tempests or the like. The signs to come will be cosmic, and not earthly. When the cosmic bodies (commonly thought in the ancient world to be heavenly powers) collapse, this will be the prelude to the Son of Man arriving in a cloud with power and glory. So, the obvious question is: what is the appropriate thing to do when this happens? It is apparent that earlier advice on what to do when faced with the destruction of the Temple - run for your life, escape to the mountains - is no longer appropriate. The return of the Son of Man means judgement for the entire world, and there will be nowhere to escape. This is why 'the nations' will die of fear, but of course the question remains, what are the disciples, the followers of Jesus, ourselves supposed to do in the face of these signs? The answer is surprising and very encouraging: disciples who experience these things are to stand up straight, hold their heads high, and realise that their liberation is at hand. Paradoxically, the very thing that will strike terror into the hearts of those whom disciples may fear is the very thing that signals their salvation (liberation)

A prominent theme of the gospel of Luke, already referred to in the introduction to these notes and to which we will return from to time, is that salvation is not to be worked out in some future yet to be disclosed, but in the present. This is the note that the gospel for the 1st Sunday of the new liturgical year ends. Disciples can prepare for that future day that Jesus prophesies by their alertness now. They are to watch themselves, that is, look after themselves, or look out for themselves. They are to ensure their hearts are not coarsened by drunkenness and debauchery, or the cares of life. In Hebrew and the Aramaic language which would have been spoken by Jesus, the heart was the place where thought and moral decision was located, rather than being the seat of the emotions with which we in today's world have become more familiar. Perhaps then we should re-think Jesus' instructions in terms of our minds and thoughts being coarsened. This idea of being coarsened by drunkenness is found in earlier chapters of this gospel. In Luke 8:14 Jesus, when interpreting his own parable about the sower going out to sow seed, warned against the danger of the word of God being choked by the cares and riches and pleasures of life. Drunkenness was also mentioned in the parable about the manager in charge of the other slaves who, in the absence of the master, gets drunk and abuses the slaves (Luke 12:45). Does Luke mean literal drunkenness? Presumably he does not exclude it, but he is more likely highlighting the effect of drunkenness which is a highly diminished state of awareness. Those who are seriously intoxicated are unlikely to be in a state of readiness for anything, and the day of the son of Man will come suddenly – in fact, it will be like a trap snapping shut! Throughout the gospel, as we shall see at various points in the coming year, the Lukan Jesus

advocates praying at all times to enable us to be in a constant state of
alertness. The upshot of praying at all times, remaining metaphorically alert,
sober and awake is that we are then constantly engaged in the ministry and
life of Jesus as it unfolds for us in the gospel message. This means that we
can embrace as good news the advice that we can stand with confidence in
the presence of the Son of Man.

All of this is contained in brief in one of Luke's parables which we shall read
later in the year. In this particular parable, one of those unique to Luke, Jesus
warns, "the master of the house has got up and locked the door, you may find
yourself knocking on the door, saying, "Lord, open to us" but he will answer,
"I do not know where you come from". Then you will find yourself saying,
"We once ate and drank in your company; you taught in our streets" but he
will reply, "I do not know where you come from. Away from me, all you
wicked men" (Luke 13:25-27). The parable was told in response to the
question, 'will many be saved?' Jesus 'parabolic answer makes it clear that it
is not enough to have been in Jesus' company, to have had him 'visit our
streets', to have 'dined on the same restaurant in which he was dining'; we
need to be part of what he has taught, we need to be recognisable as his
followers. If we do this, then we can stand with confidence in his presence –
a wonderfully reassuring message to hear!

2nd Sunday of Advent, Year C; Luke 3:1-6

John the Baptist, part 1

Questions to ponder

- ☐ How do we 'knock down mountains' and 'fill in valleys'?
- ☐ Repentance means change of mind; what must we change (i.e. repent of) if we are to see the salvation of our God?
- ☐ Is there an equivalent of John the Baptist in our own day?

All four gospels present John the Baptist as the fulfilment of Isaiah 40:3-5.
For each evangelist, he is integral to the immediate preparation for the
ministry of Jesus which is imminent, but the image of John somehow seems
to fit with the themes of the gospel of Luke even more fully than it does the
other three. This is because of Luke's recurring theme of salvation unfolding
in the present, and not just in some indeterminate future. Luke reinforces this
point with a touch found only in this gospel, and that is with his inclusion of

historical detail. Not only does this add solemnity to the account that is to follow but it also roots the ministry of Jesus firmly with in the sphere of the religious and political context of his time. Luke has done this already with his (open to question) account of the census (allegedly – see the gospel for Christmas Midnight Mass for more on this) called by the Emperor Augustus prior to the birth of Jesus (Luke 2:1-5), and now he does it again as he lays open the main body of his gospel. He begins with 'universal' detail (Tiberius Caesar is the Roman Emperor), turns to the national political scene (Pontius Pilate was governor of Judaea), and finally moves on to the local political situation (Herod was Tetrarch of Galilee, and his brother Philip was tetrarch of Ituraea and Trachonitis, whereas Lysanias was tetrarch of Abilene). Having given us a snapshot of life in the Roman Empire as it affects Palestine at the time, Luke then describes the religious situation. He states that Annas and Caiaphas held the high priesthood in those days; but there is a problem with that. There could only be one High Priest at any given time, and at the time of John's ministry, Caiaphas was High Priest, holding office between 18 and 36 AD. His father in law Annas had been High Priest from 5 to 16 AD, when he was deposed. Perhaps Luke is confusing the term Chief Priest, of which there were many, with High Priest, of which there was only one. Chief Priests were members of the High Priestly Families. If John's Passion Narrative is anything to go by however, Annas appears to have been the 'power behind the throne' (c.f. John 18:3).

Luke's intention is not primarily to write an historical treatise of the period however; his aim in listing the prominent characters of religious and political life in Palestine at the time of John the Baptist (also referred to here as John, son of Zechariah to ensure continuity with the story of John's birth in the infancy narratives), is to stress that John proclaims the Word of God in a very specific time and place. Using the Greek Septuagint Old Testament, the sources Luke usually chooses for Old Testament texts rather than the Hebrew text, John announces, or proclaims, what the Jerusalem Bible calls "a baptism of repentance for the forgiveness of sins". The Greek phrase is tricky to translate, *baptisma metanoias eis aphesin hamartiōn*. Baptism means literally immersion, and repentance means literally change of mind. So far so good: a baptism of repentance then is an immersion in a change of mind: a change of mind-set or thinking, but what about the other bit? It depends largely on what the preposition *eis* is understood to mean: it could be translated as 'for', or 'to' or 'toward', or even 'for the purpose of'. What is apparent is that for

Luke, the change of mind which is repentance is usually connected to the forgiveness of sin. The change of mind must therefore denote a different outlook in life which leads to a desire for the forgiveness of sins. Using Isaiah 40:3-5, John gives direction to the announcement of his baptism of repentance: a way is to be prepared for the Lord. To create this way, this path, every mountain must be laid low, every valley filled in. Luke alone adds these lines to the basic call to make a way for the Lord. He also adds, "and all mankind (literally, all flesh) shall see the salvation of God" (Luke 3:6). The addition serves well the Lukan theology that salvation is not a vague concept for the future, but begins to be worked out in the present, due to the proclamation of the word of God.

The main purpose of this episode about John, presenting him as a prophetic figure paving the way for the ministry of the One who is to follow him and to make clear his path by proclaiming a baptism of repentance, is to introduce him as the one called by God to prepare for the inauguration of the period of salvation which this gospel will outline.

3rd Sunday of Advent, Year C; Luke 3:10-18

John the Baptist, part 2

Questions to ponder

☐ Is there a contradiction between John's extreme appearance (wilderness dwelling, wearing animal skins and strange diet, even though these are not explicitly mentioned in Luke) and his humane ethical teaching outlined to those who ask what they must do?

☐ What aspects of John's preaching are prophetic in relation to the main body of the gospel of Luke?

☐ What does John mean when he says a more powerful (stronger) one will baptise with the Holy Spirit and with fire?

For the second time this Advent, John the Baptist is the central figure in the gospel narrative, and once more the Advent theme from the perspective of Luke focuses on the present as the time in which God's plans unfold for humanity. This time, there is no real reference to his prophetic proclamation about preparing a way for the Lord, or even directly about his baptism. Instead, John the moral teacher emerges. In response to his teaching so far, people ask the very practical question "what must we do?" This is their response to John's insistence that for repentance to be sincere, its fruits must be visible. John had addressed the crowds that came to him for baptism in very severe terms (not read on either of these Advent Sundays). He said to them "Brood of vipers, who warned you to fly from the retribution that is coming? But if you are repentant, produce the appropriate fruits, and do not think of telling yourselves, 'We have Abraham for our father' because, I tell you, God can raise children for Abraham from these stones. Yes, even now the axe is laid to the roots of the trees, so that any tree which fails to produce good fruit will be cut down and thrown on the fire" (Luke 3:7-9). These words are uncompromising, but when individuals, or particular groups ask him what they should be doing, his demands turn out to be remarkably achievable. The question "what must we do?" is put to John by three different groups of people. The first group is designated only as "all the people". They are told to share what they have; those with two tunics are to share with someone who has none. The tunic was an undergarment, usually worn beneath another one, called a *himation*, but occasionally worn in pairs in cold weather. If someone possesses a spare tunic, this is to be given to anyone who is without. Likewise, those with food are to share what they have with those who have none. These instructions, far from earth shattering in their demands, characterise John's moral teaching which is about the adoption of an attitude which results in watchfulness for, and action on behalf of those who are in need. Repentance, therefore, needs to be rooted in the change of thinking that moves away from self-focus and which instead becomes directed to an awareness of the situation of those around us. The second group to ask John what they are to do is made up of what English bible translations still inaccurately describe as tax-collectors. By this time, the Roman authorities had abolished the thoroughly corrupt system of tax collection which had remained in the hands of the patrician families of Rome. Augustus Caesar had introduced a system whereby people paid the state for the privilege of collecting taxes. They were required to return a certain amount to the Empire, and they were thereafter free to charge additionally what they needed to make their own living, and to pay for staff to do the actual collecting. Zacchaeus (Luke 19:1-10), so a better way of describing the type of person called *telōnion* in Greek - those who worked at the tolls at locations like that described when Matthew (Levi) is called by Jesus in Luke 5:27 – might be 'toll collectors'. In popular perception, they were just as guilty of corruption and fraud as the previous tax-collectors had been, and they were highly suspect because they were still employed by, or at least on behalf of the Romans. It is interesting that John does not advise toll-collectors to change occupation; instead, he presents a simple rule for toll agents seeking his baptism of repentance: they are to take in payment from people no more than they are due (Luke 3:13). John offers no opinion on what they might be due for their own expenses: that they are to work that out according to the principles of justice, and not be motivated by greed would appear to be the logical conclusion. The third group consists of soldiers, possibly either those of Herod Antipas, or Roman auxiliaries co-opted for police duties. Neither military group was held in high esteem in Jewish circles and these soldiers were usually considered to be operating outside the recognised bounds of Jewish piety by working as soldiers in either group. So John's response to their request 'what must we do' is once again surprising. He does not urge tis group to change profession any more than he had done with the tax agents; he simply instructs them not to harass or bully people – no intimidation, no threatening behaviour. They are to be content with what they are paid, and are therefore to avoid temptation to augment their salary by extortion.

These three responses to the question 'what must we do' are noteworthy. We are to presume that the questions are asked almost in despair, given John's proclamation of a baptism of repentance. Surprisingly though, John's suggested reforms are remarkably accessible. At no stage does he try to persuade anyone to adopt his own rigorous, not to say extreme, lifestyle; indeed, his advice to those who approach him in this passage is that their repentance is to be rooted very firmly in the daily lives with which they are familiar. Once again, we are confronted with the idea that the plans of God are always unfolding in specific times in human history, and in the daily and concrete expressions of the lives of real and specific humans. For Luke, salvation is worked out in real time, and has an immediate effect in the lives of real people, even if it will not be completed in them or for them in this life. John has a final word to say about his own role. Luke tells us that, presumably due to the success of his preaching, and his popular appeal to the otherwise marginalised (we have already heard of the positive response of toll-agents and soldiers), an expectation was beginning to arise: could John be the awaited Messiah? John dissociates himself from such speculation. He declares "I baptise you with water, but someone is coming, someone who is more powerful than I am, and I am not fit to undo the strap of his sandals; he will baptise you with the Holy Spirit and fire" (Luke 3:16). The stronger one is the one who will be in a position to judge between people, and has his winnowing shovel or fork (better than fan) at the ready for the separation of the wheat from the chaff. Baptism with the Holy Spirit and fire will recur not only in the gospel, but will reappear in the second volume of Luke's work, the Acts of the Apostles, with the Pentecost narrative. In the gospel itself, Jesus will say "I have come to bring fire to the earth, and how I wish it were blazing already! There is a baptism I must still receive, and how great is my distress till it is over!" (Luke 12:49-50). Notice that in this gospel John does not say that the stronger one will come after him; Luke omits this presumably to avoid any suggestion that even though stronger, the one John speaks of is John's disciple. For the present, John now leaves the scene with Luke's comment, "As well as this, there were many other things he said to exhort the people and to announce the Good News to them" (Luke 3:18). The implication is that Luke has only scratched the surface in his description of John and his ministry.

4th Sunday of Advent, Year C; Luke 1:39-44

A Visitation that is really an Annunciation story

Questions to ponder

☐　　What insights into the nature of Mary's not yet born child in this passage do we receive only through the action of the Holy Spirit in our lives?
☐　　What prophetic action can we make (or already do make) to drawn attention to the presence of the Lord in our contemporary world.
☐　　Why do you think we never hear of Elizabeth again in any part of the New Testament after the Infancy Narratives end?

On the fourth Sunday of Advent in years A and B, the gospel is an 'annunciation' story, which is also wrapped up in prophecy and its fulfilment. Matthew 1:18-24 in year A presents the account of 'how Jesus Christ came to be born' from Joseph's perspective. The angel of the Lord, unnamed, appears to Joseph in a dream, and reveals how what has happened to Mary, his betrothed, is God's plan, and that she has conceived by the Holy Spirit. This happens in fulfilment of the prophet Isaiah, "The virgin will conceive and give birth to a son and they will call him Emmanuel, a name which means 'God-is-with-us'" (Matthew 1:23, quoting Isaiah 7:14). In year B, Luke 1:26-

38 tells the story from Mary's perspective. The angel Gabriel is sent by God to Mary with substantially the same message. She will conceive and bear a son by the power of the Holy Spirit. The element of prophecy this time is that the angel offers a sign that nothing is impossible to God. This is achieved by pointing to Mary's relative Elizabeth, long considered by all to be barren, but now in the six month of her pregnancy. Mary will be able to see this prophetic word fulfilled in the birth of Elizabeth's son. (c.f. Luke 1:36-37). The passage for year C is the continuation of Luke's narrative, and is usually called 'the visitation' (Luke 1:39-44), because it describes the meeting between Mary and her cousin which takes place in Elizabeth's home following the angel's message to Mary. The story is however about more than a visit. Commendable as it is for a young woman to look after her older kinswoman, there are riches to this story which far exceed the sentimental interpretation to which it is often restricted.

Logically, it makes much more sense to consider this story as yet another annunciation narrative, firstly because from a liturgical point of view this is in keeping with the equivalent Sunday themes for years A and B, and secondly (and more importantly from a textual point of view), because this short narrative contains elements both of annunciation and prophetic word and its fulfilment which are similar to those in the other two passages. Of course, there are some notable differences between this passage and the two we normally refer to as 'annunciations'. Most noticeably, no angel is present in this episode: in the other two, the angel of the Lord (in Matthew), or the angel Gabriel (Luke) conveys the message concerning the child to be born. Even in the similar story of Gabriel announcing John the Baptist's birth to Zechariah in the temple (a parallel and a contrast to Mary's annunciation), the angelic messenger is crucial, but not in this narrative. The similarities are more striking than the differences, however.

Luke demonstrates his considerable ability as a writer in this passage. He takes a short scene, with little by way of story line, and he uses it to convey a large amount of very important information. He also uses it to link together strands of narrative that are not yet quite connected, and to pave the way for connections not yet established. In the meeting of two pregnant relatives, he reinforces that the stories of Jesus' and John's births and their preceding announcements are linked. In two short phrases, Luke tells us that Mary sets out immediately (i.e., after Gabriel's departure, and that she goes to Zechariah's house in the hill country of Judah, to visit her kinswoman

Elizabeth. The stories of Zechariah and Mary and their encounter with Gabriel are now brought together. With an extraordinary economy of words, Luke brings 'the story so far' up to date through Elizabeth's apparently perfunctory contribution to the conversation. Mary does not speak at all in this episode, although her very full reply in the form of the Magnificat follows immediately.

The annunciation aspect of the narrative soon becomes apparent when Mary arrives. As soon as Elizabeth hears Mary's greeting, the child in her womb leaps for joy, and Elizabeth is filled with the Holy Spirit. Taking the second of these aspects first, it is only by the power of the Holy Spirit that Elizabeth can have known that Mary is to be the mother of her Lord! Her description of Mary's unborn child has connotations of the child's divinity when read in the context of the previous episode. Elizabeth takes her place among those who are informed about the birth of the one who will be called son of the most High (Luke 1:32). As in the other annunciation passages in this gospel and in Matthew's, there is a strong element of prophecy at work here. At the outset, Mary is able to witness the fulfilment of the angel's prophecy about her kinswoman Elizabeth bearing a son, despite the common perception that she is barren. Elizabeth's own greeting to Mary has the appearance of a prophetic utterance, and even in his mother's womb, Elizabeth's son makes a 'prophetic statement' of annunciation, leaping for joy as soon as Mary's greeting reaches Elizabeth's ears (Luke 1:44). Even before his birth, John performs the function that he will later define as the hallmark of his ministry: pointing to the stronger one who will come after him, just as we heard on the third Sunday of Advent.

On the final Sunday of the Advent season, we see an important characteristic of the Infancy Narratives; they contain in miniature so many aspects of the main body of the gospels for which they act as prologues. The material they contain are prophetic, pointing the way to the full ministry and ultimate destiny of the one who was to come. Within one week of this particular Sunday, we celebrate Christmas. Before we do, it is important to read all of the Infancy Narrative passages that are presented in the liturgy between 17 and 24 December for what they are: Advent passages, rich in imagery and prophecy about the one whose birth we will eventually – but not quite yet – celebrate.

Chapter 2

Christmas: The Fulfilment of Prophecy

(Since many of the Christmas texts do not change from year to year, a large proportion of these notes are reprints of those offered for Year A)

Questions to ponder:

☐   As the Christmas Liturgies unfold, do we learn more by a fuller appreciation of the art of the evangelists in crafting the narratives?

☐   Or to put it another way, does the collection of traditional images help or hinder our appreciation of the effect of the Incarnation of our lives?

☐   And how far do the evangelists' portraits of society at the time of Jesus' birth inform our understanding of our own society?

The Christmas season packs a lot of celebration into a few weeks, or from a biblical point of view, draws on many rich biblical images and themes from a relatively small portion of the gospels: almost, but not entirely from the second chapters of the gospels of Matthew and Luke. The problem for preachers at Christmas, of course, is of trying to find something new to say about such familiar stories, at precisely the time when the luxury of opportunity to reflect on these is distinctly limited. In these notes, I'll try not so much to present something new (which arguably is near to impossible to do), as to seek out motifs and images that link the very familiar ideas together in a way that allows them to speak freshly to us.

To begin, it may be useful to return at least one of our themes for Advent: the theme of the closeness of the Lord in the very ordinary circumstances of daily life. The Advent readings used prophetic images (Jesus' own prophetic words in Jerusalem about the reality of his return, and how it will impinge on ordinary living, John the Baptist and his insistence that the Lord is very near, and finally, the power of the Holy Spirit empowering Elizabeth to recognise the unique nature of the child her kinswoman Mary bears. The liturgies for Christmas take up those ideas strongly. The gospel for the Christmas Vigil Mass includes Matthew's genealogy of Jesus, before going on to gives the account of how Jesus Christ came to be born – or more accurately, how Joseph became involved in the process. It is unfortunate that in the growing enthusiasm for the Christmas Vigil Mass, there is less enthusiasm for the full text of the gospel! An impassioned appeal: please read the WHOLE passage! Midnight Mass and the Christmas Dawn Mass divide up the story of Jesus' birth and the first set of reactions to this event (Luke 2:1-14, and 15-20 respectively). Finally, the Christmas Day Mass uses the Prologue to John's gospel, which, as well as giving advance notice of the major themes of this gospel, also gives us material for reflection in the form of poetic writing which covers all the ingredients of the Christmas story. All of these show that the prophecies which had dealt with the nearness of the Lord being so close that lives would change, have now become a reality in the lives of those who were first challenged to engage with the birth of the One who is Saviour, Christ, and Lord.

Christmas Vigil Mass, Matthew 1:1-25.
How many people would rush to the Christmas Vigil if they realised in advance that they were to be treated to the 42 generations listed in Matthew's version of the 'genealogy of Jesus Christ, Son of David, and Son of Abraham' (Matthew 1:1)? And yet, there is a lot that can be done with this passage, even if there is time only for a short homily on a very busy night. To begin with, it could be worth noting that the generations serve to present the credentials of the one who is to be born of Mary, but whose natural father is not Joseph. Joseph's descent from David is presented in the list, and as Mary's betrothed, Joseph is able to pass descent from David onto her child, who is also Son of God by the dynamic, creative activity of the Holy Spirit (see notes for the 4th Sunday of Advent for a fuller treatment of this).
There is another important facet of the genealogy that may repay a further look, again drawing on the theme of the nearness of God to humanity. As we examine the list, we find that Jesus' ancestors were far from perfect! Even his greatest ancestors had some very shady aspects to their personality: the great Abraham our father in faith, was not averse to telling quite big lies to his own skin: Abraham passes off Sarai his wife as his sister, because he fears if the Egyptians know he and Sarai are married, they will kill him and spare her (Genesis 12:12-13), so he persuades Sarai to lie for him! Jacob cheated his brother Esau out of the latter's birth right; not content with that, he made himself wealthy at the expense of his kinsman Laban, and had to flee for his life. David is well-known for behaviour with Bathsheba which we probably should not elaborate on at Christmas! Solomon and Ahaz were disasters as kings (the former after a very promising start and the help of his father David's vast wealth). This is only a sample of the shortcomings of some of the best known in the list! The moral of this story is that God's dealings with

humanity are not restricted to the highly virtuous. Nor are God's dealings predictable. At significant stages in the Royal line, discontinuity occurs – always marked in the genealogy by the introduction of a woman who cause the line to take a different route (Ruth and David, Bathsheba – who is not actually named - and Solomon, Mary and Jesus). So, the passage which leads in the Christmas season makes plain that it is the ordinary if the often unexpected features our human living which provide the precise locations of where the Lord has chosen to dwell among humanity, and the Christmas season allows us to explore this in fuller detail, and to ponder the responses of those confronted with that reality.

Christmas: Midnight Mass. Luke 2:1-12

Question to ponder:

☐   The Christmas story is about of the things of God being ignored by the people of the world in which they take place. Many would say that nothing has changed. How can we attempt to change this?

In this passage, Luke seeks to locate the events of the birth of the Saviour firmly within the real world of the time – even if he is not particularly accurate in his detail! For Luke, it is important to stress that all of this occurred within the Great power of the Roman Empire, when Augustus was Emperor, and *Pax Augusta* prevailed. Luke falls down in accuracy in places, but the gospel is not a treatise on Roman history: its interest in matters Roman is confined to locating the human birth of the Saviour in a rea period of human history, and not in some mythical past. Luke's text provides the opportunity for us to develop further the Advent theme that the arrival of the Messiah was an event with concrete consequences for all who would engage with it.

Luke alone among the evangelists lists the very concrete realities of the birth of Jesus, citing those aspects of the story that are so well known: the census, no room at the inn, swaddling clothes, and of course a manger, but we must ask what these actually refer to. The word used by Luke for the place where Mary and Joseph unsuccessfully sought accommodation, and which is traditionally - and inaccurately – translated as 'inn', is also the word (*kataluma*) which he uses to describe the room in Jerusalem where Jesus gathered with his disciples to celebrate the Passover (2:11). In the latter case, this room clearly refers to a place within a house, in the present example, it is usually understood as an open shelter, where travellers would literally lay down their baggage for the night. There is another intriguing feature that we will return to later in the Christmas gospels: in Matthew, the magi visit Mary and Joseph and Jesus in a *house*; could it be that Mary and Joseph had eventually found accommodation, after the birth of the child, in the place where their first attempt had been unsuccessful? This is of course mere speculation, but perhaps it does no harm to have a second or third think about some of the details surrounding this most familiar of gospel stories, to help us appreciate what the texts actually say.

The text tells us that when Mary gave birth to her child, she wrapped him in swaddling clothes, and laid him in a manger. The manger could have been outdoors, or it may have been located in part of the house where animals were kept, so its reference does not determine that Jesus was born in a stable. There have been various attempts to trace the significance of swaddling clothes. One suggestion has been a reference to the Book of Wisdom, attributed to king Solomon, although written many centuries after his time, and who describes his birth like that of any other human; "I too, when I was born, drew in the common air, I fell on the same ground that bears us all, a wail my first sound, as for all the rest. I was nurtured in swaddling clothes, with every care. No king has known any other beginning of existence; for all there is one way only into life, as out of it" (Wisdom 7:3-6). Or is that to read too much into the reference to swaddling clothes? After all, it has to be acknowledged that the correct translation should read something like 'strips (or bands) of cloth'. The Jerusalem Bible, RSV and some other translations, have opted to remain with the 'swaddling clothes' which are found in the King James Bible. Language aside, does the expression say anything about kingly birth? Perhaps not. The Palestinian custom seems to have been to wrap the limbs of a new-born baby tightly with bands of cloth to ensure that they grew straight. There is therefore the distinct possibility that the reference to this practice in 2:7 is simply a reflection on the typical scene of human birth: yet again the text appears to emphasise that the unique event of the birth of the Messiah inserts itself into the far from unique circumstances of daily human life! If anything, this is reinforced in the first mention of the shepherds, 2:8. A simple statement introduces them to us: they were working in shifts through the night to watch their flocks. In other words, this was an ordinary night's work for the shepherds, just as they would have done every night. The shepherds will merit a closer look later, but this first reference to them certainly reinforces the commonplace nature of the story's setting. There is, however, at least the possibility that in these details of Jesus' birth, we have prophetic allusions to what is to follow. It is always possible, for example, that the reference to 'no place at the inn' is a foreshadowing of Jesus' own words to a would-be disciple that the son of man has no place to lay down his head (Luke 9:58), or that the reference to his being bound in strips of cloth foreshadow Joseph of Arimathea wrapping Jesus' dead body in a shroud (Luke 23:53). However, it is far from clear that Luke intends such an explicit connection between these other episodes.

If it is true that Luke has so far been trying to accentuate the unremarkable in the birth of Jesus, the same cannot be said of what now follows. The shepherds may have expected a night's work like any other, but they could scarcely have expected the appearance of the angel of the Lord (unnamed), and the shining of the glory of the Lord all around them. This description of the glory of the Lord is of course completely in accord with the Old Testament concept of an experience of the nearness of God, bound up in the Hebrew word *kabod*, which also means 'heavy'. The angel's appearance, the glory of the Lord, and the content of the message presage the fulfilment of the prophetic prediction uttered by Zechariah (1:78). However, this is initially lost on the shepherds: they are quite simply terrified. And they are in good company here: terror at the glory of the Lord is mentioned elsewhere, e.g. the prophet himself at Isaiah's call to the prophetic role (Isaiah 6:1-5), and Peter, John and James at the Transfiguration (Luke 9:34).

That the angelic manifestation is far from common-place is evident from the content of the message which follows. Firstly, that the message is good news is stressed. Secondly, the good news is about the previously indicated saviour: the child who is born is also Messiah [Christ] and Lord (*Christos* and *Kyrios*). Thirdly, in true Biblical fashion there is a sign attached to the words (this is reminiscent of Isaiah 7:7, which we read on the 4th Sunday of Advent). This time, as we shall see, the sign is not so much the circumstances of the birth of the child (unlike the Isaiah scenario already mentioned), but that those circumstances are exactly as the angel described them. When the sign is witnessed, the angel's prophecy will be fulfilled.

For the remaining verses of the chapter found in the Midnight Mass liturgy, the shepherds are not to be seen or heard. Attention now turns to the heavenly host (army?) whose sole intent is to focus on the glory of the Lord, and to sing the hymn which will recur as Jesus prepares to enter Jerusalem before his Passion (19:38), "Glory to God in the highest heaven, and peace to men who enjoy his favour". If their focus is on the glory of the Lord, then their task is surely to draw attention to the presence of God among humanity. The glory of the Lord has never been more evident; not because of the angels, but because the presence of God had never been so close among people. The result: peace to those who have been favoured by God, or rather, those who are well-disposed towards God. At any rate, this is the last time that angels will bring such messages to humanity: from now on, the angelic messenger (a tautology in itself) is redundant.

So, in the first episode of the Christmas Gospel story, we have a curious mix of the so conventionally human (in the persons of the very ordinary Mary and Joseph, complying with the decrees of the all-powerful Roman empire, and having to adapt to the difficult circumstances they face in their family life, in the shepherds, who are carrying out their normal work practice, and also, we must infer, in the overcrowding in Bethlehem caused by the census) and in the supernatural, in the angel of the Lord, the glory of the Lord, the entire heavenly army, in the announcement of peace to all of good will because there is born to us a saviour, who is Christ and Lord.

Christmas Dawn Mass. Luke 2:15-20

Questions to ponder:

☐   There are two parts to the passing on of news of the Saviour's birth: those who carry the message (shepherds) and those who receive it (including Mary). How do we manage to do both in our own lives?

This is clearly the continuation of the narrative begun at Midnight Mass. The shepherds come into focus once more. For the first time, they speak; "Let us go to Bethlehem and see this thing that has happened which the Lord has made known to us" (Luke 2:15). Notice that the angel had given no explicit order that they must go to see the new-born child; they were simply told what they would find, should they decide to go and see for themselves. The shepherds are the first humans, not only to hear the announcement of the birth, but also to make any kind of response.

At this stage, we should say some more about the shepherds and their role in the story, in order to separate what the gospel text says about them from what popular Christmas 'midrash' has made of them. To begin with, it is unlikely that they figure in the story because they are poor – or worse, the poorest of the poor; we are told from the outset that they are watching 'their' flocks; they are not therefore poorly paid. Rather, they are owners of livestock. There is no reason to suppose that they were any greater sinners than anyone else in their locality or of their time, so they do not represent those whom the saviour came to save from their sins any more than anyone else. That having been said, there is a strong body of opinion that would equate them with the vast numbers of people who would be excluded from public worship, simply on account of the professions they belonged to. This 'exclusion list extended to traders, shop-keepers, camel-drivers, shepherds, sailors, and even physicians. These would have found themselves barred from the synagogue and the temple because their line of work would bring them into contact with possible causes of ritual contamination – goods not prepared in the proper manner, animals (always suspect), people in foreign places visited by sailors (about as suspect as the animals), or because their profession would have put them in contact with blood. The hypocrisy of the system is self-evident; the very people excluded were those relied upon by the ones doing the excluding – from traders to physicians! There is certainly a strong theme in the gospel of Luke as a whole about Jesus reaching out to those whom the system rendered outcasts, so shepherds as such outcasts may be a relevant motif here also.

There are enough strong biblical allusions to shepherds to be able to make something of these. David, Jesus' ancestor, was minding sheep in the fields when the prophet Samuel searched among his family for a successor to the disgraced king Saul. David himself, the shepherd, is the one anointed by the Lord's prophet. See 1 Samuel 16:11; 17:15 for the shepherd theme surrounding David. That the events being described are in Bethlehem only serves to strengthen the shepherd-connection between the new-born saviour, born in descent from David, who is Lord, Saviour, and the Anointed (i.e. 'Christ', or 'Messiah').

What is certainly true is that the shepherds are the first humans who are faced with making a decision in the light (literally, thanks to the heavenly host!) of the birth of the Messiah. The angel of the Lord has told them what they would see, should they go to the place where the child was, but they are free to go and see, or to stay where they are. They discuss their action among themselves, and decide to "go to Bethlehem and see this thing that has happened which the Lord has made known to us" (Luke 2:15). For the first time, there is a human response to the announcement of the Saviour's birth, but there is more to the shepherds' action yet to come. They are not only the first to respond to the angel's message; they are the first to describe what the angel had said. They are the first witnesses to the word of God that the saviour has been born, and they introduce a sequence of three different reactions. The first is from the shepherds who carry out the angel's instructions, the second is the undefined but astonished "everyone"; a reaction that is met later in the gospel, where crowds are often astonished at what Jesus says/does, but their astonishment does not apparently lead to response. The crowd merely look on while Jesus is being crucified. They may stand with mouths open, but they don't actually *do* anything. Finally, there is the reaction of Mary and Joseph, whom we may assume had not heard what the angel had to say, and who apparently were unaware of the appearance of the heavenly host. This seems most likely, because "Mary treasured all these things and pondered them in her heart" (Luke 2:19); literally, she turned all these things over in her mind, or she debated them within herself. However the phrase is rendered, it suggests that Mary too is only gradually coming to term with the Revelation of the works of God unfolding before her. Mary may have been told of the birth of her child by Gabriel; but she still has much to learn about what it means for her.

Again, we are reminded that the things of heaven and the things of earth meet in this event in an unprecedented way. When the commonplace of day to day life meets the splendour of the eternal, we cannot fail to marvel at the level of God's involvement in the affairs of humanity.

This point is stressed in the last verse of this passage: the shepherds went back glorifying God for all they had seen and heard, which was exactly what they had been told. Notice that this last action from the shepherds echoes the song that is sung by the heavenly army in verse 13, but these shepherds still have to look after their sheep, and it is dark once more. Later, and in other places, when humans have had an insight into the depths of Jesus, they soon find they must come back to mundane reality. The Transfiguration is perhaps a good example of this: Peter, spellbound at what has happened, wants to preserve the image of Jesus transfigured, with Moses and Elijah, but must come to realise that the mountain must be descended once again, that the vision will fade, and the real task ahead lies in the day to day work of following Jesus.

Christmas Day Mass John 1:1-18

Questions to ponder:

☐   What does it mean to us to say that through the Word all things came to be, and that not one thing came to be without him? How does this tie in with the Word who became flesh?

This is the one passage for the Christmas liturgy that, notoriously, doesn't tell the familiar story! Of course, the significance of the Christmas story is well laid out in this famous part of the fourth gospel. That one phrase "The Word was made flesh, he lived among us" sums up this liturgy's focus, but there is so much more within this prologue that could be explored that it would be a pity not to try to do justice to the many deeply theological themes included here. This is a gospel passage which points the way forward well beyond the Christmas season, with hints of all that the gospel will reveal to us in the year ahead, and not only from John's account. It is often claimed that the Prologue to John contains the entire gospel in miniature; it begs to be explored, even when preachers are challenged with a church full of over-exited children with presents that that they wold no doubt rather explore!

It is also often pointed out that each gospel's individual theology can be identified by the way it sets its own beginning. Mark chooses to begin with the adult Jesus following John the Baptist and proclaiming the Good News that the kingdom of God is at hand. Matthew and Luke take us further back to Jesus' human origins (as we have already explored in some detail), whereas John takes us back to before creation itself! John's beginning provides the setting to where the third Christmas day liturgy takes us. Here we are told from the beginning of the eternal relationship between the Word, and God. The key concepts are in fact: beginning, Word, with God, all things created through the Word, the Word was a light for all, a light that darkness could not overpower (John 1:1-5). These words, with their reminder of the creation narrative (Genesis 1:1), also tell us about Divine Communication. Before the Word became flesh (that comes later), the Word was with God. To be with God itself indicates intimacy and communication; this is enhanced by saying it was *THE WORD* who was with God. Whatever is communicated between the Word and God is now to be present in creation. Through the Word, i.e.

Divine Communication, all things came to be, and Light comes into the world, a light that darkness simply cannot overpower.

The Word became flesh and dwelt among us. Now, God will communicate with humanity as never before. What was shared between God and the Word is now shared between God and humanity, *through* the Word. It's official, and it's permanent, because the Word became flesh, and stayed with us, but the tragedy is that the Word was not always accepted: to those who did accept him, he gave power to become the children of God. This is where we see a preview of the rest of the Gospel. In John, there is much talking (what else could the Word do?), but there is little acceptance of the Word, but to Peter, and those who associate with his sentiment, where else is there to go? Who else has the word, the message, of eternal life? Peter says that they believe, they know that Jesus, the bearer of the message of eternal life, is the Holy One of God (c.f. John 6:68-69).

If the whole business of the Word made flesh seems remote, then another look is called for. The language may be highly theological, and the Christology it expresses is itself very high, but fundamentally, we have no more and no less than a return to our theme of the nearness of God in the Incarnation of Jesus. The God of the infinite, with whom the Word has existed and communicated from the beginning, is bound up in the affairs of humans. The Word which speaks is the word that transforms lives – from a couple whose wedding celebration was compromised through bad catering, to a court official with a son nearing death. From a cripple beside a pool who has lost hope, to a hungry crowd of 5000, and a boat-load of frightened disciples from a man born blind, to Lazarus brought back from the dead. The lives of all of these are dramatically transformed through the Word, who is God's communication in human form, Jesus. No one, nowhere, and at no other time, could reveal God like the Word of God Incarnate, in the flesh, Jesus *IS* the Word of God Incarnate, and the conversations that Jesus has with Nicodemus, the Samaritan woman at the well, the Jews and his own disciples after the feeding of the 5000, all surely highlight the significance of the life changing events that follow the 7 signs laid out in this gospel. Follow the story through, and there is more. Come to believe in the Word, to accept him among us, and see the glory of God – or, to put it in terms we have already used, be aware of the presence of God in the most fundamental and commonplace aspects of life.

Feast of the Holy Family, Year C; Luke 2:41-52

On the threshold of adulthood: the child who will be the teacher

Questions to ponder

☐　　Are you convinced by Luke's explanation of why Jesus chose to stay behind in Jerusalem after his father and mother had left?

☐　　What may we be expected to take from the concept of the Holy Family as a model for Christian living today in the light of this gospel?

☐　　What lessons should we learn from Mary's habit of pondering on what has happened, and storing them in her heart?

This story is unique in the canonical gospels since it is the only passage which tells us anything of the life of Jesus when he is, by the Jewish standards then and now, on the verge of adulthood. This kind of narrative is frequently found in Hellenistic biographies of heroes, where the early days of the hero are set out, showing that even at an early age, he already displayed all the characteristics which became so apparent in adult life. There is an element of this in Luke's account of Jesus' visit to the Temple as a twelve year old too. In Luke's hands though, the story functions as a transition between the first days of Jesus' life and his adult ministry in a way which is not found in the other three gospels.

This passage is used as one of three 'crisis' stories from Jesus' early life which are read on the Feast of the Holy Family one for each year of the liturgical cycle. All of them involve the family unit of Jesus, Mary and Joseph in danger, or a prophetic notification of suffering, or as in this case, family conflict. No one looking for a sentimental picture of an idealised Holy Family will have much success in finding source material in the gospel passages for this feast! Rather, these gospel stories all have in common the prophetic indication of what the adult life of Jesus will entail: in year A, the threat to his life by King Herod the Great in Matthew 2:13-15. 19-23 is a prophetic indication of the threat to his life posed by the leaders in Jerusalem, this time ending in his death. Likewise, the prophecies of Simeon in Luke 2:22-40 in year B are a foreshadowing of Jesus' own passion, and the association with his cross to be accepted by his followers. In year C, an episode in Jesus' early life is a prophetic indication of a series of events in the final stages of his life.

Luke once again displays great talent as a writer as he unfolds this relatively short narrative. Not only does he tell the story of a family crisis – parents of children around the age of twelve will not be the only ones who sympathise with the adults in this story when they discover their son is missing – but he skilfully and briefly puts into place so many of the elements which will be key to his gospel narrative. Hence, we are again brought to Jerusalem, where the gospel began with the story of Zechariah in the Temple. There are overtones of gospel themes in the losing and finding of Jesus, paving the way for the parable of the Lost Son who was lost and is found (Luke 15:24. 32). In this story, the young son who was lost and is found is also described by his father as having been dead, and is now come back to life. It is not too far-fetched then to see in Jesus, lost and found in Jerusalem and the Temple, a foretelling of his death and resurrection.

Luke is the only synoptic evangelist who recounts a visit by Jesus to Jerusalem other than in the context of his passion, death and resurrection. He records the presentation in the Temple, and now the visit to the Temple from Nazareth in Galilee (Luke 2:39), where Luke says they returned to after they had done all for the infant required by Law. The occasion of this visit is the feast of Passover, and they appear to travel as part of a family pilgrimage, perhaps also with neighbours taking part. It is only when they have travelled a full day on the way back home that they discover the twelve year old Jesus is not with them. The child is lost. Three days later, he is found. This is the allusion to death and resurrection already referred to. When they do find him, he is seated among the teachers in the Temple, asking them questions, and impressing them with his learning and understanding. This is a foreshadowing of how Jesus' ministry will end, with him teaching in the Temple every day (Luke 19:47), and where the chief priests, scribes and elders try unsuccessfully to get the better of him in argument. Here however, he is the extremely perceptive pupil, and not the teacher.

Eventually, his family catch up with him and take him to task for going missing, because they have been worried about him. Notice that the twelve year old Jesus has stayed behind, and it is not his family who have lost him. The point of the story is that Jesus at this age is on the verge of adulthood, and is therefore responsible for his actions. Later rabbinic teaching states that at twelve, a boy is old enough to be told the law; at thirteen, he is old enough to observe its obligations. There may well be some indications of this way of thinking in the present story. Nonetheless, the parents ask him why he has stayed behind like this, causing them so much worry in the process. Again, there is a prefiguring of an episode from later in the gospel, when the women who arrive at Jesus' tomb on the morning of resurrection are questioned as to why they "look among the dead for someone who is alive" (Luke 24:5). Jesus' rebuke to his parents suggests similar lack of comprehension, "Did you not know that I must be busy with my Father's affairs?" (Luke 2:49). Or at least, that's how the Jerusalem Bible translates the phrase which is highly enigmatic and really says only that Jesus must be about that of his father's. Some translations render this as Jesus must be about his Father's affairs, or business, which would suggest a prophetic statement about the next time that Jesus appears in Jerusalem, i.e. for his own death and resurrection, whereas others suggest that Jesus means he must be about his Father's house, which is the Temple. Perhaps all that is significant is the incomprehension of his parents, which is more than a little strange, given that they have heard in the lead up to the child's birth the angelic announcements that the child would be Lord and Saviour, and would assume the throne of his father David. Perhaps the parents feel that since he is still their responsibility, his disappearance like that is unacceptable. Once again however, Luke shows his artistry in turning a humanly very understandable situation into a vehicle for making a more profound point. We learn two things as a result of this exchange between parents and son; first, Jesus himself remains with them and grows in wisdom and stature, and in the favour of God and humans, and second, Mary once more stores all these things in her heart, just as she had done at her son's birth, and when Simeon had made his prophecy about the child's destiny and her own suffering.

Luke thus ends his infancy narrative prologue; there will be much more storing and pondering in the heart of things pertaining to Jesus' words and actions as the main body of the gospel story unfolds in the course of the year ahead.

Mary, Mother of God Luke 2:2:16-21

Question to ponder:

☐   What does Mary's pondering and treasuring in her heart of the things she has seen and heard suggest as a resolution for our own New Year intention?

This passage repeats much of what was read at the Dawn Mass on Christmas

Day. The additional elements are in the final verse, the circumcision of Jesus on the eighth day, and in the naming of the child. This verse adds two elements. Firstly, it places the upbringing of Jesus firmly within the Jewish tradition. Secondly, we are re-introduced to Mary turning things over in her mind. This time, we might want to read the text in the light of the carrying out of the Angel Gabriel's initial instruction that the child is to be called Jesus. The verse also repeats similar events from the birth of John the Baptist, except that in Jesus' case, there is no debate about the name, and we are not told who actually named the child. It is difficult not to conclude that the whole process of shepherds and their account of what they had seen and been told, and the fulfilment of the Law of Moses as it applied to new-born children. How could this ancient law be reconciled with all the new information that is now coming about?
Luke does not try to resolve whatever debate Mary may have been having in her mind; Matthew will, however, stress later in the year the importance of reconciling the Old and the New in the proclamation of the kingdom of God.

Second Sunday after Christmas. John 1:1-18

Question to ponder:

☐   The Prologue to John's gospel is used several times in the Christmas season. What new insights can we gain on this occasion by reading it in conjunction with the first reading from Ecclesiasticus and its portrayal of Wisdom?

The prologue to John's Gospel has already featured in the gospel for Christmas Mass During the Day (see above, pp. 20-22). It also features on the 7th day of the Christmas Octave, the day before the Solemnity of Mary, the Mother of God, 1 January, although that particular liturgical celebration is not featured in these notes. All in all, it is possible that in the Christmas season, we could find ourselves reading this passage three times in little more than a week! Fortunately, there is such a wealth of ideas in the Prologue that there is no chance of us ever reaching the end of what this magnificent text has to say to us.

As noted in the previous paragraph, John 1:1-18 has already been considered above, so the passage will not be given further attention here. It will perhaps be useful however to consider it afresh in the light of the other two readings offered for the liturgy of the word today. When the Second Sunday of Christmas is celebrated (which is not the case when the Epiphany is celebrated on a Sunday rather than on 6 January), it is coupled with both a passage from Ecclesiasticus and a composite passage from Ephesians. These two passages highlight for us two important ideas which are also to be found in among the many contained in John's Prologue.

It may for once be helpful to begin here with the second reading. This is a 'composite' passage in two sections from Ephesians with both sections coming from chapter 1. Verses 3-6 are about out adoption as God's children through God's son, a free gift given to us in the Beloved. The second section (verses 15-18) turns to a theme which is so closely related to Christmas themes: it is the theme that we come to the knowledge of God only through what is revealed. What the passage does not say explicitly is that it is through Our Lord Jesus Christ that we come to know God. The author of the letter prays that "…the God of our Lord Jesus Christ, the Father of Glory, give you a spirit of wisdom and perception of what is revealed, to bring you to full knowledge of him". Wisdom and perception take us nicely to the first reading.

Ecclesiasticus, the work of Wisdom teacher Ben Sira, devotes a section of the work to the subject of Wisdom (chapter 24; an extract provides the first reading for this occasion). Interestingly, Sira is concerned with the concept of Wisdom taking up residence, in accordance with the designs of the Creator, in Jacob. She is instructed by the creator of all things "Pitch your tent in Jacob, make Israel your inheritance". Although created by God, Wisdom has existed from eternity, and will exist until eternity. Wisdom is God's minister in the tabernacle (Temple), and has taken root in God's inheritance, his people. This extract is enough to show that the Prologue to John's gospel has borrowed heavily from Ecclesiasticus' portrayal of Wisdom – existing with God from the beginning, dwelling among humans, and especially among the Lord's inheritance. John's portrait of the Word has similarities with Ecclesiasticus' view of Wisdom, but there are significant differences. First, Wisdom is created; the Word was God and was with God from the beginning. Wisdom dwells in Jacob, among God's inheritance, i.e. his people; the Word became flesh and dwelt among US. To those who accepted the Word made flesh was given the power to become children of God.

So, the other reading, easily forgotten in among the familiar Christmas stories from the gospels, give us a prompt, as it were, to reflect on Jesus, the Revelation of God, and Jesus, the Word of God. The concept of Divine Wisdom may aid our reflection on the Word made flesh; but the differences are important to note as well!

Epiphany. Matthew 2:1-12
Question to ponder:

☐   Once again, the dream provides the vehicle for divine communication here. How do we re-discover the ability to dream the things of God – if not in sleep, at least in the sense of having a vision of what God desires for us?

Royal connections are laid down from the very first verse of this text: the story is set in the reign of King Herod the Great, and the magi enquire after the infant King of the Jews. With two opposing alleged royal factions there will be no easy resolution of this episode. Characters and events are worth exploring, because each person, or category of person, each title, and indeed each place name is of symbolic significance. The figure of King Herod is well known –so much so that it is quite easy for inexperienced readers of the New Testament to confuse later Herods, and especially Herod Antipas, with the one in this story. A very brief guide to the Herod dynasty is given in the Excursus below.

Herod's personal history is easy to trace, because of the impact he had in Palestine during his reign. The same cannot be said about the enigmatic figures who come from the East to Jerusalem, seeking the 'infant king of the Jews', because they saw his star rising and so they want to pay homage to him. There have been so many misleading titles given to these visitors that it is probably simpler (and safer) to stick to the term used in the gospel, magi. This term 'Magi' was originally applied to Persian priests who claimed to be able to interpret dreams. Of course, this is a feature of the story here, but these people are also depicted as astronomers/astrologers, people who sought to predict major events in human history according to the movement of stars. And they are also bearers of gifts. As the Excursus explains, each of these features suggests a slightly different place of origin for these visitors. All we can say for certain however is that the gospel does not give any further hints about where in the East they emerged from. So much is hinted at, but not developed, in a single verse.

EXCURSUS: The Herods, Magi and Gifts from the East

Herod the Great was the most prominent member of the Herodean dynasty, and he reigned from 40 until 4 BC, although he did not take control of Jerusalem until 37 BC.

Herod (73-4 BCE) was the pro-Roman king, whose career began as a general, whom the Roman Senate made king provided him with troops to enable him to seize the throne. As a Roman ally, he was never a truly independent king; however, Rome allowed him a domestic policy of his own. Herod undertook an extensive building programme, most notably new walls around the city of Jerusalem and the citadel which guarded its Temple, which he also reconstructed. Other building projects included Caesarea Maritima, Masada, and various other fortresses.

Herod's position was always insecure. His building programme cost his subjects dearly in taxes, and his projects won him the bitter hatred of the orthodox Jews, who disliked Herod's Greek tastes, shown not only in his building projects, but also in several transgressions of the Mosaic Law. Sadducees hated him because he had curtailed their own influence in the Sanhedrin. The Pharisees despised any ruler who despised the Law, and all his subjects resented his excessive taxation. Herod often resorted to violence, employing mercenaries and a secret police to enforce order. Herod concluded ten marriages, all for political purposes, and all probably unhappy. Herod's reign ended in terror. The story about the slaughter of infants of Bethlehem in Matthew is not known from other sources, but it would have been totally in character for the later Herod to commit such a terrible act.

Disease (probably a cancer-like affection called Fournier's gangrene) made acute the problem of Herod's succession, and the result was factional strife in his family. Shortly before his death, Herod decided against his sons Aristobulus and Antipater, who were executed in 7 and 4 BCE, and after his death in 4 BCE, the kingdom was divided among his sons. Herod Antipas was to rule Galilee and the east bank of the Jordan as a tetrarch; Philip was to be tetrarch of the Golan Heights in the north-east; and Archelaus became the ethnarch ('national leader') of Samaria and Judaea.

Archelaus: ruled Samaria, Judaea and Idumea between 4 BCE and 6 CE. His rule was disastrous and he was sent into exile by the Roman emperor

Augustus.

Philip: ruled between 4 BCE and 34 CE in the southwest of what is now Syria. He was married to his relative Salome. (In the *Gospel of Mark* 6.17, Philip is mentioned as the first husband of Herodias. This is a mistake; Herodias was never married to Philip.) Among his subjects, the Jews were a minority; most people were of Syrian or Arabian descent. Philip died in 34 AD, having ruled his dominions for thirty-seven years. According to the Jewish historian Flavius Josephus, he had been a person of moderation and quietness in the conduct of his life and government (*Jewish Antiquities*, 18.106).

Herod Antipas: Jewish leader, ruler of Galilee and Peraea between 4 BC and 39 AD, was full brother of Archelaus and half brother of Philip, and was appointed tetrarch of Galilee and Peraea (the east bank of the Jordan). According to the *Gospel of Mark*, John the Baptist criticized the king and was consequently killed. Antipas' daughter Salome had been dancing in public, much to the delight of her father, who asked her to ask a present, and was shocked to learn that she demanded the head of the Baptist. In 37 AD, Herodias' brother Agrippa became king of the realms of Philip. She thought that the royal title ought to be given to her husband and made a plan to make Herod Antipas king, but the emperor exiled Antipas to Lyon in Gaul.

MAGI This term is used to describe the visitors from the East who came to do homage to the new-born king. The expression was first applied to a sect of Persian priests who claimed to have the ability to interpret dreams. But the Magi in Matthew's gospel combine the interpretation of dreams with another attribute, and that is the study of stars, either as astronomers or as astrologers. This in itself would suggest that their origin was Babylon. But there is another facet to their character, and that has to do with the gifts they bring, which seem best associated with Arabia! The reflection in this commentary for the Feast of the Epiphany suggests that rather than look for evidence of either these magi, or the star they followed, it is more profitable to identify the Biblical allusions that are connected with them and their gifts. The star has already been linked with Balaam's oracle in Numbers 24:17. But there are other possible allusions: Psalm 72:10 refers to kings of Sheba and Seba brining gifts (this may be where the tradition that the Magi were kings grew from), and Isaiah 60:6, which provides the first reading for the Epiphany, also refers to visitors from Sheba, bringing gifts of gold and frankincense.

Perhaps the Magi thought they were asking an innocent question in their enquiry, but 'King of the Jews' was Herod's official title. Supporters of Herod could only see its use as a challenge to Herod's reign, and of course the title King of the Jews was inscribed and mounted when Jesus was crucified. The Magi have travelled thus far because they saw the new king's star rising. Belief that astral phenomena signalled the births and deaths of prominent people was widespread among the ancients, and many attempts have been made to identify what it was that caught the attention of the Magi – was it a planetary conjunction, or a supernova, or a comet. More significant than any of this however is the Biblical connection between this star-story and the Old Testament – particularly Number 24:27, and the selection from the prophecy or oracle of Balaam, the pagan seer, "I see him - but not in the present, I behold him - but not close at hand: a star from Jacob takes the leadership, a sceptre arises from Israel."

The Magi say that they have come to pay homage to the new king. The expression is used three times in the narrative, and so is a dominant motif in the passage. To pay homage is to bow, or prostrate oneself before, e.g., a king. The term can also denote the proper attitude of humans before God, so the Magi might be making a theologically significant statement here as well, a recognition of the new king as Son of God.

That Herod is dismayed is not hard to imagine; that the 'whole of Jerusalem' shares his dismay is perhaps less so. The term presumably refers to a considerable number of the most influential people in Jerusalem, and not literally to every single inhabitant. The term is vague, but the next verse is specific: and utterly appalling! It involves the "chief priests and the scribes of the people". Chief priests apparently refers to members of the high priestly family, and perhaps even former high priests – about seven people held the office during the reign of Herod, and up to four of these may still have been alive around the time when this story would have taken place. The designation 'chief priest' would, of course, have included the current high priest himself. Scribes would have been able to give an answer to the question 'where was the Christ to be born?' These were the scripture scholars of their day. Their certain knowledge regarding the birthplace of the Messiah makes even more pointed the opposition that they and the chief priests will later mount against Jesus. They can cite a combination of Micah 5:1 and 2 Samuel 5:2 for what Matthew describes as 'the prophet'.

When Herod summons the wise men, in the light of the information his advisors have provided for him, it is with the intention of sending them to find out more. His professed reason is so that he can 'do homage' to the new king (the second occurrence of the phrase), which is, of course, the exact opposite of his true intent, which turns out to be murderous.

The star reappears now, and its movement specifies the precise location of the child, information which has been lacking so far. Notice that the place where it rests is described as a 'house'. The reflection on the Christmas Midnight Mass gospel on pages 14 and 15 above noted that this need not be seen as contradictory to Luke's account which includes the words *kataluma*. And for the Holy Family gospel, reflection, we noted that Matthew makes no reference to a journey from Nazareth to Bethlehem prior to Jesus;' birth in the latter town (c.f. p. 21). Paying homage is mentioned for the third time, and this time, it actually happens: the Magi pay their homage and present their gifts, again with Old Testament allusions which are listed in the Excursus. Finally, a dream once more provides the vehicle for divine communication. This very Persian feature, which is also very biblical, is the impetus for the Magi to return home by a different route. But notice that this time. There is no presence of an angelic messenger to accompany the dream.

This story is one of clear contrasts. The pagans, following signs of at best questionable reliability, and without the prior aid of biblical information possessed by the scribes, are prepared to put themselves to considerable inconvenience, not to say danger, to do homage to the one they believe to be the rightful king of the Jews. Those with the heritage of the prophets show no sign of moving toward the one they profess to have awaited all these many long years; indeed, any intent they have is hostile. The association of the chief priests with Herod, and their subsequent behaviour toward Jesus prevents any suggestion that they be dissociated with Herod's desire to do murder. Our overall theme for Advent/Christmas returns: the arrival of the Son of God needs more than theoretical assent; it requires a submission that will inevitably mean substantial changes to daily life. Mary and Joseph had already discovered this: now the Magi are to find it out for themselves. Knowing about the new born king and wishing to do him homage will require some abrupt and often dramatic changes to our otherwise formulated plans.

Feast of the Baptism of the Lord, Year C; Luke 3:15-16. 21-22
At the end of Christmas, and on the threshold of the beginning of Jesus' ministry

Questions to ponder

☐   What does Jesus' baptism in this version tell us of our own baptism?
☐   What is the significance of John's prophecy of one who will baptise with the Holy Spirit and with fire?
☐   What do you make of Luke's attempt to describe the appearance of the Holy Spirit?

The season of Christmas ends with this feast, even though the episode it celebrates belongs to Jesus' adult life – a stage far removed from Bethlehem, shepherds, wise men, and visits to the Temple! There is a logic in this episode being considered in the context of Christmas, because it represents the last of what we might call the preliminary subject matter of Jesus' life story. Once the narrative of his baptism is concluded, the narrative of his ministry and its culmination in his passion, death and resurrection can begin. Accounts of Jesus' baptism are found in all four gospels, although his baptism is not actually described in John, where the nearest we get to a direct reference is when John the Baptist explains, "'This is the one I spoke of when I said: A man is coming after me who ranks before me because he existed before me. I did not know him myself, and yet it was to reveal him to Israel that I came baptising with water.' John also declared, 'I saw the Spirit coming down on him from heaven like a dove and resting on him. I did not know him myself, but he who sent me to baptise with water had said to me, "The man on whom you see the Spirit come down and rest is the one who is going to baptise with the Holy Spirit". Yes, I have seen and I am the witness that he is the Chosen One of God'" (John 1:30-34). Luke's version of Jesus' baptism follows closely the account fond in Mark, but at the same time he makes significant changes to the narrative. The first noticeable change is that Luke does not mention John the Baptist at all in his version. This may initially seem strange since we have heard so much about John in the various stages of the Infancy Narrative, but in fact Luke here is addressing in his own way a problem connected with Jesus' baptism that Mark did not seem to be

aware of, and which Matthew solves in a different way. The problem is one which looks as if it preoccupied the early Christians, and may even have led to a rival movement of those who hailed John as the awaited one rather than Jesus. The four gospels are all at pains to quote John himself as saying that his own role is no more than to pave the way for the stronger one who follows him, as we saw on the 3rd Sunday of Advent this year; "'I baptise you with water, but someone is coming, someone who is more powerful than I am, and I am not fit to undo the strap of his sandals; he will baptise you with the Holy Spirit and fire" (Luke 3:16). The problem is this: if Jesus is the stronger one, the more powerful one, why does he agree to baptism at the hand of John?" Mark apparently saw no problem; Matthew resolves the issue through the exchange where John replies to Jesus' request for baptism with, "It is I who need baptism from you' he said 'and yet you come to me!' But Jesus replied, 'Leave it like this for the time being; it is fitting that we should, in this way, do all that righteousness demands'. At this, John gave in to him" (Matthew 3:14-15). Luke's solution is not to describe the actual mention at all, so there is no need for John to be mentioned, and Jesus is at the very centre of the story. We move ahead too far, and too soon, however.
The gospel text chosen for today recalls an earlier passage which was read in Advent, where John counters the feeling of expectancy that he might be the Christ, by stressing, "I baptise you with water, but someone is coming, someone who is more powerful than I am, and I am not fit to undo the strap of his sandals; he will baptise you with the Holy Spirit and fire" (Luke 3:15-16). Notes for these two verses can be found for the 3rd Sunday of Advent, but now before Luke moves on to Jesus' baptismal experience, he introduces a note that is not found in the other two synoptics. He tells us that Herod the tetrarch, whom he criticised for his relations with his brother's wife Herodias and for all the other crimes Herod had committed, added a further crime to all the rest by shutting John up in prison" (Luke 3:20). No other gospel introduces this information at this point, and it appears that as the evangelist is describing something which is not to happen yet, the intention behind its the insertion here is to create an impression of further distance being placed between Jesus and the Baptist. Already, John is being moved from centre stage which is occupied by Jesus alone from now on. There appears to have been an issue in the early church where Apostles encountered a group who had only received John's Baptism, and who had never heard there was such a thing as a Holy Spirit (c.f. Acts 19:2). Luke may be using this scene in his

first volume to make clear the relationship between John and Jesus.

Luke, as we have seen, does not stress the baptism of Jesus itself. After the other people have been baptised, and after his own baptism, Jesus is found at prayer. This is a dominant theme in the gospel of Luke, where Jesus will repeatedly be found at prayer when the major events connected with his life take place. He will spend the night in prayer before he chooses his Twelve associates, when he asks 'who do the crowds say I am', when he is transfigured, when his disciples ask him to teach them to pray, just as John taught his disciples, and of course at his so-called agony in the garden of Gethsemane. In Luke, Jesus also prays for the forgiveness of his executioners. In this gospel Jesus repeatedly urges his disciples to pray not to be put to the test. Here, after his baptism when he is at prayer, the Spirit descended on him. The connection between prayer and the Spirit will be returned to in the post-Pentecost setting in the second volume of Luke/Acts; "As they prayed, the house where they were assembled rocked; they were all filled with the Holy Spirit and began to proclaim the word of God boldly" (Acts 4:31), and "they went down there, and prayed for the Samaritans to receive the Holy Spirit" (Acts 8:15). Each time Luke tells of the arrival of the Holy Spirit, he struggles to describe it, and we should avoid drawing he conclusion that he is giving an accurate and details account of what happened. Thus, at Pentecost, Luke says that what happened was that "suddenly they heard what *sounded like* a powerful wind from heaven, the noise of which filled the entire house in which they were sitting; and something appeared to them that *seemed like* tongues of fire; these separated and came to rest on the head of each of them" (Acts 2:2-3 my italics). Likewise, after Jesus' baptism, although the Jerusalem Bible says "the Holy Spirit descended on him in bodily shape, like a dove", a better translation would possibly express this as "a bodily appearance" with the same sense of grappling with the reality of what the spirit resembles in the description of what the apparently corporeal appearance of a dove actually represented. We may never discover what imagery the evangelist was calling upon here; it does not resonate well with any known biblical image. What Luke appears to be trying to convey is the reality of the descent of the Holy Spirit and its consequences. Again, a link with Pentecost is helpful. Just as the Pentecost descent of the Spirit will lead to the ministry of witness to the Risen Christ of the early church, so the descent of the Holy Spirit here will lead to Jesus' ministry, which we will announce himself in the synagogue at Nazareth in the words of Isaiah, "The spirit of the Lord has been given to me, for he has anointed me" (Luke 4:18).

Finally, there is a similarity between this descent of the Holy Spirit on Jesus, accompanied by the voice form heaven which declares him to be the beloved son, with the annunciation when Mary is told that the Holy Spirit will come upon her, that she has found God's favour, and that her child will be called the Son of the Most High (i.e. God). Now, Jesus, with the Holy Spirit upon him, is described by God as the beloved Son on whom rests God's favour. Thus, the story of Jesus' formative years from the announcement of his conception until his baptism places him on the verge of his ministry – the entire sweep of the Christmas narrative, in fact, begins and ends in the same manner; the 'coming upon' people by the Holy Spirit.

Chapter 3. Sundays of Lent 1-5, Year C

Introduction

It's reasonable to assume that we will not derive the best from major liturgical seasons if we approach them without some overall sense of their direction. Each year, the Sundays of Lent give us a particular emphasis for the season, and if we can identify the themes that hold the Sundays together, then we have something which can be developed in preaching, catechesis and systematic reflection on these gospels. There are always a variety of ways in which we can do this and no theme is likely to be the only one or even the best one. In Year C, the year of Luke, we will consider an overall Lukan theme which is one of the major themes also found in Ordinary Time: Jesus, the ultimate prophet. The gospel of Luke offers us various portraits of Jesus – as saviour, teacher, healer, one who reaches out to the marginalized, but above all as one who is The Prophet that Moses had promised God would send to the people after Moses' departure: "the Lord your God will raise up for you a prophet like myself, from among yourselves, from your own brothers; to him you must listen...and the Lord said to me, "All they have spoken is well said...I will raise up a prophet like yourself for them from their own brothers; I will put my words into his mouth and he shall tell them all I command him" (Deuteronomy 18:15. 17-18). In Luke, Jesus' first public appearance of his ministry is as The Prophet who in the Nazareth synagogue fulfils the words of Isaiah, only to find them rejected. This is because, as he himself acknowledges, no prophet is ever accepted in his own land (Luke 4:24). Much later in this gospel, he will even go as far as to assert that "it

*would not be right for a prophet to die outside Jerusalem" (Luke 13:33).
Here are examples where Jesus' prophetic ministry is highlighted in the Lent
gospels:*

1st and 2nd Sundays of Lent

Gospels for these follow the same theme each year:
☐ *Week 1 is the Temptations (testing) of Jesus following his baptism,
and his identification by the heavenly voice as God's beloved Son. In year
C, it is Jesus the prophet who is put to the test;*
☐ *Week 2 is the Transfiguration. In Luke's version there is an
additional association of Jesus with the legendary prophetic figures of
Moses and Elijah in that Jesus is engaged in conversation with them about
his passing (exodos) which he, the Prophet, will accomplish in Jerusalem.*

3rd, 4th and 5th Sundays of Lent

*Jesus the Prophet reveals the attitude of God the Father to sinners in each of
the passages on these Sundays:*
☐ *Week 3 is the parable about the fig tree in response to the
presumption that those who have died as a result of Pilate's brutality or
natural disaster are somehow being punished for sin. The parable
counters that supposition, and presents God as the forgiving, loving
Father, as well as the reminder of our need for repentance.*
☐ *Week 4 is the parable of the Prodigal Son, really a parable about a
father who will go to great lengths to win back, not just one lost son, but
in fact both his estranged children.*
☐ *Week 5 is a passage from John which most scholars believe does not
really belong in this passage, and which may even originally have been
part of Luke. In this, Jesus the prophet speaks of mercy and forgiveness
over and above justice and condemnation.*

For those who will be using the Year A readings, notes on the gospels for the
3rd 4th and 5th Sundays from previous years are included at the end of these
notes.

1st Sunday of Lent, Year C. Luke 4:1-13

The Prophet put to the Test

Questions to ponder:

☐   Do these three episodes constitute temptations as we normally understand them?

☐   What are the real issues of the trial that Jesus undergoes in this passage?

☐   How does Jesus demonstrate he is *The Prophet* in resisting these temptations?

In both Matthew's and Mark's accounts of Jesus' return to his home town and his preaching in the synagogue, the episode is placed well into Jesus' ministry. In Mark (6:1-6a), it actually closes the first stage of Jesus' ministry. In Luke however, this is Jesus' first public action. The synagogue story is placed immediately after the passage we read today, and the two are connected. When Jesus speaks in the Nazareth synagogue, he quotes Isaiah: "'the spirit of the Lord has been given to me, for he has anointed me...this text is being fulfilled today even as you listen'" (Luke 4:18. 21). Thus, he associates himself with the Spirit empowered/Spirit filled prophetic ministry. Jesus did not invent this designation for himself, though. After his baptism had taken place we were told that the Spirit descended on him in bodily form (Luke 3:22). Today's text opens with the words that Jesus was 'filled with the Holy Spirit...' (Luke 4:1). All of these allusions to the Spirit are reminiscent of Old Testament prophetic utterances where the prophets were filled with, or driven by, the power of the Spirit. The prophet exile Ezekiel is a good example of this (c.f. Ezekiel 2:2; 3:12. 14. 24; 8:3 etc.). Whatever else today's gospel episode tells us about the Jesus who is put to the test, it portrays him as The Prophet, driven into the wilderness by the Spirit, put to the test and emerging victorious, i.e. one who is qualified to speak the word of God.

From the background to Jesus' role as the Prophet promised by Moses, we now take up the narrative in today's gospel passage. Filled with the Holy Spirit, we are told, Jesus left the Jordan and was led by the Spirit through the wilderness – the implication is that he was led for a purpose, just as Israel, on its release from slavery in Egypt, was led into the wilderness to journey and be tested for 40 years. The Jerusalem Bible tells us that he was "being tempted there by the devil for forty days" (Luke 4:2); this could be expressed more strongly, because the text appears to suggest that it was precisely for the purposes of testing that Jesus was led into the desert: just had been the case with the nation Israel, as it states in the Greek Septuagint (LXX) Old

Testament version of Exodus 16:4; 17:2; Deuteronomy 8:2, and Psalm 94.9. Luke calls the one doing the testing here 'the devil' (*diabolos*), which means 'accuser' or 'slanderer' or even 'deceiver'; Mark and Matthew use the name 'Satan' (*satanas*). Satan gets his reputation as the 'tester' in Job 2:3, but Luke's use of 'devil' introduces the additional feature of deceitful opponent who represents a counter-kingdom (which is the realm of demons and unclean spirits) to that inaugurated by Jesus. Luke states that Jesus was hungry from lack of food, but refrains from calling this 'fasting', as in Matthew 4:2.

In Luke's account of events, the testing takes place at the end of the forty days, when Jesus is weak with hunger. The first test, following the information about his hunger, is the challenge that Jesus should turn stone into bread with a verbal command. This gives the sign of the counter-kingdom to which the devil belongs. In Luke's version of John the Baptist's preaching the Baptist declared that God could "raise children for Abraham from these stones" (Luke 3:8); Jesus is challenged now to raise up bread from the same source; if he does so, not only will he alleviate his hunger but he will demonstrate his divine power. The deception inherent in the devil's attempt here appears in Luke 11:11, when Jesus, declaring the totally trustworthy nature of his Father, appeals to the integrity of even flawed human parents, "What father among you would hand his son a stone when he asked for bread?" Jesus however will not be drawn by the deception underlying this first test by the devil; nor will he be motivated by selfish desire. He quotes Deuteronomy 8:3, "man does not live on bread alone". Luke omits the additional phrase which is included by Matthew 'but on every word that comes from the mouth of God'.

The second test takes on a visionary aspect in Luke's version. Jesus is taken up – we are not told where - and in a moment of time he is shown all the kingdoms of the world. This test is left to the end in Matthew's version. In Luke's version, all of these kingdoms are in the devil's gift; to take possession of them, all Jesus has to do is to worship the devil, and their glory and power will be his. It is a test of allegiance between kingdoms; will Jesus remain loyal to the kingdom of his Father, for which he, as Paul puts it, "did not cling to his equality with God but emptied himself to assume the condition of a slave, and became as men are; and being as all men are, he was humbler yet, even to accepting death, death on a cross" (Philippians 2:6-8)? Or will he accept the power and the glory which match his equality with God

(Philippians 2:6)? Again, Jesus' answer is given in terms of scripture, "You must worship the Lord your God, and serve him alone" (Deuteronomy 6:13). Thus Jesus rejects the kingdom offered by the devil, in favour of the kingdom which has been bestowed on him by his Father" (c.f. Luke 22:29).

The content of the tests is the same in both Matthew and Luke, but the order of the second and third examples is different. Matthew places second the visit to the temple in Jerusalem, whereas Luke keeps this to the end, making it the climax to the set. This is very much in keeping with the prominence given to Jerusalem and its Temple by Luke the evangelist: this is the gospel which begins and ends in Jerusalem and in the Temple, (c.f. Luke 1:8; 24:53); it is the gospel in which Jesus the Prophet declares "it would not be right for a prophet to die outside Jerusalem!" (Luke 13:33); Luke's gospel is the most explicit in its description of Jesus deliberately setting out on a journey to Jerusalem which will take up almost ten chapters of the gospel, and which will culminate in his death and resurrection (9:51-19:27). It is understandable, then, that this evangelist places last the test which takes place at Jerusalem and in particular, on the temple parapet. This one has the devil at his most subtle, basing his attack on an allusion to scripture, quoting the Greek LXX text of Psalm 90:11; "He will put his angels in charge of you to guard you, and again: They will hold you up on their hands in case you hurt your foot against a stone". Thus, he challenges Jesus to throw himself off the high edge of the temple, thus demonstrating his trust in God, who having promised in the Psalm to send angels to protect David (about whom the Psalm is apparently referring) from so much as stubbing his toe, will surely do so much more to protect his son. The challenge is the deceiver at his best: why not demonstrate faith in God in this way? To carry out his suggestion however is to infringe a fundamental commandment given to Israel by Moses, which Jess offers as a counter quotation from scripture, "You must not put the Lord your God to the test" (Deuteronomy 6:16). Indeed, *not* to put the Lord to the test is the ultimate expression of faith; complete trust eliminates any need to provoke the Lord into a show of fulfilling his promise. The devil, the deceiver, the slanderer, withdraws, defeated, but ready to return at a later time. There will be explicit reference to this later in the gospel at 22:3; "Satan entered into Judas, surnamed Iscariot", and 22:31; "Simon, Simon! Satan, you must know, has got his wish to sift you all like wheat". The reference to Satan's withdrawal, but later return may, however, simply be a way of saying that there will be continued conflict between the two kingdoms: that bestowed on Jesus by his Father, and that of the devil, which he too has the power to give to others.

There is much for us in this passage which will resource us for our reflections at the beginning of Lent. The tests that Jesus faces are, rather than temptations as we might normal understand them, trials which highlight to which kingdom our allegiance is given. The tests present opposite poles:

	Kingdom of God	**'kingdom' of the devil**
1. Stone to bread:	denying self	giving in to self
2. World kingdoms personal power	desire for God's will	desire for
3. Temple parapet proof from God	complete trust in God	demanding

Full acceptance of the kingdom of God requires knowledge of God's will, of the true meaning of scripture. Lent is a time for exploring God's will, perhaps especially through scripture reading and reflection.

2nd Sunday of Lent, Year C. Luke 9:28-36

The Prophet Transformed

Questions to ponder

☐ What is the significance of Jesus at prayer as a prelude to the Transfiguration?

☐ This is the only gospel version of the Transfiguration in which the actual content of Moses' and Elijah's conversation is recorded. This is coupled with the voice from heaven. How do the various voices help us understand Jesus' identity?

☐ The Transfiguration is often presented as an event which was designed to prepare Peter James and John for the Passion. If so, did it work? If not, what do you think its purpose is?

Just like the first Sunday of Lent each year, the second Sunday always carries the same theme: the Transfiguration of Jesus. Matthew, Mark and Luke tell substantially the same story – Jesus, accompanied by Peter, James and John, is on a high mountain somewhere in Galilee (there is no gospel evidence for the tradition that this mountain is Mt Tabor). There, in the presence of Moses and Elijah, Jesus is transformed, his clothing changes appearance and a voice from heaven, speaking for the benefit of the three disciples, identifies Jesus: "This is my Son, the Chosen One. Listen to him" (Luke 9:35). Peter wants to set up three tents, and on the way down from the mountain and beyond the disciples remain silent on what has happened. In each gospel version of the story, the transfiguration takes place after both Peter's confession at Caesarea Philippi and Jesus' first passion prediction. So much for the similarities; the differences between the gospel accounts are often significant, and nowhere more so than here. Luke includes many of his major themes in this strange episode which takes place near the end of Jesus' Galilean ministry: Jesus is at prayer before the experience begins; that he is cast as the Prophet is reinforced by the company of the prophetic figures from the past, Moses and Elijah. This is developed in a uniquely Lukan way; Jerusalem is the focus for what will soon begin, Jesus' 'passing' (*exodos*; and finally, Peter is treated more sympathetically than in Mark or Matthew: Luke makes no mention of his fear.

In Luke there is a clear separation between this episode and what has immediately preceded; this is about all that can be concluded from Luke's assertion that eight days had passed (Mark says that it was six days), so this episode is not closely linked to what has gone before (which for the record was the outline of the conditions attached to following the Christ). Luke stresses the importance of this episode by stressing that the transfiguration happened as Jesus was praying. This is always an important *motif* in Luke: Zechariah was at prayer in the Temple when the angel appeared; Jesus was praying after his baptism when the heavens opened, the heavenly voice spoke and the Spirit descended in bodily form. Likewise, Jesus prayed before he called the Twelve. Luke avoids stating that Jesus was transfigured, or transformed as Mark chooses to describe his change, and restricts himself to stating only that the *appearance* of his face was altered. In Exodus 24:17, the Israelites saw the glory of the Lord *appear* like a devouring fire before Moses; at Jesus' baptism, the Holy Spirit *appeared* (*eidos*) in bodily shape. Now, Jesus' face *appeared* to be altered, and his clothes were white and dazzling. This also recalls the *appearance* of the Ancient of Days in Daniel 7:9, who had garments as white as snow, and paves the way for the 'men in dazzling clothes' at the Resurrection (Luke 24:4) and the 'men in white garments' (angels?) at Jesus' Ascension (Acts 1:10).

In all three synoptic accounts, Moses and Elijah are with Jesus, but only in

Luke is the content of the conversation recorded. Here, they also *appear* in their glory, and are discussing Jesus' 'passing' (*exodos*) which he was to accomplish in Jerusalem. These two unique details provide a link between the Transfiguration and Jesus' passion (surprisingly, the only direct reference to this on any of the Sundays of Lent in Year C with the obvious exception of Palm Sunday's Passion Narrative), and also to Jesus' prophecy about the Son of Man in 'his glory' which is found two verses before this passage begins (Luke 9:26), even though, as was discussed earlier, the evangelist sets out to create a separation between the two passages. The discussion about Jesus' 'passing', his '*exodos*', provides a clear link between him and Moses who led the 'passing' of Israel from Egypt to the promised land. Before his own departure from this life and prior to the entry to the promised land, Moses told the Israelites that "God will raise up for you a prophet like myself, from among yourselves, from your own brothers; to him you must listen" (Deuteronomy 18:15). A significant aspect of Luke's portrayal of Jesus is as the Prophet whom Moses had promised. This Prophet, Jesus, is now about to begin his own 'passing' which will involve not only a physical journey (which will be dealt with extensively in Luke 9:51- 19:27), but with his passing through death to resurrection. This passing is itself 'fulfilment' – an activity very much associated with prophets and prophecy.

Meanwhile, Peter and the other two were heavy with sleep (as they will be in the garden of Gethsemane, Luke 22:45-46). The Jerusalem Bible translation is strange here, suggesting that they struggled to stay awake, but the text seems to suggest that as they woke, or became fully awake, they saw Moses and Elijah in their glory; apparently they did not however hear the conversation. Perhaps Peter is impressed by the sight of glory, because he wants to construct three tents ('shrine' would be an acceptable translation here): one each for Jesus, Moses and Elijah, thereby preserving the image he has just witnessed. Luke gives no indication of fear on the part of the three at this point: that comes later!

The fear of the three comes as the scene changes. Moses and Elijah depart from the mountain and a cloud appears – another reference to the Exodus where the cloud signified the present of the Lord as the Israelites travelled through the desert; "Yahweh went before them, by day in the form of a pillar of cloud to show them the way, and by night in the form of a pillar of fire to give them light: thus they could continue their march by day and by night" (Exodus 13:21). The cloud was a frequent symbol for the presence of the

Lord among the people while on their desert journey. While teaching in the Temple at the end of his ministry, Jesus will predict "the Son of Man coming in a cloud with power and great glory" (Luke 21:27). Now, a voice comes from the cloud, repeating almost exactly the words heard at Jesus' baptism. This time, however the voice says, "This is my Son, the Chosen One. Listen to him" (Luke 9:35). There are two features here. One is explicit; the voice addresses Peter, James and John, whereas after Jesus' baptism, he was the one addressed. Here the three disciples are commanded to listen to Jesus, which is an implicit reference to the command of Moses when he told the Israelites that God would raise up for them a prophet just like himself. They were to listen to that prophet. Here, the command is repeated, but from an authority higher than Moses! Now the disciples are afraid, and not without cause! Finding themselves once more alone with Jesus, they descend the mountain in silence, which they maintain.

Of course, it is one thing to piece together the component parts of the story; it is another to see its relevance for us today, and especially for our Lenten journey. Luke stresses the prophetic connection. This is one theme that we could preach about and link to the 'testings' of the previous Sunday's gospel: the Prophetic Beloved Son, having shown his loyalty to the kingdom of his Father is the one qualified to teach us; we need to take seriously the heavenly command to listen to him. Listening will be particularly important over the next three weeks of this season as Jesus, the Chosen Son, tells us about the Father he knows so well. Jesus is moreover the Prophet whose passing is from death to resurrection, and who challenges his followers to take up the cross and renounce themselves in imitation of him. Finally, Peter's suggestion of building three tents (shrines) to preserve the memory of the image was inappropriate, because his challenge was, with the other two, to come down from that mountain and get on with the business of following the Prophet Jesus – almost immediately, because in a few verses he will embark on that (literally) fateful journey to Jerusalem. Our own Lenten challenge is therefore about us taking our religious experiences and insights and making sure they are not retained only as memories, but are lived out in our own journey of discipleship.

3rd **Sunday of Lent, Year C. Luke 13:1-9**

The Prophet Jesus teaches of the Father's patience and the need for

repentance

Questions to ponder

☐   Which part of the parable of the fig tree do you think is the ore important – that the gardener will wait another year? Or that at the end of another year, if there is still no fruit, the tree is to be destroyed?
☐   What kind of repentance does Jesus require here?
☐   Which aspect of the parable of the fig tree applies to Jesus himself?

The issues brought to Jesus' attention in this passage might seem a little remote to present day readers, concerned as they are with the historical matters of the cruelty of the Roman governor and the collapse of an unstable tower. We would have no problem empathising with the poor people who suffer from these tragic circumstances, but it is unlikely we would assume that those caught up in the atrocities were in any way responsible for their own fate. There is equally no indication from the text itself that those who reported Pilate's cruelty to Jesus believed that the sufferers were being punished for their own wrongdoing. Something else therefore must provide the clue to the reason for the inclusion of this particular passage for Lenten reflection. One possible way of identifying that 'something else' may perhaps be found in the first reading. Normally, first readings don't receive much attention in these notes, but on this Sunday an exception to that rule is in order.

The first reading for this week is from the foundational passage for Israel about Moses' encounter with God at the burning bush (Exodus 3:1-8. 13-15). Central to the understanding of the liturgy of the Word for today are verses 7 and 8, which contain the ultimate expression of God's response to humanity's suffering: an expression which is found time and again throughout the Old Testament in times of crisis, and where in effect God says "I have seen the miserable state of my people in Egypt. I have heard their appeal to be free of their slave-drivers. Yes, I am well aware of their sufferings. I mean to deliver them…" In this case, deliverance will be from slavery in Egypt. It will lead to settlement in a Promised Land, flowing with milk and honey; at other times in Israelite history it will result in a different type of deliverance. 'Fast forwarding' to the central idea of the Easter Triduum, we find that it is Jesus in his death and resurrection who is shown to be God's final response to the cry of his people in their distress. Final, in the sense of never to be exceeded and never to end, rather than in the sense of God's last every intervention, because in God's final intervention, Christ's death and resurrection, God is now constantly intervening to counter human distress. The Eucharist is God's final intervention is human affairs, because the Eucharist makes present in every age of history Jesus' death and resurrection. Thus, in today's liturgy, we set in place the first link in a chain of events that culminate in this Paschal Mystery – the first intimation that God has heard his people in their cry of distress, and the promise that he will respond to liberate them. Returning to today's gospel and Jesus' response to the two stories of innocent suffering, we should keep in mind the fact that Jesus himself will be the one who suffers the ultimate penalty, even though he is completely blameless. The Lenten readings help us to focus on this fact, culminating in the Servant Song from Isaiah 53, which is the first reading for Good Friday.

We are now in a position to consider today's gospel in more detail. The two incidents described at the beginning of the passage are found only in Luke. The one involving Pilate's mingling of the blood of Jews with that of their sacrifices is not recorded in any literature of the time, but it does seem to be entirely consistent with his known readiness to bear down swiftly and cruelly on any insurrection, real or imagined. There was a popular pious belief of the time, based on a narrow interpretation of Deuteronomy chapters 28-30, that disaster was a punishment for sin. This conviction finds expression in the question to Jesus from his disciples in John 9:2-3 about whether the man who was born blind was being punished for sin he may have somehow committed in the womb – or was he paying the price of his parents' sin? The same train of thought is clearly present in the minds of the Pharisees when they assume that the cripple brought to Jesus for healing, and whom Jesus forgives, is a sinner through and through and hence reduced to his crippled state (Luke 5:20-24). Jesus does not dwell on the matter in this instance, but simply that those who suffered in this cruel act were no more sinful than any other Galileans at that time. The issue, he makes clear, is not the extent of sin, but whether people are prepared to repent or not - and what will be the ultimate consequence of refusal to repent. To reinforce his argument, he adds a story of his own: a tower at Siloam had collapsed and killed eighteen. Is it to be supposed that they were any more sinful than anyone else in Jerusalem at the time? Again, the issue is whether or not people will repent; if not, they will be sure to perish. Given that Jesus has just insisted that in neither case are the victims suffering divine retribution, the warning that the non- repentant will surely perish. The words used in several English translations to convey the Greek *apoleisthe* cannot mean they will necessarily face a similar sudden and violent death. The original term is actually based on a wider meaning of the Greek, which can also refer to loss, or ruin. Those who do not repent, then, are those who face the prospect of losing the fullness of life (at the final judgement?) in the sense of the saying, "anyone who wants to save his life will **lose** it; but anyone who **loses** his life for my sake, that man will save it. What gain, then, is it for a man to have won the whole world and to have **lost or ruined** his very self?" (Luke 9:24-25). The words in bold type here are translated from the same Greek expression as in 13:3. 5 in today's passage. It is also essential to recall 'repentance' is the English word for *metanoēte*, which first and foremost means a change of mind, i.e. a change of outlook which embraces in its totality the kingdom of God.

Hence the parable which follows immediately. This is quite different in meaning from the episode of the fig tree found in Mark 11:12-14. 20-21, and Matthew 21:18-20, although all three have in common the unproductiveness of the fig tree. In Luke's parable, the unproductive fig tree has been planted in a vineyard. This coupling of the fig tree and the vine has prophetic overtones; both are found in Micah 4:4, "Each man will sit under his vine and his fig tree, with no one to trouble him. The mouth of the Lord Sabaoth has spoken it", and Joel 2:22, "the trees bear fruit, vine and fig tree yield abundantly as signs of God's blessing". In the gospel story, the fig tree has failed to yield fruit for three years, and the vineyard owner decides it should be cut down, presumably instead of leaving it to use up valuable space that could be given over to more productive plants. Is this the owner's real intention, or is it a literary device to flag up the 'common sense' position? Why should an unproductive tree take up space in a vineyard whose purpose is to bear fruit? This owner however is easily persuaded to give the fig tree another chance to become productive. The man who tends the vineyard (notice that he is not given a specific job title – perhaps we are not required to identify him with any specific task) suggests giving it another year in which he will make every effort to encourage it to bear fruit: he will dig around and fertilise the earth on the off chance that the tree may bear fruit the following year. If not, and if everything has been done to no effect, then it can be cut down.

It will not be helpful to search too much for allegorical meaning here, but it is not difficult to see where various allusions may lie. The unproductive fig tree is surely a symbol of Israel, which has been given opportunity to bear the fruit of returning to God but has repeatedly failed to do so. There are two contrasting themes that result from this. One is the almost ludicrous patience that the owner of the vineyard has with the fig tree, and the inefficient use of resources that he is prepared to see squandered on what he apparently deep down knows to be a lost cause. We can see the history of Israel contained in this, in a parable which now begins to resemble the parable of the wicked tenants in the vineyard: Matthew 21:33-46. The other is about realistic expectations. The patience of the owner is extreme, stretching well beyond what is reasonable; but it cannot and must not be taken for granted. The reason the fig tree is given so much attention is based on the hope – even if it is not entirely realistic – that it will eventually bear fruit. When that hope no longer exists, there will be no reason to continue the care.

The obvious conclusion therefore would appear to be this: God hears and responds with lavish generosity to the cry of his people in their distress. Those who do not respond to God's generosity through repentance (i.e. the change of mind-set toward the things of God) must however carry personal responsibility for any loss or ruination of life that may result. Jesus will lament at such lack of response when he sees Jerusalem at the end of his journey to the city: "If you in your turn had only understood on this day the message of peace! But, alas, it is hidden from your eyes" (Luke 21:42).

The relevance of this passage to us in Lent is of course its revelation to us of the God who has heard and responded to the cry of his people in distress, and who responds in the person of Jesus. The chilling 'background' to the discussion about those who die innocently is that it is a prophetic statement by Jesus on his own death. He, the sinless one, will be condemned to death without any guilt but nevertheless subjected to the cruelty decreed by Pilate! The episode is therefore located entirely in the Lenten journey by the Exodus motif from the first reading, and the implicit prophecy of Jesus' own death.

4th Sunday of Lent, Year C. Luke 15:1-3. 11-32

The Prophet Jesus answers his accusers; he associates with sinners because they too are children of God.

Questions to ponder.

☐ Which of the two sons in this text evokes the more sympathy from you?

☐   Is the father's behaviour in this parable reasonable? What does his behaviour tell us about the attitude of God the Father?
☐   Which of the two is really the lost son?

This is the year in which we read during Lent what is perhaps the most famous of all Jesus' parables. We will read the story again on the 24th Sunday of Ordinary time, but on that later occasion, we will consider the full collection of the three Chapter 15 parables: the shepherd who loses one sheep out of a hundred, the woman who loses one coin of ten and the father who loses a son – or perhaps two sons. On this Sunday in Lent however we read only the parable commonly called the Prodigal Son. We might begin by posing the question: is this really the most appropriate title for the parable? The question should be raised in our minds as we ponder the full extent of themes and motifs in this story. Before we begin to look at the parable itself, it is important to take full account of the first three verses of the chapter in which it occurs since these set the scene for Jesus' teaching as well as providing the context for all three parables and especially the last and longest. The issue is this: the tax agents and sinners were looking to spend time with Jesus, wanting to hear what he had to say. Meanwhile the scribes and Pharisees complained: this man, according to them, was in the habit of welcoming sinners and eating with them. Two very different groups are thereby identified. First, the tax agents and sinners, who are actually listen to what Jesus has to say and who want to spend time with him. They fulfil Jesus' prophetic words at the end of the previous chapter "Listen, anyone who has ears to hear!" (Luke 14:35). Those who hear Jesus may have been outcasts by virtue (if that's the right word!) of their profession. In fact, tax-collectors (or to be more accurate in our use of terminology, tax-agents), were included among the wider group of people known as sinners, not so much on account of their immoral behaviour (although most people assumed that they were guilty of this), but on account of their professions. Tax-agents, soldiers, all who worked with animals, traded with gentiles, came in contact with blood (which of course included physicians) and many other classes of people were deemed to be ritually unclean and therefore were forbidden to worship in synagogue or temple. These constituted the group known collectively as 'sinners. In the gospel of Luke the theme of reversal of fortunes is major: in the Magnificat Mary proclaims that the Lord has 'cast down the mighty…and raised up the lowly' (c.f. Luke 1:52). The first humans to hear the news that the Saviour has been born are from among this group known as 'sinners' – the shepherds, who would not be allowed to enter synagogue or temple! These people are now being gathered into the people of God restored by Jesus because they are the ones who listen to what he has to say. The scribes and the Pharisees on the other hand, the ones who pride themselves on lives dedicated to the service of God, refuse to listen to the prophet who uniquely speaks of God and God's plans for the salvation of humanity. They are complaining (*diagogguzon*), or grumbling against Jesus: just as their ancestors did in the desert in Moses' time (e.g. Exodus 17:3). Just like their ancestors, the hearts of the scribes and Pharisees of Jesus' time are not with the God they claim to serve. Therefore, Jesus tells them three parables about God's delight over the return of what was lost. The third parable expresses the father's delight at the return of his wayward son, but it also has something to say to the 'grumblers'.

This parable, which is one of those unique to Luke, is more like a short story than any other parable we read in any of the gospels. Its depiction of the characters of the two sons and their father who loves them both 'to a fault' goes well beyond most parabolic characterisations.

The story opens with a straightforward enough statement: a certain man (i.e. someone who is not going to be named or identified in a more specific way) had two sons. This is no sooner made clear than we are straight away into the story – and the mind set - of the younger son. There is nothing in the description of the younger son that it intended to persuade us to like him; rather, the narrative goes out of its way to make him totally repugnant. He is selfish, without thought for the needs or feelings of others and ruthless when it comes to serving his own purposes. The first words we hear him utter are in the form of a demand that his father will give him his share of the inheritance immediately. This of course should not have come to him until after the father's death, but this son is not prepared to wait that long. He wants his money now, and in demanding it is treating his father as if the old man was already dead – which is presumably the option this young man would have preferred! His rapid downfall thereafter is briefly sketched, but still with sufficient detail to give us a clear picture of the extent of his decline. He left the region with everything he had, and moved to a distant country. While there he squandered his money, according to the Jerusalem Bible translation; more accurately, he scattered it through loose living, with the implication that it was carelessness that led to his poverty rather than excess of moral dissolution. His timing was not good either, because a famine hits the land (an apparently common occurrence in the Ancient Middle East, if biblical accounts are accurate), and he is reduced to near starvation. His degradation reaches its lowest at this point because he, a (presumed) Jew is forced to work at feeding pigs - the ultimate in unclean animals - and indeed he would gladly have eaten the pigs' food, except that none was offered to him. He has reached the lowest depths of marginalisation and exclusion from the life he had previously known, and it is all of his own doing.

The next stage of the story relates how he comes to his senses, literally he 'comes to himself'. He will regain life itself through the plan that he now formulates, but at first this is on his own terms. He thinks of the servants who are both paid and fed in his father's house. He will try to seek a position as one of them. This has consequences which are not immediately obvious. The young man has come to the conclusion (wrongly, as it turns out) that he could no longer enjoy the father-son relationship he previously knew, so he decides that he will try to gain employment as a servant. Unlike slaves, servants had no relationship with their employers, and no rights apart from the right to be paid for the work they had done. Slaves had a permanent relationship with their masters, albeit as property rather than as persons. Slaves, if they were bought by a sufficiently well motivated master, would be provided with accommodation, food, clothing etc. Some slaves rose to positions of trust in the household – the steward in many of the parables (e.g. Luke 16:1-8). Servants were hired – and fired – on a casual basis. The young man concludes that this arrangement will suit him well: a relationship with his father which will require no personal commitment on his part, but will provide him with enough money to live on. He prepares his speech for the father, and sets out.

The story then turns to the second character: the father. This man has evidently been looking out for his son to return throughout his absence. He sees the boy a long way off (he is clearly not caught unprepared by his son's return!) and is moved with compassion. This response was attributed to Jesus in Luke 7:13 when he saw the distress of the widow at Nain, and to the Good Samaritan who saw the ambushed man in 10:33. It is that attribute of God which has been described as being somewhere between God hearing the cry of his people in their distress and acting out his response on their behalf. Likewise with Jesus compassion is also the 'half-way stage' between awareness and action. Here, the father is moved with that same kind of compassion, and he takes action by going out to meet the boy. His response is dynamic – he sees the boy, embraces him, hears him, kisses him, orders him clothed in finery, fitted with a ring and sandals and fed with the fatted calf – literally, the calf that has been fattened by feeding with grain. The father pays no heed to the son's request – seeing him alive and returned is all that matters, and he lavishes the finest of everything he has on his son, because, "this son of mine was dead and has come back to life; he was lost and is found" (Luke 15:24). The prophetic nature of the words 'dead' and 'alive' cannot be missed, nor can the reference to 'lost' and 'found', which were also used of Jesus at the story of his finding in the temple at the age of twelve (Luke 2:45-46). This second part of the story ends with the words "they began to celebrate" (Luke 15:24).

The third and final part introduces us to the elder son for the first time, although it is soon made clear that he has been in the background of the story all along, unknown to the reader. This character so often draws the sympathy of the readers of this gospel, and yet, it pays to look very closely at his portrait as Luke paints it. The first time we hear about him, he is outside in the fields and asks a servant what the noise is about. When told that his brother has returned home and that the father has had the fattened calf killed, he is angry (just like the scribes and Pharisees?), refuses to take part and stays outside. His father goes out to meet him, just as he had done earlier to greet the younger son. When the father tries to plead with him, he protests, "Look, all these years I have slaved for you and never once disobeyed your orders, yet you never offered me so much as a kid for me to celebrate with my friends. But, for this son of yours, when he comes back after swallowing up your property - he and his women - you kill the calf we had been fattening" (Luke 15:29-30). Notice the detail in these two sentences. First, the elder son feels estranged from his father: like a slave and not like a son. Second, he resents the fact that he has never been given so much as a young goat (kid) to celebrate – a much more modest offering than the fatted calf – but on his own admission, he wanted to celebrate with his friends and not with his family. Third, he adds to the detail of his young brother's misdeeds; he is the first to make any mention of women. He has invented sins that neither the young brother nor the evangelist have mentioned! In these three details we learn that although he has stayed at home, the elder son is just as lost to his father as was his young brother. This therefore is not so much the story of one prodigal son, as it is a story of two lost sons, only one of whom is found again. The elder son cannot accept that he shares the life and luxury of his father; he is consumed by jealousy. Unlike his brother, he refuses to turn back to his father, and again his language betrays his true thoughts: whereas his father refers to 'your brother', the elder son insists on referring to him only as, 'this son of yours'. The father however insists, "it was only right we should celebrate and rejoice, because your brother here was dead and has come to life; he was lost and is found" (Luke 15:32).

There can be no doubt as to whom the two sons represent; they are symbols of the two groups of people mentioned at the beginning of this chapter. The younger son is the symbol for the tax agents and sinners – and as we have already seen, no attempt is made to lessen the sense of the sin that the young man has been guilty of – and the resentful, ungrateful, unforgiving elder son is a warning to the scribes and Pharisees about their own attitude. They run the risk of being just as estranged from the God they claim to serve as the sinners they so much despise, and just as the elder son will hear nothing of his father's pleading, the scribes and Pharisees will hear nothing of Jesus the Prophet's words on God the Father's desire which is only that all his lost children be found; that those as good as dead are brought back to life.

This is arguably the most powerful gospel example of Jesus the Prophet's revelation of the attitude of God to the sinner – to welcome back, to embrace, and even to celebrate the return of anyone who has been lost to him. It is customary for readers of this gospel to try to identify themselves in relation to the main characters. To do this effectively, it is necessary to read the story in the light of the first three sentences of the passage, in which we are told that Jesus spoke the parable for the benefit of scribes and Pharisees who not only refused to hear his words, but who refused to countenance his outreach to those they considered to be unworthy of Jesus' (and God the Father's) attention.

5th Sunday of Lent, Year C. John 8:1-11

The Prophet Jesus shows compassion to a sinful woman rather than condemning her.

Questions to ponder

☐   Do you think the sentence should have been carried out on this woman, and why (or why not)?

□ What, if anything, does the passage tell us about 'punishment' for sin?
□ Why does Jesus tell the woman to sin no more?

This is the only time this year on the Sundays of Lent that we have a gospel which is not from Luke. There is an anomaly, though. This gospel passage is found in our bibles as part of the gospel of John, but most commentators are agreed that the passage doesn't really belong in this gospel. For various reasons, mostly based on the use of language, they conclude that it may have originally been included elsewhere, or might even have stood independently from the gospels we now possess and was only later incorporated into what we now know as the Fourth Gospel. Ironically, it appears to have more in common with the theology and writing of Luke than it does with John – so perhaps it's appropriate that it is read as part of a sequence in which Jesus the Prophet figures so prominently in Luke's gospel readings for Lent. The setting is almost typically Lukan. Whatever its original context and location of this particular passage and no matter how little it fits the context into which it is placed in John's gospel, this is an ideal passage for Lent, bringing to a close as it does a series of passages which have presented Jesus the Prophet progressively revealing God's desire for the repentance of his children, the return of the lost, and now divine compassion which exceeds anything that humans can offer.

Given that the passage did not originally belong in this part of John's gospel, it begins on a strange note: Jesus went to the Mount of Olives. At daybreak he appeared in the Temple again. This is the kind of thing he did in the synoptic accounts after his entry to Jerusalem prior to his passion and death; a useful reminder to us of the proximity of Holy Week and the Easter Triduum. The episode then opens on a new day, with Jesus in a setting more typical of the Synoptics gospels' last week, teaching in the Temple with people coming to hear him. Into this appear the scribes and Pharisees, leading a woman who has been caught in adultery, bringing her into the gathering of Jesus and the crowd. The text is explicit that the woman was caught in the very act; the scribes and Pharisees have dragged her from this situation into the public glare, realising as they do so that she faces certain death as a result of her conduct. The Scribes and Pharisees shown no concern for the woman herself; she is merely an exhibit in their plan to trap Jesus. They know exactly what the scriptures say Moses ordered in this case: she should be condemned to death by stoning. They challenge Jesus on his opinion, but it is not precisely clear at this point what it is they want him to comment on. Is it on their judgement of the woman based on the Law of Moses, or is it on the passing and carrying out of sentence? The point may sound academic, but there are issues involved which would have been contentious at the time, since either question could, depending on how Jesus responded, put him in conflict with either Mosaic or Roman law. There is some question as to whether in Jesus' time the Jews had already lost the right to carry out capital punishment. If that right had already been lost, then it would have been dangerous for Jesus or anyone else to advocate, or worse, to participate in a stoning. The only Jewish piece of evidence in existence about the loss of this right is found in the Jerusalem Talmud, but this dates from a later period, and states that 'forty years before the destruction of the Temple the trial of capital cases was taken away from Israel'. John 18:31, refers to a ban on the Jews putting someone to death; but would this place the ban prior to the events of this gospel passage? Given that the origin of the passage is shrouded in such mystery, it cannot be certain that this would be the case. Clearly, if the ban was in place by this time, then Jesus, had he upheld the sentence handed down by Moses for such cases, would have fallen into the trap of opposing Roman Law; in addition he may also have left himself open to the accusation that his supposed compassion was nothing more than empty speech. If Jesus was to speak against Moses' prescription of death by stoning for the crime of being caught in the act of committing adultery, then he would be accused of speaking against Moses.

Meanwhile the poor woman waits in terror, wondering what fate awaits her. In fact, she faces a grim end. Deuteronomy 22:21 specified stoning for the adultery of a betrothed woman (this would have been the penalty for Mary if Joseph had not decided to settle for informal divorce; c.f. Matthew 1:19), but the manner in which this was to be carried out was not specified. Death by stoning could equally mean being thrown from a height onto rocks, just as the synagogue congregation attempted to do to Jesus when he spoke to them in his home town (Luke 4:29. Alternatively, stones could be thrown at the condemned person. The punishment had to be seen to be carried out by the people as a whole, and so, beginning with the one making the accusation, the assembled group would take part in a symbolic laying of hands on the offender. The ones making the accusation would be the first to cast a stone, in order of seniority, followed by the others. This practice was derived from Leviticus 24:14. This is evidently what is happening here and presumably also at the death of Stephen in Acts 7:58-59. In the present story, there are plenty of accusers ready to condemn the woman, but their determination to uphold the Law of Moses is secondary to their determination to trap and discredit Jesus. They pose the question to Jesus, "'Master, this woman was caught in the very act of committing adultery, and Moses has ordered us in the Law to condemn women like this to death by stoning. What have you to say?" (John 8:4-5). We are not told whether the woman is married or betrothed, although her crime would be adultery in either case. The Scribes and Pharisees who make the accusation do not seem to care. Initially, Jesus feigns total indifference to their machinations, and starts to write something on the ground. There has been much speculation as to what he actually wrote. The text gives us no clue, although various suggestions have been made. Was this an allusion to Jeremiah 17:13: "those who turn away from thee shall be written in the earth, for they have forsaken the LORD" (RSV translation). Jerome and some mediaeval writers surmised that Jesus was writing down the sins of the woman's accusers. Perhaps more probable, given Jesus' initial refusal to answer his questioners, is that he was doodling in the dust while feigning indifference to their ploy. When pressed, he does offer an answer but not one they could ever have expected. He wants them to take personal responsibility for what follows – in a sense in the manner in which such executions would normally be carried out, as referred to already – and he alludes to, rather than quote directly from the scriptures. Witnesses were to throw stones in order of seniority. Jesus issues a challenge which will be responded to in order of seniority; but it is a challenge to each to recognize first his own sinfulness: "If there is one of you who has not sinned, let him be the first to throw a stone at her" (John 8:9). Jesus then returns to writing on the ground again. One by one, the accusers and would-be executioners depart, beginning with the most senior. It is only after a while that Jesus looks up, and becomes the only person in the story to address the woman as a person, "Woman, where are they? Has no one condemned you?" (v.10). Jesus has no concern about the legal arguments with which the scribes and Pharisees had tried to trap him; he only notes the absence of anyone other than the woman, and asks her where her accusers have gone. She replies that there is no one remaining to condemn her; no accuser to lay hands on her head, no one to throw the first stone. Jesus makes no comment on whether the judgement or the sentence would have been just; he merely introduces a whole new element into the episode: neither is he prepared to condemn her.

He is prepared to forgive, indicated by his exhortation to her 'not to sin any more'; only if she is forgiven can she be told not to sin again. So many phrases from the Old Testament come to mind: "though I struck you in anger, in mercy I have pitied you" (Isaiah 60:10); "he has shown us in his mercy and in his boundless goodness" (Isaiah 63:7); "To the Lord our God mercy and pardon belong, because we have betrayed him" (Daniel 9:9); "The Lord is compassion and love,

slow to anger and rich in mercy" (Psalm 102(103):8) and "He does not treat us according to our sins nor repay us according to our faults" (Psalm 102(103):10) all come to mind, although many other examples could be cited. St. Augustine coined the phrase that describes the end situation in this passage. In a literal translation in English, it is powerful enough; 'Two are left: the wretched woman, and mercy'. In the original Latin, it has a poetic ring: *'Relicti sunt duo, misera et misericordia'*

The Prophet Jesus has demonstrated that the will of God is to be compassionate in preference to demanding justice that will end in the destruction of any of his children. This is expressed so fully in the last gospel passage for the Sundays of Year C before Holy Week begins, turning our focus to the events leading to the passion, death and resurrection of Jesus. Paul's letter to the Romans offers what might be the last word we need to say at this stage: "what proves that God loves us is that Christ died for us while we were still sinners. Having died to make us righteous, is it likely that he would now fail to save us from God's anger?" (Romans 5:8-9).

Appendix: Notes for the Year A gospels (reproduced from Volume 1 of this Commentary)

3rd Sunday of Lent, Year A. John 4:5-42

Questions to ponder

☐ Does the Samaritan woman finally manage to make a genuine profession of faith in Jesus? Do the other Samaritans? Do Jesus' own disciples?

☐ What implications does Jesus' insistence on the need to worship God in Spirit and in Truth have for today's Church?

☐ Why is the passage, and the two that follow it, so important for the final stages of preparation of Catechumens (You could ask the same question over the next two weeks as well!)?

(Note: where the Fourth Gospel refers to the Jews, I will follow the convention of many commentaries and use inverted commas. This is to preserve the wording of the gospel but at the same time to avoid any sense of anti-Semitism. Those designated 'the Jews' are a specific group of people who mounted opposition to the works of God made manifest in the person of Jesus).

Preamble

For many, the passages from John's gospel that we read on the 3rd, 4th and 5th Sundays of Lent are not easy to penetrate. For a start their length is against easy reading in church, and then the texts have little by way of a good story that is easy to follow. In each of them, there is much dialogue, and within the dialogue, apparently much repetition. And yet, these passages are so full of wonderful imagery that they deserve the best possible 'opening up' that we as preachers can give them. Mind you, that takes us to yet another problem: these texts are also open to many different readings! All I can do here is to give some suggestions for a reading within the church's liturgy during Lent, which I hope will be able to say something to ourselves as preachers, and to congregations listening to our attempts to let the texts speak to the Church of today.

Jesus and the Samaritan woman

The very title that I have used here highlights yet another problem with these long passages; they are much more extensive in their scope than the title we commonly give them will suggest: the Samaritan woman, the cure of the man born blind, and the raising of Lazarus. In fact, in many ways, each of these passages give only scant mention of the people and events in the title, as we shall see. Each one of these is a complex mix of interpersonal exchanges between Jesus and individuals and groups, interchanges which are placed in opposition and contrast to each other. This may become clearer as we consider each passage in turn.

The evangelist is at pains to place the encounter between Jesus and the Samaritan woman against a clear background: Jews and Samaritans and their differences. The gospel puts it rather succinctly, "Jews, in fact, do not associate with Samaritans" (John 4:9). There is some debate over the exact location of Sychar, but the important reference for the evangelist is that the episode that we are about to consider is placed near the well that Jacob gave to his son Joseph (v. 5). This in itself gives clues to the themes we can expect. Jacob was also known as Israel, and the gift of water that is implicit in the providing of the well forms the basis for the conversation that takes place between Jesus and the woman. Like so many Johannine episodes, this one begins at the basic level of human living and necessity, and develops into a discussion of something much more profound. Practical considerations determine the how and why of the encounter. Jesus has been travelling up until the 6th hour, the hottest part of the day (v. 6). He needs a rest, and he needs a drink. Where better to sit than at a well? Likewise, the woman's arrival is governed by necessity, although that is not explained. We can surmise. She arrives at the well at a time when she expects no one else will be there (women usually gathered water in early morning). Presumably her reputation, which will emerge shortly, prevents her from mixing with the other women. On a human level, what follows should not occur for two reasons. First, Jesus should not speak to the Samaritan because she is a woman, and second, he should not speak to her because she is a Samaritan! Notice that the disciples are absent. We might well ask why all of them had to go to the village to buy food; but already we begin to see signs that divine plans are at work here, setting up an unlikely scenario which will nevertheless enable the narrative to progress.

The conversation begins with an imperative from Jesus to the woman, "Give me a drink". We might be taken aback by the abruptness of the command; the woman certainly was! She is all too aware of the irregularity and incongruity of the situation; Jesus, a Jew, asking her, a woman and a Samaritan, for a drink! There is an element of insult in her reply. This is the only place in this gospel where Jesus us called *Ioudaios*, 'a Jew'. There is not much room for interchange so far!

The woman is in for even more surprises. Jesus informs her that if only she knew what God is offering her at this time she would be the one to ask, and Jesus would himself give her something to drink – not from the well, but from living water (Verse 10). However, the woman is locked in the world of the practical. This Jew has no bucket, and the well is deep; how could he give her living water (v. 11)? What she fails to understand in Jesus' words are the two special ingredients that he has introduced: who is doing the giving, and the nature of the living water that comes from God. These form the basis of the remainder of the discussion. Her misunderstanding of 'living water' can come from two possible meanings of the expression. First, she may be looking for the natural phenomenon of a stream of flowing water, which, if she could find, would mean an end to the trips to the well to carry water home. Second, it can mean life-giving revelation which gives life in abundance. This builds on Biblical themes like Ezekiel's vision of living water pouring from the Temple, giving life to all that come into contact with it (c.f. Ezekiel 47:1-12). This is an expression for the experience of the life of God, which of course Jesus has come to offer. The woman opts for the physical interpretation of running water. She is still stuck with her lack of comprehension. Despite what this Jew says, the well is still deep, and the stranger still has no bucket! However, her tone towards him is changing. First, she had called him "Jew"; now, she calls him "sir" (*kyrie*), a more reverential form of address (John 4:11).

This is where we first encounter a theme that is so important for a reading of this passage, the idea of movement. This is a text in which people's ideas move. The only question is: will the various characters move sufficiently in their faith journey to be able to make a proper identification of Jesus? We have already seen the Samaritan woman's tone change as she converses with Jesus. As the story moves on, so does the woman's level of awareness. When she first replies to Jesus, and dismissively calls him "Jew", she also dismisses his request (command?) for a drink of water. Now, she calls him "sir", and wonders how he can produce the living water he speaks of since he has no bucket. Then she wonders, could this Jew possibly be greater than Jacob, who provided this well for his children and his cattle (which must shed some doubt on the quality of the well's contents – with animals present we might wonder what also went *into* the well!). Now, although the woman herself is almost certainly unaware of this, she is setting out on a theological journey, reflecting on both Jesus and Jacob. When Jesus says, "Whoever drinks this water will get thirsty again; but anyone who drinks the water that I shall give will never be thirsty again: the water that I shall give will turn into a spring inside him, welling up to eternal life" (John 4:13-14), she makes a request of Jesus; "Sir, give me some of that water, so that I may never get thirsty and never have to come here again to draw water" (John 4:15). She has moved on in her response to Jesus, but sadly, she has not moved enough: the issue is still rooted in her drudgery of having to draw water from this all too familiar well. A change of direction is needed, and Jesus initiatives this by turning to the woman's personal life.

Jesus' next instruction at first seems irrelevant, but it is a necessary prelude to the next stage of the encounter. He tells the woman to fetch her husband, and she truthfully replies that she has no husband. Jesus commends her for her honesty, but then shows he knows more than she realised: "You are right to say, 'I have no husband'; for although you have had five, the one you have now is not your husband. You spoke the truth there" (John 4:14-15). What are we to make of this woman's marital history? Feminist writers have suggested that for the woman to have had five husbands would have been virtually impossible under the social conditions of the time. They suggest that the five husbands and the non-married partner she is currently with are symbolic of her futile search for fulfilment in various ways which have ultimately failed her. Her search for elusive happiness in failed relationships stands in marked contrast to the promise of living water and a fulfilled life that Jesus is now offering her. Such a perspective may well contribute to the understanding of the issue, but another aspect should also be considered, and this is the possibility that her marital infidelity is linked to her Samaritan nationality, with its history of infidelity to the Covenant with God. There was constant suspicion among the Jews as regards the Samaritans. Their history had at one time been as part of the Northern Kingdom of Israel, notorious for its dalliance with the religious practices of the neighbouring nations and which had led the prophet Hosea to speak out against its behaviour. Here are a couple of examples of Hosea's preaching: "The inhabitants of Samaria are trembling for the calf of Beth-aven; yes, its people mourn for it, its so-called priests bewail its glory, now this has vanished. The calf itself shall be carried off to Assyria as tribute to the Great King. Ephraim will reap the shame, and Israel blush for his idol. Samaria has had her day. Her king is like a straw drifting on the water. The idolatrous high places shall be destroyed-that sin of Israel; thorn and thistle will grow on their altars. Then they will say to the mountains, 'Cover us!' and to the hills, 'Fall on us!'" (Hosea 10:5-8), and, "the more I called to them, the further they went from me; they have offered sacrifice to the Baals and set their offerings smoking before the idols" (Hosea 11:2). The woman in the story, with her dysfunctional private life, is the embodiment of all that was inadequate in the Samaritan race itself.

The woman's first reaction to Jesus' revelation of her private affairs is to say, "I see you are a prophet, sir" (John 4:19). Her estimation of Jesus has moved further. She calls him 'sir' once again, but now accords him the status of a prophet. This is her conclusion on the strength of her discovery that he can know more than she has told him. This is quite a move forward, because she knows that there are the differences between Jews and Samaritans in terms of religion: "Our fathers worshipped on this mountain, while you say that Jerusalem is the place where one ought to worship". Her reaction to Jesus reminds us of the reaction of Nathanael to Jesus' statement that he had seen him under the fig tree in John 1:48. Nathanael goes from calling Jesus 'Rabbi' to, "you are the Son of God, you are the King of Israel" (John 1:49). In both cases, Jesus promises more to the person he addresses. To the Samaritan woman, he sums up the reason for the religious suspicion that Jews and Samaritans retain of each other, all rooted in their respective traditions. Although there will be serious conflict between Jesus and the Jewish people in this gospel, he can still maintain the superiority of Jewish traditions to those of the Samaritans: "Believe me, woman, the hour is coming when you will worship the Father neither on this mountain nor in Jerusalem. You worship what you do not know; we worship what we do know: for salvation comes from the Jews. But the hour will come - in fact it is here already - when true worshippers will worship the Father in spirit and truth: that is the kind of worshipper the Father wants. God is spirit, and those who worship must worship in spirit and truth" (John 4:21-24).

This last statement is one that the woman will not yet be able to understand. He is the reason why worship is now to be 'in spirit and in truth'; he is the 'place' for true worship. The woman takes another backward step (metaphorically), retreating to her familiar traditions, "I know that Messiah - that is, Christ - is coming; and when he comes he will tell us everything" (John 4:25). Whatever her understanding of Messiah, she clearly relates this to Jesus' having told her everything about herself. This will continue to be her points of fixation, no matter where Jesus tries to lead the discussion. Jesus now makes a statement about who he is – the Messiah, a disclosure he makes through one of the 'I AM' statements so prevalent in this gospel, "'I who am speaking to you," said Jesus "I am he" (John 4:26). In these statements, which recall the revelation of Yahweh to Moses at the burning bush, "say to the sons of Israel: 'I Am has sent me to you'" (Exodus 3:14). When Jesus uses an I AM statement in this gospel it frequently carries some predicate, adding to the listener's understanding of the One who reveals himself as God, e.g. I AM the bread of life/light of the world/the Good Shepherd/the Way, Truth, Life, and in this case, I AM he (= the Messiah); but he is Messiah because he brings streams of living water, because he provides the focus and the place for worship of god in spirit and in truth; not because he tells a woman all that she had ever done.

The narrative is interrupted here, without any sign being given of a resolution of the woman's failure to comprehend fully Jesus' words. At this stage, the disciples return from the village with food and the woman disappears. Is this because the disciples have appeared? Does she flee because she senses they will conclude something scandalous has occurred between Jesus and her? As far as the narrative is concerned, the evangelist now takes the opportunity to take us back over some of the ground covered so far by uncovering the same lack of faith in the disciples as we witnessed in the woman. Her story began with an inappropriate use of a title for Jesus (a "Jew"); they now call Jesus "rabbi", whereas Jesus has demonstrated he is so much more than any rabbi. The woman was obsessed with the problem of Jesus obtaining (and offering her) water without proper provision (a bucket); the disciples urge Jesus to eat, and wonder if he has managed to obtain food in their absence, food that they knew nothing about. Are they taken aback that perhaps Jesus knows more (i.e. about how to get food) than they previously thought he did, just as the woman was impressed by his knowledge of more of her life than she had thought he would?

Jesus' food is to do the will of his father, and to complete his work (John 4:34); and this is the clue as to why the whole episode has taken place. The details of this narrative are fraught with difficulties. No attempt is made to explain why Jesus should have gone to Samaria in the first place; Luke in particular testifies to the hostility Jesus and his disciples met at their hands (Luke 9:52-53). There is likewise no explanation why the Samaritan woman comes to the well at the most improbable hour of the day. I have already suggested that, given her reputation, she would probably have to collect water at a time when other women were unlikely to be present, but does it have to be at the very hottest hour of the day? However, Jesus' speech to his disciples indicates that this whole encounter has taken place because God's work is to be done. He quotes a proverb which seems to advocate a leisurely approach to life, "four months, and then the harvest" (v. 35), but for Jesus, urgency is the order of the day; the harvest is already ripe. The harvest clearly is the Samaritans, and the task is not just Jesus'. The disciples are associated with his work; missionary activity has begun. This story concentrates on characters beyond the familiar world of Judaism - notice also that disciples are only present in the absence of Samaritans. It is this previously despised race that are the focus of the story, which becomes perhaps a commentary on John 3:17, "For God sent his Son into the world not to condemn the world, but so that through him the world might be saved".

There is a final part to the narrative. The woman, who may have been avoiding the company of her fellow Samaritans at the beginning of the story, had progressed sufficiently on her faith journey to have the confidence to say to the villagers, "Come and see a man who has told me everything I ever did; I wonder if he is the Christ? (John 4:29). She is still unable to progress beyond the wonder of Jesus, the prophet who could tell her everything she had ever done. It appears she never goes beyond this. However, on the strength of her testimony, the villagers are prepared to approach Jesus themselves. And they are able as a result of a two-day stay with him to say to the woman, "Now we no longer believe because of what you told us; we have heard him ourselves and we know that he really is the saviour of the world" (John 4:42). The Word of Jesus (=the Word who IS Jesus) is much greater than the word of the woman ABOUT Jesus. Do the villagers come to a true faith in Jesus? It would appear so at first: they call him the saviour of the world. However, in the gospel passages for the next two weeks we will have occasion to question the depth of statements of faith like this one, but that discussion must wait for the present.

4th Sunday of Lent, Year A; John 9:1-41

Questions to ponder

☐ The dialogue in this narrative centres time and again on *how* Jesus healed the man born blind. Where might the Church of today become obsessed with *how* God works, rather than why and where?

☐ Try to identify the stereotyping of characters that goes on in this narrative. Do we apply the same stereotypes today?

☐ The cure of the man born blind leads to much division in the Jerusalem community. Where does the work of God cause division in our communities?

☐   Does the formerly blind man become a 'full-blown' believer? What is the evidence for or against?

This narrative will draw on many of the ideas of faith journey that we already encountered in the story of Jesus and the Samaritan woman last week, but unlike last week's narrative, this one is set firmly in Jewish territory, in Jerusalem in the vicinity of the Temple. Main features include Pharisees, Jews, the synagogue, and debates about points of law. The immediate context of the passage is the Jewish Feast of Tabernacles, the final stages of which involved the sprinkling (washing) of people with water from the pool of Siloam. It also involved the lighting of lamps in the Temple precincts. This is one of the many times in John's gospel when Jesus is present in Jerusalem during a major feast, and in which he shows himself to give the true significance of the feast. This time, he declares himself to be the Light for the world, and the issue of giving glory to God, i.e. recognising the presence of God in his works, is also evident.

This passage is the only occasion in Jesus' ministry in which he is not the main player: the various other characters are more evident in the course of events than Jesus is. The text itself provides instances of a commentary on scripture. The disciples open the discussion with a question about a man who has been blind from birth. They want to know who was responsible for this man's condition: was it the result of his parents' sin, or had the man himself sinned while still in the womb? The question sounds crass today, but it highlights a biblical principle, that God will punish evil that is done, (Exodus 20:5; Numbers 14:18; Deuteronomy 5:9; Tobit 3:3-4). Conversely, God cannot be blamed for the evil that befalls people. The belief was that evil was the punishment for wrongdoing. Returning to the disciples' question, notice that Jesus does not give them a direct answer. Instead, he describes the man's plight as an occasion for showing forth the works of God. This reminds us of the Samaritan experience, which was also the occasion for God's work to be done, which in itself is what nourishes Jesus. This man has never seen light, but now Jesus declares, "I am the light of the world" (John 9:5), another I AM saying with a predicate to develop further Jesus' self-disclosure. In the Samaritan narrative, Jesus associated his disciples in his work; now he does the same once again: "we must carry out the work of the one who sent me" (John 4:4a). The Jerusalem Bible translation misses the point when it has this verse refer to Jesus' activity alone: the Greek begins the sentence with the plural pronoun *hemas*, 'we'. There is an important consequence of this involvement of the disciples. As long as Jesus is in the world, he is the light of the world, but if his disciples are to do the father's work along with Jesus, then they are to make the presence of Jesus the light of the world one that is continuous. The evangelist states that Jesus sent the man to wash in the Pool of Siloam, and adds the commentary, "a name that means 'sent'". John's exegesis is much briefer than mine, but it is, I think, important to make the link between the work of the one who has sent Jesus, and the water which reinforces the notion of being sent to do God's work. So there is nothing random in this cure; it is the work of God which is being revealed. Further, it is not the waters of Siloam that effect the cure; it is effected by God, the one who has done the sending in the first place. As is so often the case in John's gospel, the actual miracle is treated almost perfunctorily: the action is covered in one verse, "he spat on the ground, made a paste with the spittle, put this over the eyes of the blind man" (John 9:6), and the next verse covers the command to wash, and the effect of his obeying the Word made flesh. Is there a biblical link in the paste that Jesus makes and applies to the man's eyes – possibly an allusion to creation of humanity in Genesis 2:7? If so, the point is not laboured here.

The immediate result of Jesus' action and the man being sent is, of course, that he is given sight. What follows is surprising, though. The cure not appear to give glory to God but to cause immediate division on a number of levels, some more serious than others. To begin with, there is division among the neighbours. The question is raised "Isn't this the man who used to sit and beg?" Opinion is divided. Some say it is; others say, no, it just looks like him. In last Sunday's narrative at the Samaritan well, Jesus made a self-declaration (John 4:26); now, the formerly blind man does the same; "I am the man". In other words, he speaks for himself. People want to know how he received his sight. Just as the Samaritan woman became fixated on Jesus' knowledge of her personal life, so the *how* of the blind beggar's cure will become a fixation here. The question being asked no less than six times in the chapter. The man can only answer, "The man called Jesus made a paste, daubed my eyes with it and said to me, 'Go and wash at Siloam'; so I went, and when I washed I could see" (John 9:11), and when he is asked who healed him, he can only answer "the man called Jesus". The man does not know that he has been healed by the one who was 'Sent by God'; but he is at least prepared to admit he does not know where the man is.

The next division is found between the man and the Pharisees, they become involved because the neighbours take the man to them (John 9:13). At this point, the narrator informs us, as if in passing, that the day on which Jesus cured the blind man was the Sabbath. Don't we just know there is going to be trouble! The Pharisees ask the same question: how did this happen. The blind man reports that the man named Jesus put clay on his eyes, and he washed, and he can see. The Pharisees realise the heart of the problem: Jesus has broken the Sabbath by making and applying clay – doing work! This man cannot be from God, because he does not keep the Sabbath (c.f. 9:16). But there is division among the ranks of the Pharisees; some say, "How could a sinner produce signs like this?" (John 9:16). So, in their division, they go back to the man and ask him what he has to say about the man. Once again, the formerly blind man has to speak for himself, he who has already had to declare that he is the one who used to be the blind beggar. Now, his assessment of Jesus is that, "He is a prophet" (John 9:17). Just as we saw in the story of the Samaritan woman, the formerly blind man makes a transition in his understanding of who Jesus is; at first, he was 'the man Jesus'; now, he is 'a prophet'. The Samaritan woman concluded Jesus was a prophet because of what he knew about her; the man in this story reaches the same conclusion because Jesus made him able to see.

The next case of division among people occurs between the man's parents and the Pharisees. We can see in this scene that as the man progresses in awareness (sight?), the Pharisees are in fact moving in the opposite direction. This will continue until the end of the chapter. 'The Jews', as they are now described, still refuse to believe that the man has been cured: they are still demanding facts, wanting to know *how* the man had been cured. Belief is beyond them, and they will settle only for hard facts. They summon the people best able to testify to these facts: the parents of the man, but their questioning is laced with subtle threat and abuse, suggesting that they have been lying all along, and the man was not born blind at all. The parents are not prepared to make any statement beyond declaring that yes, this is their son, yes he was born blind, and yes, now he can see. They haven't a clue how he can see, and suggest that they go and ask the man himself: he is, after all, old enough to speak for himself (John 9:19-21)! The story has been told and re-told repeatedly; but facts do not lead to faith. This can only come about through the true identity of Jesus, the Light of the World, the Sent One of God, who is at this stage of the story on trial in his absence (a foretaste of the trial that he will undergo in the passion narrative, John 18-19).

The parents remain static characters throughout the narrative. The once-blind man is already moving closer to the Light which is Jesus; the Pharisees are receding further into the darkness. The parents do not move. They don't want any trouble; they don't want to be asked to commit themselves, and they certainly don't want to be expelled from the synagogue, which 'the Jews' had used to threaten anyone who claimed that Jesus was the Christ. So, to avoid further trouble, they tell 'the Jews' to go and ask their son for any further information.

'The Jews' summon the man, and go over the same ground once again, but they open this discussion more formally, with the phrase "Give glory to God!" (John 9:24). It is ironic that they use this phrase, which was used legally before taking a testimony from someone – or a confession of guilt. The concept of the glory of God was an Old Testament one related to a sense of the presence of God among his people. In John's gospel, the miracles (signs) that Jesus works are manifestations of the glory of God, a glory that is shown to belong to Jesus himself (c.f. John 2:11). When Jesus; hour comes, his glory will be seen, that is, when he undergoes death and resurrection, God is truly present and at work in this. But 'the Jews' who demand that the man give glory to God show that they are blind to that glory. The God they say they give glory to, is not the God who is being revealed to them in the works of Jesus.
The man had earlier stated that he did not know where Jesus was; 'the Jews' are most definite in what they claim they know. They express this in different ways: a) they 'know' that Jesus is a sinner; b) they 'know' that God spoke to Moses; c) they 'know' that the man born blind is a sinner through and through since his birth. What they don't know is where Jesus came from. This lack of knowledge is going to be compounded by their continued insistence on enquiring *how* the man received his sight.

The man's argument is also rooted in the miracle, but in a different way. He notes the inconsistency in the argument of 'the Jews': they say they don't know where he comes from, but, he says; "He has opened my eyes, and you don't know where he comes from! We know that God doesn't listen to sinners, but God does listen to men who are devout and do his will. Ever since the world began it is unheard of for anyone to open the eyes of a man who was born blind; if this man were not from God, he couldn't do a thing." (John 9:30-33). The man has made extraordinary progress in his faith journey – earlier, he had said he didn't know if the man who cure him was a sinner or not; all he knew then was that this man had opened his eyes. Now, he insists that anyone who could do such a remarkable thing as open the eyes of someone born blind – something never before seen in the world. There is more than a hint of irony when the man, whom they have asked yet again to explain how he got his sight, wonders, "do you want to become his disciples too?" (John 9:27). They then state their true position: they are disciples of Moses! The very people who claim to listen to the words of Moses are the ones who fail to listen to the prophet that Moses promised would come after him (Deuteronomy 18:15, 18, 20) the Word made Flesh, the Son of Man, who has come down from heaven (John 3:13).

When Jesus ask the man if he believes in the Son of Man, he answers, "tell me who he is so that I may believe in him" (v. 36). When Jesus replies, "You are looking at him; he is speaking to you" (v. 37), the man professes belief and worships him. However, can we conclude that he has completed his journey of faith? Perhaps not. In his own way, he too is still suffering from a fixation on how the miracle was worked; not on the idea that he believes what Jesus speaks of, because of what he has seen. Certainly, the formerly blind man has made significant progression from calling Jesus "the man" who gave him sight, to 'a prophet'', to someone who must come from God because of what he has done. He has done all of this in the face of doubt and opposition from neighbours, parents, co-religionists. And yet, he has finally bowed down before the Son of Man, the one Sent by God, the Light of the World. It does after all look as if the man has made Jesus' earlier words come true: his condition, and his transformation to sight and to belief in the one God has sent have indeed allowed the Works of God to be made manifest in him.

This passage also shows how people place themselves in judgement before the works of God. The man has made a transition from blindness to sight, but also from darkness to light. 'The Jews' have gone in the opposite direction. They reject the words and actions of the one who was sent. They protest vehemently when Jesus suggests that they are still blind, but their refusal to accept the one who was sent shows the true depth of their blindness. They claim to have all the knowledge they need in Moses, therefore they shut themselves off from the revelation that God offers them in Jesus. There is no need for external judgement to be passed on them; by their actions, they demonstrate the full extent of their profound blindness.

Before concluding, let's go back to the beginning of the passage. In retrospect, we can now appreciate how the image of seeing permeates the text in ways we might not have been initially aware of. For instance, society 'sees' the man born blind as an outsider, marginalized by his contemporaries, made to beg, because he had the misfortune to be born blind. The disciples 'see' him as a possible sinner because of his condition, the religious leaders are in no doubt about his status; they 'see' him as a sinner through and through, and as a result, expel him from the synagogue on account of his sinful – in their eyes – adherence to the person of Jesus, whom they 'see' only as a law-breaker, and therefore a sinner. Only Jesus looks at the man afflicted with blindness form birth, and sees in him the opportunity to make visible the works of God. Earlier, we discussed the involvement of the disciples in the ministry of Jesus, i.e. in the task of making visible the works of God. Inevitably, this leaves us with the question of how well equipped we are today to see in the afflicted and the needy the opportunity to make known the works of God.

5th Sunday of Lent, Year A. John 11:1-45

Questions to ponder

☐   Do you consider that Martha and/or Mary come to full faith in this passage?

☐   If the answer to the above is 'no', what are the signs that their faith is limited? And do they have equal faith?

☐   What does this passage have to say to those on the verge of baptism?

In last week's gospel, the miracle (sign) came near the beginning of the narrative. This week it comes at the end. The passage is redolent with themes of death (and resurrection). At the beginning, there is the discussion between Jesus and his disciples about his decision to go to Judea. When Jesus announces this intention, the disciples remind him that it is not that long since 'the Jews' there wanted to stone him. Later, Thomas advocates mass-suicide, as he invites his fellow-disciples to accompany Jesus and die with him, and of course the death of Lazarus forms the background to the whole narrative. The rest of the chapter, which is not included for reading in the liturgy for this Sunday, tells how the response of the Pharisees and the Chief Priests to the raising of Lazarus is to plot to kill Jesus, and in the episode following that, they decide they want to kill Lazarus too, since it was on his account that many were leaving them and believing in Jesus. Related to this is an important Johannine theme: the 'hour' of Jesus. In the encounter with the Samaritan woman, Jesus had spoken of the hour to come, "- in fact it is here already - when true worshippers will worship the Father in spirit and truth: that is the kind of worshipper the Father wants" (John 4:23). As this narrative unfolds, it becomes clear that the 'hour' of Jesus is rapidly approaching. This story brings the series of Johannine miracles (or signs) to a dramatic climax, and yet once again the miracle itself plays only a small part in the scene. As we saw in the story of the cure of the man born blind, the miracle itself should not become the focus for attention: it is faith in Jesus that is the key issue. As in the gospels for the previous two Sundays, the details of the narrative are particularly illuminating, even though through familiarity, these can sometimes be overlooked. We forget, for example that we are introduced at this late stage in the gospel to three entirely new characters, in a new setting: Mary, Martha and Lazarus, all from Bethany. These must have been well-known to the early readers of the gospel because we are told that this was the Mary who anointed Jesus and wiped his feet with her hair BEFORE the episode is actually recorded in the gospel (the incident won't be related until the beginning of the following chapter). Some have suggested that this is because the original order of the gospel of John has been lost; others more sensibly conclude that the episode was so well known that it could be referred to before it is reached in the narrative. Interestingly, Jesus is absent from the scene of the main activity at the beginning of the narrative, and after the episode concludes, he will have to withdraw again.

Lazarus' condition receives extensive coverage. Jesus may be away from Bethany, but Mary and Martha (notice the order in which they are mentioned: Mary appears to have been the more prominent of the two sisters) are able to send word to him, "Lord, the man you love is ill" (11:3). That Lazarus is ill is mentioned five times in the first six verses. Jesus stays where he is for two more days, before announcing that he is going to Judea: that is where Lazarus is resting, and Jesus is going to wake him (John 11:7-11). The disciples show their lack of understanding in two different ways. First, they call Jesus "rabbi", just as they had done in 4:31. Despite the fact that there have been many examples where people have grown in their understanding of who Jesus is, reflected in the titles they use, the disciples are back where they were at the start. This is a feature of the present story: even where people seem to make progress in their faith, there is still a tendency for them to regress. The second way in which they misunderstand is in not realising that Jesus is speaking of Lazarus' death. "Lord, if he is able to rest he is sure to get better". Jesus has to clarify the situation, "Lazarus is dead" (John 11:14). Once again, an event which is the occasion of so much misunderstanding, will have consequences which are to do with God's work. Lazarus' death will have two consequences. First, it will be the means by which God's glory is seen and second, through it Jesus himself will be glorified. Again, the concept of the glory of God draws from the Old Testament idea that the glory of God somehow referred to the sense of God's presence and action; it has nothing to do with the splendour that is associated with Jesus' divine nature. In the next chapter, Jesus' glory will be linked to 'his hour', "Now my soul is troubled. What shall I say: Father, save me from this hour? But it was for this very reason that I have come to this hour. Father, glorify your name!' A voice came from heaven, 'I have glorified it, and I will glorify it again.'" (John 12:27-28).

When they finally arrived at Bethany, Lazarus was already four days in the tomb. This will be stressed again later. There is to be no doubt that Lazarus is well and truly dead. When Martha hears that Jesus has arrived, she ruses out to meet him. Her first words are understandably in rebuke of Jesus, "If you had been here, my brother would not have died". Even now though she accepts that God will do whatever Jesus asks (John 11:21-22). Jesus immediately takes the opportunity to affirm the truth of the resurrection of the dead, "Your brother will rise again". Martha has no problem with this; she clearly is one of those who believe in the resurrection on the last day – unlike those who followed the parry of the Sadducees, who did not accept the resurrection. Perhaps Martha's problem is that she only accepts resurrection as a future, detached event. What happens in the here and now is what causes her grief. Jesus teaches her a bit more. With another I AM phrase, he says, "I am the resurrection. If anyone believes in me, even though he dies he will live, and whoever lives and believes in me will never die. Do you believe this?" (John 11:25-26). Martha replies "Yes, Lord,' I believe that you are the Christ, the Son of God, the one who was to come into this world" (John 11:27), but we cannot yet be sure that her faith is complete. Like Nicodemus, like the man born blind, she can accept that Jesus is someone with special access to God, who can work wonders, who is the Lord's anointed – even that he is the one awaited; but there is still Martha's rebuke that none of this need have happened if only Jesus had hurried up. She displays no recognition that the entire event of Lazarus' illness and death are about the work of God unfolding. Like the disciples, she fails to understand the full significance of Jesus' ministry.

Now the attention turns to Mary. Whereas Martha ran toward Jesus, she now tells Mary that the Master wants to see her (John 11:28): Martha runs to Jesus, but Mary is called by him. Mary uses similar words to Martha, but they do not appear as a rebuke: she knows that had Jesus been present Lazarus; death could have been avoided, but she also falls at Jesus' feet – an act of worship which Martha did not think to perform. Does Mary possess a faith that is lacking in Martha? The initial signs are good; whereas 'the Jews' in attendance think that when Mary runs from the house that she is going to the tomb to weep, she in fact goes out in answer to Jesus' call. She has heard the voice of the Lord and she responds. When she does throw herself at Jesus' feet, she does not add Martha's remark, uttered in desperate hope perhaps, that even now, God will do what Jesus asks: she seems to accept Jesus as he stands before her, and she submits to whatever he will do next.

So far, we have every sign that Mary expresses a faith that has not been seen in any other part of the gospel, but then the narrative takes an extraordinary turn. This verse has been variously interpreted. Many see in this the human dimension of Jesus, and his reaction at the death of his friend, and the grief of his family and neighbours. But another reading has also been suggested. Firstly, Jesus is moved at Mary's tears. We need to ask why? The answer may come following his next question, "Where have you put him?" (John 11:34). Why does Jesus sigh from the heart? In his prayer to the father some verses further on, he will say "Father, I thank you for hearing my prayer. I knew indeed that you always hear me, but I speak for the sake of all these who stand round me, so that they may believe it was you who sent me" (John 11:41-42), so it does not make sense that Jesus would be expressing emotion at the death of Lazarus. His cry from the heart may be more realistically interpreted as a heartfelt sorrow that 'the Jews', his disciples, and Martha have not yet understood what he has come on earth to do. This view is reinforced by what happens next. Jesus asks to be shown where they have put Lazarus. Verse 35, which follows, is the shortest verse in the Bible, as is well-known by quiz fans. It is shorter in English than it is in Greek. "Jesus wept". It tells us what he said, but it does not tell us why. 'The Jews' give an interpretation, "and the Jews said, "See how much he loved him!" but others wondered why the one who could give sight to the man born blind could not have prevented Lazarus' death. It has been suggested that Jesus' distress comes, not from the death of Lazarus, which he could have prevented, and which he will overcome, but by the fixation of all around him with the apparent finality of Lazarus' death. Mary worships Jesus, but weeps for one who is dead to her: her brother, Lazarus. No one, it seems, has realised that what is going on is that God is being glorified in Jesus' actions. Lazarus; death should not have been the centre of everyone's attention, if they had penetrated the truth of Jesus' identity, that is. But despite Mary and Martha's apparently impressive words, they are unable to move beyond the death of their brother. Thus, when Jesus tells them to remove the stone covering the tomb, Martha is shocked! This is the fourth day since Lazarus was buried. To put not too fine a point on it, he will smell by now! What happened to Martha's earlier insistence that whatever Jesus asked of God would be granted? Martha's words are her statement to Jesus that he has no authority over one who has lain in the tomb for such a long time. So, are Jesus' cry from the heart and his tears an expression of frustration that so near to his own death, no one has yet understood his mission? Are his tears rather of anger and disappointment?

It should perhaps be noted that the evangelist uses two different verbs to describe the weeping of Mary and the Jews (*klaiō*), and that of Jesus (*dakyrō*), as if he wants to distinguish between two types of weeping, or two different reasons for these expressions of emotion. Up until she meets Jesus, nothing has been said of Mary's tears, or of her mourning, but now, she shows in reality that she has joined 'the Jews' who came to comfort her.

No matter how disappointed Jesus may have been, his task has to be completed. He reminds Martha; "Have I not told you that if you believe you will see the glory of God?" (John 11:40). Jesus takes complete charge of what follows; others offered to show him where the tomb was; but Jesus reaches the tomb himself – no one takes him. When they have removed the stone, Jesus prays for all to hear. This prayer, as Jesus himself says, is not for his own benefit; he has complete confidence that his prayers are heard; but he prays that those around, who have been sadly short of faith, may believe that it was God who sent Jesus (just as he was the Sent One in the tale of the man born blind).

The focus so far has not been on Lazarus. We have now reached verse 43, and only now does the miracle occur. In a perfunctory manner, Jesus, the Word of God, Sent by the Father, utters a loud word of command: "Lazarus, here! Come out" (John 11:43). At the command of the Word of God, Lazarus gets up to his feet, and emerges from the tomb, still wearing his 'funeral clothes'. That Lazarus has been freed from death by another is emphasised by the fact that he needs to be freed from the cloths that bind him by the command of the one who called him from the tomb. At another – this time empty - tomb, disciples will see the grave clothes that had bound Jesus are lying neatly rolled up. No one freed Jesus. He had the power to lay down his life, and the power to take it up again (c.f. John 10:17). Finally, we are told many of the Jews who had come to visit Mary – there is no mention of Martha here – came to believe in Jesus because they saw what he had done. Again, the fixation is on the miracle: on what Jesus has *done*, not on *who he is*.

This story is the dramatic climax of Jesus' ministry. It shows how God is glorified in the works of Jesus, but what is not yet clear is how Jesus is glorified in this. The missing information will come in the next chapter, where we read, "Jesus said, 'Now my soul is troubled. What shall I say: Father, save me from this hour? But it was for this very reason that I have come to this hour. Father, glorify your name!' A voice came from heaven, 'I have glorified it, and I will glorify it again.' People standing by, who heard this, said it was a clap of thunder; others said, 'It was an angel speaking to him'. Jesus answered, 'It was not for my sake that this voice came, but for yours. Now sentence is being passed on this world; now the prince of this world is to be overthrown. And when I am lifted up from the earth, I shall draw all men to myself.' By these words he indicated the kind of death he would die" (John 12:27-33).

Now sentence is being passed on the world, that is, Jesus' long-awaited 'hour' has come (c.f. 2:4). This 'hour' is when God will be glorified in Jesus' death, in which Jesus himself will be glorified, that is, in his death, God will be revealed in Jesus. This is why when the Fourth Gospel presents its version of the Passion Narrative, Jesus, when on trial, effectively becomes the focus for the judgement that people call on themselves. When confronted with the Glory of God, sentence is passed on the world for its refusal to accept the One that God has sent – but that's material for another time – Good Friday, to be precise.

Passion (Palm) Sunday, the Triduum, and Easter Sundays 1 & 2 C

Introduction: why bother to preach on the Passion?
It's understandable that some preachers are inclined not to preach on Palm Sunday or Good Friday. The usually reason/excuse is that there is too much going on in the Passion narratives for anyone to make sense of it in a homily; in any case, everyone knows the story. The opposite argument, though, is that given the complexity of these long narratives, we owe it to congregations to give at least a few pointers on the main characteristics highlighted by each of the evangelists. Can we afford *not* to say a few words? As readers, can we afford *not* to take the opportunity to deepen our understanding of such rich texts? At the beginning of Holy Week, we have the added factor of the extra gospel on Palm Sunday – the entry into Jerusalem, which needs some explanation if it is not to be brushed aside immediately after it is read to make way for the longer passion gospel.

This year, Luke gives us very carefully crafted narratives for both passages, and brings to a focus many of the themes of the main body of his gospel that we have already encountered this year. Particularly prominent in both the Entry Narrative and the Passion in Luke's gospel, is the theme of Jesus the Prophet, the fulfilment of the one Moses had foretold, "the Lord your God will raise up for you a prophet like myself, from among yourselves, from your own brothers; to him you must listen" (Deuteronomy 18:15) and "I will raise up a prophet like yourself for them from their own brothers; I will put my words into his mouth and he shall tell them all I command him." (Deuteronomy 18:18). One way to read Luke's passion, I suggest, is effectively to consider the themes from the end to the beginning of the passion account, identifying fulfilment of prophecies, and then tracing back to find their first utterance by Jesus. For example, the death of Jesus is the fulfilment of his prophecy that he will not celebrate with them again until it is fulfilled in the kingdom of God. For Luke, this fulfilment is in his death and resurrection, because he does break bread again with the disciples after the resurrection.

In this collection of notes, those for the celebrations which involve texts used each year are repeated from previous years.

Palm Sunday – Jesus' entry into Jerusalem: Luke 19:28-40

Any comments made on this passage will need to be brief, given liturgical constraints on this day. Perhaps two main observations could be made. The first is that Luke tells much the same story as we find in all four gospels: the agreement is that Jesus enters Jerusalem on a colt, or a donkey. In doing so, he re-enacts the procession of newly crowned kings coming in peace, as the donkey betokens (a king intent on war would enter the city on a war horse, and be accompanied by an army). An additional feature of the kingly entry is that disciples threw their garments on the animal to provide a makeshift saddle: a sign of respect for the royal personage show by placing the owner's property at the king's disposal.

The second observation is that the differences between Luke and the other narratives are very significant. Luke makes no mention of palms or other branches being cut down. Perhaps having given subtle hints at the recognition of Jesus' royal status, the evangelist also wants to play down any detail that might have prompted the authorities to read Messianic intentions into Jesus' actions. The leaders tried to makes these very charges against Jesus, but the evangelist is at pains to point out that they had no foundation. Also noteworthy is that Luke omits from the song of the disciples the word 'hosanna': a Hebrew word which may not have been understood by Luke's Greek speaking readers.

Finally, the scribes and Pharisees (possibly being friendly on this occasion?) ask Jesus to silence his disciples, perhaps for fear of them drawing attention from the authorities at a time of tension prior to the Passover when crowds (including Jesus and his disciples) are gathering. Jesus' reply takes on the form of a prophetic utterance, one which will not however, need to be fulfilled, "if these keep silence the stones will cry out" (Luke 19:40). This statement will be fulfilled in this real sense: at Jesus' death, various groups of people will bear testimony to the righteousness of the one whose death they have just witnessed, and in Acts, the Sanhedrin find it impossible to silence those who bear witness to the Risen Christ; on this note, we turn to Luke's version of the Passion Narrative itself.

Palm Sunday - The Passion of Our Lord Jesus Christ. Luke 22:14-23:56
An outline of the sections of this Passion narrative might be helpful. In the table below, the references to verses, the section themes or headings, and connections with the rest of the gospel are outlined.

	references	Section description	Fulfilment of earlier
1.	22:14-23	Passover meal (Last Supper)	Luke's gospel sets great observation of Jewish fe and makes frequent refei Jerusalem and the Temp gospel opens and also cl
2.	22:24-38	Teachings at the Last Supper Table	This recalls Jesus teachii the leading Pharisee, Lui
3.	22:39-53	The Time of testing	c.f. Luke 11:1-4, the Loi not put us to the test"; "\ Man find any faith on hi 18:8
4.	22:54-71	Hearing before the Sanhedrin	c.f. Luke 21:12, "men w to the synagogues and tc
5.	23:1-12	Delivered to Prefect and King	c.f. Luke 21:12 "men wi before kings and govern my name"
6.	23:13-31	Jesus condemned to death	3 passion predictions in
7.	23:32-46	The Death of the Prophet	3 passion predictions in
8.	23:47-56	Reactions to the Prophet's Death	c.f. Isaiah 52:13-53:12; ‹ The contents of this are : death, according to Luke

The plan here is to begin at the end, with reactions to the death of the prophet, and to work to the beginning, seeing were the prophetic indications were building up. Luke devotes more time and space to these reactions than do the other evangelists, although at the same time he deals with his material with economy, making this an accessible presentation of the material from the tradition about Jesus' death.

8. Reactions to the Death of the Prophet; Luke 23:47-56

There are four main reactions to Jesus' death. First is the centurion, who
having seen what had happened, gave glory to God and proclaimed "this was
a great and good man" (Jerusalem Bible version; a more literal rendition
would be, this was a righteous man", i.e. a man who did God's will in every
way). Next are those standing by and who had turned up to watch the
spectacle of the executions and who afterwards went home beating their
breasts. Literally, they turn back to the city; the Greek for this is used later in
Acts to indicate conversion, which the beating of breasts here also indicates.
These are the people who will ask Peter in Acts 2:37 what they now must do,
and are told that they must repent and be baptised. It is noteworthy that Luke
does not consider the crowd to be hostile during the passion narrative; they
are neutral as they had tended to be in the travel narrative (Luke 9:51-19:27).
Next come friends and the women who had followed Jesus from Galilee.
They remain at a distance but they are still eyewitnesses. Finally, Joseph of
Arimathea and the women carry out a hasty burial for Jesus. Luke describes
Joseph as a member of the Council who disagreed with the decision of other
members to have Jesus arrested. The reactions of all four groups mentioned
here are all favourable to Jesus, in contrast to the position of the Jewish
authorities, whom Luke blames for his death.

7. The death of the Prophet; Luke 23:32-46

This is above all the fulfilment of three prophetic statements by Jesus that the
Son of Man must be put to death. In the story of Jesus' death, Luke sets his
own particular emphases once more, while still working firmly within the
tradition. He makes a clear distinction between the leaders of the people and
soldiers who mock Jesus, and the people who observe. As the soldiers crucify
him, the Prophet Jesus exclaims "Father, forgive them, they do not know
what they are doing". He is mocked by the leaders who also challenge him to
save himself, but not by the people standing by. Luke even introduces
division into the statements of the two crucified beside Jesus: one wants Jesus
to save himself – and them as well; the other maintains that whereas they are
being legitimately punished for their crimes, Jesus has done nothing wrong.
He turns to Jesus and asks "Jesus, remember me when you come into your
kingdom", to be told, "I promise you, today you will be with me in paradise".
The Prophet is makes prophetic statements about salvation to the very end of
his life. This is a major theme in this gospel, not in terms of escape from

physical danger (which as we saw, the leaders challenged Jesus to do for himself), but in the promise of fullness of life. When Jesus dies, Luke's accompanying details are minimal compared with those in Matthew's and Mark's narratives; darkness is attributed to an eclipse, the veil of the temple is mentioned almost in passing (possibly another instance of Luke's great respect for Jewish traditions. C.f. no. 4 below), and Jesus' last words are a simple "Father, into your hands I commit my spirit" said in a loud voice – no anguished cry misinterpreted as a calling in Elijah. The Prophet's death is described with more of the calm and control of the fourth gospel than with the very human details of anguish and suffering of Mark/Matthew.

6. Jesus condemned to death; Luke 23:13-21

In this episode, Jesus is brought back to Pilate after he has been to Herod. Pilate had originally found Jesus innocent of the charge brought against him (political agitation) and now, in the open air and with a large crowd assembled, Pilate again declares twice more that Jesus is innocent, making a total of three times that Pilate has declared Jesus' innocence. The first was that Jesus was innocent of the charge brought by the leaders; next that he was innocent of leading people astray, and finally that he was innocent of any wrongdoing deserving death. Pilate cites Herod as being of the same opinion on Jesus' innocence. Notice the charges become less specific and wider in scope on each occasion. Pilate and Herod, not previously on amicable terms, are united in finding no fault with Jesus! Thus, Luke stresses that Jesus is the one who is innocent but who suffers, fulfilling the prophecy of Isaiah 52:12-53:21. Pilate attempts to resolve the situation by having Jesus punished (not specified, but presumably by flogging) and released. Only when the crowd demands that Pilate release another (not specified) does Pilate give in and the demands of the leaders be met. As he is led out, aided by Simon of Cyrene large numbers of people follow and mourn: in particular, women. Jesus resumes his prophetic role by predicting the misery they will have to face; if this is how they have treated the messenger of peace, what will happen when vengeance is visited on those who have so treated him? Readers of the gospel will see the destruction of Jerusalem foretold here.

5. Delivered to Prefect and King; Luke 23:1-12

Jesus is for the most part silent in his trial before Pilate; a fulfilment of Isaiah 53:7, "Harshly dealt with, he bore it humbly, he never opened his mouth, like a lamb that is led to the slaughter-house, like a sheep that is dumb before its shearers never opening its mouth". Pilate can find no case against him. When the leaders say that Jesus has been leading people astray from his days in Galilee, Pilate tries another approach and has Jesus sent to Herod because Galilee was within the latter's jurisdiction. Luke had earlier mentioned Herod's desire to see Jesus; he also cited warnings given to Jesus by Pharisees that Herod's intent was malicious. Now that this prophecy is being fulfilled and Herod's orchestrated mockery of Jesus has taken place, there is still no sign of there being any case to bring against him. The attempts of the Jewish authorities to bring about Jesus' death are increasingly laid bare as having no legitimate foundation whatever.

4. Hearing before the Sanhedrin; Luke 22:54-71

There is much debate as to whether or not the Sanhedrin had the right to put someone to death. The gospel tradition is clearly based on the understanding that the Jewish leaders had to find a way to persuade the Roman authorities to have Jesus crucified, which meant they needed to identify a political and not a religious charge. The added advantage for the Sanhedrin would be that if they were successful in persuading the Romans of the truth of such a political charge, the Romans would have to bear full responsibility for the execution. This section of the narrative also includes Peter's denial. Unlike Mark, Luke does not intertwine Peter's denial with Jesus' trial before the Sanhedrin. The result is perhaps less stark, but the emptiness of Peter's 'prophecy' at table that he would be prepared to go to prison and even death for Jesus is evident (c.f. Luke 22:33). At the same time, Jesus makes the prophetic statement to Peter– one which is fulfilled - that "by the time the cock crows today you will have denied three times that you know me".

Luke's version of the Sanhedrin trial is interesting in that it omits any reference to false witnesses or to the High Priest. These references are retained for the trial of Stephen in Acts 6:11-7:60. Luke is widely thought to have been a gentile convert - perhaps a 'God fearer', someone who did not convert to Judaism, but who supported Jewish religious causes primarily through financial donation. Perhaps this is reflected here in Luke's apparent unwillingness to describe so important a Jewish figure as the High Priest, of accusing the Son of God of blasphemy!

3. The Time of testing; Luke 22:39-53

The New Testament attests that Jesus underwent a powerful testing of faith and obedience before his death. Hebrews 7:5-8 says "During his life on earth, he offered up prayer and entreaty, aloud and in silent tears, to the one who had the power to save him out of death, and he submitted so humbly that his prayer was heard. Although he was Son, he learnt to obey through suffering". John omits any reference to prayer in the garden, but does have Jesus exclaim "Now my soul is troubled. What shall I say: Father, save me from this hour? But it was for this very reason that I have come to this hour" (John 12:27). Luke places the emphasis on Jesus during the garden scene, with no account of Jesus needing companionship from his disciples. His prayer is earnest and concentrated, reminiscent of the *agonia*, i.e. something like the focussed concentration of an athlete before a contest. There is no suggestion of fear from Jesus (to the Greek mentality, this would indicate weakness and cowardice), which is applied only to the disciples who sleep through fear. They have failed to pray for the strength to survive the test as Jesus had instructed (c.f. Luke 11:1-4; 18:8). There is a contest but Jesus emerges victorious, ready to confront his adversaries. When they arrive, he addresses them with some humour, virtually saying "do you think you have come to arrest a brigand with all these soldiers?" Jesus demonstrates that he is still in control, even when he is apprehended: he brings his disciples under control in the midst of the chaos, and has power to heal the ear of the High Priest's servant, cut off by the sword of one of his disciples. He even offers a last opportunity to Judas, effectively saying 'Judas, do you really want to betray the Son of Man with a kiss?' (C.f. Luke 22:48). The charge will be that Jesus led people astray, but as he points out, he taught in the temple every day and everyone who heard him knows what he taught: but now is the hour of darkness, so he gives them permission to take him into custody.

2. Teachings at the Last Supper Table; Luke 22:24-38

Alone among the synoptic evangelists, Luke provides a Last Supper Discourse. Admittedly, it is much shorter and less theologically profound than John's, but it is still a significant feature of this particular passion narrative, and it provides a useful contribution to Luke's portrayal of Jesus as The Prophet. The discourse deals with several important issues, the first of these prompted by a dispute arising among the disciples as to which of them was the greatest. A similar incident is recorded by Mark during the travel narrative (Mark 9:34-37). For Luke, not only does the episode afford Jesus the opportunity to instruct them on the nature of true greatness, but he also uses the occasion to stress that he comes among them as one who serves, although he is the ruler of a kingdom conferred by his father and in which he will confer on them the right to judges the twelve tribes of Israel, because they have stood by Jesus in his trials.

The prophetic statement about Peter's denial follows, although there is the assurance that Jesus has prayed, and not just for Peter, but for all of them, that their faith may not fail, and that when all this is over, Peter may be able to strengthen his brothers.

Finally, a time of crisis is prophesied. When Jesus sent out the Twelve and the Seventy (or Seventy Two), he told them to make no preparations because God would provide for their needs; they were under Jesus' protection. Soon, that protection will have been removed, and they will have to take purses and haversacks if they have them and, in a figure of speech (although the disciples take him literally), he even advises that those lacking a sword should if necessary sell a cloak to buy one. Presumably this is said with the ironic tone that when this happens, they would be better off if they went looking for swords instead of cloaks! This is because, in fulfilment of scripture, he will be taken for a criminal (another passion prophecy) and so disciples will have to fend for themselves. This will be fulfilled in the various circumstances in which they will find themselves in the post-Pentecost era, when they will need to rely on their own resourcefulness. Bang on cue, the disciples misunderstand: "Lord, there are two swords here!" Jesus draws the discussion to an abrupt close by saying in effect, 'that's enough of this for now!' Prophetic statements at table over, they head for the Mount of Olives, and the beginning of the fulfilment of Jesus' prophetic words.

1. Passover meal (Last Supper); Luke 24:14-23

Luke's understanding of the Last Supper sets the tone for the rest of the Passion Narrative. He sees it as a celebration of Passover at which Jesus is joined by his disciples. This is however one of those important places in the overall narrative where what Luke omits is also significant. For example, there is as little mention as possible of betrayal, and Judas as betrayer is not mentioned by name: he is simply called the one by whom the Son of Man is to be betrayed; Judas will not be named until the act of betrayal takes place. The highlight of the meal is when Jesus takes the cup, blesses it, and shares it with his disciples. This is a kingly gesture: the king only shared his cup with his most trusted associates. This then is a prophetic gesture which points to Jesus' words in the discourse, described in the section above, where he calls his disciples the ones who have stood by him in his trials. The prophetic gesture is much more profound as well. The content of the cup that Jesus shares is his blood which will be poured for them. Likewise the bread which he takes, breaks and passes round is his flesh which will be broken for them. They are to do this in his memory, because this cup and this bread are not just reminders or mementos of his death; they *are* the new covenant in his blood, the blood shed for them; the bread *is* his body, given for them. These prophetic words will be fulfilled throughout the rest of the passion narrative; Jesus words will be shown to be true. This is why at the very end of his life, the Prophet can say "Father, into your hands I commit my spirit". He has begun the fulfilment of all that he has spoken; the rest will be fulfilled in his resurrection.

There is an additional advantage to considering the Pasion According to Luke in this 'back to front' manner. Although there are the days of holy Week before the Easter Triduum begins, the next chapter in these notes covers the huge area from the Mass of the Last supper (where the Luke Passion Narrative began on Palm Sunday).Itis important to remember that from the Mass of the Last supper until the Easter Vigil, we are celebrating the EASTER Triduum – not the final days of Lent!

Chapter 4

Easter: From the Triduum to Pentecost, Year C

Introduction: Summoning the Energy for the Easter Season

These notes are arranged in a way which recognises that Holy Thursday Mass of the Last Supper is the beginning of the EASTER Triduum, and is not a last fling for the season of Lent. This makes for a long chapter and an unrivalled wealth of Biblical material to be covered, so be prepared for a long chapter! Following the rigours of the Easter Triduum with its utter wealth of biblical themes from both Testaments and all packed into a few short days, it will be tempting to wonder: where do we go next? How can we keep up the same momentum for the next seven weeks? The good news is that we do not need to maintain that level of intensity, but it is also true that we have a challenge ahead of us if we are to make the most of each of the Sundays of the season. The biggest challenge we face is probably related to the gospel which dominates these Sundays – John. This gospel has traditionally been used extensively in the major seasons of the liturgical year, and the Post Vatican II lectionary has exploited to the full the use of the fourth gospel during these seasons. This means that we are to be exposed to some wonderfully inspiring concepts, but it also means that most of the gospels are singularly lacking a good story! The good news however is that we can identify and develop a thread which runs through these Easter gospels and which allows us to follow the progression of a series of reflections on the Resurrection.

Each year, the Easter gospels follow a similar pattern:-

- 2nd Sunday. As we saw, this always has the gospel of the appearances of the Risen Jesus in the upper room on the day of resurrection and one week later; Thomas is absent from the first, but present for the second.

- 3rd Sunday. This always contains a late post-resurrection appearance. This year, it is Jesus' appearance at the seas of Tiberias, which is followed by Peter's commission as the one to shepherd the flock after Jesus' departure.

- 4th Sunday. The gate of the Sheepfold, Good Shepherd, and the Listening Flock. In year C, the focus is on the sheep that belong to Jesus and their listening to his voice

- 5th Sunday. The commandment and gift of love, the defining quality for disciples of Jesus, and the way in which his continued presence is assured, and through which he is revealed in the world by successive generations of disciples

- 6th Sunday. The sending of 'another Paraclete' who will have a special relationship with Jesus' disciples in the period between the Resurrection and the end-time when Jesus will return.

From this outline we can detect a theme which unfolds from week to week, and that is the theme of continuity from the Father, who sent his Son into the world so that the world may have life and have it to the full: through the Son, the Shepherd who has power to lay down his life for his sheep and to take it up again; continuing on to the definition of the true flock of Jesus which listens to his voice and which make his presence known through living out his commandment to radical love. All of this is made possible through the gift of the 'other Paraclete' who will accompany, teach, remind, and empower disciples to continue the work that originated, not even in Jesus himself, but in the Father and from the very beginning, when the Word was already with God and was God (c.f. John 1:1).

Mass of the Last Supper (John 13:1-15)

It no longer comes as a surprise to most of us that the Mass of the Last supper does not contain the gospel account of the institution of the Eucharist, but instead has the gospel account of Jesus washing his disciples' feet. This has led many to conclude that the feet-washing is really a commentary on the Eucharistic institution narrative which is entirely missing from John. However, in reality, this is probably not accurate at all. If there is a Eucharistic narrative in John, it is surely Chapter 6, and the discourse on Jesus, the Bread of Life. The real significance of John 13:1-15 is its exploration of the true meaning of the death of Jesus, which takes place the following day. Now, of course, the death of Jesus has obvious Eucharistic connections, so it would be absurd to suggest that the feet-washing had nothing to do with Eucharist; however, its main purpose is to elaborate the death of the Lamb of God.

The other two readings, of course, offer the background to the occasion: the instructions for the celebration of Passover (including the choice of animal and its preparation), and the New Testament's earliest account of the institution of the Eucharist, from 1 Corinthians 11:23-26.

The first few verses of this passage set the scene for the next seven chapters. The occasion is linked to Passover, but also to the 'hour' for Jesus' passing from this world to his father. His love had always been evident but now it was to be demonstrated in its perfection.

The setting is supper. Already, the devil had put it into the mind of Judas Iscariot to betray Jesus, or at least, that's how the Jerusalem Bible renders this: the Greek, reflecting Hebrew thinking, says that the devil had put into Judas' heart to betray him. For the Hebrew, the heart was the organ for intellectual activity and moral judgement and decision-making. The link between the devil and Judas was made more explicit at the end of the Eucharistic narrative in chapter 6; 'Have I not chosen you, you Twelve? Yet one of you is a devil.' He meant Judas son of Simon Iscariot, since this was the man, one of the Twelve, who was going to betray him (John 6:70-71).

The action of Jesus' washing disciples' feet is easy enough to interpret, given the extensive account of Jesus leaving the table, removing his outer garment, wrapping the towel round his waste and beginning to wash the disciples' feet. This is emphasised by the insistence that Jesus knew that the Father had put all things into his hands, that he had come from God, and that he was returning to God (John 13:3). Not so apparent though is the reason for Peter's outrage at Jesus' actions. His vehement repulsion at what Jesus is trying to do here reminds us of his reaction to Jesus' first passion prediction (Mark 8:31-33; Matthew 16:21-23). So why is Peter so outraged? To understand this, we must consider something of Jewish etiquette regarding washing and service. It was customary for Jewish people to wash on entering the house – feet, shod only in open sandals, might have been particularly in need of refreshment from the dust of the way, so washing one's feet on entering the house was required. Servants (or more likely, slaves) were required to assist their masters in the process of washing their feet, but, according to Mishnah, on no account was a slave ever to be asked to wash the feet of his master; this would be too demeaning even for a slave. Now there was one occasion on which a person might wash the feet of another, and that was the honour accorded by the master of the house to a very distinguished guest.

These two observations help us to see why Peter is so upset at Jesus' actions: his master wants to do for him what no slave should ever be asked to do. Either that, or Jesus is treating Peter as a distinguished guest. In either case, Peter is scandalised. He cannot get his head round that, but of course this is exactly what the death of Jesus is all about. Later in the narrative, he will say that no one has greater love than to lay one's life for another, and that is what is symbolised by the washing of feet. It is a powerful prophetic gesture and Peter, for once, knows exactly what it means: Jesus is placing himself below the lowest member of the human race in his abject service of humanity. He is the Lamb of God, the good sheoehrd who has the power to lay down his life, and the power to take it up again, a life that he places at the disposal of others. On the following day, Jesus' death will be the demonstration and the reality of how perfect is his love. There is a consequence as well: disciples must follow his example. He, the Lord and Master, has given them an example that they must follow. Later in the narrative, he will insist that this is no more and no less than the sign that they are his disciples: the love they show for one another.

The prophetic gesture has been made. The next stage of the Triduum liturgy, the commemoration of the Lord's Passion, gives John's account and interpretation of those events to which the prophetic gesture of the feet-washing have pointed.

Good Friday: Commemoration of The Lord's Passion. John 18:1-19:42

The dominant theme in this account of the Passion can be related to what we have seen already of Jesus as the Lamb of God, the Shepherd, who has the power to lay down his life, and the power to take it up again. The Passion According to John tells substantially the same tale as the other gospels; after the supper, Jesus is taken into custody, is tried by the Jewish authorities, is handed over to Pilate, sentenced to death, crucified, dies, is taken from the cross, and is buried. This evangelist however weaves his own very well-developed theological programme into the familiar narrative. Some examples will be given here to illustrate how he does this.

<u>1. Jesus is taken into custody</u>. This description is used deliberately, because we can scarcely speak of Jesus being arrested. Here, as in the other gospels, Jesus goes to the garden after supper although only John supplies details of the route he takes. Historically, Judas is of course associated with this episode, but John limits references to Judas to two observations. First, Judas the traitor knew the place well and is therefore well-placed to bring the cohort, together with a detachment of guards provided by the chief priests and Pharisees - all well-armed and equipped. Second, Judas the traitor is among them as Jesus asks, 'who are you looking for'. John omits any suggestion that Judas identified Jesus with a kiss, or even that he took an active part in the proceedings. There is good reason for all of this. Jesus' hour has arrived, and he is in full control of what will now take place. The Passion Narrative in John is the fulfilment of Jesus' own prophetic statement earlier in this gospel: "The Father loves me, because I lay down my life in order to take it up again. No one takes it from me; I lay it down of my own free will, and as it is in my power to lay it down, so it is in my power to take it up again; and this is the command I have been given by my Father." (John 10:17-18). Therefore John wishes to avoid any suggestion that Jesus was taken by force, or that he was tricked by Judas. Notice however that this evangelist does nothing to contradict the synoptic tradition of Judas the betrayer.

Far from being taken by force, Jesus controls what now happens. Knowing everything that was going to happen (18:4), Jesus asks the would-be arresting party, "Who are you looking for?" and they reply, "Jesus the Nazarene". He utters one of the famous I AM statements found so often in John, and drawn from Exodus 3:14 "I am he". When Jesus utters these words his would-be assailants fall to the ground, powerless to do anything. Jesus, after saying 'I am he' for the third time, demands that the others be released. This is in fulfilment of his prayer at the supper, "I have watched over them and not one is lost except the one who chose to be lost". Peter's futile attempt to intervene by cutting off the ear of the high priest's servant Malchus, is rebuffed with Jesus' insistence that he drink the cup the Father has given him. Only then, is Jesus taken into custody.

2. Jesus and Peter, both on trial. John follows the basic plan of Matthew (and of course Mark) in interweaving the story of Jesus before Annas and Caiaphas, with that of Peter, in the courtyard, by a charcoal fire. It should be noted at this point that another charcoal fire will figure in the post-resurrection narrative of chapter 21, where Peter is questioned three times by Jesus on his love, so clearly whoever penned what is thought by most commentators to be an appendix to the gospel, wanted to reinforce the connection between Peter's triple denial, and his triple protestation of love for Jesus.

The contrasts between the performances of Peter and Jesus under questioning could not be more marked. Jesus' replies to Annas are measured and considered – even to the point that his acute observations provoke the violence of a guard, to which Jesus again has a considered answer. If Jesus' answers are assured, Peter's answers do not impress us at all. The real parallel in John's account is not only between Jesus' answers to the High Priest and Peter's in the courtyard: it is really between Jesus' reply in the garden of 'I am' (or 'I am he' in the Jerusalem Bible Translation) and Peter's 'I am not' when asked if he is a disciple of Jesus. If 'I am' in Exodus means (as is usually stated) that God is the one who always is: the one who is eternally present and eternally consistent, and if Jesus takes this title to himself in a claim to divinity, then Peter's very stark 'I am not' significantly heightens the impact of Peter's denial. Jesus identifies himself totally with his Father in saying 'I am'; Peter dissociates himself totally from Jesus by saying 'I am NOT'! Later, before Pilate, Jesus will bear witness to the truth, as he has done before Annas, but Peter's lies amount to his rejection of Jesus, even when he has been positively identified from the relative of the man whose ear

Peter had cut off. Truth and witness are important themes in John: Jesus is visibly faithful to both; Peter hides behind to falsehood and denial.

3. Jesus before Pilate. John tells that Annas sent Jesus, still bound, to Caiaphas, but tells nothing of what happened. He does however add that Jesus was taken in the morning to Pilate and that the Jews would not enter the Praetorium itself, since doing so would defile them and prevent them from being able to eat the Passover. This leads to a dramatic situation which this gospel exploits to the full. In a scene which would be almost comical if the stakes were not so high and the setting less dramatic, John depicts a feeble, ineffectual governor, representative of the most powerful nation on the earth at that time, reduced to running between the main protagonists in the drama: the Jewish authorities outside the Praetorium; Jesus inside. Pilate is almost reduced to carrying messages between the two, as he shuttles back and forward. Notice that the legal case is presented rather differently in this gospel from that outlined in the synoptic gospels. The charge is still that Jesus claims to be the King of the Jews, but in answer to Pilate's question, "Are you the king of the Jews?" Jesus responds with another question: "Do you ask this of your own accord, or have others spoken to you about me?" In the John chapter 4 narrative about the Samaritan woman, the villagers had said to the woman that they now believed in Jesus, not because of what she said, but because of what they heard Jesus say. Is this echoed in Jesus' question to Pilate? The niceties are lost on the governor: "Am I a Jew? It is your own people and the chief priests who have handed you over to me: what have you done?" when Jesus is further pressed to answer whether he is a king, he replies in the formula now familiar to us from Matthew's passion, "It is you who say it". Literally, Jesus says "You say I am a king" (*su legeis oti basileus*). Jesus' next remark can be misinterpreted, depending on how well it is rendered in translation. When Jesus says: "Yes, I am a king. I was born for this, I came into the world for this: to bear witness to the truth; and all who are on the side of truth listen to my voice", there is a danger of reading Jesus' words as meaning he was born to be a king. In fact, Jesus is stressing that he was born, that he came into the world to bear witness to the truth. Pilate's famous answer follows, "Truth? What is that?" This should not be read as a philosophical question: Pilate the pragmatist is simply not interested in truth: the nearest he comes to being concerned about the truth is when he decides what is expedient for his own security, as we soon find out. Pilate goes back outside and declares there is no case to answer. He offers to release the King of the Jews, but the crowd shout for Barabbas' release.

4. Sentence. Pilate now orders Jesus to be scourged, and he is mocked much in the way we heard described in Matthew, but there appears to be a big difference. In the synoptic accounts, Jesus is scourged and mocked with the trappings of royalty AFTER sentence has been passed: in John, this is done BEFORE sentence is passed.

There are in fact three different nuances in the gospels regarding Jesus' flogging, suggesting the three different reasons why flogging was administered in the first place. The first, which we read in Matthew, was a severe beating almost to the point of death to weaken the condemned prisoner and thereby reduce the time spent hanging alive on the cross. The second seems to be the motive suggested in Luke: Pilate offered to have Jesus scourged, rather than crucified. This was sometimes done as a punishment in its own right, as was the case for Peter and the apostles in Acts 5:40, after which the apostles could go home again with a warning. The third was a severe beating to make the prisoner serve as an example to others, a deterrent or in Jesus' case to make him into a figure of pity, fulfilling Isaiah 53:3. This would appear to be how John understood Pilate's decision to have Jesus flogged. It didn't work: if anything, the crowd became more insistent in their demands for crucifixion.

Pilate has now lost what little control he had retained over the events. The Jews insist that Jesus must die for calling himself the Son of God. Pilate is now becoming increasingly frightened. He re-enters the Praetorium (still shuttling back and forward) and asks Jesus; "Where do you come from?" He is greeted with silence. Earlier in the gospel, there was a debate about where Jesus came from, as people in Jerusalem debated, "Isn't this the man they want to kill? And here he is, speaking freely, and they have nothing to say to him! Can it be true the authorities have made up their minds that he is the Christ? Yet we all know where he comes from, but when the Christ appears no one will know where he comes from" (John 7:25-27). Of course, for the reader, the prologue has already solved the problem of Jesus' origins: "He was with God in the beginning" (John 1:2) but Pilate knows nothing of this. In a last ditch attempt to regain some dignity, he says in response to Jesus' silence, "Are you refusing to speak to me? Surely you know I have power to release you and I have power to crucify you?" Jesus' final comment to Pilate is devastating, "You would have no power over me if it had not been given you from above; that is why the one who handed me over to you has the greater guilt." Pilate has to return yet again to the gathering outside the Praetorium, wishing to release Jesus, but the Jews use their ultimate threat: "If you set him free you are no friend of Caesar's; anyone who makes himself king is defying Caesar". The best he can do now is to ask, "Do you want me to crucify your king?" The answer is shocking in the extreme: The chief priests, the highest ranking officials in the religious system of God's chosen people answered, "We have no king except Caesar". God's chosen people has finally abandoned its God as sovereign, and proclaimed allegiance to the foreign emperor, the head of a family renowned for taking upon itself divine honours, although Tiberius himself declined these. This rejection of God as king was already hinted at in the prologue: "He was in the world that had its being through him, and the world did not know him. He came to his own domain and his own people did not accept him" (John 1:10).

5. Crucifixion. In John's account of Jesus' crucifixion, there is great dignity and Jesus is totally in control. He accepts no help on his way to Calvary: no Simon of Cyrene to carry the cross, no mention of wine mixed with gall to deaden the pain. The scenes are described in such a way as to recall the scriptures, e.g. the soldiers casting lots for Jesus' robes, in fulfilment of Psalm 22:18. Jesus sometimes takes the initiative here too, such as when he says "I thirst", and they give him vinegar to drink, fulfilling Psalm 22:15.

Prior to this, Jesus speaks the famous words to his mother and the disciple standing near the cross; neither are named. The two appear in the gospel as the ideal disciples, and many commentators see in the handing over of each to the other's care as John's way of describing the origins of the church, the community of disciples that Jesus leaves behind. This community is identifiable by their service of each other after the pattern laid down by the Master at the Last supper in his washing of the disciples' feet, and his accompanying instruction that they are to do the same for each other. This idea of the birth of the Church is reinforced by what happens next. First, Jesus announces that "it is accomplished", and bowing his head, he gives up his spirit. This is not to be understood as an equivalent to saying, 'he gave up the ghost'; rather, it indicates that he gave over (handed over, *paradidōmi*) his spirit to the fledgling community gathered at the foot of the cross. When Pilate is approached about breaking the legs of the crucified (to hasten death), since a particularly solemn Sabbath was approaching, it is found that Jesus is already dead, again in fulfilment of scripture (Psalm 34:20. So instead of breaking his legs, the soldiers pierced his side, and blood and water flowed out. This has the effect of yet another fulfilment of scripture (Zechariah 12:10), but it also suggests the beginning of the sacramental life of the church – water and blood symbolising Baptism and Eucharist, poured out on the fledgling community gathered beneath the cross (mother and disciple).

6. The funeral. John now adds details not found in the other gospels. Like Matthew, he calls Joseph of Arimathea a disciple but adds that he was a fearful, secret disciple. The other addition is of Nicodemus, who had appeared in chapter 3, coming to Jesus 'in the dark' – a great Johannine theme, and who had also offered an important but unheeded argument against condemning Jesus without a trial (John 7:50-51). Now Nicodemus brings a mixture of myrrh and aloes, about a hundred pounds in weight - Roman measure, that is! A Roman pound equalled about twelve ounces, therefore the weight in today's units would be around 75 pounds, or just under five and a half stone; about 35 kg – still rather a lot! At last, the king of the Jews receives in death what was denied him in life: a lavish burial! The references to the linen cloths will be returned to in the next chapter: but that comes later!

Appendix: A suggestion for the Old Testament Readings at the Easter Vigil

What can be done with the readings at the Easter vigil? How can some sense be made of seven (or more!) Old Testament readings, without having to spend half the night talking about them?

Here is a suggestion that might help, one I have run past a few people. Let me stress that I am not suggesting that the order in which the readings be read is altered in any way: these are of course presented in the lectionary in the order we find them in the Bible. We can't even say they are presented chronologically; only according to their traditional placing.

The theory is this: why not group these readings together, at least notionally, according to their themes? If we are to do this, I suggest we find that we discover readings follow themes, sometimes standing alone, usually in pairs going together thus:

    a. **Abraham and Isaac; the beloved Son**: Genesis 22:1-18 [lectionary reading 2]; Abraham was not required to sacrifice his only, beloved Son – but God did! Central to the entire Triduum

    b. **God's Powerful, creative word**: Genesis 1:1-2:2 [lectionary reading 1] (God said, let there be…and there was…and it was good); Isaiah 55:1-11 (the word that goes forth from my mouth does not return without carrying out my will);

c. **<u>God has never abandoned his people – not even in exile</u>**: Isaiah 54:5-14 [lectionary reading 4] (mountains may fall, hills be shaken, God's love will never leave his people); Baruch 3:9-15. 32 – 4:4 [lectionary reading 6] (Israel in exile because of unfaithfulness, but by returning to God, it may find the light).

d. **<u>Life-Giving Water</u>**: Exodus14:15-15:1 [lectionary reading 3]; Ezekiel 36:16-28 [lectionary reading 7], both passages about new life for Israel, brought about by water – the Red Sea at Exodus, living water in Ezekiel.

Easter Vigil Gospel, Year C: Luke 24:1-12

The gospels provide us with insights into various and differing traditions concerning the resurrection of Jesus, making it difficult to provide a complete harmony of the narratives. As in other parts of his gospel, Luke presents his account of the resurrection narrative to serve the overall purpose of his gospel. There are of course common features to be found in all four gospels, most noticeably those surrounding the first discovery of the empty tomb. Other ways in which similar emphases are made is in stressing that, even though disciples do not immediately recognise the Risen Jesus, when awareness does dawn, he is *more* rather than *less* present to them; his power is more apparent among them than ever before. A further common feature is that Jesus' word is a significant factor in disciples' recognition. They usually 'hear' (i.e. recognise) the voice of the Risen Christ before they can recognise him by sight.

Luke shares with Matthew and Mark much of the tradition's material concerning the empty tomb. On the first day of the week, the women bring ointments they had prepared to perform the burial rites that had not been possible immediately after his death. Luke, like John, notes that the stone had been rolled back, but he hadn't mentioned the stone before this. There is economy in detail, with no discussion on how the stone will be moved, or Matthew's account of the earthquake. Only Luke mentions that they did not find the body of the Lord Jesus. As they mull this over this, two men appear. These are wearing shining clothes. Who are they? Luke does not specify, but they are clearly supernatural beings. The description of shining clothes is the same as the description of both Moses and Elijah at the Transfiguration. Presumably, while Luke is clearly not suggesting that the two now standing near the empty tomb are Moses and Elijah, he invites the reader to make some connection between the two sets of heavenly figures. The point is that, in an age where resuscitation of the supposed dead was not unheard of, or where grave robbers and body snatchers were active, this evangelist (and others) wants to stress that the story of Jesus' resurrection was not invented by disciples and friends, but was endorsed by heavenly visitors. We might recall that something similar took place for the benefit of the shepherds at Jesus' birth (Luke 2:9-12). The message of these visitors is explicit, "Why look among the dead for someone who is alive? He is not here; he has risen. Remember what he told you when he was still in Galilee: that the Son of Man had to be handed over into the power of sinful men and be crucified, and rise again on the third day" (Luke 24:5-7). The recurring theme of the Prophet's words being fulfilled is apparent here, and of course the statement of the two heavenly strangers provides the basis for the earliest preaching of the Christian community we read about in the Acts of the Apostles.

In Mark, the terrified women do not pass on to the disciples the (much shorter) message they are given; in Luke, they remember the words of the strangers, so they return to tell the Eleven all that they had heard. The reaction they receive is a bit extreme: the Eleven consider what they have reported as sheer nonsense. This reminds us of Thomas' refusal to believe in John 20:24, but in fact it might carry other overtones as well. The Eleven's laughter at the very suggestion that these women, whom Luke actually names, had held this conversation with two heavenly strangers, may just remind us of Sarah's laughter when she overhears the messengers tell Abraham that his wife will have given birth to a son by this time on the following year (Genesis 18:1-15). It may also recall Zechariah's incredulity at the angel's message at the beginning of this gospel (Luke 1:5-24). In this post-resurrection episode Luke literally says that the Eleven are' delirious with joy': the meaning appears to be: 'howling with laughter'!

Peter, however, gets up and runs straightaway to the tomb. In a way that reminds us of John 20:6-7, Peter examines the cloths, but nothing else (no Jesus: no clues?), and goes back home, amazed, apparently none the wiser. The narrative breaks off at this point, and next comes the story of the two disciples on the road to Emmaus, but that is a story for another time!

EXCURSUS – burial customs in Jesus' time. The stone: how it got there, and who could have moved it!

Ancient Jerusalem has been described as a city surrounded by a gigantic cemetery. This is not in fact accurate. Tombs are to be found on three of the four 'sides' to the ancient city, not on the fourth. The west side of Jerusalem which is exposed to winds, lacks ancient tombs. In Jesus' time, the custom, as is borne out in gospel accounts of his own burial, was to cut burial caves from the soft limestone rock. The corpse of the newly-deceased would be placed in the cave, perhaps on a shelf or a niche, cut out in the process of digging the cave, or on a kind of plinth which would have been against the wall on one side but in such a way as to permit access to the body from the other three sides. The body would be left to decompose for a year or so, after which the bones would be gathered and placed in a container ('ossuary') which might bear inscriptions of the names of those whose bones had been placed here. This explains the detail in Luke 23:53 that Joseph of Arimathea put the body of Jesus in a tomb hewn from rock *in which no one had yet been laid.* Luke stresses that the bystanders at the burial noted the position both of the tomb and of the body. It was not usually expected that tombs would have only a single occupant. John also says that there was a garden with a new tomb in which no one had yet been buried (John 19:41).

The gospels all record the placing of a large stone. This was intended as a deterrent to grave robbers and wild animals, was probably circular and flat and set in a groove to allow it to be rolled in front of the entrance to the tomb. If it could be rolled in front of the tomb, could it not be rolled away as well? Would it be such a great deterrent to robbers? Perhaps it would have needed a sufficiently large number of people to move it that would render it beyond the capability of robbers working individually or in small groups to have any reasonable hope of moving it unaided. Certainly, the women who came to the tomb first thing in the morning were taken aback to see the stone moved, and according to Matthew, it required an angel to shift it.

What purpose could the women's visit to the tomb on the morning after the Sabbath had ended possibly serve? Since the purpose of anointing was to keep down the stench of decomposing bodies, would they not have been too late? There is evidence that a belief of the time held that the soul did not fully depart from the body until about the third day. It's just possible that this belief is reflected in John's account of the raising of Lazarus, where Jesus delays arrival at the tomb until four days have passed, as if to establish beyond all doubt that Lazarus was really dead. When he calls for the tomb to be opened, Martha is aghast, for he has been there for four days, and by now will smell! Perhaps in the case of Jesus' burial, the women are at least hopeful that putrefaction would not yet have set in – the cool spring climate of Jerusalem may have helped here. It is however more likely that they would just have wanted to try as best they could to give the one they loved as decent a burial as circumstances would permit, since it was a duty for anyone who could do so to ensure that a fellow Jew was properly buried. This obligation even extended to the High Priest himself to do this if necessary: even if his attention to a corpse made him ritually unclean and unable to perform his religious duties! In Mark, there is no real suggestion that Joseph of Arimathea did any more than a pious Jew would feel obliged to do for any dead Jew with no one to bury him or her. Mark does not suggest that Joseph was an admirer of Jesus, still less that he was a disciple – even a secret one as do other gospels.

Easter Sunday. John 20:1-9

No motive is given by John for Mary's arrival at the tomb, although from the accounts in the other gospels, we would assume it is connected with the deferred burial rites. It is interesting that John makes no mention of Mary of Magdala's companions listed in the other accounts either. Yet the two versions of that first visit are not mutually exclusive: John may simply omit some of the detail provided by the other evangelists. All John tells us is that she arrived early on the first day of the week and it was still dark. She sees the stone has been removed and she runs to tell Simon Peter and the other disciple, the one Jesus loved: "they have taken the Lord out of the tomb and we don't know where they have put him." No attempt is made to define who 'they' and 'we' are: just panic in Mary's voice. Time for action! Peter and the other disciple run to the tomb; the other disciple arrives first but giving Peter his place, he stands back to let the slower Peter go in first. Both see the same thing: the cloths have been arranged and are not left in a haphazard fashion. Both see the same thing but understand what they see in different ways. Peter can only see the facts of the cloths, but the 'other disciple' sees them as a reminder of scripture; "he saw and he believed. Till this moment they had failed to understand the teaching of scripture: that he must rise from the dead."

So, what is the clue? The other disciple realises perhaps that this is a different scenario from the raising of Lazarus, who could emerge from his tomb, still bound by his grave clothes, only after being called from outside by Jesus. In the resurrection story, Jesus is not called from the tomb, and has not been released from his burial cloths: this disciple has seen Jesus' grave cloths and understood, if not scripture (it is not at all clear what scripture the other disciple is supposed to have been thinking of here), then at least the substance of Jesus' earlier words: that he had the power to lay down his life, and the power to take it up again. This is exactly what has happened: the Lamb of God who takes away the sins of the world, the Good Shepherd, the Grain of Wheat, the one who says I AM…the light of the world, the bread of life, the Gate of the Sheepfold, the Good Shepherd, the Way, the Truth and the Life, has indeed laid down his life (as we have heard), but has also taken it up again. This is a significant departure from the way the resurrection is described in the synoptic gospels. In those accounts messengers by the empty tomb inform the women that Jesus whom they are looking for is not there; he *has been raised*. For John, however, the Son of Man has the power to lay down his life, and he has the power to take it up again. These two ways of describing the agent of the resurrection are not in fact exclusive, so there is no contradiction here. For John, this is precisely why the whole episode can be called HIS HOUR, WHEN HE IS GLORIFIED, because in laying down his life and in taking it up again, power given to him by the Father, Jesus makes the presence of God more fully felt in human affairs than ever before. And that is what is meant by the expression, the Glory of God, which now we see is exactly the same as the Glory of the Son of Man who has been lifted up.

2nd SUNDAY OF EASTER, John 20:19-31

This is one of those passages which is read on the same Sunday for each year of the cycle. There are superficial reasons why this is so: it refers to one week after the resurrection, but it also highlights for us many themes that are important to take into consideration in reading the post-resurrection narratives.

The first of these is the repeated failure of the disciples to recognise the Risen Christ, even after they have already sighted him. It appears that the issue is seldom, if ever, about disciples believing because they have seen. Rather, it is those who hear the voice of the risen Lord (literally, or in the understanding of scripture) who come to believe. This is what we find in the Thomas story in today's gospel. The story has many of the hallmarks of post-resurrection narratives, not least in the gathering of fearful disciples behind closed doors -

understandable, especially on the day of the resurrection itself, given the hostility to Jesus they have witnessed in the events leading to his death. The Easter morning gospel indicated that the Risen Christ was not bound either by the tomb even with a huge stone over its entrance, nor by the cloths that bound his dead body: now we find that he is not bound by closed doors either.

When Jesus appears, he repeats his earlier words that he has been sent by the Father: this was met on the 4th Sunday of Lent, "I must carry out the work of the one who sent me" (John 9:4). Now, in the same manner, Jesus sends the disciples. They are to be equipped with the Holy Spirit, who descended on Jesus, as witnessed by John the Baptist, "I did not know him myself, but he who sent me to baptise with water had said to me, "The man on whom you see the Spirit come down and rest is the one who is going to baptise with the Holy Spirit" (John 1:33). The one on whom John saw the spirit descend is also identified as the Lamb of God who takes away the sin of the world (John 1:29); so it's not surprising that the disciples are given the power to take away sin also.

A question arises: is this power to forgive sin limited to this generation? Not according to this story. Thomas is the vehicle for making the point. When Jesus first appears, Thomas is absent, and his subsequent reaction to the tale of his fellow disciples that Jesus appeared has earned him the reputation of Doubting Thomas, even though the gospel only ever calls him Thomas the Twin (who was 'the other' twin?). Much as Thomas may have regretted that outcome, he plays an important role in demonstrating the continuity of disciples sent by Jesus even beyond those who have actually seen the Risen Lord. Thomas wants to carry out a post-mortem on Jesus before he believes in the Resurrection. He is a pragmatist; he wants hard facts (so did the Pharisees when trying to discover how the man born blind was cured in John 9:10 etc.). Jesus offers to let Thomas do what he had asked for, but there is actually no suggestion in the gospel text that Thomas takes up Jesus' offer! In fact, it seems that Thomas makes his very profound profession of faith only as a result of hearing the voice of the Risen Lord. We are possibly misled once again by the Jerusalem Bible translation with its rendition: "Jesus said to (Thomas): 'You believe because you can see me. Happy are those who have not seen and yet believe'. This would be better expressed as a question than as a statement. Jesus in effect says something like 'Is it because you see me that you believe? Blessed are those….'" (John 20:29). Logically, there must be a link between disciples of Jesus' own generation and the future disciples, and that link can only be found in the 'hearing the voice of the Lord' - not literally, but in the words of scripture where we encounter the Word of God in so far as it is consigned to writing (c.f. *Dei Verbum 9*). As the concluding section of this chapter (which is probably the original ending of the gospel) makes clear, "These are recorded so that you may believe that Jesus is the Christ, the Son of God, and that believing this you may have life through his name" (John 20:30-31). These words are the means by which the voice of the Risen Lord continues to be heard whenever the scriptures are proclaimed within the Church. It is in this way that subsequent generations of disciples, empowered by the Spirit of Christ, are sent out to bring forgiveness, just as he himself was sent by the Father, as the Lamb of God who takes away the sin of the world.

3rd Sunday of Easter Year C. John 21:21:1-19
Questions to Ponder:

☐   Why did Peter and the other disciples decide to go fishing?
☐   Why is it a constant theme in post resurrection narratives that disciples do not recognise Jesus when they see him? How could this be the case?
☐   What is the significance of 153 fish, all held in the net that did not break?
☐   Why would Jesus speak of Peter stretching out his hands and letting others lead him where he would rather not go, when the tradition already held that Peter died by crucifixion?

Most commentators agree that there are many indications in this passage to suggest that John 21 is an addition to the original ending of the gospel. The fine details of the argument are not relevant for our present purposes, but a couple of observations might usefully be made before we consider today's passage at some length. The first point is that, as we saw at the end of last Sunday's gospel, there are clear signs at the end of John 20 that this is where the gospel would originally have ended. Following Thomas' confession of the risen Jesus as his Lord and God and Jesus' reply, "happy are those who have not seen and yet believe", the evangelist adds a couple of verses: "There were many other signs that Jesus worked and the disciples saw, but they are not recorded in this book. These are recorded so that you may believe that

Jesus is the Christ, the Son of God, and that believing this you may have life through his name" (John 20:30-31). So, it's rather odd that the gospel would then proceed to another lengthy tale. This however is precisely what happens with today's episode, set in the vicinity of the Sea of Tiberias and ending with another concluding remark, this time with the additional testimony of the disciple who witnessed these things: "This disciple is the one who vouches for these things and has written them down, and we know that his testimony is true. There were many other things that Jesus did; if all were written down, the world itself, I suppose, would not hold all the books that would have to be written" (John 21:24-25). There are other clear signs of lack of continuity between chapters 20 and 21; one example is that in chapter 21, at the conclusion of the miracle and the breakfast offered by Jesus, it is stated that this was the third time Jesus had shown himself to his disciples after rising from the dead: actually, it is the fourth! The second point to be made is that although the material of Chapter 21 is clearly an addition to the original ending, it is still evidently material which has been composed in and from the Johannine tradition. It refers to the unnamed disciple, first referred to in John chapter 13, and who is prominent throughout all major events from then on. The language and terminology of chapter 21 differs in certain ways from the rest of the gospel, but also shows continuity with the language of the rest of the gospel. A good example of the differences is when Jesus "shows himself", or reveals himself (*phaneroō*). This is a phrase used widely in the main body of John's gospel, but never in relation to resurrection appearances prior to chapter 21. It is the verb used when the evangelist writes of Jesus revealing his glory (e.g. John 2:11). In John 21 the verb is used with the phrase "This was the third time that Jesus showed himself to the disciples after rising from the dead" (John 21:14). The expression is also used at the marriage feast of Cana, "This was the first sign given by Jesus…He let his glory be seen and his disciples believed in him" (John 2:11). It implies that in this appearance of Jesus there is more than physical sighting: a component of the revelation of God in Jesus is in evidence as well. This is of course in keeping with the gospel of John's depiction of Jesus as the One whom the Father has 'sent', the One who makes the Father known. Jesus' glory is a term which is used to convey the concept of Jesus' divine nature being made manifest in his actions.

It is important to stress the continuity between John 21 and the rest of the gospel, even though the chapter is almost certainly a later addition, since this will have repercussions for our reading of the fishing miracle which features in the first part of today's passage. Before the narrative proper begins, the scene is set. Unusually, we are given introductory detail: "Later on, Jesus showed himself again to the disciples. It was by the Sea of Tiberias, and it happened like this:" (John 21:1). The narrator goes on to inform us that seven disciples were there, three are specifically named: Peter, Thomas the Twin, and Nathaniel from Cana in Galilee. This is the first time we have heard that Nathaniel was a native of Cana, and it helps explain Nathanael's outburst "Can anything good come from Nazareth?" in John 1:46. Cana and Nazareth were adjacent and perhaps rival towns. A further two other disciples are identified, not by name, but as the sons of Zebedee and two more disciples, not identified in any way, make up the remainder of the list. Peter decides he is going fishing: the others decide they'll join him. This is the only place in the gospels where there is a gathering of seven disciples. The number clearly has symbolic significance, reminiscent of the way 'The Twelve' suggested the Twelve Tribes of Israel. The number twelve carries connotations of completeness in biblical literature; perhaps numbering this group as consisting of seven carries similar connotations, denoting the fullness of the post-resurrection community and perhaps recalling that Matthew and Mark both recount two feeding miracles, one resulting in 12 baskets of left-overs and the other 7 baskets when the miracle is repeated in Gentile territory. We might therefore have here a symbolic representation of the Christian community with Peter initiating the action. It would not be helpful to press the analogy too far, however: suggestions that Peter is here launching a post-resurrection ministry in his prophesied capacity as a 'fisher of men' is not borne out by the text, and there is no commission from Jesus to Peter or any other disciple to become 'fishers of men' anywhere else in the fourth gospel. A more appropriate link may be found through the unnamed disciples, listed as the last pair among this seven. When the narrative proper of the fourth gospel gets underway, two disciples, initially those of John the Baptist, follow Jesus once John has identified him as the Lamb of God: "Jesus turned round, saw them following and said, 'What do you want?' They answered, 'Rabbi,' - which means Teacher -'where do you live?' 'Come and see' he replied; so they went and saw where he lived, and stayed with him the rest of that day" (John 1:38-39). This story is followed by the disciples' claim when they discuss that happened with Simon Peter, whose brother Andrew happened to be one of the pair, that they thought they had found the

'Messiah'. They have actually missed the whole point, because disciples *do not* choose Jesus. Quite the reverse happens: Jesus *always* chooses those whom he would call to discipleship (c.f. John 15:16, "You did not choose me, no, I chose you; and I commissioned you to go out and to bear fruit, fruit that will last"). Throughout the four gospels the failures of Jesus' disciples are usually related to their wish to take an inappropriate initiative, rather than to follow the lead of the one who called them. Are the two unnamed disciples here the same two as were present in John Chapter 1? It doesn't really matter whether or not they are; what does matter is that here Simon Peter, followed by the rest of this group of seven, embark on an initiative of their own, one which did not originate with Jesus. Hence, it failed – all through the night! They stay out all night, but catch nothing. It is only when Jesus appears early in the morning (a reminder of his appearance to Mary Magdalene, also first thing in the morning) that their fortunes change. In typical fashion, at first none of them recognise Jesus on the beach. He addresses them with the question, 'children, do you have any fish?' This is a literal translation, rather than the Jerusalem Bible's "Have you caught anything, friends?" The term 'children' shows a level of affection for the seven. They have no option but to answer 'no' and Jesus instructs them, 'cast your net to the right side of the boat and you will catch something'. The evangelist tells us that they were unprepared for the catch that they net – one hundred and fifty three fish: big ones! There have been many ingenious suggestions on the significance of the number. Obviously it had some significance for the evangelist but its true significance may never be known to us. Perhaps more important is the fact that the net, although strained to breaking point, did not in fact tear. Is this, like the reference to the seamless garment which was not divided at Jesus' death, a symbol of the unity of the community he leaves behind, despite the very real diversity of those who belong to it? Before we are informed of the number of fish, we are told something else of importance. Of all the seven, only one understands the true identity of Jesus – the Beloved Disciple, the unnamed one who has been present since the beginning of the Last Supper account, who was known to the High Priest and therefore was able to gain access to the courtyard of the High Priest's house when Jesus was on trial there. This disciples was also present with the mother of Jesus at the foot of the cross and who first understood the significance of the grave clothes and their arrangement when he reached the empty tomb. He is the first to recognise who Jesus is, because he hears the voice of the Risen Lord. This is always the key to faith in the Resurrection in the Fourth gospel. Repeatedly, disciples fail to recognise Jesus on sight; those who hear his voice (i.e. who listen to the Word) are those who believe he has risen.

When they come ashore, they discover a charcoal fire, and that Jesus has already cooked some fish, along with some bread which is there. The allusions to the feeding of the 5000 with bread and fish cannot be missed. They have particularly Eucharistic overtones in chapter 6 of this gospel and the feeding of the 5000 which in turn lead into the long discourse on Jesus, the Bread of Life. There is another connection with a previous incident however and this is made through the reference to a charcoal fire. This was first mentioned earlier during the Passion Narrative, when Peter warmed himself in the courtyard of the High Priest's House: "it was cold, and the servants and guards had lit a charcoal fire and were standing there warming themselves; so Peter stood there too, warming himself with the others" (John 18:18). This was when Peter made his scandalous triple denial of any knowledge of Jesus. Now, again around a charcoal fire, Peter will be asked three times about his relationship with Jesus and now by Jesus himself. The issue is about the extent of Peter's love. Peter is not asked if his love is superior to that of the others as the Jerusalem Bible wrongly suggests; "Simon son of John, do you love me more than these others do?" (John 21:15), but rather does Simon love Jesus more than he loves his friends? There has been much speculation as to why the words for love and the words for sheep change, but the evangelist appears to intend no more than finding three different ways to say exactly the same thing. The point is that Peter having denied three times that he knew Jesus, is now asked how much he loves Jesus. He repeatedly insists that his love for Jesus is greater than it is for anyone else, and he appeals to Jesus' knowledge of all things as his witness that Jesus knows he is telling the truth. Peter is at each stage of his threefold answer commanded to continue what Jesus began – tend, or feed His sheep. Peter is commissioned to continue Jesus' mission to be the Good Shepherd. Chapter 20 of the gospel had told of Jesus' appearance on the day of resurrection in the room where the disciples were gathered in fear. He said to them, "As the Father sent me, so am I sending you" (John 20:21). Now, the nature of the sending out is made explicit. Peter is to assume the role of the Good Shepherd; but the Good Shepherd would lay down his life for his flock, and that is why Peter is told that whereas in his earlier life he would take charge of his own affairs (put on his own belt and walk where he liked), in later life he would stretch out his hands to allow others to fasten his belt and make him go where he would rather not go. By the time this gospel was written, it would have been widely known that Peter had died by crucifixion, so this is a prophetic expression of Jesus' prophecy of Peter's ultimate mission for the sheep entrusted to him; he would lay down his own life for them and by that death, he would give glory to God (as Jesus had done in his death). This passage opened with Peter making his own decisions, tying his own belt (perhaps when he jumped into the water semi-clad?) and go where he wanted (out to fish?). Peter's own initiatives were always less than successful; in accepting Jesus' commission, which is also rooted in Peter's love for Jesus, a whole new mission is open to the former fisherman.

This is the last post resurrection story we read on the Sundays of Easter (with the exception of John 20:19-23, repeated on Pentecost Sunday. The rest of the Sundays of the season use passages which, with only one exception (and that is next Sunday), come from the Last supper Discourse, and which we now read in the light of Jesus' death and resurrection.

4th Sunday of Easter Year C. John 10:27-30

Questions to Ponder

☐ To whom is this discourse of Jesus addressed today?

☐ Is this passage about the relationship of Jesus to his Father, or that between Jesus and his flock?

☐ In what sense does this passage, correctly read, pave the way for discussion on Vocations to Priesthood and religious life?

There are assumptions made about this central Sunday of the Easter Season which are not always fully supported by an accurate reading of the gospel text which must therefore be approached with some caution. The 4th Sunday of Easter has been the occasion for the annual Word Day of Prayer for Vocations since the 1960s.This is based on the usual designation of this Sunday as "Good Shepherd Sunday" which is really a bit of a misnomer, because only on one of the three years of the cycle on this Sunday does the gospel explicitly deal with Jesus, the Good Shepherd who lays down his life for his sheep (Year B). On other years, it is true that related themes are presented: in Year A Jesus is cast as the authentic gate of the sheepfold and also as the gate keeper whereas in the current year of the cycle, the passage deals with the response to the voice of the shepherd, which is given only by the sheep who belong to him. There is an additional exegetical difficulty in that the gospel for years A and B are directly connected with each other in respect of chronology and continuity of text, but in the passage for Year C, we have not only a separation in the text (Year B's gospel ends at John 10:18, and that for Year C does not resume until John 10:27), but the setting of the events at which these passages take place is also separated by some months. This is because the Good Shepherd Discourse is set in Jerusalem during the celebration of the Feast of Tabernacles (the account runs from the beginning of chapter 7 until 10:21), whereas the beginning of Tabernacles took place on the fifteenth day of the seventh month, which would mean it fell somewhere in the region of September-October in today's calendar. The discourse which we therefore read this year (the sheep who listen to the voice of Jesus) takes place in winter and during a totally different feast: Dedication.

The whole of chapter 10 in the fourth gospel is wedged between two major pilgrimage feasts. The first is Tabernacles, which provides the backdrop of the healing of the man born blind and Jesus' dismissal of the Pharisees as blind guides and unworthy shepherds of God's people. The second is Dedication, when he presents himself as the gate of the sheepfold, the gatekeeper and ultimately as the Good Shepherd who unlike the hired man who abandons the sheep when danger looms, who is prepared to lay down his life for his flock. The first readers/hearers of this gospel must have had two historic events in mind as they encountered these words. There was the memory of Jesus' death for the salvation of humanity, which of course fulfilled Jesus; prophetic statement that he lays done his life, but there would no doubt have been the memory of the behaviour of the Pharisees just before the destruction of the Temple in September – October of 70 AD (coincidentally, about the time of the Feast of Tabernacles) – when they abandoned Jerusalem and its population and relocated in the safety of the city of Jamnia, not returning until the siege of Jerusalem was well and truly over! John 10 also looks forward to the Feast of Dedication or Hanukkah which provides the necessary background for the last section of the chapter. This feast commemorates events from Jewish history when the people revolted against yet another wave of pagan oppression and persecution aided and abetted - according to biblical accounts (1 Maccabees 1:11) - by influential and leading Jewish figures who colluded in the suppression of the Temple worship. The events are alluded to in the book of Daniel, although this book purports to be set in the earlier time of exile and are more fully described in the books of Maccabees. Various responses occurred. Break away religious communities formed in protest at corrupt Temple worship, the best known of these to us being the Essenes at Qumran, the Hasidim movement, and the Maccabean revolt. The very identity of the Jewish people was at stake during this time of profound crisis, and the search was on for the authentic people of God. This sets the scene for the gospel passage we consider today and for that matter the preamble to it which is not read in the liturgy. John 10:25-26 places Jesus in the Temple area, specifically at the Portico of Solomon. This was the man point of entry to the Temple for most people, and it would figure as the gathering place of the early post-resurrection community, according to Acts 5:12. It is also mentioned in Acts 3:11, in the immediate aftermath of the first miracle worked in the name of the Risen Christ by Peter and John. Its specific identification, and the public nature of the dispute that follows adds later to Jesus' insistence that he also taught openly in the Temple where people meet, and all were able to hear him (c.f. John 18:12).

The Feast of Dedication (or Consecration) signifies an anointing and of the Jewish nation for the exclusive worship and service of God. Jesus enters the scene as the one who gives true meaning of this feast, as the One who is totally dedicated and anointed for God's purposes and so the narrative proper begins as Jesus is walking in the Portico of Solomon already mentioned, and where a dispute between himself and "the Jews" breaks out. It begins when the Jews demand of Jesus "How much longer are you going to keep us in suspense? If you are the Christ, tell us plainly." The Christ is of course the 'anointed one' (or Messiah), and the connection with the feast is immediately established. They are not at all happy at his reply. Jesus insists, "I have told you, but you do not believe. The works I do in my Father's name are my witness; but you do not believe, because you are no sheep of mine". Notice it is the works of Jesus which are yet again identified as the witnesses to his role as the Anointed One: the Christ or the Messiah. Having set the scene, we are now in a position to understand more fully the significance of Jesus' next discourse, when he identifies just who are to be included in the definition of who qualify as his sheep. The answer is simple: the sheep that belong to him are those who listen to his voice: therefore those who do not listen to him are not his sheep. This is a new development within the gospel of John. Until now when Jesus faced opposition and lack of acceptance from an audience, he would attribute this to their lack of knowledge and understanding of the

Father who had sent him into the world; to their lack of love for the Father; to the fact that the Word is not within them; that they are afraid to come into the light lest their evil deeds be exposed; or that they do not come to Jesus because they are not drawn to the Father. Now he says that their unbelief, characterised by all of the above reasons, is really summed up in the single concept that they are not his sheep, and this is amply demonstrated by the fact that they do not listen to his voice.

This means that questions of who do or do not respond to Jesus are now expressed in terms of the relationship between Jesus and his flock, which in turn depends on the relationship between Jesus and his Father. This is because the flock has been given to Jesus by the Father, and no one can ever take them away from (steal them, snatch them away) from Jesus. They will remain in relationship with Jesus because just as sheep recognise the voice of their shepherd and follow the sound of that voice and only that voice, so Jesus' flock will listen to his voice and follow him. The flock then are Jesus' disciples, because they have been given to him and not because they chose him initiative. In listening to Jesus' voice and following him, Jesus' flock will be led to eternal life - that is, a fullness of life through which they will never be lost and no one will ever steal them from Jesus: because no one can steal from the Father. This becomes clearer in the light of the nature of the relationship that exists between the Father and the Son, a relationship that has been and will continue to be at the very heart of this gospel. From the opening verses of the Prologue, we learned that "In the beginning was the Word: and the Word was with God and the Word was God. He was with God in the beginning" (John 1:1-2). At the end of this passage Jesus will insist that "The Father and I are one" (John 10:30), although puzzlingly he will say during the Last Supper Discourse, "The Father is greater than I" (John 14:28). Can the two statements be reconciled? One of the best suggestions as to how this might be done appears to be in the recognition, not of superiority in nature of the Father over the Son, but in the primacy of action of the Father with respect to the Son, that is, the Father is the greater in that he sends the Son. There is however no competition between the two, because the one who is sent does everything that the Father wills, and himself wills everything the Father wills. The works done by the Son therefore are the works desired by the Father: the words of the Son are the Word of the Father. It has been pointed out that the original Greek makes clear what Jesus means by saying that he and the Father are one: they are one (*en*) in action, but they are not one as a single (*eis*) person.

This gives even deeper significance to the importance of who does or does not listen to the voice of Jesus. To hear the voice of Jesus is to hear the voice of the Father; to ignore the voice of Jesus is to ignore the voice of God. It is this relationship that makes clear what is meant by the Word of God, who was with God in the beginning, and who was God and who has now become flesh. No wonder a recurring theme in the post-resurrection narratives is the importance of the disciples hearing the voice of the Lord as the means of recognising that he has risen: Thomas on the 2nd Sunday of Easter, the Beloved Disciple on the 3rd are two clear examples of this.

In next week's gospel, another category will be introduced which is crucial for the identification of Jesus' disciples – that quality of love demonstrated by Jesus himself, which will not only identify them as followers of Jesus, but will in fact reveal Jesus in the world, just as he revealed the Father.

5th Sunday of Easter Year C. John 13:31-35

Questions to Ponder

☐ Can a requirement to love really be expressed in the terminology of a commandment?

☐ Why does love according to Jesus' definition identify those who are truly his disciples?

☐ How does the love of disciples give glory to God (that is, according to the theology of this gospel)?

To some extent, almost every verse of every book in the Bible will depend on the one which precedes it, but this is particularly true of the gospel passage for the 5th Sunday of Easter. It is a pity therefore that the text to be read in today's liturgy does not begin one verse earlier! There is no doubt good reason why the Lectionary editors omitted John 13:30 from this passage; it refers to Judas and Jesus' betrayal, and may be thought of as not appropriate for the Easter season. It also may be difficult to comprehend without even more verses tacked on before it; but it definitely sets the scene for what we do read - at least according to the minds of some contemporary writers who insist that Jesus' response to Judas' departure is really a shout of triumph; because now his hour has arrived, and now he gives glory to God and is himself glorified in an unprecedented way. Here is the text both of the first

verse of today's gospel, and the one which immediately precedes it: "As soon as Judas had taken the piece of bread he went out. Night had fallen. When he had gone Jesus said: 'Now has the Son of Man been glorified, and in him God has been glorified. If God has been glorified in him, God will in turn glorify him in himself, and will glorify him very soon." (John 13:30-32).
What follows in the rest of this passage is bound up in the concepts of glory and glorification of Jesus and of God which are to be achieved when the Son of Man is lifted up (c.f. John 3:14; 8:28). The change from Judas' departure to Jesus' proclamation that his Hour has come lead some writers to conclude that Jesus' announcement is a shout of triumph! Jesus has frequently used the expression "Son of Man" to point towards his crucifixion: with Nicodemus, "the Son of Man must be lifted up as Moses lifted up the serpent in the desert, so that everyone who believes may have eternal life in him" (John 3:13-15); in the Bread of Life discourse, "if you do not eat the flesh of the Son of Man and drink his blood, you will not have life in you" (John 6:53); when Jesus said: 'When you have lifted up the Son of Man, then you will know that I am He" (John 8:28); and especially when the Greeks ask to see Jesus and "Jesus replied to them: 'Now the hour has come for the Son of Man to be glorified'" (John 12:23). At the beginning of today's gospel passage as it stands for liturgical reading, Jesus proclaims, "Now has the Son of Man been glorified, and in him God has been glorified. If God has been glorified in him, God will in turn glorify him in himself, and will glorify him very soon" (John 13:31-32). A better translation would end, 'and will glorify him immediately'. Having made his very dramatic statement, Jesus addresses his disciples with the affectionate term "little children" (*teknia*). He reminds them of what he said to the Jews, "You will look for me, and…where I am going, you cannot come" (John 13:33; c.f. 7:34). The Jews did not understand what Jesus meant; "The Jews then said to one another, 'Where is he going that we shan't be able to find him? Is he going abroad to the people who are dispersed among the Greeks and will he teach the Greeks? What does he mean when he says: "You will look for me and will not find me: where I am, you cannot come"? (John 7:35). Jesus' disciples are no clearer in their understanding of what he means either and yet Jesus still calls them his 'little children'. He has something to pass on to them before he goes: his testament. It is a gift, but it is also a commandment, "I give you a new commandment: love one another; just as I have loved you, you also must love one another. By this love you have for one another, everyone will know that you are my disciples." (John

13:34-35). It is also an example to follow. He has already mentioned the example that they are to follow earlier in this chapter, after he had washed his disciples' feet. This was to be an example through which they were to copy him, but can a commandment be a gift? Can love be commanded? To explore this further we must go back to Jesus' announcement that the time has come for him to be glorified, and for God to be glorified in him. The author of the fourth gospel consistently uses the terms glory and glorification as a vehicle for the revelation, the self-disclosure of God. So when God is glorified in the Son of Man being raised up, it means that God is revealed in Jesus' raising up on the cross, and thus Jesus is glorified, because he is revealed as God in his raising up. The terminology draws heavily on the imagery of Moses receiving the Law from God on Mount Sinai. When the Covenant was ratified, God instructed Moses, along with Aaron, Nadab and Abihu, and seventy of the elders of Israel to go toward the Lord and bow down in worship from a distance, although Moses alone was to approach the Lord. Moses informed the people of the Lord's commands, and the people accepted them, promising to obey all that the Lord had commanded. Moses wrote the commands down, and he offered a holocaust to the Lord, sprinkling the blood on the people to ratify the covenant. Moses then obeyed God's commandment to go up to the mountain and receive the stone tablets of the commandments. The glory of the Lord rested for six days on the mountain in a cloud, and on the seventh day, the Lord called Moses to enter the cloud (c.f. Exodus 24)

The glory of God dwelling on the mountain is the revelation of God given its full expression to the people of Israel in the commands that the Lord had given: the defining conditions of the Covenant that God had made with his chosen people; that unique people to whom God had given the Law through Moses. This gives the background to Jesus' reference to a new commandment. It is not that the commandment to love - even to the extent of Jesus' love - that is new; it is rather that the commandment to love is the new gift which is the defining condition of the new covenant which is sealed in the blood of Jesus. Jesus' disciples cannot follow him as he departs from this life, but they can be instrumental in revealing Jesus and God, and the way they do this is by keeping his commandment to love. Just as the people of Israel were given commandments which ensured their love for God and love for one another, and just as the Law which God gave them identified them as God's chosen people and therefore revealed God to the other nations in their keeping of that Law. In Deuteronomy 4:5-8, Moses addresses the people:

"See, as Yahweh my God has commanded me, I teach you the laws and customs that you are to observe in the land you are to enter and make your own. Keep them, observe them, and they will demonstrate to the peoples your wisdom and understanding. When they come to know of all these laws they will exclaim, "No other people is as wise and prudent as this great nation". And indeed, what great nation is there that has its gods so near as Yahweh our God is to us whenever we call to him? And what great nation is there that has laws and customs to match this whole Law that I put before you today?" Likewise, Jesus' commandment to his disciples to love each other as he has loved them is the defining quality by which they will be recognised; but it is also the way in which Jesus and God are glorified, that is, revealed, in Jesus' disciples. This is because of the extent of the love the commandment urges: it is love after the example of Jesus himself, a love that as he will make clear later in the discourse, cannot be surpassed: because no one can have greater love than to lay down life for friends. The commandment is new because the covenant is new, but like the commandments of the old covenant, this commandment is a gift from God, or most accurately, a gift from Jesus, whose glory is revealed as he glorifies God. Throughout the fourth Gospel, Jesus is described as the One whom the Father has sent; after the resurrection, on the first day of the week, in the room behind closed doors, the Risen Jesus appears to his fearful disciples, "Peace be with you. 'As the Father sent me, so am I sending you.'" (John 20:21). Jesus' ultimate act of love is on the cross. It is how he reveals God, the One who sent him into the world. Thus, it will be the way Jesus' disciples reveal both Jesus and his Father to the world.

6th Sunday of Easter Year C. John 14:23-29

Questions to Ponder

☐ How can our love for one another draw us into the very life of the Trinity?

☐ In what sense does the love that Christians show for each other reveal God to the world of today?

☐ What is the role of the Paraclete as teacher of everything and reminder of Jesus' words in our own relationship with Father, Son and each other?

☐ How essential is the Holy Spirit, the Paraclete, the Instructor, the Reminder necessary to make love a truly Christian phenomenon?

Last week's gospel introduced us to a new commandment – not new in the sense that it had not been around before, but new in the sense that its implementation would do what had never been done before. The commandment was for Jesus' disciples to love one another according to the model that he set down; the newness of the commandment lay in the fact that such love continued what Jesus' action of love had done, and that was to reveal God ('glorify God'). If we stop for a moment to think some more about last week's passage, we realise that one element was not spelled out in detail and that was the question of what it means in practice to love one another as Jesus has loved us. What exactly has to be done if the commandment is to be put into practice? This week's passage addresses the issue with a very simple answer, and then spells out more fully the consequences of living out the commandment.

Precisely how Jesus' commandment is to be put into practice is easily explained. Jesus says "If anyone loves me he will keep my word, and my Father will love him, and we shall come to him and make our home with him" (John 14:23). The opposite is also true, "Those who do not love me do not keep my words. And my word is not my own: it is the word of the one who sent me." (John 14:24). To love is to keep Jesus' commandments; not to keep his commandments is not to love him, and since his commandments (words) are not his own, but the words of the one who sent him (he is the Word of God), to reject Jesus' words, to refuse to love is to reject God. To love therefore, is to put into practice the word he has spoken. In the Synoptics, Jesus famously pairs the commandments on love of God and love of neighbour as what underpins the meaning of the whole of the Law (Mark 12:30-31; Matthew 22:37-39). Paul says something similar; "the whole of the Law is summarised in a single command: Love your neighbour as yourself" (Galatians 5:14). In John, the centrality of love for the disciples of Jesus is spelled out in more detail: whoever keeps Jesus' commandments loves Jesus, but is also loved *by* Jesus (c.f. John 14:21, a couple of verses before today's passage commences). What was expressed as a commandment in last week's passage (John 13:31-35) and came to be understood as a gift is also highlighted as the beginning and the end of a relationship – or rather of a series of relationships which are quite extraordinary in their scope. Thus, those who keep Jesus' commandments 1) not only love Jesus, but 2) they are loved by the Father, and 3) they are loved by Jesus and are known by Jesus because 4) he makes himself known to them (i.e. to those who love him,

Jesus is revealed for who he really is). So, the relationship is not just between the disciple and Jesus: it is equally between the disciple and the Father because it also involves the relationship between Jesus and the Father. This passage is of course from the Last Supper Discourse which at an earlier stage had turned to the departure of Jesus from the world (c.f. John 14:2-3). Jesus had promised to prepare a place for his disciples in his Father's house, and that he would return to take them with him so that where he is, they would be too. In today's text, it is clear that he will still have to leave them, but the links between Jesus and disciples, between and the Father and disciples will still be maintained. This will be achieved by the Advocate (*paraclētos*), the Holy Spirit, whom the Father will send in Jesus' name. The role of the Paraclete, the Spirit will be twofold, according to this section of the discourse. It will be a) to teach disciples everything they will need to know and b) to remind them of all that Jesus has said to them (his words, his commandments, the very things by whose implementation they will love him and be recognised as his disciples because his commandments are about loving one another as he has loved them and are about revealing God (give glory to God) in the process). In the Johannine Passion Narrative which we read on Good Friday, Jesus, at the moment of his death, will hand over his Spirit to the two representative disciples, unnamed but identified as his mother and the beloved disciple (John 19:30) stationed at the foot of the cross. On the Day of Resurrection (in the passage for the 2nd Sunday of Easter), he will breathe on his fearful disciples in the room behind closed doors saying, "Receive the Holy Spirit". He will follow this by saying "For those whose sins you forgive, they are forgiven; for those whose sins you retain, they are retained" (John 20:22-23). The gift of the Spirit, who will teach all they need to know and remind them of Jesus' words is linked to the gift of being able to forgive, surely the highest expression of love, as Jesus shows in his ultimate expression of love, giving his life so that humanity may be free from sin and may have life, so that the world might be saved (c.f. John 3:16-17). Jesus is the One whom the Father sent into the world; he now says that the Father will send the Paraclete, the Advocate, the Holy Spirit, but this is done in Jesus' name. During that resurrection appearance, when Jesus breathes the Holy Spirit and empowers disciples to forgive he also sends them as the Father had sent him (John 20:21). In 14:16-17, Jesus had said, "I shall ask the Father, and he will give you another Advocate to be with you for ever, that Spirit of truth whom the world can never receive since it neither sees nor knows him; but you know him, because he is with you, he is in you". On trial before Pilate, Jesus will say that he came into the world for this purpose: to bear witness to the truth (John 18:37). In 14:6, he proclaims that he is "the Way, the Truth and the Life". These observations show that whereas it would be unhelpful to try to discover in any of the gospels a well-developed Trinitarian theology (that would not be worked out until much later), we do find in the Last supper Discourse in John a careful working out of the relationships which exist in God who is Father, Son and Spirit: relationships into which disciples of Jesus are themselves brought.

Behind those closed doors, on the day of resurrection, Jesus will also pass on to the disciples the gift of his unique peace which is unobtainable from the world, along with the gift of the Holy Spirit and the gift of forgiveness. In the discourse we are considering now he promises his peace which is beyond the world's capability to give. This paves the way for an almost exact repeat of his initial words in this chapter, "Do not let your hearts be troubled or afraid (John 14:27; c.f. 14:1). The reason for their fear and troubled hearts is Jesus' departure, just as it would be on the day of resurrection, but Jesus reassures them. Although he is going away he will return, and if they loved Jesus (kept his words/commandments?) they would realise that he is going to the Father who is greater than he is. He has already said to Philip, who said that if they (i.e. the disciples) could see the Father then they would be satisfied; "To have seen me is to have seen the, Father, so how can you say, 'Let us see the Father'? Do you not believe that I am in the Father and the Father is in me? The words I say to you I do not speak as from myself: it is the Father, living in me, who is doing this work. You must believe me when I say that I am in the Father and the Father is in me; believe it on the evidence of this work, if for no other reason" (John 14:9-11). Can the two statements be reconciled? Can Jesus and the Father be one, and at the same time the Father be greater than Jesus? It was pointed out in the notes for the 4th Sunday of Easter this year that the Father is greater than Jesus, not in the sense of greatness of person, but in greatness of action, i.e. the Father is the one who sent the Son into the world, therefore his action is one of priority. Likewise the Father, on Jesus' request and in Jesus' name (an indication of equality of person?) will send the Paraclete, the Spirit, through whom the Father and the Son will be in the lives of disciples from whom they are physically absent. If disciples truly loved their master, that is had listened to his word, had heeded his commandments, they would have realised that Jesus returns to the One whose will he obeys implicitly, not as a command but in a unity of wills; that he returns to the One from whom he came so that the world might be saved, so that people might have life. Since achieving this is the purpose of Jesus' return to the Father, his Hour, his Lifting Up, his unique way of giving glory to - revealing – God, there is nothing for disciples to fear in Jesus' departure and that is why he has told them all of this before it happens, so that they may believe when it does happen (c.f. John 14:29).

EXCURSUS: ANOTHER PARACLETE – Hebrew and Greek backgrounds

A rather glib answer to the question 'what is a *paraclete*' would be to say 'an agent of *paraclesis*'. *Paraclesis* can have two different meanings depending on whether we are considering its Greek or its Hebrew connotations. In the Hebrew tradition, God is Israel's comforter; Israel's '*paraclete*', according to the Greek version of the text. The Septuagint (LXX) translation of Isaiah 51:12, uses the Greek word *paraclitōn* for the Hebrew for the English 'comforter'. Now the Hebrew *nḥm*, which here becomes in English 'to comfort' can in other 'moods' be rendered as 'to repent', that is, the *metanoeō* in Greek, meaning to change one's mind. Confusing? Perhaps there is a link in that the person who is comforted is enabled to think of the world that causes so much pain (in Isaiah 51, for example, the excruciating pain of exile for Israel) in a new light. Simeon gives an example of *paraclesis* in Luke 2:25, "Now in Jerusalem there was a man named Simeon. He was an upright and devout man; he looked forward to Israel's *comforting* and the Holy Spirit rested on him". So, according to the Hebrew way of thinking, it is God who is Israel's comforter, or *paraclete*. By implication, Jesus is *paraclete*; see, for example Matthew 11:4-5, "Jesus answered, 'Go back and tell John what you hear and see; the blind see again, and the lame walk, lepers are cleansed, and the deaf hear, and the dead are raised to life and the Good News is proclaimed to the poor". Hence, the first *paraclete*, implied in John 14:16, is Jesus himself. The second *paraclete* is therefore one who will continue Jesus' ministry of comfort, for the disciples that he has left behind. There is also another understanding of *paraclete*, found more frequently in the word of Greek and Roman thinking and which has more to do with the language of the courtroom. In this use, *paraclete* was understood to refer to a legal advisor, or an advocate (the latter being the term often used in English translations of John 14:16). This is also appropriate for the one Jesus promises to request from his Father for the disciples. Especially in the 4th gospel, Jesus' ministry is presented as, among other things, a trial scene usually carried out in the presence of the religious leadership, but also latterly before Pontius Pilate. Jesus frequently cites witnesses – his Father, the work he does, John the Baptist. Before Pilate, Jesus declares that his purpose in this world is to bear witness to the truth. After his departure, as will be made clearer in the prayer that makes up John 17, the disciples will be on trial, since they are in the world but not of the world. This is where the *paraclete* is needed as an advocate, as one who will teach them everything and remind them of all that Jesus had said (John 14:26). Since Jesus came into the world to be witness to the truth, it is therefore understandable that the *paraclete* is also called the "Spirit of truth" (John 14:17). This other *paraclete* then will combine the roles of comforter and legal advisor for disciples.

Solemnity of the Ascension of the Lord. Luke 24:46-53

Questions to ponder

☐　Why would Luke give two different times for the Ascension: the day of the resurrection in the gospel, and 40 days later in Acts?

☐　If the timescale is not important, what does the Ascension really signify?

☐　Matthew's gospel cites Jesus' last appearance as on a mountain in Galilee, whereas Luke has it take place just outside Jerusalem. Why does the Jerusalem setting suit Luke's purpose (and why might Galilee better suit Matthew's)?

None of the four canonical gospels places Jesus' Ascension 40 days from the Resurrection: this information is found only in Acts 1:3, "He had shown himself alive to them after his Passion by many demonstrations: for forty days he had continued to appear to them and tell them about the kingdom of God". It is strange therefore, that the same author would give two different occasions for the same event – or is it? Perhaps the reference to 40 days in Acts has more to do with the frequent and clearly symbolic use of the number 40 in the Old Testament and in the gospels – the 40 days following the flood, the Israelites wandering for 40 years in the desert, Moses fasting for 40 days on Mount Sinai, Elijah walking for 40 days and 40 nights to Mount Horeb, and of course Jesus' own fast of 40 days following his baptism. In each case the period of forty days, months or years denotes a period of preparation, growth and the emergence of a symbolic expression of new life at the end of the time (the birth of the nation Israel, a new start for humanity after the flood, the onset of Jesus' ministry etc. It seems likely that the number takes on this symbolic significance from the natural human cycle of giving birth: every mother knows the significance of 'waiting' for forty weeks, after which new life emerges. This symbolic reading of the number 40 would make sense in the case of the Ascension forty days after the Resurrection. As the verse in Acts says, Jesus used the period of forty days to appear to his disciples and to tell them about the kingdom of God. That means therefore that the period between the resurrection and the Ascension, however long or short it may have been, was a period of post-resurrection instruction for the disciples before Jesus is finally no longer visible to them. So perhaps it will be more helpful to see the period between the resurrection and the Ascension as a process of transition, rather than an exact period of time. As Joseph Fitzmyer suggests, what is important is for us to develop an accurate impression of what the Ascension represents in New Testament writing. The word itself means 'upward motion'. The essential features of the New Testament accounts is that now Jesus is with his heavenly Father in glory, and that he sends the Holy Spirit on his disciples, investing them with 'power from on high' (the 'upward' theme again). The Ascension itself therefore is nothing more than the cessation of Jesus' visibility to his disciples, making way for his presence being perceived in the 'breaking of bread', and through 'what his Father had promised'. The '40 days' then become the period of gestation for the new community of disciples which will no longer see Jesus, but who testify to his continued presence among them in the proclamation of his word and the breaking of bread. With these points in mind, we can now turn to Luke's account of Jesus' Ascension.

The account opens with Jesus appearing among the Eleven, after he has appeared to the two disciples on the road to Emmaus. The part of the narrative where Jesus eats food to prove he is no ghost is omitted (c.f. Luke 24:37-43), as is the evangelist's comment that he opened their minds to understand the scriptures (Luke 24:45). Instead, Jesus immediately reinforces the point he has made earlier: that everything written about him in the Law of Moses, the Prophets and the Psalms (i.e. the whole of Scripture) had to be fulfilled, and that it was written that the Christ had to suffer, die and on the third day rise again (although the Lukan Jesus does not make it clear exactly where in scripture these things are said. Here Luke is merely offering a distillation of various scriptural sources to produce a background statement from scripture which has now been fulfilled. From the beginning of this gospel, Jesus the prophet and the fulfilment of his prophecy have been prominent themes, and there is still room for more because Jesus now moves on to a programmatic prophecy, outlined in stages: a prophecy which will see its fulfilment in the second volume of Luke's work, the Acts of the Apostles. The prophecy is that a) in Jesus' name b) there would be preaching of c) repentance d) for the forgiveness of sins, e) preached to all nations, f) beginning from Jerusalem. Among Jesus' final words to his disciples will be the instruction that they are to stay in Jerusalem until they are clothed with the power from on high. When that happens, they will be 'witnesses to this', that is, once they are clothed with the power on high they will become the prophetic voice that was Jesus' role during his earthly life. Notice the hints of the prophetic ministry that the disciples are about to take on. They are to be clothed with the power on high; yet another allusion to the prophetic ministries of Elijah and Elisha, already a feature of the gospel of Luke. When Elijah was taken from Elisha's sight, the latter took possession of the prophet's cloak, with which he was able to continue the former's prophetic ministry. The first sign of this is seen when Elisha uses Elijah's cloak to make the waters of the Jordan roll back and allow him to pass through dry-shod, just as Elijah (and of course Joshua and the Israelites in Joshua 3:7-17) had done earlier. Before departing, Elijah asked Elisha "What can I do for you before I am taken from you?" Elisha answered, "Let me inherit a double share of your spirit". It was with Elijah's spirit that Elisha was able to use the prophet's cloak to part the waters. This was recognised by the brotherhood of prophets who concluded "The spirit of Elijah has come to rest on Elisha" (c.f. 2 Kings 2:1-15). It is easy to see this episode as background for Jesus' instruction to the disciples to stay in Jerusalem until they are clothed with the power from on high. In Acts 1:4-5 it becomes clear that the power from on high is the Holy Spirit with whom they will be baptised (i.e. in whom they will become immersed).

The basic instructions having been given, Jesus now takes the eleven to Bethany, which was reckoned to mark the outskirts of the area of Jerusalem. In an action recalling Moses lifting his hands to give Israel victory in battle (Exodus 17:11), Jesus lifts his hands in blessing (c.f. also Aaron raising his hands and blessing the people (Leviticus 9:23). Jesus is then taken upwards and away from them – a dual motion. The reaction of the disciples is perhaps surprising: they prostrate themselves in worship, an action reserved for the recognition of divinity. Such recognition of the divinity of Jesus is coupled with their departure and return to Jerusalem full of joy where they were continually in the Temple praising God (c.f. Luke 24:52-53). Joy is a frequent accompaniment of peace, both which were considered to be messianic gifts. In obedience to Jesus' instructions, they return, awaiting the power from on high, whose arrival will be described in volume 2 of Luke's work: the Acts of the Apostles. The wait is necessary because Jesus has departed from sight, and the fulfilment of his extended programmatic prophecy about the preaching of repentance for the forgiveness of sins.

7th Sunday of Easter Year C. John 17:20-26

Questions to Ponder

☐   How can disciples give glory to God?

☐   In John's gospel, what does it mean to give glory to God?

☐   How should the unity of disciples make known to the world the life of the Trinity?

John Chapter 17 brings the Last supper Discourse to an end and makes way for the 'hour' of Jesus to reach its climax. The discourse closes with Jesus' extensive prayer for himself and for those whom he will leave behind once he has departed from this world. In the earlier stages of the prayer, read on the 7th Sunday of Easter Years A and B, we are made aware of the anomaly that Jesus is still physically present in the supper room, and yet he declares that he is no longer in the world. The prayer begins with a summary of what Jesus has achieved, looks to what he will achieve and turns to the ones that the Father has given to Jesus and who will remain in the world when he has departed.

The passage for year C is short, but even in its brevity it consists of two distinct sections. The first section begins with the clear statement about those for whom Jesus is praying – not only for those who have been his disciples during his ministry, but also for those who will hear his word and believe in him as a result of the activity of these first disciples. The content of this prayer is that they (i.e. in every generation) may be one as Jesus and the

Father are one. The reason Jesus prays that they may be one is so that in their unity, disciples may demonstrate to the world that Jesus is indeed the One who has been sent by the Father, the recurrent theme throughout the gospel of John. There are many occasions when Jesus' origins are debated, and on which he is asked directly where he is from, but there is almost total failure among those whom Jesus addresses to recognise that he is the One whom God has sent. The notable exception is at the end of the Bread of Life discourse of Chapter 6, when disciples leave Jesus because they find his sayings about the Bread of Life too hard, and Jesus asks the Twelve, "do you want to go away too?', and Peter replies, "Lord, who shall we go to? You have the message of eternal life, and we believe; we know that you are the Holy One of God" (John 6:68-69), that is, the One whom God has sent. So, in this prayer, it becomes clear that the missionary task of the disciples of Jesus is to make God known. This purpose, which is developed in second section of the prayer, is to be achieved by disciples displaying the kind of unity that exists between the Father and the Son. That unity is not about absolute identicality – the Father and the Son are not identical; they are distinct persons, but Jesus stresses that the Father and he are one. The synoptic gospels also explore this idea: "no one knows the Son except the Father, just as no one knows the Father, except the Son and those to whom, the Son chooses to reveal him" (Matthew 11:27; Luke 10:22). It is this unity between Father and Son that allows Jesus to proclaim "I AM the Way, the Truth and the Life" – specifically, the truth (c.f. John 18:37). It is this unity between Father and Son that makes it possible for Jesus to say to Pilate: "I came into the world for this: to bear witness to the Truth" (John 14:6).

After the reason for the prayer is made clear –what we might call the intention for which Jesus is praying – the second section tells us what will be the outcome if Jesus' prayer bears fruit. This has to do with glory. Rather than simply offering a prayer, quite uncharacteristically for him, Jesus makes his own will in this matter known. He does not simply petitioning his Father to answer his prayer: he asserts that it is his own will, his desire, that his disciples will see the glory that the Father has given to Jesus, because the Father has loved him since the foundation of the world. Once again, we have the theme of 'glorify', and once again it means what it usually means in this gospel; the glory of God is always in some sense about an awareness of the presence of God on earth: the revelation of God, that is, the making known of God in words and in actions. In the fourth gospel, there are seven miracles or signs as they are called, and each of these are ways in which Jesus reveals his glory; that is, in which he reveals God in his works. For Jesus, to reveal his true nature, his glory, is to reveal God, or God's glory, because he is the One whom the Father has sent; he and the Father are one. It is this unity between Father and Son that makes it possible for Jesus to reveal his Father in his own works, and this also explains why Jesus desires or wills that his disciples display among themselves that unity that exists between Father and Son. Since it is through the unity of the Father and the Son that the glory of the God is revealed Jesus desires, wills that his disciples will be with him where he is and that they will always see the glory that God had given him, because he loved him before the foundation of the world (John 17:24). Now we see a link emerging between the unity of disciples, through which God is known in the world, and Jesus' early indication of how Jesus is known in the world – the love which is gift and commandment, and which we read about on the 5th Sunday of Easter this year. The new commandment is the formulation of the new covenant whereby the glory of God is manifested in the world (c.f. John 13:31-35). By living the new commandment, disciples give glory to God, that is, become the vehicle for God's self-revelation, expressed in the love of his Son, whom he has loved since the foundation of the world. So, the Last Supper Discourse ends as it had begun. God is to be made known in the love that defines people as disciples of Jesus, that love which follows the example of Jesus' love, to the extent of laying down his life for his friends. This was why Jesus spoke of being glorified and giving glory to God when the Son of Man is raised up. Jesus' love gives glory to God because of the unity between Father and Son. The Son reveals the Father's love for those he has given to Jesus; likewise, the unity among disciples which can only be founded on that new commandment, reveals Jesus and reveals his Father because such unity is nothing less than the unity between Father and Son.

Pentecost, Vigil and Feast. John 7:37-39/20:19-23.

Pentecost or Tabernacles?

Questions to ponder:

☐ Given the multiple instances of disciples receiving the Holy Spirit throughout the New Testament, how much prominence should be given to the Pentecost account in Luke/Acts?

☐ From the Vigil gospel, and from the John Passion Narrative account of

Jesus' death, are we to link in some way water and the Holy Spirit?
☐ What link do the two gospel passages offered for Pentecost suggest
between Baptism and Confirmation?

The Last Day of the Feast: The Vigil of Pentecost
A prominent feature of the Fourth gospel is that is regularly presents Jesus as
the one who give fulfilment to the major feasts of the Jews. There are three
references to Passover in this gospel, and in each of them Jesus gives the true
meaning of the feast. Around the time of the first reference to this feast, at the
end of chapter 1 and into chapter 2, John the Baptist describes Jesus as the
Lamb of God who takes away the sins of the world (John 1:29. 36), and we
are told of events that take place around the time of Passover (the marriage
feast at Cana, 2:1-11, and the cleansing of the Temple 2:14-22). In chapter 6,
the feeding of the 5,000 and the Bread of Life Discourse chapter, the setting
is again the Passover (6:4), and finally, at the time of Jesus' Hour, his
passion, death and resurrection is set against the Passover backdrop. 'Lamb
of God', 'Bread of Life', 'the Son of Man raised up' – these motifs all
indicate how the ancient celebration of Passover is made fuller (fulfilled) in
Jesus. The Feast of Tabernacles provides the backdrop for John 7 – 10, with
its dual themes of light and water, fulfilled in Jesus who is the 'Light of the
World', and who promises 'streams of living water'. Chapter 10 concluded at
the time when people were celebrating the Feast of Dedication. This
originated from the time of the Maccabean revolt: Decdication's themes are
the restoration of the Temple and the apostasy of those who abandoned the
Law and the ways of God – failure to listen to the voice of the Lord. Hence
Jesus' insistence on that occasion that "the sheep that belong to me listen to
my voice" (John 10:27; c.f. 4th Sunday of Easter Year C). Pentecost does not
figure at all in the gospel of John! Perhaps the reason for this is that although
important in its own right, Pentecost was the concluding act of the Passover
season, occurring 50 days after Passover began: hence the title 'Pentecost',
which means 'fiftieth'. A brief explanation of the significance of these feasts
is given in the **EXCURSUS: Three major feasts of the Jews** below.
The Vigil of Pentecost. The gospel tells us the exact setting for this –
Tabernacles. The evangelist tells us, "On the last day and greatest day of the
festival, Jesus stood there and cried out" (John 7:37). As we shall see in a
moment, the action of Jesus is dramatic. It takes place in the Temple at the
climax of a major Jewish feast. It is an illustration of one of the recurring

motifs in John's gospel we considered in the previous paragraph: that Jesus gives the true meaning to the feasts that the Jews had been celebrating in the Temple for years. Here, Jesus chooses the final and - according to the evangelist but with apparently no real basis in Jewish custom, thinking and practice - most important day of the Feast for his gesture and speech in the Temple. On this day, the ritual involves Temple Priests passing through the Water Gate in procession and circling the altar seven times, sprinkling water from the Pool of Siloam (there's a name to recall from Lent, and the cure of the man born blind, John 9). Against a ceremony that reminds us of Ezekiel's vision of a Temple which would be a source of living water Jesus proclaims himself the source of living water. Life-giving water for Zion was a theme of the readings from scripture chosen for use during the celebration of Tabernacles (e.g. Zechariah 14:8, Ezekiel 47:1f), and the liturgy for this feast also included prayers for rain. The procession from Siloam recalled the episode in Exodus 17 when Moses brought forth water from the rock. The evangelist has added significant layers of interpretation to this short passage. His reference to scripture is not really a quotation, but it does hint at the 'transfer' of the source of water from a building (the Temple envisioned by Ezekiel) to a person: Jesus. This, as we have already noted, is a frequent theme in John where Jesus rather than the Temple or a ritual from the Temple liturgy, demonstrates the true significance and purpose of the feasts. The evangelist gives a second interpretation for Jesus' invitation to all who believe in him to come to him in thirst and to drink from streams of living water. This ties up with we heard in John 4 where Jesus encountered the Samaritan woman, saying at one point: "anyone who drinks the water that I shall give will never be thirsty again: the water that I shall give will turn into a spring inside him, welling up to eternal life" (John 4:14). Now we are given additional information about this spring of water. According to the evangelist, Jesus is speaking about the Spirit, who has not as yet been given to people because Jesus had not yet been glorified. When that happens, as we know from reading John's account of Jesus death which was read on Good Friday, Jesus will hand over the Spirit as his last living act. After death, blood and water will gush from his side. Spirit and Water clearly are linked here: the sending of the Holy Spirit and the waters of baptism are strongly linked in the theology of this gospel - c.f. John the Baptist's testimony, "The man on whom you see the Spirit come down and rest is the one who is going to baptise with the Holy Spirit" (John 1:33). But all of this is in the future because, as the evangelist says in comment on Jesus' proclamation: "for there was no Spirit as yet because Jesus had not yet been glorified" (John 7:39).

EXCURSUS: The three major feasts of the Jews

The Gospel of John sets the ministry of Jesus against the background of Jewish feasts: Passover, Tabernacles, and Dedication. Jesus is presented as the 'fulfilment' of these feasts. Therefore, significant events in the ministry occur to coincide with these. For example, there are three occasions on which Jesus' actions are set against the background of Passover, beginning at John 2:13; 6:4; 11:55, the last of these providing the context of his 'hour'. Likewise, 7:2 tells us that the Feast of Tabernacles was drawing near, and 10:22 tells us it was winter, and the Feast of Dedication was being celebrated in Jerusalem. One feast which is missing from the Johannine list is Pentecost, or the Feast of Weeks, which is not mentioned in any gospel, but which was one of the three 'Great' Feasts of the Jews, the other two being Passover and Tabernacles. Their greatness comes from their identification in Deuteronomy 16:16, "Three times a year all your males shall appear before the LORD your God at the place that he will choose: at the festival of unleavened bread, at the festival of weeks, and at the festival of booths. They shall not appear before the LORD empty-handed".

These three feasts operated as follows. The first, Passover, was celebrated during the season of spring, and combined the sacrifice of the Paschal Lamb and the Feast of Unleavened Bread. Instructions for this feast are to be found in Exodus 12, part of which makes up the first reading at the Mass of the Last Supper on Holy Thursday Evening.
The second of the great feasts occurred seven weeks after Passover, and is Pentecost (literally the fiftieth [day]), and signified the end of the grain harvest which began with the presentation of the first sheaf of barley at the time of Passover. Therefore, Pentecost was celebrated around May-June.
The last of the three is Tabernacles, which lasted one week (although an eighth day is mentioned in Leviticus 23:34, and Numbers 29:35, neither of these texts refers to this eighth day as the greatest day of the festival as John 7:37 does), and which was held commemorated the time spent by the Israelites in the desert, during which time they dwelt in tents (tabernacles, booths). During this time, the Ark of the Covenant also dwelt in a tent. Solomon dedicated the first Temple during this festival. This feast was

celebrated in autumn.

Pentecost Sunday (John 20:19-23)

There are two ways we can speak of the Day of Pentecost here. One is to refer to the Christian feast we celebrate, and the day of the feast itself (as opposed to the vigil of the feast which we have already considered). The second is to take the lead from the first reading today, from Acts, and talk about what happened in the room where the disciples were gathered on the *Jewish* feast of Pentecost. What we cannot do of course is to use the gospel to talk about what happened on that particular day of Pentecost!

There is the danger that because we are so familiar with the account of the Pentecost gathering of disciples given in Acts 2:1-11, we might tend to ignore the other readings for today, especially the gospel with its particular description of how Jesus gave the Holy Spirit to the Apostles on the day of resurrection, or that we might fail to be aware of the repeated experience of the Spirit in Acts and the New Testament letters (Acts 20:16, and 1 Corinthians 16:8 both refer to Paul and the celebration of a later Pentecost). If we are to do justice to this feast, we need to take into account the multiplicity of texts available, as indeed the full background to Pentecost – the Jewish feast that was being celebrated when the Apostles were gathered as described in Acts 2 - and the rich biblical imagery that feeds Luke's narrative there.

Let's start with that particular imagery. It is presumably safe to assume that Luke highlights the Pentecost event for several reasons. One might be that it gives him a useful platform for Peter's Pentecost speech which is given to a wide range of Jews from the Diaspora who are in Jerusalem for the festival (remember, Pentecost marked the end of Passover, just as for Christians it marks the end of Easter). So, Pentecost provides the setting for the first apostolic preaching of the Good News of the Risen Christ. Perhaps more important however is that it allows Luke to bring together all sorts of images from biblical and non-biblical sources (e.g. the Jewish philosopher Philo's *Decalogue*) which describe what would happen when the Holy Spirit came. Hence when Luke in Acts describes what sounded like a powerful wind from heaven, he may be alluding to Exodus 19 as re-worked by Philo to include a sound on Sinai which then became fire. Exodus 19:18 says that Sinai was wrapped in dense smoke, and God descended in the form of fire, and the whole mountain shook violently. When Philo writes about the giving of the

Law on Mount Sinai, he explicitly links the giving of the Law by God to the communication of speech through the fire, "And a voice sounded forth from out of the midst of the fire which had flowed from heaven, a most marvelous and awful voice, the flame being endowed with articulate speech in a language familiar to the hearers, which expressed its words with such clearness and distinctness that the people seemed rather to be seeing than hearing it." Luke says that at Pentecost, a noise like that from a powerful, or even a violent wind came from the heavens, so presumably the house shook! Only the noise is important here: the wind is only a vehicle to explain the noise. Perhaps this also recalls Elijah on Mt Sinai (1 Kings 19:11-12). What seemed like flames were distributed in tongues upon the disciples. This suggests a sharing in the one gift of the Spirit, what in the 2nd reading Paul refers to as the variety of gifts, but only one Spirit (c.f. 1 Corinthians 12:4). The biblical images extend even further. The immediate ability of those on whom the tongues of flame descended and are now able to converse with people of different nations and speak different languages suggests that there has been a reversal of Genesis 11:1-9 and particularly the 'Tower of Babel' narrative. Peter's speech contains prophetic utterances that also echo the vision in Joel 3:1, "I will pour out my spirit on all mankind. Your sons and daughters shall prophesy, your old men shall dream dreams, and your young men see visions". The prophecies of Luke's own writings are fulfilled as well. John the Baptist had foretold the one who would baptise with the Holy Spirit and with fire (Luke 3:16), and in Acts 1:5, Jesus had prophesied, "John baptised with water but you, not many days from now, will be baptised with the Holy Spirit." So, it might not be too much of an exaggeration to say that Luke is more interested here in the consequences of the reception of the Holy Spirit than with describing in strict detail what form the descent of the Spirit took.

No examination of Acts 2:1-11 would be complete without taking into account the audience who are attracted to the scene by the sound and then by the ecstatic utterances in tongues. This is not the usual crowds or bystanders who so often feature in Luke's gospel; who grow in number but so often remaining non-committal while Jesus is engaged in teaching his disciples, instructing the Pharisees etc. (see, for example, Luke 11:29; 14:25; 23:27; 23:35). This crowd consists of the first hearers of the proclamation that Jesus is Messiah, the descendant of David, and the list of those who hear this proclamation is both extensive and specific: "Parthians, Medes and Elamites;

people from Mesopotamia, Judaea and Cappadocia, Pontus and Asia, Phrygia and Pamphylia, Egypt and the parts of Libya round Cyrene; as well as visitors from Rome" (Acts 2:9-10). This is Luke's way of saying that the gospel was preached to Jews from all over the world, all of whom are invited to accept Jesus as the promised Descendant of King David. There is a parallel here with Luke's gospel, as is so often the case in his two-volume work. In the gospel, following Jesus' baptism and the descent of the Holy Spirit has descended upon him, Luke traces Jesus' ancestry back to Adam, beginning with the observation that when "he started to teach, Jesus was about thirty years old, being the son, as it was thought, of Joseph son of Heli" (Luke 3:23). Now Jesus, whom Peter says the 'Jews' had put to death having believed he was a criminal, has his ancestry traced back to David. Jesus' ancestry is not made explicit in this present passage, but those who have read the genealogy in the gospel will recall the importance of that lineage, and which underpins the motif of Jesus' descent from David in Peter's first sermon.

The gospel for the day of Pentecost has a very different account of the arrival of the Holy Spirit, although the two accounts are not mutually exclusive. John's account takes place on the evening of the day of resurrection and begins with a scene that shows all the hallmarks of fear, hiding behind closed doors in the semi-darkness of twilight: an inward-looking, guarded, terrified gathering seeking to avoid the outside at all costs. Into this scene comes unexpectedly the Risen Jesus, breaking through the closed doors and the attempts of the disciples to hide away. Jesus comes with gifts. The first is the gift of peace promised in the Last Supper Discourse and assured in the last words of that discourse. It is Jesus' final offer to the disciples before he begins the prayer that precedes their departure from the Last supper Room and journey to the Mount of Olives, where he will be taken into custody. Jesus' next words in the upper room on the evening of the day of resurrection immediately counter the defensive, secretive, fearful attitude of the disciples. If they had determined to lock themselves indoors, Jesus tells them that they are to be sent, just as the Father had sent him. Jesus breathes on them to impart the gift of the Holy Spirit. We have already heard of what the Holy Spirit will do for them (6th Sunday of Easter): the 'other Paraclete' will teach them all things and will remind them of all that Jesus has commanded them. Finally, they are given the power to forgive sins. This must be the ultimate gift that comes with the Spirit and which empowers disciples in their sending out to continue the work that Jesus had begun. They are not enabled only to forgive those who offend them: they are empowered to forgive all sins. Using a typically Aramaic phrase, Jesus says, "for those whose sins you forgive, they are forgiven; for those whose sins you retain, they are retained" (John 20:23). To our ears, this sounds ominous, because we are attuned to hearing the bit about retention; to the Semitic ear, this is just a way of emphasising that disciples who are given this power have complete control over the forgiveness of sins. This should not be so surprising. They are being sent out to continue the work of the one who came into the world as the Lamb of God who takes away the sin of the world (c.f. John 1:29). They are to bring to the world in Jesus' name that power over sin and death which he demonstrated in his ability to enter the room despite its closed doors. As Francis Moloney puts it, the disciples "are to be to the world what Jesus has been to the world". This is only possible through the gift of the Holy Spirit.

Easter ends for another year!

Chapter 5

Sundays 2 – 5, Year C: Setting out on a Mission

INTRODUCTION

Each year, Ordinary time no sooner gets underway than it is interrupted by the combination of Lent, Easter and the Feasts of Trinity Sunday and Corpus Christi. This year, after a mere five weeks of the Ordinary season, Year C, this first phase of Ordinary time ends on Sunday 14 February, and we do not return to the Ordinary Sundays until 13 June 2010. In the process, Sundays 7 – 10 are omitted. Once we reach Sunday 11 C, on 13 June, it's going to be rather difficult to remember where we left off! There is an obvious negative side to this, where such a long interruption takes place between the two sections of the longest period of the liturgical year, in which each year one of the synoptic gospels is offered for the Sunday liturgy over some thirty weeks in a semi–continuous series of readings.

There is, however, a positive element in this as well, evident at least this year, because the four gospel texts for this first section of Sundays 2 – 5 give a comprehensive introduction to the ministry of Jesus as it unfolds. The pattern is: first a passage from John's gospel – always the case of the 2ⁿᵈ Sunday of Ordinary time, and this year it is the passage about the wedding feast at Cana in Galilee – which annually gives us a pointer to where the story of Jesus' ministry will conclude, with Jesus accomplishing his 'hour'. Sunday 2 is followed by two weeks which focus on Jesus' visit to the synagogue at Nazareth (Luke chapter 4). Next comes Luke's highly individual version of Jesus' interaction with his disciples in which Simon is the central figure.

2ⁿᵈ Sunday, Year C. John 2:1-11

That Wedding Feast and The Hour of Jesus

☐	What is the significance of the gospel of John referring to incidents like the changing of water into wine as 'Signs' rather that as 'Miracles'
☐	What does this sign tell us about the nature of Jesus' ministry?
☐	How does the portrait of the mother of Jesus in this gospel equate with Marian devotion in the church today? Is our Mariology truly formed by the gospels?

Famously known as the location for first of the signs worked by Jesus, Cana is also the setting for his second sign in the 4ᵗʰ Gospel. It should perhaps be noted that not only does this 'Sign' not appear in any of the other gospels as Jesus' first; it is not found at all in the others! The point that Jesus' first two signs (John does not use the expression 'miracle') is stressed in John 4:45 and again in verse 54, and suggests that the two signs are to be considered as a pair – providing new wine at the wedding feast, and healing the son of a royal official who was ill with a fever. Between these two signs comes the narrative of the cleansing of the temple, the discourse with Nicodemus and John the Baptist's final statement, and finally the discourse with the Samaritan woman at the well. There is also a 'third day' motif present when Jesus' stay among the Samaritans comes to an end. On the day which follows two days spent among the Samaritans, the healing of the court official's son takes place, and Jesus gives the child a new lease of life. The two Cana miracles, therefore are signs of that fullness of life which Jesus discusses with Nicodemus, and which he, the Son of Man, came to bring (c.f. John 10:10).
This first sign begins with the information that 'three days later, there was a wedding' etc. The narrator tells us that "The mother of Jesus was there, and Jesus and his disciples had also been invited" (John 2:1-2). This sentence

gives notice that the mother of Jesus will be a significant player in the narrative, but it not an excuse for an exaggerated Marian piety created from this miracle story. The mother of Jesus is mentioned only here and at the foot of the cross in John's gospel. In both cases, she is cast in the role of the ideal disciple; in neither case is she named – strange since John's gospel gives the names of many people, including some who are not named in the synoptics (e.g. Nicodemus, Lazarus (not the one of whom the parable is told in Luke 10) and Malchus). The crucial role that the mother of Jesus plays in this narrative is emphasised by the fact that she is mentioned before Jesus and his disciples; precisely what that role entails will become clearer as the passage unfolds.

Famously, the pretext for the miracle is the absence of wine. Some commentators have offered the interesting suggestion that Jesus and his disciples had turned up at the wedding uninvited, and so they were the ones responsible for the wine running out. Ingenious as this theory may be, it has absolutely no basis in the text itself. When the wine ran out, the mother of Jesus turns to him and says "They have no wine" (verse 3). Jesus' reply is difficult to render exactly, since it involves a typically Semitic expression, and it defies any attempt to soften the abrupt retort from son to mother. The Jerusalem Bible translates his reply as 'Woman, why turn to me?', but this is not quite accurate. The expression *ti emoi kai soi* is translated in the RSV as "what have you to do with me?". Other translations suggest that it could mean *'what have I to do with you?'* or *'what have we in common?'* Some suggest it might even mean *'leave me alone!'*, or *'never mind!'* or even, *'this is no affair of yours!'* The harsh tone of the phrase (it is not even clear whether it is a question or a statement) is evident, however, and is reinforced by the manner of address Jesus uses for his mother, calling her "woman". The phrase occurs in various places in the Greek Old Testament, and in the gospels in Mark 5:7 where the Gerasene demoniac speaks the phrase before continuing "Jesus, son of the Most High God? Swear by God you will not torture me!" It is also found in the Lukan version of the same incident (Luke 8:28). A similar phrase is found in Jesus' first miracle in Mark's gospel, the exorcism in the Capernaum synagogue, 1:24. In these examples, it invariably denotes a distance between the person uttering the phrase and the adversary being addressed, such as between the demon about to be exorcised and Jesus the one who will carry out the exorcism. There is therefore no mistaking the harshness of tone in Jesus' retort to his mother. The reason for his words must lie in his next phrase, "my hour has not come yet" (verse 4). Jesus' "hour" and its significance will unfold throughout the course of this gospel. For the major part of his ministry, his hour is 'not yet'; it makes its first appearance, however, at the first of Jesus' signs, located during the highly significant and symbolic 'wedding feast', a frequent image of the kingdom of God in Jesus' teaching in three of the four gospels (c.f. also Matthew 22:2-14; 25:1-13; Luke 12:36; 14:8). The 'hour' which first appears at a wedding will soon come to be associated with violence, as in John 7:30, "they sought to arrest him; but no one laid hands on him, because his hour had not yet come" and "John 8:20, "These words he spoke in the treasury, as he taught in the temple; but no one arrested him, because his hour had not yet come" (both of these quotations are from the Revised Standard Version translation). As Jesus' ministry develops, and as the threat of violence intensifies, 'the hour' paradoxically becomes associated with Jesus' glorification (John 12:23, 27). The hour gives glory to the Father because glory is associated, not with splendour, but with a sense of the presence of God. Disciples will struggle throughout Jesus' ministry to come to terms with the significance of his hour, and its implications for themselves.

At the wedding feast, the response of Jesus' mother is not to her son, but to the servants, "do whatever he tells you". Frequently, this is piously interpreted as a mother's expectation that her son will not refuse her request; however, not only is there no hint of this in the text itself – indeed as the narrative unfolds, we see that Jesus' mother is the one who acquiesces to her son's wishes – but she emerges as the one human being associated with Jesus at this early stage of his ministry who is prepared to wait for the unfolding of what he has just called his 'hour'. Her discipleship is exemplary, because she has complete trust in whatever action her son will take, and she therefore instructs the servants to do to the letter what he asks of them. She even goes so far as to tell the servants to 'do what he tells you'. The mother of Jesus has implicit faith in the Word made flesh; and she tells others to put that same faith into practice! There have been no prior 'signs' in this gospel, so Jesus' mother can have no way of anticipating the outcome of her son's word. She nonetheless awaits it as the proper consequence of the actions of him who later in the gospel will describe himself as the one sent by his Father, and whose life is committed to doing the will of his father. Jesus' mother awaits an element of a 'new creation'; in Genesis chapter 1, God repeatedly uttered a word and it became action, e.g. "God said, 'Let there be light', and there was light" (Genesis 1:3). This transition from word to action works better in Hebrew than in the Greek of the gospel, since the Hebrew verb 'to speak' also means 'to do'. The reader of this gospel has already discovered in the prologue that Jesus is the Word now made flesh (John 1:14), but who from the beginning existed, was with God, was God, and through this Word everything came into being (c.f. John 1:1-3). Therefore, when Jesus speaks the word of command, the word becomes deed, and now his mother acknowledges as much in her instruction to the servants. There will be only one more appearance of the mother of Jesus, and that will be when she and the disciple whom Jesus loved (also unnamed in this gospel) are together at the foot of the cross. At that point, Jesus hands each of these two exemplary disciples, the only two now present as his hour reaches its climax, into the care of each other, thereby constituting the community that he leaves behind to the same - indeed even greater- work as he has done. At Jesus' death, he breathes on them, i.e. passes over to them his Spirit, whom he had promised at the Last Supper, and after death, when his side is pierced, 'blood and water pour out' (c.f. John 19:34): symbols of the sacraments of Baptism and Eucharist that take effect as a result of the hour which Jesus has undergone. Back at the wedding feast at Cana, however, a different symbolism is at work. The details in the narrative are significant. To hand is only water for Jewish ritual washing, contained in six stone jars. The water is inadequate to the needs of the gathering; being for ritual washing, it is unlikely to be suitable for human consumption even as water. Stone was considered to be a suitable substance for ritual containers, since it was thought to be free from any kind of contamination. The jars are large; most English translations state they could hold between 20 and 30 gallons. A rough calculation suggests that they would hold around 1000 or more bottles of wine. Even so, the jars number only six. In the symbolic language of the Jewish people, the number 7 denoted perfection; 6 therefore denoted something less than perfection. We are not told *HOW* the miracle was 'worked'; only that Jesus instructed the servants to fill the jars with water to the brim, and then to draw some of the contents, which of course is now wine of superlative quality. This lack of explanation of how the change came about places the reader in the same position as the steward at the wedding, not knowing where the wine came from.

A conversation then ensues between the steward and the bridegroom, with a mixture of irony (a frequent feature in John's gospel) and a statement whose truth goes much further than the speaker could possibly comprehend. The steward addresses the bridegroom with the perceptive but unconscious comment, "People generally serve the best wine first, and keep the cheaper sort till the guests have had plenty to drink; but you have kept the best wine till now" (John 2:10). The bridegroom makes no comment whatever. The irony of course is that the image of bridegroom is frequently used for Jesus in the gospels, and indeed, John the Baptist, in his final statement in this gospel, gives his last act of witness to Jesus as the one he calls 'the bridegroom' (John 3:29). The steward is seeking an explanation as to why the good wine has been kept to this late stage in the wedding feast, instead of being served first and the stuff of lesser quality kept until such times as when the guests' palates may be less discerning. But the steward is not only questioning the wrong person (or at least the wrong bridegroom!); he is assessing the whole situation according to the earthly standards that will be encountered time and time again in this gospel. Repeatedly, people will want to know of Jesus where he came from, how he works his miracles, where he intends to go, and so on. The deep irony is of course that the steward is closer to the truth than he knows. The 'bridegroom' is responsible for the new wine, but not the bridegroom that he is addressing. The new wine has been kept until now because only since the arrival of the Word made flesh is the new wine, which is a symbolic expression of Jesus' hour and what it brings, becoming a reality, and one that will only reach a climax when Jesus reaches his hour. The wedding at Cana forms an inclusion with the crucifixion scene where Jesus reaches the 'hour' first introduced at Cana. In the hour of the Son of Man, the Father is glorified, and in him, the Son is glorified (c.f. John 12:23-28). The present episode at Cana draws to a close with the narrator telling us that this was the first of Jesus' signs, and that in his signs Jesus lets his glory be seen. In other words, according to the underlying meaning of the phase 'glory of God', it is in these signs that the presence of God in human affairs can be seen through the eyes of faith. On a few rare occasions, disciples of Jesus gain insight into his true nature: Peter will say at the end of the bread of life discourse, "you are the Holy One of God" (John 6:69), and at the Last Supper, the disciples will say, "we believe that you came from God" (John 16:30). The signs are pointers to some of the true origins of Jesus, and where he has come from; they are never to be seen as an end in themselves, but always as pointers to who Jesus is.

An evangelist's statement of intent and visit to the synagogue

Questions to ponder

☐ What are the consequences of Luke's presentation of Jesus as The Prophet?

☐ How do you expect scripture to be fulfilled for us as we hear it today?

☐ How can we look more fully to the Old Testament prophets to be fulfilled for us today?

Both volumes of Luke's two-volume work usually called Luke-Acts open with a formal prologue of a kind not found elsewhere in the New Testament. The prologue identifies the work's dedicatee, Theophilus, and sets out the evangelist's purpose, "I in my turn, after carefully going over the whole story from the beginning, have decided to write an ordered account for you, Theophilus, so that your Excellency may learn how well founded the teaching is that you have received" (Luke 1:3-4). There is much debate about what Luke means by this introduction, but perhaps all that is really of importance for us in terms of its liturgical setting is the realisation, reinforced by a similar introduction to the Acts of the Apostles with the same dedicatee identified, that Luke-Acts is not two works as often assumed, but a single work in two volumes. There is a consequence of this realisation which has a particular significance in the year of Luke: that the theology of the gospel of Luke carries on into Acts, and the themes found in Acts are a continuation of those already outlined in the gospel. We will read the gospel of Luke in a more or less systematic way throughout Ordinary time, and Acts on the Sundays and Feasts of Easter; themes originating in the gospel of Luke concerning the ministry of Jesus will find their continuation and complement in Acts in the lives of the early Christians, who live out the principles introduced in the life of Jesus in the gospel.

Once we have read the first four verses of the prologue to the gospel, we move straight on to chapter four, and the inauguration of Jesus' ministry, which according to Luke takes place in the synagogue in Jesus' home town. This episode follows on immediately from the Temptations narrative, read on the first Sunday of Lent, and is introduced with the phrase "Jesus, with the power of the Spirit in him", which provides a lead in to Jesus' return to Galilee following his temptation experience. The phrase 'power of the Spirit' has already been used in 3:22, at his baptism and in 4:1, twice, at the beginning of his time of temptation. These references to Jesus, empowered by the Spirit, set the scene for the self-application Jesus makes of the prophet Isaiah in the episode which will soon unfold. Before that, however, we are given another reminder of Jesus' Jewish origins, and his habitual practice of his religion, "He taught in their synagogues and everyone praised him. He came to Nazara, where he had been brought up, and went into the synagogue on the Sabbath day as he usually did." (Luke 4:15-16). The implication is not only that Jesus taught, but that it was his habit to teach in all of the synagogues in the area that he visited. He has therefore gone around the local towns before he returned to his home town. His travels resulted in his reputation growing, and he drew the praise of everyone who heard him. Then he arrived at his home town, to a very different reception!

This passage is important for the way it presents the Lukan vision of the significance of Jesus' ministry, but also in the way it informs us of synagogue practice in the first century AD. This is thought to be the oldest account in existence of a synagogue service, the shape of which is outlined in the **excursus: what happened in the synagogue at Nazareth?**

Excursus: what happened in the synagogue at Nazareth?

The account of Jesus in the synagogue at Nazareth may well be the oldest account of a synagogue service in existence. Luke tells us that Jesus stood up to read, and so they handed him the scroll of the prophet Isaiah (Luke 4:16-17). The gospel tells us little else about the procedure at a 1st Century AD synagogue service, however. Here is a possible reconstruction of such a service, however, as offered by H. Howard Marshall.

"After private prayers on entry to the building by the worshippers there was a public confession of the Jewish faith from the *Shema* (Deuteronomy 6:4-9; 11:13-21), followed by prayers which included the *Tephillah* (ed. literally prayer, or petition, said in the morning and evening) and *Shemoneh Esreh* ('Eighteen Benedictions'). Then came the centre of the worship, the reading of the Scriptures. A passage from the Pentateuch (*Torah*) was read, according to a fixed scheme of lections, by several members of the congregation in turn, with an Aramaic paraphrase. There was also a lesson from the prophets; in later times this too was according to a fixed lectionary, but it is a matter of dispute whether this system existed in the 1st Century AD, and if it did, what form it took. It is safest to assume that there was at least some freedom of choice of prophetic reading in the 1ˢᵗ Century. Following the readings there was a prayer and then came a sermon if there was somebody competent present to give one (Acts 13:15). Finally, the *Qaddish* prayer was recited. (A short version of this ancient prayer is, "Magnified and sanctified be his great name in the world He created according to His will. May He establish His kingdom during your life and during your days, and during the life of all the house of Israel, speedily and in the near future. And say Amen.")The readers for the day were appointed before the service began.

The passage that Jesus read, if Luke is correct, was a composite and edited version of Isaiah 61:1; 58:6; 61:2. It shows, as does Isaiah 40:3-5 which are quoted in Luke 3:4-6, something of the importance of the later Isaiah texts for early Christians. Luke has Jesus omit the words 'to heal the broken hearted'; his focus is on Jesus empowered by and anointed with the Spirit of the Lord. For Luke, the term Messiah is literally to do with anointing, which has already been indicated at Jesus' baptism, and is now confirmed by Jesus himself. Being anointed by/with the Spirit, the Lukan Jesus is commissioned as Prophet, and charged with proclaiming good news. Jesus will acknowledge that he is sent by God in 10:16, and that those who reject him also reject the One who sent him. The Good News is to be announced to 'the poor', not to those who are economically deprived, but, as will become clearer in the gospel, all who are marginalized or excluded from full expression of human existence and fellowship. The full implications of 'the poor' will be considered when we come to Sunday 6 C and Luke's beatitudes and woes of chapter 6. Here, we are given some early insight into the prophets' (Isaiah and Jesus) understanding of 'the poor'. It is addressed to captives, the blind and the downtrodden. To reinforce the point that 'the poor' is not limited to a financial interpretation, it should be noted that nowhere in Luke/Acts is there any hint of a mission to the impoverished which resulted in new disciples. Luke here uses the same word for liberty (to captives) and set free (downtrodden), *aphesis*, which he also uses for forgiveness of sins (Luke 1:77) and for freedom from debts in his version of the Lord's Prayer (Luke 11:4). It is the expression used in Deuteronomy 15:2 for the release from debt and slavery that was to occur every seventh year in Israel, and in Leviticus 25:8-12, for the 50ᵗʰ year of Jubilee in which all debts would be 'released'. There appears to be no evidence that a Jubilee year was ever actually held.

Having read the passage, Jesus hands the scroll to the 'assistant' and sits down. The word which Luke uses, and which the Jerusalem Bible translates as 'assistant' is the same one that Luke uses for 'ministers of the word' in his introductory prologue; *oupēretē* (Luke 1:2). In sitting, Jesus is taking his seat once more after reading, he is also about to teach, having taken up the traditional posture of the teacher. There is an air of expectancy: all eyes are fixed on Jesus. The passage ends with Jesus' assertion that the words they have heard are being fulfilled at that very point, almost literally 'the words which are in their ears'. This section of the passage answers a fundamental question about Jesus' ministry: what would its nature be. The answer becomes clear: in Jesus' own terms, realising the vision of Isaiah, he will be a Spirit empowered prophet who proclaims the word of God, the good news for the poor. This mission will be continued in the successors of Jesus in that mission; the church which will be spirit filled at Pentecost, and which will continue to proclaim the good news of the Risen Lord. In the gospel passage for the following Sunday, which is the continuation of the Nazareth synagogue narrative, Jesus will explicitly assume the title of prophet for himself, albeit in a negative way (Luke 4:24), and he will do so during the journey to Jerusalem narrative as well. In the gospel for next week, the continuation of the passage we have been considering here, Jesus will equate his mission with that of the famous prophets of old, Elijah and Elisha, and it is to these that we turn now.

4th Sunday, Year C. Luke 4:21-30

Jesus, fulfilment of the prophets Elijah and Elisha

Questions to ponder

☐   Should we still find Jesus' insistence on Good News to the poor 'a scandal' because of its implications for our lives – or have we become too used to the words without necessarily taking seriously their implications

☐   Is a preferential option for 'the poor' as defined in the gospel still an obstacle to discipleship?

☐   Who are 'the poor' in our society (perhaps this can only be properly asked after we reflect on Luke's beatitudes in a couple of weeks' time)?

To reinforce the continuity from last week's gospel to this, the final verse from the preceding Sunday becomes the first verse of today's gospel. This also means that what unfolds in today's passage is all about fulfilment; about the actualisation in the hearing of the synagogue congregation of the stories about Elijah and Elisha. Initially, Jesus' words are well received, and all who hear them are astonished at the gracious words that come from his mouth. This is a major departure from the Mark/Matthew version of this episode (Mark 6:1-6a; Matthew 13:54-58) in which opposition to Jesus comes about because his hearers cannot reconcile his wisdom with his local origins (or at least, with the origins they suppose he comes from). For Luke, however, there is as yet only a non-committal response: in this gospel astonishment does not necessarily betoken faith and here it merely indicates that what Jesus said has been noted. The Jerusalem Bible says that "he won the approval of all" (verse 22); other translations say that all spoke highly of him. Luke uses the Greek verb *emarturoun*, which normally is used where people bear witness to Jesus, but here probably means no more than that they confirmed that they had heard his words. Likewise, gracious words do not necessarily have theological content to them. The combined phrases are probably little more than an indication that initially, Jesus faced no hostility in the synagogue – unlike the Markan and Matthean scenarios where hostility awaits Jesus' on his arrival.

Jesus provokes the change in mood which will soon come about. He says "No doubt you will quote me the saying, 'Physician, heal yourself' and tell me, 'We have heard all that happened in Capernaum, do the same here in your own countryside'" (Luke 4:23). The word for 'saying' is *parabolēn*, but it has the sense of a proverb rather than what we would normally recognise as a gospel parable. The reference to Capernaum is problematic. Nowhere has a ministry for Jesus in Capernaum been mentioned so far. The reference looks as if it must be a 'handover' from Luke's source for the background to this episode, Mark 6:1-6a. Perhaps Luke's editorial skills deserted him momentarily here, and yet it is difficult to imagine Luke allowing this to remain by accident! No obvious solution to the problem presents itself, however.

Having put words of objection into the mouths of the synagogue congregation, Jesus now goes on to make a solemn (prophetic?) statement: "I tell you solemnly, no prophet is ever accepted in his own country" (Luke 4:24). Literally, it reads "Amen, I say to you that no prophet is acceptable (favourable) in his own land". Amen is a word that would normally be used by someone in response to a previous speaker. It is intended to convey the meaning of 'yes', or 'so be it'. The phrase is one which is peculiar to Jesus alone, and here he uses it before his statement, highlighting its true significance. This prophet validates his own prophetic statement *beforehand*, and makes an assertion that a prophet will never find approval, or will never be acceptable in his own land. The world for acceptable or favourable, *dektos*, is the world that was used in the Isaiah quotation about an acceptable day for the Lord. In Luke's version of the narrative, it is Jesus himself who instigates opposition and his own rejection. This prophecy will soon be fulfilled, but before it is, he cites two examples from Israel's history to illustrate his point about a prophet not finding favour in his own land. The first example is the story of Elijah and the Canaanite woman (1 Kings 17:1-16), and the second is that of Elisha and the Syrian general Naaman (2 Kings 5:1-14). The prophets Elijah and Elisha will provide models for Jesus' ministry in Luke 7:1-16 as well: specifically, 7:3 referring to 2 Kings 5:3, and 7:11-16 to 1 Kings 17:20.

The reaction is great. Everyone in the synagogue is enraged at the implications of Jesus' statements. The only other time Luke uses this expression to describe the reaction of a crowd in Acts 19:28, fired up by Demetrius the silversmith who fears that Paul's preaching against idolatry will cause he and his fellow silversmiths to lose business in crafting idols for temple worship, and will ruin the town's reputation as a centre for craftsmanship. Perhaps something similar is intended here; the people of Nazareth take exception to the preaching of someone whom they know as the son of the local carpenter and claiming that his mission is to reach out to the very people they have been brought up to consider as outcasts; the poor, the blind, the oppressed. As far back as Luke 2:34, Simeon had promised that the child Jesus, brought to the temple by Mary and Joseph in order to do what the law required of them, was destined for the rise and fall of many, destined to be a sign that is rejected. He is to be the fulfilment of the promise that the Lord has pulled down princes from their thrones and exalted the lowly (Luke 1:52). The reader has heard of all of these, but the congregation in the synagogue has not! They are only familiar with the traditional view that they were God's chosen people. They presumably feel cheated that the one who teaches in their synagogue and was brought up among them, would preach a message which reaches beyond them, and worse, a message that embraces the marginalized (there was a prohibition on the poor, the blind and the lame from serving in the priesthood (Leviticus 21:18), and were to be excluded from fighting in the eschatological Holy War according to the literature of Qumran. This reversal of the accepted order of things perhaps explains the extent of the rage of the crowd; they reject Jesus in no uncertain manner: they rush him out of the synagogue and forcibly take him (*exebalon*) to the hill their town was built upon, intending to throw him off. This is a lynch mob at work, enraged by what they have heard. They are intent on murder – even on the Sabbath! It is surprising that they do not try to stone Jesus for his comments which they will have perceived as blasphemous, that is, insulting to God. However, this is purely academic, because Jesus passes through the crowd unharmed. We are not told whether or not his passing is miraculous. As an epilogue to the episode, we might briefly consider another occasion when Jesus speaks of his mission as Good News to the Poor, when the disciples of the imprisoned John the Baptist ask if he is the one they have been awaiting, or do they still have to wait for another. Jesus replies to them, 'Go back and tell John what you have seen and heard: the blind see again, the lame walk, lepers are cleansed, and the deaf hear, the dead are raised to life, the Good News is proclaimed to the poor' (Luke 7:22). Jesus adds an interesting postscript to this list by saying 'and happy is the one who is not scandalised in me (*skandalisthē*)' (Luke 7:23 – Jerusalem Bible, 'happy is the man who does not lose faith in me'). To be scandalised, is to fall foul of a *skandalon*, a stumbling block. Jesus' teaching on Good News to the Poor, the blind, the lame etc. is a stumbling g block to those who are not open to the words of the prophet. In two weeks' time, we will have occasion to examine in more detail the implications of this mission, when we read Luke's version of the beatitudes.

5th Sunday, Year C. Luke 5:1-11

A call to discipleship

Questions to ponder

☐   In what sense could Simon be ranked among 'the poor' to whom Jesus proclaims his gospel?

☐   What does Peter mean by declaring that he is a sinner?

☐   Jesus makes two prophecies: the first is of a miraculous catch of fish; the second is that Peter will be 'capturing people'. How is the second prophecy fulfilled in the New Testament?

Mark (and Matthew, following his example) has crafted a standard format for Jesus calling disciples in his gospel. The call always goes through the same stages: 1) Jesus is always on the move, 2) his eye catches the ones he will call, 3) he invites them to follow him, and 4) they leave what they are about and walk after him (c.f. Mark 1:16-20; 2:13-14). The process is not quite as straight forward in Luke, as we see in the present account of the call of Simon, although here too we can see the basic steps of the call to discipleship still present. In Luke's telling, we are taken more into the character of the one being called. Luke does, however, retain that aspect of the authentic call to discipleship where it always begins with the initiative of Jesus, and never with the initiative of the individuals involved in the encounter with Jesus. This passage is a superb illustration of that point.

In some ways, the Lukan account of the call of Simon is much less dramatic than that found in Mark and Matthew. In these other two gospels, Jesus issues an invitation to follow him (almost a command) without any suggestion him having had a prior meeting with the ones he is calling. Luke places his version of the episode in the setting of a ministry already begun in the Capernaum area, and precedes it with the account of Jesus healing Simon's mother in law, and in Simon's house too. After this episode, Jesus leaves the area and continues his preaching in the synagogues of Judaea (Luke 4:44). There is a clear gap in time between these episodes and the call of Simon, but there is still a prior relationship between the one called and Jesus. This enables Jesus to interact with Simon at the latter's place of work, and in his profession before issuing the call, and inviting Simon to a whole new sense of vocation, expressed as capturing people rather than fish.

This episode, like others in Luke, begins with Jesus cast in the role of the prophet, this time with a crowd pressing round him to 'hear the word of God'. The 'crowd' is a neutral term; when they respond positively to the word of God, they become part of 'the people' which forms around the prophet. Jesus catches sight of two boats and of the fishermen cleaning their nets, indicating that they have all but finished their night's work. This is different in detail from Mark's version of events, when Peter and Andrew are still at work, casting their nets. The fishermen are left aside in the narrative for a moment, and we are told that Jesus got into one of the boats and started teaching. As in the synagogue at Nazareth, Jesus sits down to teach. We are not told the content of the teaching (a similarity this passage shares with Mark, who frequently reports that Jesus taught, but who seldom gives the content of the teaching, e.g. Mark 1:21-28). When he has finished teaching, Jesus turns his attention back to Simon, instructing him to put out the boat out into deep water, and for the nets to be paid out. Jesus engages with the person he is about to call by inserting himself in the very professional life of Simon, and in having the temerity to instruct the latter on his own profession! There are some other points worth noting here too, which are not immediately apparent from the translation we use. First, Jesus commands, rather than asks for the boat to be put out into the deep water. Second, the command to put the boat out is given in the singular, therefore it applies only to Simon. Third, the command to pay out the nets is in the plural, indicating that there are others in the boat apart from Simon. Only one person answers and that is Simon, cast in the familiar role of the spokesperson for the group. Not only does he speak on behalf of the others; he takes the responsibility for putting out the nets again, even though he points out that they have worked all night and caught nothing. Jesus had ordered a collective effort in putting out the nets again. Simon addresses Jesus as master – not as *kurios*, which is often translated as Master, or Lord, but as *epistatēs*; a recognition of a person in authority, and is only found in Luke, and used either by disciples or by those who approach Jesus seeking his help. Simon said he would pay out the nets, but again the narrative changes to the plural, to when 'they' had paid out the nets (verse 6), the nets were full to bursting with fish. No time scale is given, but the miraculous and abundant nature of the catch seems to suggest a very quick result. The occupants of the first boat are so overwhelmed that the call for the help of their companions with the second boat, and both are filled to the point of almost sinking. Later in the narrative, Simon will be linked with the sons of Zebedee as business associates. This language suggests something of a sharing of possessions and resources which might be a prophetic indication of the attitude of these and other members of the initial Christian community as described in e.g. Acts 2:41-47; 4:32-37.

Simon falls to his knees when he sees the size of the catch, and exclaims, "Leave me, Lord; I am a sinful man" (Luke 5:7). Simon uses the same word to Jesus that Jesus had used to the demon in 4:35, *exelthe*. Simon designates himself a sinner (*hamartōlos*); this is not a confession of misdemeanour so much as a statement of unworthiness in the face of the glory of God. It means that Simon locates himself in the tradition of prophets like Isaiah who responded similarly when faced with the sight of the glory of God (Isaiah 6:5 LXX, although Isaiah claims to be a man of unclean lips). Simon now addresses Jesus as 'Lord' (*kurie*). Simon is the first of the long list of sinners, outcasts and marginalized who will receive a favourable response from Jesus. Jesus' response to Simon is positive, and Simon is given a new commission; from now on he will capture (alive) humans: a prophetic statement of the mission Simon will exercise in Acts, and which the reader will see fulfilled in the second volume of Luke's work. Simon and his companions then bring the boats back to the shore – necessary for their next step: to leave everything and follow Jesus. This detail follows Mark's version of the call of the first disciples more closely than any other stage in the narrative, but with the distinctively Lukan touch that they left everything. This will be an indicator of true disposition to the teaching of Jesus throughout the rest of Luke-Acts. For Luke, without this action, they cannot follow Jesus. It betokens the leaving behind of more than physical possessions; it is a symbol for the true spiritual allegiance of all disciples, detached from anything which is not of Christ. They undergo a change of outlook, a change of mind ending in dispersal of possessions: they undergo *metanoia*, repentance – a change of mind or change of outlook.

Given that Jesus clearly has prior knowledge of Simon in this Lukan text, and that which succeed the call of the first four disciples in Mark/Matthew have already taken place (especially the incident of Jesus' visit to the Nazareth synagogue), it might make much more sense to consider this story as Jesus' renewal of Simon's call to discipleship. Simon is not disbarred because he is a sinner; he is fully qualified to follow Jesus the moment he recognises his sins and shortcomings. It may be worth noting that in Luke, there is no attempt by Simon to correct Jesus after he has proclaimed him as "the Christ of God". Likewise there is no retort from Jesus to Simon "get behind me, Satan". Is it feasible then that just as when Jesus in Mark 8:33 uses exactly the same Greek words to tell Simon to get behind him as he did when he told him to "follow me"; *opisō mou*. It is, after all, noteworthy that, although Luke uses a different expression for following, still calls the disciples including Simon, to follow him.

Chapter 6.

Sundays 6 – 12 Year C

INTRODUCTION AND BACKGROUND

The 'back story' is important for a proper understanding of these passages. This is because the narrative of Luke's gospel approaches a significant stage in which Jesus' ministry reaches fulfilment. In this chapter's selection of passages, we follow from the proclamation of Jesus' prophetic ministry on the occasion of his visit to the Nazareth synagogue, where he made the words of Isaiah (or 3rd Isaiah, as we might more accurately say today) his own. He particularly associated himself with the prophets Elijah and Elisha, and the series of passages we will consider in this chapter will include Jesus' close association with these two legendary figures in his miracles, in the stories of the cure of a pagan military leader's servant, recalling Namaan the Syrian general Jesus cited in Luke 4:27, followed by the raising from the dead of the widow's son in the town of Nain, recalling the widow of Zarephath mentioned in Luke 4:26. Before that, we encounter the prophetic teaching of Jesus in the Sermon on the Plain – thought by many writers to be the earlier of the two versions of this sermon found in the canonical gospels (the other version being found in Matthew).

On the final Sunday of this chapter, Jesus reaches the end of his Galilean ministry, and asks the questions "who do people say I am?"…. "Who do you say I am?" and receives bizarre answers to the first, but answers which nevertheless accentuate Jesus' prophetic ministry to date. The prophet brings to a close this stage of his ministry – a ministry which began with his presentation of his prophetic credentials in the Nazareth synagogue in chapter 4 – by adding vital information on the nature of this ministry: the Son of Man is destined to suffer, die and rise again, and anyone who would be his follower is challenged to renounce self, take up the cross daily and come after him.

6th Sunday, Year C. Luke 6:17. 20-26

Beatitudes and woes: who are the poor in question?

Questions to ponder

☐   From the very first verse of this gospel, what would you say are the implications of prayer before understanding the beatitudes?

☐   Who are 'the poor' today to whom these beatitudes apply?

☐   Why does Luke also supply a complementary series of 'woes'

Matthew's equivalent of this section of Luke's gospel is known as the Sermon on the Mount, for the simple reason that it begins with Jesus going up the mountain to teach his disciples as the one who fulfils the law and the prophets. In this way, Matthew presents Jesus once more as the New Moses, the New Law-Giver. Luke, on the other hand, has Jesus come down from the mountain where he has been with the disciples, and where he had spent the night in prayer. Next, he chose twelve of them, to whom he gave the name 'apostles'. When Jesus descends with these twelve, he sees a large group of disciples and a "great crowd of people from all parts of Judaea and from Jerusalem and from the coastal region of Tyre and Sidon" (Luke 6:17). In his own way, Luke sets the same scene as Matthew, because Jesus the teacher is once again at work, and presenting the law to his disciples. Just as Moses had gone up Mount Sinai to receive the law (indicated in Matthew, in the fulfilment of the law presented by Jesus on the mount), so Moses also came down the mountain with the Law which he then passed on to the Israelites (indicated in Luke by Jesus' descent with those who will be the New Israel, the Twelve Apostles). When he stops on a piece of level ground, he fixes his eyes on his disciples, or better, raises his eyes to them. This is a stylised way of saying that the content of Jesus' teaching is first and foremost directed to his disciples. The multitudes are of course not excluded from his teaching, but the disciples are the primary audience. This is reinforced by Luke's use of the second person, "Blessed are YOU..." as opposed to Matthew's "Blessed are...THEY shall be..."

The precise audience addressed by Jesus is immediately relevant when he launches into the first beatitude, because he calls his addressees 'poor'. Time for two definitions! Firstly, what does Jesus mean when he addresses disciples as 'blessed; (*makarioi*) – probably a better translation than merely happy. The word carries with it a whole biblical tradition which is related to a state of righteousness before God. In Luke, Jesus then proceeds to tell his disciples what it is that renders them righteous before God. It is never anything to do with their actions; it is to do with their situations or conditions, and always those over which they have no control: the 'blessed' are i) the poor, ii) the hungry, iii) those who weep, and iv) the hated, cast out, abused and criminalized. In contrast, the Lukan Jesus lists a corresponding series of 'woes', to you who are i) rich, ii) well-fed, iii) who laugh and iv) generally well-spoken of. All of the categories mentioned in the beatitudes/woes have strong biblical roots. Isaiah 65:13-14 contains a mixture of very similar blessings and woes, "Therefore, thus speaks the Lord Yahweh: You shall see my servants eat while you go hungry. You shall see my servants drink while you go thirsty. You shall see my servants rejoice while you are put to shame. You shall hear my servants sing for joy of heart, while you will moan for sadness of heart; you will wail for distress of spirit". The hungry and well-fed found in 6:21 and 6:25 respectively are an echo of Luke 1:53, "The hungry he has filled with good things, the rich sent empty away"; 6:22 and 6:26 recall Jesus' prophetic words in the Nazareth synagogue, "on the fate of a prophet in his own land; "I tell you solemnly, no prophet is ever accepted in his own country (Luke 4:24).

It is clear that the beginning of this discourse, the beatitudes and woes, marks a turning point in Jesus' ministry. Having chosen his twelve apostles, he will not send them out until another couple of chapters have passed and then, they will be sent to do precisely what Jesus himself has been doing, "he sent them out to proclaim the kingdom of God" in word and action (Luke 9:2). So the preliminary statement of this inaugural address sets the parameters for inclusion in the kingdom of God.

Luke's beatitudes and woes, four in number, can be subdivided. The first and the last of each make a pair, as do the second and third: the poor are told they are blessed, as are those who are hated and rejected; woe is prophesied for the rich and for those who find a favourable hearing in the world. The same is true for the second and third: the hungry and those who weep are blessed; in their cases, their fortunes will be reversed. Woe is prophesied for the satisfied and those who laugh now will also have their fortunes reversed. Notice that the direct reversal of fortune is restricted to these inner pairs.

The questions remain: who are the poor (or the rich) that Luke has Jesus address, and what constitutes them as such? We have already seen that Jesus addresses his disciples. Therefore, they have the potential to be in all four double-categories that he mentions: poor/rich, hungry/satisfied, weeping/laughing, and despised/admired. The pairings are divided between those in tune with the values of the kingdom of God (hence the kingdom of God is for the poor; the rich on the other hand have their consolation in their riches). Likewise, the final pairing explores whether disciples are indeed closely replicating the life of their master – they are in solidarity with the prophets, including Jesus the Prophet, when they are hated, driven out, abused, denounced as criminal on account of the Son of Man. On the other hand, if the world speaks well of them, they are following in the steps of the false prophets! The 'internal pairings' prophesy that the wrongs disciples suffer will be righted in their favour, in due time. Jesus will return to this theme later, during the Travel Narrative, "will not God see justice done to his chosen who cry to him day and night even when he delays to help them? I promise you, he will see justice done to them, and done speedily" Luke 18:7-8).

We are still left with the problem of what constitutes 'the poor'. Already it seems clear that the term is no reflection of a person's financial situation: we have already seen Simon, James and John as patterns in a fishing business, able to employ workers (c.f. Luke 5:9-10). As the gospel unfolds, we find that Jesus and his disciples are supported from the resources of some well-to-do people (Luke 8:3). There seems to be a clue in the word that Luke (and Matthew) uses for 'poor', *ptōchoi*, which literally means 'beggar'. This word applied to those who were completely dependent on others for their very survival. They may have been reduced to begging because they were orphaned, widowed, afflicted with illness, lameness, blindness or any condition that made it impossible for them to work. Beggars had no family to rely on for support. They had no control over their own lives, and really only lived thanks to those who gave them alms. On the other hand, the rich are those who have control over their own lives, can provide for themselves, to a degree, they can shape their own futures. They are not utterly dependent on others. In spiritual terms the poor, then, are those who are like beggars; not in any sense that they are persistent in their demands, but in the sense that they recognise their dependence on God. The rich, in spiritual terms, are those who see no need for God in their lives. We see examples of both of these in the gospel of Luke; indeed, we have already seen the poverty Jesus extols as a virtue in Peter, who in recognising the power of God in his life and his own inadequacy, described himself as a sinful man, that is, someone who is dependent on God. Peter thought this excluded him from Jesus' mission; he soon found that such recognition allowed for his inclusion in his ministry. In the terminology of the beatitude, Peter's recognition of his sinfulness means he already possessed the kingdom of God. Later in the story, we will meet a rich aristocrat who is unwilling to part with his riches, his self-sufficiency

(Luke 18:18-23), and we will hear the parable of the rich man and Lazarus, where the latter is utterly dependent, and the former is so self-sufficient in his wealth that he does not even know of the existence of the poor man at his door (Luke 16:19-31). We can see the implications of this in the beatitude and woe about being hated/lauded by the world: those who court the approval of the world seek the same present satisfaction as do the rich, whereas the poor seek only the approval of God – as did the prophets of old.

Perhaps we can begin to understand why Matthew chooses to set his first beatitude as "Blessed are the poor *in spirit*" (Matthew 5:3). This qualification may mean no more than an insistence that it refers, not to the material poor, but to those whose poverty enables them to recognise their total dependence on God for their lives. In which case, both sets of beatitudes seem to be saying the same thing.

This is where we depart from the Sundays of Ordinary time for some three months, turning instead to Lent, Easter, and the Feasts of the Lord Trinity Sunday and Corpus Christi. When we return to Luke, on Sunday 11, Year C, we take up the narrative with Jesus at a meal in the house of one of the Pharisees. That in itself spells trouble!

7th Sunday, Year C. Luke 6:27-38

From revenge to compassion

Questions to ponder

☐   Why does Jesus focus on love as an action rather than love as an emotion?

☐   What is the difference between mercy and compassion?

☐   Is Jesus suggesting that God's love for us is contingent upon our love for others? The answer is patently not so; but what then does Jesus mean when he says that the amount we measure out is the amount we will be given?

This episode is also found in almost exactly the same form of wording in Matthew's Sermon on the Mount, but Matthew includes it among the 'antitheses' in 5:21-48, whereas it is a 'stand-alone' commandment in Luke: the saying opens with Jesus' words only, and not, as in Matthew, a reprise of what has been said in the past: "You have heard how it was said.. but I say to you…(Matthew 5:43-44)". The saying leans heavily on the use of the word which translates as 'love' in English as a verb rather than a noun. This means that what Jesus has to say here has to do with actions rather than with feelings. The command 'to love' requires action on behalf of and directed toward the good of another, and not just a general feeling of goodwill to that other. Luke makes this clear in the very first verse of this saying: "*Love* your enemies and *do good* to those who hate you". The challenge to action here is radical because it is based on a paradox: effectively it says 'love those who hate you; do good to those who do you harm'! This calls for a reversal of the accepted order of behaviour, and this is presented in terms of positive action toward enmity and hatred. Thus, disciples are to bless and pray for those who curse them and treat them badly: the disciple is to do the exact opposite of the one who wishes or causes them harm. In all gospels, but in Luke among the synoptics in particular, the shadow of the cross is never far away, and perhaps the reader cannot fail to remember that Jesus himself was subjected to the ultimate curse of crucifixion, accursed by being 'hung on a tree' (c.f. Deuteronomy 21:23). The problem with the so-called wisdom of the contemporary approach to the question of permitted retaliation is that it results in an escalation of the violence it seeks to limit. As J B Caird once commented, 'When one man wrongs another, the other may retaliate, bear a grudge, or take his injury out on a third person. Whichever he does, there are now two evils where before there was only one; and a chain reaction so started, like the spreading of a contagion. Only if the victim absorbs the wrong, and so puts it out of currency can it be prevented from going any further. And this is why the great ordeal is also the great victory". This is of course precisely why the cross of Jesus is the way in which the power of sin is destroyed.

Jesus' argument goes further than the mere statement of the command however. His argument extends to a challenge to the accepted principles governing and controlling retaliation in his own day. Unlike in Matthew antitheses, in Luke, Jesus does not quote the (non-biblical) adage 'eye for eye and tooth for tooth', but he does offer some extraordinary statements of the principle of loving enemies. If someone slaps you on one cheek, offer the other cheek as well.

Matthew's version specifies 'if someone strikes you on the right cheek, offer the other cheek as well (Matthew 5:39)'. Some writers point out that Matthew's version presupposes that striking someone on the right cheek, if done by a right handed person (90%) of the population, then the chances are that this is an insult rather than a serious blow. Luke draws no such distinction: whenever a disciple is stuck, in earnest or in insult, the appropriate response is not to retaliate, but to go so far even as to allow the assailant the opportunity to land a second blow! Likewise, if a person takes from a disciple his cloak (outer garment), far from retaliating or treeing to wrest back the taken (stolen?) garment, the disciple is to give the rest of the clothing he is wearing: his tunic! Even if one is robbed, he/she should not demand back the property that was taken. Finally, disciples are to treat others as they would like to be treated themselves.

Such outrageous demands require the underpinning of a remarkable principle, and Jesus will shortly outline this. Before that, however, he appeals to reason. What merit can there be in loving those who love you? Disciples are called to a higher righteousness than sinners, who love those who love them! Even sinners do good to those who do good to them (honour among thieves?), and even sinners lend to other sinners in order to get as much back. Instead – and here is the principle – disciples are to love their enemies, to do good and to lend without any hope of return. In short, they are to be compassionate as their Father is compassionate. The word *oiktirmōn* has connotations of 'mercy', which is the practice of releasing from obligation (including sin), and again carries with it the sense of action rather than feeling. Most English translations use the word 'merciful' rather than compassionate here, leaving the word 'compassion' to describe the feeling of sympathy for another in need which the Good Samaritan of the parable felt on Luke 10:33, where the Greek expression is *splangchnisthē*, literally a 'gut feeling' towards the man who had been ambushed. So, those who are compassionate (merciful) as God is merciful will have a great reward, and they will be true children (literally, 'sons' [*uioi*] of the Most High – a term already used of God in Luke 1:32 when Gabriel announced to Mary that her child would be 'Son of the Most High'. In this present context, the sons (children) of the Most High are urged to behave as the Most High does: God is kind to the ungrateful and the wicked!

The final series of injunctions, following on the order to be compassionate/merciful as God is compassionate/merciful, are all in two parts. It is important that disciples do not judge so that they may not be subject to judgement themselves; they are not to condemn lest they leave themselves open to condemnation. On a more positive note: if they grant pardon to others, they will receive pardon themselves, and if they give, they will be the recipients of gifts. The implication is that what is given will be returned in a fuller form, because disciples who carry out these instructions will receive a full measure, pressed down, shaken together and running over. This may or may not appeal to contemporary readers since the terminology does not resonate with current use of language. Its meaning is quite simple, however. The Greek word *metron* means 'measure', and is clearly behind the words metre and metric and their derivatives in our measures in use today. In the ancient world, *metron* was the term for a standard of measurement for e.g. the measuring of grain or the like which is implied in this proverbial saying. The abundance of the reward for acting toward others as God acts toward his children is expressed in the imagery of a measuring vessel whose contents are shaken to allow settling, are then pressed down to allow even further capacity, and then filled to the point of overflowing. It is a figurative description of the goodness of God. There is cause and effect implied as well: the amount that disciples measure out in terms of goodness to others is the amount they can expect to receive in return – anything other than that would be illogical: the phrase' you will be given' is an example of what is often termed the 'Divine Passive' and is a Semitism for saying 'God will give'. This might lead us to a further reflection. Earlier in this passage, Jesus had said "Treat others as you would like them to treat you". This and its equivalent in Matthew 7:12 have come to be known as the 'Golden Rule'. It could be argued though that Jesus finally goes beyond even that rule. The object of the exercise is not to treat people as you would like them to treat you, but to treat them as God treats them! Can this really mean that God would refuse to forgive us if we refuse to forgive others? Or rather does this really amount to arousing in disciples (and readers of the gospel) that it is supremely illogical not to forgive others, not to judge but to pardon when we consider how bountiful is God's love, pardon and complete care for those who are already 'children of the most High'?

8th Sunday, Year C.

Luke 6:39-45

Ending the Sermon with a parable: the problem with blind guides

Questions to ponder

☐   What kind of disciple today would be the equivalent of the 'blind guide' of today's gospel?

□   Does Jesus' teaching make it virtually impossible for the Church to correct the faults of others? Presuming that this is not the case, how must fraternal correction be carried out?

□   What splinters in the eyes of others do you see, and what plank in your own eye remains unnoticed by you (this is probably not a question for discussion with others!)?

When is a parable not a parable? Surprisingly often in the Gospels, it would seem! Today's passage opens with what the evangelist describes as a parable, but which is closer to what we would understand as a proverb. A further complication lies in the fact that there are several proverbs, rather than a single offering as the evangelist suggests! The distinction between parables and proverbs is perhaps less clear in Greek that it is in English. In Greek, the word *parabolē* means literally 'thrown together' and the term can be used for a parable as we understand it, or an illustration, a proverb, a figure of speech etc. It might be clearer if we thought of Luke's opening remarks as meaning something like: 'Jesus spoke to his disciples parabolically'. Certainly the entire text for this week's gospel reading consists of a variety of these parabolic saying.

The first of these is short and to the point. Jesus asks: "can one blind man guide another?" In this form (and in virtually every English translation), the implication we would draw is that guiding has to do with physically leading on a given path. This meaning also exists in the Greek word (*odēgein*), but there is an equally valid alternative, where the word translated in English as 'guide' can also mean 'instruct'. When two blind people are mentioned in a proverb, and one is challenged with 'guiding' the other, a physical act is what immediately comes to mind, especially since Jesus adds "Surely both will fall into a pit?" The aspect of instruction will also provide a helpful link into the next phrase that Jesus utters: "the disciple is not superior to his teacher; the fully trained disciple will always be like his teacher". It is clear therefore that Luke, beginning with a saying that implies showing the way in a literal sense, is developed into a teaching that has to do with 'showing the way' spiritually. It is with noting that Matthew not only uses both the saying about blind guides and that about a disciple not being above his teacher, but he also places them in different parts of his gospel and in different contexts. In Matthew 15:14, the Pharisees are described as blind guides, and in 10:24, we are told that a disciple is not above his teacher, nor a slave above his master.

Luke takes a very different approach by listing all of these saying together at the end of the Sermon on the Plain.

The implications of these sayings are many and varied, and we may be led to the conclusion that the sayings are to be taken as a whole, building up a picture of disciples who will be called upon to teach in the future, and who must therefore not forget their own limitations and the need to learn from the master – otherwise they may forget that they teach message which is not theirs, and attempt to lead others on paths they themselves cannot see clearly. In other words the true disciple is one who must always strive to learn first, and to lead others along paths which they know only because they have been led along these paths themselves by the master – Jesus himself.

Disciples who would lead others must keep in mind their own limitations and failings. Not to do so is to cease to learn, and when a teacher no longer learns, that teacher is apparently more interested in personal status than in the teaching that is learned from Jesus. This is precisely the kind of teacher who is like a blind guide who will inevitably lead the blind person he tries to guide into the pit along with him. This is the kind of disciple who forgets that his master is greater than he is, whose teacher is above him (or her). The consequences of such an error are brought out in the next saying that Jesus utters: "Why do you observe the splinter in your brother's eye and never notice the plank in your own?" It is clear that Jesus' own observations on human nature are both insightful and accurate! Notice the contrast in this proverbial saying and the first in this series, where blind guides were unable to see the way to guide their blind charges. Now, the emphasis is on seeing, but in a distorted and unproductive way – blind guides cannot see the plank (of wood?) on their own eyes, but paradoxically seem to be of the opinion that they can see and offer a remedy to a brother (or sister) who has a tiny splinter in his (or her) eye! The person who thinks he can detect the minute splinter but who claims not to be able to see the plank in his own eye is fully deserving of the description 'hypocrite' – a term for a false person (see below **EXCURSUS: Hypocrites**).

The 'cure' for the hypocrisy of someone who sees the splinter in the eye of a brother while being oblivious to the plank in his own is simple: the plank of one's own faults has to be removed before making any comment on the faults of others – especially when a brother or sister's faults are considerably less than our own! The truth about a person will out, as the saying goes. People's virtue or vice will lead to consequent fruit which can easily be identified.

This may seem a bit simplistic in our sophisticated age, but in the ancient world there was the firm belief that a person's actions will always been firmly in keeping with that person's character. So, just as a sound tree cannot produce rotten fruit, or a rotten tree produce good fruit, neither can the actions of a bad person be good, nor of a good person be bad! No matter how much the hypocrite strives to cover up the intentions of a bad heart, the camouflage will never be sufficient to block out sight of the evil deeds which will emerge from such a heart.

EXCURSUS: Hypocrites

Jesus uses the word 'hypocrites' to describe his adversaries 11 times (9 in Matthew, and 1 each in Mark and Luke), and the singular 'hypocrite' on another 2 occasions (1 each in Matthew and Mark). Matthew makes fullest use of the expressions therefore, and applies them constantly to Jesus' onslaught against his opponents. The terms are normally reserved for the Pharisees, but in Matthew, Jesus also uses the terms in the Sermon on the Mount (Matthew 6:2, 5, 16) for those whose prayer, almsgiving and fasting are carried out to draw attention to themselves. The English word 'hypocrite' is derived from the Greek expression used in the gospels, *hupokritēs*. This word is a composite of others: *hypo* = 'under' and *krinein* = to 'decide', which in turn gives rise to *krisis* = 'judgement', *kritikē* = 'critics'. When these terms are combined to become *hypokritēs*, meaning under, or deficient judgement, critical faculty, decision making ability. *Hupokritēs* became an expression associated with the theatre, and in particular with actors. It's not too difficult to see the connection: actors in drama, hiding behind masks, were called upon to play people who were not themselves, to suspend their own opinions, judgements, values. 'Play actors' were playing people other than themselves, and indeed their own identity was hidden from the audience before whom they performed. This is of course precisely the accusation that Jesus lays before Pharisees and other opponents to whom Jesus applied the description 'hypocrites'. Their greatest fault was that they presented to those who saw them a persona which was not genuine; that no one saw the real person behind the mask of self-importance, self-publicity, and more seriously, sheer malice which was in complete opposition to the very false image of perfection and propriety which they ensured those who saw them were likely to perceive.

These proverbial illustrations provide an interesting commentary on the various expressions concerning love of enemies and doing good to those who hate you. Now, the principle is extended to enemies and those who hate, but who are also members of the community. Disciples are required to teach and correct those who err, but the principles of love must govern how that teaching, that correction is to be carried out. Any disciple who is required to correct the errors of a brother or sister must above all avoid the pitfall of hypocrisy. No disciple is above the master, therefore every disciple must first and foremost examine his or her own faults, otherwise that disciple is a blind guide, a hypocrite.

9th Sunday, Year C. Luke 7:1-10

The Prophet Jesus cures a gentile.

☐   Does Jesus respond to the delegation of elders' suggestion that the centurion 'deserves' the favour of a cure for his slave? Does 'deserving' ever play a part in the action of Jesus to another?
☐   Why does Jesus not take the slave by the hand and raise him up as he does in some other cures?
☐   What does the episode say about faith in Israel according to Jesus' perception? (A comparison with Matthew 8:10 may be instructive here: see the end of these notes).

The opening phrase of this weekly's gospel passage links us to last week's passage, but also to the entire Sermon on the Plain from which we have been reading over the past three Sundays: "When Jesus had come to the end of all he wanted the people to hear…" The phrase occurs only here in Luke, but its equivalent is found in various forms no less than five times in Matthew; in fact its occurrence at the end of five blocks of teaching in Matthew is what led to the designation of these as 'Sermons' or discourses, beginning with the Sermon on the Mount (Matthew 5 – 7) and ending with the Eschatological Sermon (Matthew 25). In each case, in both Matthew and Luke, the saying appears to point in the direction of what follows rather than what has just been taught. This is certainly the case here, where the phrase ends: "…he went into Capernaum". A new scene is set!
The setting of Capernaum takes us to the place where in Mark (and Matthew) a significant part of Jesus' early ministry is located. The synagogue is the scene of Jesus' first miracle in Mark, and the town is the location of the house of Peter and Andrew, where Jesus stays on several occasions, and

where he cures Simon's mother in law of her fever (Mark 1:29-31). Like Matthew, Luke tells the story of the centurion with a sick servant. Luke however tells the story with significantly more detail that Matthew. In this version, the centurion, hearing about Jesus, sends appear odd that these elders would respond to the orders of a Roman centurion, but we are soon made aware of the reason. The elders in question are probably the synagogue's board of elders making up the body of local senior figures who administered the affairs of the local community. These elders are very different from the 'elders of the people' of the Sanhedrin before whom Jesus was brought for trial (Luke 9:22; 20:1; 22:66) and who caused problems for the early Christians (Acts 4:5, 8, 23; 25:15). It seems clear that this gentile was one of those who were known as 'God fearers': gentiles with a very high regard for the Jewish religion, although they did not become Jews themselves. These were very often substantial benefactors of the local Jewish institutions, and this turns out to be the case with the centurion in this story, who loves the Jewish nation and who built their synagogue – presumably metaphorically speaking, and not as the actual layer of bricks! There is at least one other 'God-fearer' in Luke's writings: Cornelius, also a gentile centurion (Acts 10:1, 22). Some writers are of the opinion that the evangelist/author of the Acts of the Apostles may have been a God fearer himself, basing their conclusion on the assumption that his origins were gentile, and observing the high regard with which he appeared to hold the Jewish traditions. For example, Luke apparently cannot bring himself to accuse the Jewish High priest of charging Jesus, the Son of God, with blasphemy, so he omits any suggestion of this from his account of Jesus' trial before the Sanhedrin. Given that these elders are indebted to this centurion in the present story, and that he and the elders presumably had a very close relationship, it sounds as if they had agreed to make representation to Jesus, asking for a cure for the centurion's servant (slave), rather than the centurion having ordered them to do so.

Luke alone adds these details about the centurion and the Jewish delegation, but for very good theological reason. As in all instances in the narrative of this gospel, this evangelist casts Jesus in the role of the ultimate prophet whom Moses had foretold (Deuteronomy 18:15), and in this episode and the one which immediately follows, Luke is more specifically linking Jesus' prophetic ministry to the ministries of the legendary prophets Elijah and Elisha. When Jesus inaugurated his prophetic ministry in the Nazareth synagogue he cited both of these prophets – Elisha as the one who cured the Syrian (i.e. gentile) general Naaman, and Elijah who raised from the dead the only son of the widow at Zarephath. In next week's gospel, Jesus will raise to life the only son of a widow in the town of Nain, fulfilling the feat of raising a widow's son to life by the prophet Elijah. In this week's episode, a Jewish delegation make representation to Jesus to cure a gentile with military connections, thus fulfilling the story of the Jewish slave girl who intercedes on behalf of the gentile general cured of leprosy by Elisha the prophet. These two stories recall Jesus' prophetic words in the Nazareth synagogue in Luke 4.

Jesus responds to the delegation of elders, but before he reaches the centurion's house, he is met by some of his friends who bring a personal message from the gentile man to Jesus. This in itself suggests that the earlier Jewish delegation had not been ordered and had not been required to demand a cure from Jesus, because the centurion's message is "Sir, do not put yourself to trouble; because I am not worthy to have you under my roof". Once more, the Jerusalem Bible translation lets us down a bit here since the actual mode of address is *kurie* which is at least a term of respect for Jesus which is much stronger than 'sir'. It is also most probably used by Luke to imply some sign of faith that in Jesus there is some divine connection.

The speech which follows, "for I am under authority myself, and have soldiers under me; and I say to one man: Go, and he goes; to another: Come here, and he comes; to my servant: Do this, and he does it" exists in almost exactly the same form in the Greek in both Matthew and Luke, but in Luke, the power of the word of those who have authority is accentuated when we take into account the allusions to the prophet Elisha in the earlier verses of the narrative. The centurion speaks as one who is used to his word being carried out, and who recognises in Jesus one whose word is powerful enough to effect the cure of his slave. There is no need for Jesus to demean himself by entering the house of a gentile (a 'God fearer' would have understood the implications of potential uncleanness for an observant Jew who entered the house of a gentile); all he need do is proclaim his authoritative word, and the illness will be banished. Later in this gospel, the Pharisees will object that Jesus spends time with tax collectors and sinners who wish to 'hear what Jesus has to say' (Luke 15:1). It is perhaps also worth recalling the fact that in Hebrew the word to speak and the word to do are the same (*dabar*). Whether the Roman centurion would have been aware of this is debatable;

clearly, Luke the evangelist was, despite writing his gospel in Greek. There is no contact between Jesus and the slave; nor is there any entry into the gentile house. There is however astonishment from Jesus: "I tell you, not even in Israel have I found faith like this". This is interesting, because in Matthew's version, the Greek text does not include the phrase 'not even'. Here again, Luke demonstrates his affection for the faith of Judaism: perhaps he argues his case too far here, and Jesus really only wanted to compare Israel's lack of faith with the impressive faith of the gentile. The centurion's slave is cured, not because the elders suggested that his master deserved a favour from Jesus because of his generosity toward the synagogue, but because of his faith. This reinforces the suggestion that the centurion does intend a religious significance when he calls Jesus 'Lord' (*Kurie*). To the reader of this passage, if the connection to the prophet Elisha and Naaman has been recognised, there is also the allusion to Jesus' earlier words in the Nazareth synagogue that in the prophet Elisha's time there were many lepers in Israel, but Elisha cured none of them: he only cured the Syrian Naaman. Jesus, the prophet, has just fulfilled his own words!

10th Sunday, Year C. Luke 7:11-17

The Prophet Jesus restores to life a widow's only son.

☐ Prophecy and its fulfilment in Jesus was clearly an important theme to Luke, and presumably to his initial readers. How important is it to you that Jesus fulfils the prophets from of old, or that his own ministry is prophetic?

☐ In what way should the prophetic action of Jesus shape the prophetic role of the Church today? In other words, what does it mean to say that the Church must be prophetic (hint: this has nothing to do with predicting the future!)?

☐ How are Jesus' prophetic acts fulfilled today in your life?

It's a pity that the lectionary version of this passage omits the phrase which the gospel text itself uses to open the story. Had this been included, it would have made clear that this text is to be read in in conjunction with the previous episode, read in last week's gospel text. The phrase, when translated literally, gives us that famous biblical link expression which is well known to us from the King James translation: 'and it came to pass…' This is followed by 'the day after…'. In contemporary translations this is usually expressed as something like 'soon afterwards…', or even 'the next day'. It is clear therefore that Luke intends to link this episode with the one immediately preceding, and that's why it is unfortunate that the lectionary does not make the connection explicit: not least because the passages follow one after the other in the sequence of Sundays. Perhaps the omission was due to the realisation that there are times when one or other of these Sundays may be omitted from the Sunday lectionary due to the Easter season or the Solemnities that follow Easter. So, if Sunday 9 is missing, it makes no sense to begin the reading of Sunday 10's gospel with the phrase 'soon afterwards', since this would then relate to nothing we have already heard. Nevertheless, it is important for us to be aware of the link between these two passages. The story at the heart of today's gospel is unparalleled in any other gospel text: Jesus restores to life and returns to his mother the only son of a widow. It is not unparalleled in biblical literature, however. In 1 Kings 17:20-24, Elijah raises a dead man to life, returning him to his widowed mother. The details of the Elijah story are replicated in Luke's gospel to such an extent that we must assume the evangelist intends us to see Jesus' miracle as a prophetic action which mirrors and fulfils Elijah's deed in history long past. It may also be helpful at this stage to recall that although the Lukan story set in the town of Nain is not found in any other gospel, stories of Jesus raising the dead to life occur in all four canonical gospels. In Matthew and Mark (as well as in Luke) Jesus raises Jairus' 12 year old dead daughter to life. In John chapter 12, he famously calls the dead Lazarus from his tomb. Raising the dead to life is the ultimate act that Jesus performs as an illustration of the scope of the kingdom of God which he proclaims. It is the ultimate expression of the Good News Jesus announces – until his own resurrection, that is.

The text we are now considering shows every sign of having been carefully edited, along with the previous story of the cure of the centurion's seriously ill servant, in order to present Jesus as the ultimate prophet foretold by Moses: "Moses said to the people: "The Lord your God will raise up for you a prophet like myself, from among yourselves, from your own brothers; to him you must listen. I will raise up a prophet like yourself for them from their own brothers; I will put my words into his mouth and he shall tell them all I command him" (Deuteronomy 18:15.18). Luke introduces Jesus' first declaration of his prophetic ministry in the Nazareth synagogue, quoting a combination of texts from Isaiah (c.f. Sundays 3, 4C) and stating that "this text is being fulfilled today even as you listen" (Luke 4:21; Sunday 3C).

From that point until now, Jesus' words and actions, substantially covered in the Ordinary Sundays of this year, have revealed him as the one who speaks and acts prophetically while at the same time fulfils prophecies of old. The gospels for last week and this show Jesus fulfilling the legendary prophets of old: Elijah and his disciple Elisha. Luke arranges his material in a deliberate way to highlight the connections between these two and Jesus. This does not mean, however, that Luke actually created the story. There are several features of the story, even in Luke's highly edited form, which point to it being historically rooted, and we will consider these before examining the lessons which the evangelist proposes for us in the narrative.

First, we are told that Jesus is accompanied by his disciples and a large number of people. The two groups are distinct. The crowd has a complex function in Luke. It grows as Jesus' ministry unfolds. It is normally silent, but on occasion, a member of the crowd will ask a question, or make some demand on Jesus or simply shout out (c.f. Luke 10:25; 12:13; 11:27). The crowd has particular function as Jesus moves to Jerusalem from 9:51 onwards, since it will provide the witnesses cited at Jesus' trial before the Jewish authorities about what he said and did in the open, and not in secret. Finally, this large crowd which continues at all times to grow demonstrates that Jesus is not merely an itinerant preacher who would occasionally attract the attention of passers-by. This is the leader of a new and expanding movement.

Second, Luke's description of the place makes it all the more probable that he is reporting the facts. There are episodes where Luke's geography is vague; for example, when he says that Jesus was in the house of Martha and Mary, he omits any reference to the house's location and also omits any references to the disciple's and crowds present on either side of that story (Luke 10:38-24). Luke places the story alongside its predecessor and links the two (we will consider this in greater detail on Sundays 15 and 16 of this year) by removing any difficult location identifiers. Second, in the story of the dead young man raised to life, Luke is explicit that Jesus was nearing a town called Nain (a town which has been identified), and that as he was nearing the gate, a funeral was taking place. Nain's gate has not so far been discovered by archaeologists, but burial grounds outside the town have been found. Likewise, Jewish funeral practices are indicated: the man is being carried on a bier and not in a closed coffin. This suggests Jewish practice rather than Roman custom. Third, Luke does not say that Jesus touched the body of the dead man: had Jesus done so it would have made him ritually unclean. Luke does say that Jesus touched the bier. This may have caused some ritual difficulty, but its purpose was clearly to stop the funeral procession. These and other details therefore point to an historically accurate account, edited in such a way as to highlight the prophetic significance of Jesus' action.

It has already been noted that all four gospels give accounts of one kind or another where Jesus raises the dead to life. The remarkable feature in each of these stories is that little attention is given to the person who is raised: not one of them speaks, and each of them is only mobile enough to prove that they are no longer dead. In this present story, we are made to focus on the mother of the dead man, and not on the man himself – just as in John's account of the raising of Lazarus, there is more focus on his sisters Martha and Mary than there is on Lazarus, and when Jairus' daughter is raised, the father has a more prominent role than his little girl. In the case of this young man, we are told that when Jesus saw the mother, he was filled with compassion for her. This word is used to translate a Greek expression which conveys the sense of an inner feeling that leads to an action for the good of the person who elicited a compassionate response. In this case, Jesus' compassion for the mother leads to him raising the dead son. The reason is not hard to understand when we consider the social climate of the time. In a highly patriarchal society, it was practically impossible for any woman to support herself without male assistance. Until she was married, a woman had to rely entirely on the support of her father. Once married, her husband took on that responsibility. A widow would have to look to her sons for the necessities of life. So, the tragedy of this story is that here is a woman with no husband and no son. It is not impossible that she might starve to death with no male to provide for her (the assumption seems to be that her own father will either be dead or in need of support from others). The widow is almost as dead as her only son – or could become so very soon! Hence Jesus' compassion.

For the first time in this gospel, the evangelist explicitly calls Jesus "the Lord" although the title has been used by others. It is a hint that something prophetic is about to happen. The Lord touches the bier, and the bearers stop. With a word (a prophetic word at that), Jesus, who has not touched the dead man at all, says "young man, I tell you to get up". And the young man sat up and began to walk. When Jesus raised Jairus' daughter, he said "Little girl, I tell you to get up" (Mark 5:41), and when he has instructed them to remove the stone from Lazarus' tomb, Jesus calls to the dead man, "Lazarus, come out". In each case, a prophetic word effects the raising to life. The prophetic word of God is also the creative word of God; therefore when The Lord gives the command, the word becomes deed. Also significant is the wording used for both Jairus' daughter and the young man at Nain: Jesus tells both to 'arise'. This is the word (*egeirō*) which is used of Jesus' own resurrection in the synoptic gospels. It is also the verb used when Jesus cures the paralysed man in 5:23-24, and when he heals the man with the withered hand in 6:8. There is one other example here of Luke using an expression found elsewhere. When he says that Jesus gave the young man back to his mother, he uses exactly the same words as are used in the Greek Septuagint (LXX) version of 1 Kings 17:23 (*edōken auton tę mētri autou*). The observant bystander may well have heard these words and remembered the Elijah story (or not as the case may be) but at least Luke uses the expression to lead into the reaction of the crowds: "a great prophet has appeared among us" is the Jerusalem rendition; the phrase should say that a great prophet has *been raised*, since the verb is once more *egeirō*.

This is an acknowledgement of an earlier prophecy in Luke's gospel. When John the Baptist's father Zechariah regained his speech, he proclaimed in the song we call the Benedictus, that the Lord has "raised up for us" a power for salvation – again, *egeirō*.

On a final note, this passage also looks to the next episode in Luke's gospel, although this is unfortunately not read on the Sundays of Ordinary time. It is the story of John sending two of his own disciples as messengers to Jesus to ask, "Are you the one who is to come, or must we wait for someone else?" (Luke 7:19). John does this, because reports of Jesus raising the dead man to life had gone out all through the countryside and Judea (Luke 7:17). Jesus sends the messengers back to tell John what they had seen and heard: "the blind see again, the lame walk, lepers are cleansed and the deaf hear, the dead are raised to life, the Good News is proclaimed to the poor" (Luke 7:22). With these words we are reminded of the way Jesus inaugurated his ministry: by proclaiming Good News to the poor, giving new sight to the blind etc. He insisted that these words were being fulfilled as the congregation in the synagogue at Nazareth listened, and he cited the example of two legendary prophets Elisha and Elijah who brought healing and resuscitation. Now, we have reached that part in Luke's ordered account of the things that Jesus said and did where he has fulfilled even the mighty deeds of those two prophets.

Over the next two Sundays, Jesus, the prophet will demonstrate his prophetic gifts further. He does this first by reading the thoughts of both Simon the Pharisee, who doubts Jesus 'prophetic status on the basis of his association with a woman who had a 'bad reputation' in the town. Jesus demonstrates his powers by reading the thoughts (heart) of both Simon, and the woman whom he pronounces forgiven for her many sins. Next, when he asks who the crowds say he is, the disciples say that they state 'John the Baptist (a prophet); Elijah (the most famous of all ancient prophets – perhaps because he raised the dead to life); or any of the ancient prophets come back to life'. These may sound far-fetched, but the crowd have perceived the prophetic nature of Jesus' work. Following these two episodes, we will read that the prophet has concluded his Galilean ministry, and will head to Jerusalem: the rightful place for a prophet to die.

11th Sunday, Year C. Luke 7:36-8:3
Questions to ponder

☐　　What kind of prophet do you think Simon the Pharisee considers Jesus to be?

☐　　Is forgiveness of sin a trait usually connected with prophets?

☐　　Do the crowd who ask "what kind of man can forgive sin" display faith or doubt?

☐　　What kind of salvation does Jesus offer? Does it belong to this life? The next? Both?

This week's gospel opens with a reference to people reclining at table: the same posture that was attributed to the crowd of 5,000 as described in Luke's account of the feeding from loaves and fishes (c.f. Luke 9:11-17 Corpus Christ, Year C). The two references are no more than coincidence however since the episodes in question are separated by two full chapters! It is true to say, however, that events taking place at table in Luke's gospel are often extremely significant, and frequently provide a vehicle for Jesus' teaching – as in today's passage. There is an additional episode in today's passage, which concludes with a summary of Jesus' travelling companions, giving a miniature biography of each. Once again, the appeal goes out: please do not us the shorter version of the gospel which omits this final short but highly significant piece which complements the previous story.

In almost all of the passages which are read on the Sundays of Ordinary Time this year, the focus is on Jesus as The Prophet whom Moses had foretold in Deuteronomy 18:15-18. This is a major feature in Luke's gospel and the prophetic component of Jesus' words and deeds will frequently be highlighted and set against the background of Old Testament Prophets, very often Elijah and/or Elisha. In this week's gospel passage, a Pharisee who has invited Jesus to dinner wonders to himself whether or not Jesus can be a prophet, since he allows himself to be approached by a woman 'with a bad name', who then begins with great ostentation to wash his feet with her tears and dry them with her hair. The Pharisee's 'question' to himself is, "If this man were a prophet, he would know who this woman is that is touching him and what a bad name she has". Prophets were widely thought to have the ability to read other people's minds. Jesus, in knowing what his host was thinking, demonstrates the validity of his prophetic credentials. This provides Jesus with the opportunity to teach those present on a whole range of topics. In the process, he once more demonstrates his status as The Prophet whom Moses had promised. As a coda, Luke gives a list of the regular companions of Jesus, as well as providing a very short biography for some of them.
The present passage opens with an invitation to dinner being extended to Jesus by one of the Pharisees; later in the narrative, we learn that his name was Simon. The diners are arranged in a way typical of Greek meals; reclining (as we are supposed to conclude that those at the feeding of the 5,000 were doing), with their heads facing the table and each other, and their feet pointing away from the table. The Jerusalem Bible's translation which says that Jesus 'took his place at table' doesn't convey the scene with sufficient accuracy, since it is precisely because of the reclining, feet- away- from-table posture that the next scene becomes possible. A woman enters, one who was 'a sinner'. The Jerusalem Bible's translation that she 'had a bad name in the town' is not a literal translation but actually conveys well the issues that surrounded her. Literally, she was a woman from the town ('city' is possible, but since it is not named, and cities were not so numerous, town seems more likely) and she was 'sinful' (*hamartōlos*). It is likely that Luke calls the woman 'sinful', not because she had committed sins (as had everyone else around, with the exception of Jesus), but because she did not carry out her religious duties. People could be sinners in this sense for a variety of reasons: carelessness was one: another very common one was that they were designated as 'sinners' or 'sinful' because of their occupations.

Thus, people who worked with animals, and thus were unclean, and could not practice their religion in public settings like the Temple or synagogues; others were unclean because they worked for the Romans (tax agents and soldiers came into this category); some might also have been habitual sinners, e.g. in irregular partnerships. It is not unlikely that the woman in this story would have belonged to the latter category, and therefore had gained for herself a 'bad name'.

Simon the Pharisee, Jesus' host, is scandalised that Jesus would allow such a woman to come close to him, never mind touch him, "If this man were a prophet, he would have known who and what sort of woman this is who is touching him, for she is a sinner" (Luke 7:39, RSV translation). His logic is that a sinful person touching another would make that second person ritually unclean; a true prophet would surely want to avoid such an outcome. Since prophets were expected to be able to read the hearts of people, Simon's supposition that Jesus should be able to do so is quite reasonable, but his conclusion that Jesus, having done so, would not allow a sinful person anywhere near him is far from an accurate assessment of Jesus the prophet. In fact, Jesus the Prophet demonstrates his ability to read the minds of both the woman, as he will demonstrate shortly, and of Simon, whose inner thoughts he is now about to reveal. He begins by informing Simon the Pharisee that he has something to say, and Simon replies "speak Master". Jesus tells a very short parable, one about two creditors. One owed 500 *denarii*, and the other owed fifty, both to the same person. Both owe considerable sums of money, because the *denarius* was the recognized minimum daily wage on which a worker could survive; fifty *denarii* corresponded to one and a half month's wages; five hundred to more than a year and a half's wages. The men owing these sums were released from their debt. Jesus asks Simon, 'which of the two thus pardoned would have more love for the master who released them from their debt". Simon can only give one answer, and he does so with a measure of reluctance, because he knows that as soon as he gives the required answer to Jesus' question, he has disclosed his own secrets thoughts regarding this woman and Jesus. So, he says "the one who was pardoned most, I suppose". Simon must realise that he has uttered his own condemnation!

Jesus now turns to the woman, and shows that he, the Prophet, *can* read her heart (it should be remembered that for the Hebrew mentality, the heart was the organ that symbolised, not emotion, but thought, judgement, reasoning, decision – attributes we would nowadays associate with the mind). He demonstrates this, starting with the evidence of the extent of her love: she has shown such lavish (and probably even embarrassing) love for Jesus that she must have been conscious that she has been forgiven her many sins; the Prophet is not denying that the woman has been sinful. Jesus spells out her love, and contrasts it with the absence of love shown by Simon. It should be stressed that Simon had done nothing wrong in the hospitality he had offered to Jesus; in fact, he probably extended an invitation to Jesus to dine because he had a high regard for Jesus as a Prophet, but as Jesus points out, Simon does not greet his distinguished guest in any special way, does not offer him water with which to wash his feet, or oil to anoint his head. On the other hand, the sinful woman poured tears over Jesus' feet and dried them with her hair, showered him with kisses, and anointed his feet with ointment. Based on this evidence, Jesus concludes that her many sins must have been forgiven. To reinforce the point, he turns to the woman and says 'Your sins have been forgiven'. This is better than the translation 'your sins are forgiven' of the Jerusalem Bible, because it stresses that the woman had been forgiven before her demonstration of love. This provides the cue for the crown to ask, 'who is this who can even forgive sins?' The answer is, the Prophet is the one who can forgive sins, and he reinforces this with his prophetic statement to the woman, "Your faith has saved you; go in peace" (Luke 7:50). At the Prophet Jesus' birth, peace was proclaimed to people of goodwill, and the angel announced that a saviour has been born". It is her faith that brings the salvation of forgiveness of sin to the woman whose heart has been accurately read by the Prophet Jesus.

This episode is followed by a brief roll call of Jesus' companions through Galilee, comprising the Twelve and certain women whom he had cured of evil spirits and ailments. This list is important, because these women will be the ones who follow him all the way to Jerusalem, and are in fact the witnesses to both his death and his resurrection they are "Mary surnamed the Magdalene, from whom seven demons had gone out, Joanna the wife of Herod's steward Chuza, Susanna, and several others who provided for them out of their own resources" (Luke 8:2-3). They are mentioned now to stress that they were with Jesus while he was still ministering in Galilee, and they had all benefited from that ministry; their witness to Jesus will include personal testimony of how he had brought salvation to their lives, just as he has brought salvation to the woman in the house of Simon the Pharisee. Their names will recur in the Passion Narrative later in the gospel.

Sunday 12, Year C. Luke 9:18-24
Questions to Ponder

☐ Why might Luke omit any reference to the place where Peter's confession occurred?

☐ Why would Luke be so nervous about including any reference to Jesus as the fulfilment of Messianic hope?

☐ How can it be possible for anyone to follow Jesus by taking up the cross on a daily basis as Luke suggests?

As is often the case in this Gospel, Luke introduces here an episode of particular significance with the note that it happened when Jesus was praying privately even though he was in the company of his disciples. This happened earlier in 3:21 after Jesus' baptism, and will happen again soon after the present episode at the Transfiguration, 9:28 (which is read in Year C on the 2nd Sunday of Lent). Unlike the accounts of this particular episode found in Matthew and Mark and which situate it around Caesarea Philippi, Luke does not identify the location where it took place. Luke also gives a 'tidier' account of Jesus' interrogation of the disciples than the other two evangelists. When he lists the reports of who the crowds are saying the Son of Man is, he repeats exactly the list that had already appeared in 9:7-9. That was when Herod had begun to hear reports that "some people were saying that John had risen from the dead, others that Elijah had reappeared, still others that one of the ancient prophets had come back to life". When Herod gets to hear about Jesus, there is a chilling pointer to later tension between Jesus and Herod which surfaces elsewhere in this gospel. It is noticed when Pharisees warn Jesus that Herod means to kill him (c.f. 13:31), and of course reaches its height in the story of Jesus' trial before Herod, unique to Luke, in which Herod was unable to find anything in Jesus that could justify a death sentence being passed (c.f. 23:8-1. 14-15). Now, Jesus' own disciples repeat the same information, but without any suggestion of John being brought back to life. In Luke's account in particular, the replies carry a note of irony. This evangelist consistently portrays Jesus as the Prophet promised by Moses, but who is seldom recognised as such by his hearers; now, prophetic attributes are being applied to Jesus, but with superstitious belief rather than true faith in Jesus and his prophetic ministry. He is considered therefore – possibly more in fear than in earnest - as Elijah or one of the ancient prophets come back to life (perhaps we can even fast forward here in anticipation of the parable of the Rich man and Lazarus, where the rich man appeals to Abraham to send Lazarus back from the dead to warn his brothers, and Abraham replies, "If they will not listen either to Moses or to the prophets, they will not be convinced even if someone should rise from the dead" c.f. 16:31). As in the other versions of the narrative, Peter alone replies to Jesus' question: "but who do you say I am?" In Luke's version, he replies "The Christ of God", which means the 'Anointed of God', which is how Jesus had been identified, albeit indirectly, in the synagogue at Nazareth, when, in response to the words "the Lord has anointed me" (Luke 4:18), Jesus announced that these words are being fulfilled in their hearing (c.f. 4:21). Otherwise in this gospel so far, the use of the word 'anointed' or 'Christ' has been significantly played down. In Luke 3:15-16, John the Baptist emphatically denies that he is the Christ, and in 4:41, Jesus forbids unclean spirits to speak because they know he is the Christ.

What happens after Peter's confession is handled in a very individual way by Luke. He quotes Jesus as strictly forbidding any of the disciples to tell anyone anything about this conversation. Like the other gospel writers, Luke then goes on to Jesus' first passion prophecy: that the Son of Man was 'destined to suffer grievously, to be rejected by the elders and chief priests and scribes and to be put to death, and to be raised up on the third day' (9:22). In Luke's account, there is no subsequent account of Peter rebuking Jesus and insisting that this must not happen to him, as there is in both Mark and Matthew. The omission is not accidental: here is Luke at his most meticulous; at no stage in his gospel will this evangelist write anything which might allow for the reader to conclude that Jesus could justifiably be accused of claiming to be a political Messiah. This of course will be the charge that the chief priests will try to make stick before Pilate, and for which neither Pilate nor Herod will be able to find any justification (c.f. Luke 22:66 – 23:15). It is also the fear of the Pharisees who hear and see the jubilant chants of Jesus' accompanying crowds as he enters Jerusalem , in which Luke omits references to branches being placed before the king, as are to be found in Mark 11:8-9 and Matthew 21:8-9. Nor does Luke include the Messianic title 'Son of David' which is used in the other two synoptic accounts. In omitting Peter's outburst against the suffering Son of Man and Jesus' harsh reaction as in Mark 8:31-33 and Matthew 16:21-23, Luke emphasises that if Jesus is to be called Messiah at all, it only as the Son of Man who is destined to suffer. Peter's outburst recorded in the other two synoptic accounts is not to be allowed to interfere with or weaken in any way the essential combination in Jesus of Messiahship and suffering.

The Passion prediction is remarkably accurate in its identification of the protagonists in Jesus' suffering and death. These will be the elders, the chief priests and the scribes; Pharisees are not included in this list. Just as he has omitted Jesus' rebuke to Peter's attempt to distance himself – and Jesus – from suffering, so Luke shows that the follow-on from the Passion prediction is directed to as wide an audience as possible. We should remember that the disciples were told earlier to tell no-one about that has just happened. Now, however, Jesus addresses his words to all – reaching beyond the scope of disciples present, and states that "if *anyone* wants to be a follower of mine, let him renounce himself and take up his cross every day and follow me" (Luke 9:23). Physically, Jesus can only have addressed himself to those present, but the sense that the words are addressed to anyone who subsequently reads them is reinforced by the insistence that disciples must take up the cross 'daily'. This moves the meaning of the concept of taking up the cross from a possible, or even probable, necessity of a death by martyrdom, to an attitude which is demanded on a daily basis. Since it is not possible to undergo physical crucifixion on a daily basis, the expression must bear some relation to the second part of the saying, about renouncing self. Perhaps the reference to taking up the cross on a daily basis is an interpretative comment on the true meaning of renouncing self: something which must be more than an occasional example of self-denial, but rather a permanent, daily attitude of laying aside all self-interest. This applies to the same extent as that renunciation of self which accompanies Jesus' willing adoption of his death on the cross on behalf of humanity. To renounce self is always, on a daily basis, to put every other person ahead of oneself. It is call to a serious and hugely challenging commitment. It is precisely what Jesus himself did throughout his entire life and ministry. The words of course are not limited to the first batch of Jesus' disciples, or to the Twelve. These words have applications in the lives of 'all'. Thus will the process of following Jesus be undertaken, a process that is expressed in the present tense, and will happen on a daily basis. Nothing less will be sufficient for anyone else who would follow Jesus.

Chapter 7. Jesus the Prophet begins his Journey to Jerusalem

Sundays 13 - 17, Year C

Introduction:

On each Sunday from now until the end of this liturgical year, we will be able to follow Luke's depiction of Jesus, the Prophet whom Moses had promised. This will be done almost entirely through material which is unique to Luke; on the few occasions when this is not entirely the case, we will find either that Luke links episodes found also in other synoptics with his own unique material (e.g. from chapter 15, we will read the parable of the lost sheep which is also found in Matthew 18:12-14, but which Luke couples with the parable of the lost coin and the so called Prodigal Son), or that he includes episodes familiar from other synoptic gospels, but presented in his own way. At the very beginning of this sequence of gospel readings for the Ordinary Sundays, we open Luke's major section of the Travel Narrative, as Jesus and his disciples head toward Jerusalem. Its opening is not dramatic: it would be easy to miss the cues, but in a short sentence, Luke changes the entire thrust of Jesus' ministry. "As the time drew near for him to be taken up to heaven, Jesus resolutely took the road for Jerusalem…" (Luke 9:51). Perhaps we should not say that this is not dramatic: it is very dramatic, but understated. Dramatic, because it marks that turning point where Jesus definitively embraces his destiny, and sets out on that journey which will have no other ending but his death and resurrection. It will be in Jerusalem that the Prophet will fulfil his destiny, since "it would not be right for a prophet to die outside Jerusalem" (Luke 13:33). The Travel Narrative will take up most of the rest of Ordinary time, and will begin on Sunday 13, spanning some full ten chapters of the gospel. During this time, Luke will explore almost all of his major themes – Jesus the Prophet, who challenges to fully committed discipleship, who brings salvation, who calls those who will respond to listen to his word, who heals, who forgives and promises paradise to those who will accept him as the Prophet.

In the gospels considered in this selection, we will read some of Luke's most famous unique parables, including the Good Samaritan and the Prodigal Son. We will hear about Martha and Mary, and will be instructed in the true meaning of prayer, at least as Luke sees it.

Sunday 13, Year C. Luke 9:51-62
Questions to Ponder

☐   What possible alternatives might there have been to Jesus setting his face toward Jerusalem at this point?

☐   Why do you think that Jesus would reject the offer of James and John to call down fire from heaven on Jesus' enemies, given that this had been an acceptable course of action for Elijah?

☐   Why would Jesus prevent one of the would-be disciples from attending to his father's funeral before embarking on discipleship?

There are very few – if any - places in the gospel of Luke where so few words are so hugely charged with meaning as are those in the second half of the opening verse of this week's gospel. The phrase is very brief and immediately follows the notice that 'the time drew near for him (Jesus) to be taken up to heaven'. So, Jesus "resolutely took the road for Jerusalem". This is widely recognised to be the turning point of the entire gospel, for in those few words, Jesus chooses the change of direction, the destination being Jerusalem, to the place where he will fulfil his destiny. The passage we read in this week's liturgy continues from this statement to a series of very short episodes and saying, all of which are challenging to the people involved, and to the reader or hearer who encounters them, but which only really begin to make sense in the light of this fundamental decision of Jesus to turn toward Jerusalem which, as we will soon discover, is the only place in which it is fitting for a prophet to die – at least, according to the evangelist Luke.

The entire narrative is driven by a sense of timing. Most contemporary English translations render the first sentence much as the Jerusalem Bible does, "the time drew near for him to be taken up to heaven", but a more literal translation would be that 'it happened in the coming to fulfilment of the days of his being taken up into heaven' – very inelegant in English, but conveying the important ingredients: the time of fulfilment has almost arrived, and what is being fulfilled is Jesus being taken up (received) into heaven. Once again we have an instance of the Prophet Jesus not only *making* prophetic statements and gestures, but also *being* the fulfilment of prophetic utterances and expectations. What is to happen to the Son of Man (his suffering, death and resurrection) is not the result of human planning; it is the outcome of what has been written coming into reality. The Prophet had already announced his role in fulfilling scripture when he spoke in the synagogue at Nazareth (Luke 4:21). The gospel narrative from here until chapter 19 will unfold the move toward final fulfilment. There is of course an echo of the Elijah narrative in this sentence, and this is what Jesus is also fulfilling. At the end of Elijah's time on earth, we are informed that "when the Lord was about to take Elijah up to heaven" (RSV translation), Elijah and Elisha were on the way from Gigal. It is part of this tradition that Elijah did not die, but was taken up into heaven that led to the belief that he would return before the day of the Lord to make sure all things were in order. In the Gospel tradition, John the Baptist is presented as the figure of Elijah returned. As we shall see shortly, the Elijah/Elisha narrative provides more background to subsequent episodes in this narrative.

Against such a solemn laying-out of themes of fulfilment and of 'being taken up to heaven', it is not surprising that Jesus' decision is not take lightly: he deliberately (or 'resolutely' in the JB translation) takes the road to Jerusalem. Again the literal translation, though lacking elegance, may confer more fully the idea: Jesus 'hardens his face to go' to Jerusalem. His decision is to embrace the fulfilment of his destiny; his decision, then is his sealing of his own fate, the acceptance of his death, and indeed, setting out on the first steps that will lead to that death. His decision points to a crossroads: what should he do at this point? Should he continue with his Galilean ministry? There is still surely much he can achieve in the region, more good he can do in healing, exorcising, cleansing, raising to life, and teaching, but his destiny is not to remain as a teaching wonder worker: his destiny is to suffer, die and rise again – this is what is meant by his passing. Like Ezekiel, 'son of man', who had set his face against Jerusalem, to prophesy against the land of Israel (Ezekiel 21:7-8), Jesus too must set his face with determination.

What follows from here is very much in the prophetic tradition. Jesus sends messengers before him. This reminds us of how Zechariah described his own new born son, who would "go before the Lord to prepare the way for him" (Luke 1:76). It also recalls the story of Moses sending out messengers ahead of him in Exodus 23:20. When these reach Samaritan territory, they are refused entry, because Jesus is heading for Jerusalem. The old hostility breaks out again, and James and John propose the solution that they call down fire from heaven to consume the Samaritans. Their suggestion is not new; presumably they were recalling a similar action on the part of Elijah who threatened to call down fire from heaven to consume his enemies. Mark

3:17 informs us that in naming the Twelve, Jesus had given the nickname 'Boanerges', or 'Sons of Thunder' to James and John. Jesus does not accept their offer: he turns and rebukes them, that is, he puts a stop to, or silences, all such talk.

There follows a rapid succession of offers and calls connected with discipleship, all of which are qualified with expressions highlighting the demands of such a calling, and the episodes themselves draw from the background of OT prophetic tradition. The first is an apparently generous offer to follow Jesus wherever he will go. It is a reminder of Elisha's persistence in being accepted as Elijah's disciple (2 Kings 2:1-6); Elijah does his best to put off his would-be follower, whose persistence pays off in the end. In the gospels, offers to follow Jesus that originate in the would-be disciple are never successful; authentic calls to discipleship always originate in the initiative of Jesus. In this case, Jesus' response to the one who would follow him wherever he would go appears to founder on the grounds that the enthusiastic would-be disciple has not taken into account that the 'the Son of Man has nowhere to lay his head' (9:58). It is an early reminder of the nature of the journey on which Jesus has just embarked, a journey which has only one objective in mind: the fulfilling of the destiny of the Son of Man through death and resurrection in Jerusalem. Another man is addressed by Jesus in familiar terms of the call to discipleship, "Follow me". This one hesitates, pleading to be allowed to go and bury his father first of all. By any standards Jesus reply seems very harsh, "Leave the dead to bury their dead; your duty is to go and spread the news of the kingdom of God" (Luke 9:59-60). In Jewish piety, to bury a dead fellow Jew was among the highest obligations by which one could be bound. Even the High Priest on his way to perform a Temple duty was obliged to bury a dead Jew if no one else was available, even though by doing so he would necessarily incur ritual defilement which would prevent him carrying out his High Priestly duty. The obligation of piety to honour father and mother in their death is indicated in Tobit 4:3-4; 6:13-14; 14:11-13. Here, Jesus appears to ride roughshod through the accepted religious traditions of which he was always otherwise so observant. So why is there now such a change in tone? The answer would appear to be that the journey that the Prophet has begun, leading to the accomplishment of his destiny, and the time for which is approaching, takes priority over everything else. The Prophet will pass this way but once, and there will never be another opportunity to accompany him on this journey, or to join with him in the proclamation of the good news of the kingdom of God. Likewise, those who, like the final man in the trio of potential disciples, find excuses for postponement on the grounds of family business run the risk of missing this unique opportunity. Elisha may have been excused by Elijah to go and make his farewells to his family, but the circumstances were less pressing than they are now that the Prophet has begun his journey, and the consequences of a delayed start in ministry are now much more significant than in the past. Hence, Jesus challenges to discipleship at an unprecedented level.

Jesus the Prophet, cast in the tradition of both Moses and Elijah sets out to fulfil his destiny. As the prophet who travels to Jerusalem, he speaks the word of God and much of what follows in this major section of the gospel will consist of Jesus' teaching. The section will include some of the most famous of all parables, and most of these are unique to Luke. At every step of the journey, we will be given clear indications of Jesus' audience, and will be informed whether his teaching is accepted, or whether his prophetic utterances are rejected.

In next week's gospel, Jesus will give much more explicit instructions to 72 disciples he will send out in pairs. When we read this, we will perhaps begin to see why his rejection of the three would-be disciples in today's passage makes sense.

Sunday 14, Year C. Luke 10:1-12. 17-20

Questions to ponder

☐ Why might Luke include this additional story of 'sending out' of the seventy-two, doubling the story in 9:1-14 of the sending of the Twelve?

☐ Why are no preparations to be made by the disciples sent out?

☐ What are the similarities and the difference between the sending of the Twelve and the sending of the 72?

☐ What in daily life might then be the real reason for disciples' rejoicing?

Following Mark 6:6 where Jesus had met with opposition from the people of his own town, he re-launched his ministry by commissioning the Twelve, already called, to go out and to continue the proclamation of the Good News. This involved casting out devils and anointing the sick with oil and curing them (c.f. Mark 6:12-13). There is a parallel between the Markan text and the gospel passage for this week, although there are also several significant differences. The similarities include the fact that both texts describe a new initiative on Jesus' part in which he enlists the assistance of his delegates as he re-launches his ministry. The differences are varied: in Mark the Twelve are sent out, in Luke, the number is 70 or 72 (both of these numbers are possible, since both appear in equally reliable manuscripts, and each can draw on Old Testament background for their justification - none of this need concern us here); in Mark, the episode occurs during Jesus' Galilean ministry, whereas in Luke, it concerns his journey from Galilee to Jerusalem; in Mark, his rejection is by how own people, and in Luke his rejection is from Samaritans who will not let him enter their territory because he is heading to Jerusalem. Finally, in Mark, this is a one off mission undertaken by the Twelve; in Luke this is the second time Jesus has sent out delegates: already, in 9:1-6, Luke has given his own account of the mission of the Twelve.

There are some unusual features in these observations. Luke is an evangelist who normally avoids repetition (for example, unlike Matthew and Mark, he does not relate a second feeding miracle c.f. Mark 6:31-46 and 8:1-9; Matthew 14:13-21 and 15:32-38), but for some strange reason, he substantially repeats the accounts of Jesus sending out disciples. It is difficult to say exactly why he should include this 'doublet' here, unless it is to do two things: first, to recount the all-important Mission of the Twelve in its own right, and second, to present Jesus once more in the light of the Moses-like prophetic figure, who himself had appointed 70 elders. It is also true - and should be carefully noted - that the emphasis on major missionary activity in Luke-Acts is much more developed than it is in any other gospel. This is especially the case in Acts where two features are noticeable. First, there are frequent gatherings of disciples which involve many more people than the Twelve: we need look no further than Acts 2:1-11 and the Pentecost narrative for an example. More specifically, we are told in Acts 1:15 that when Peter addressed the assembly on the occasion of the election of a successor to Judas, there were 120 in the congregation. When Pentecost came round, they were "all met in one room". The second feature is typified in events after Pentecost, when the activities of the early community will very soon move far from the confines of that room, and then "repentance for the forgiveness of sins would be preached to all the nations" (c.f. Luke 24:47).

Unlike the Twelve in their earlier mission, the 72 (this is the number used in the Jerusalem Bible edition) are sent to the places that Jesus himself would

visit. They are sent out on an 'apostolic mission', although they are not apostles (Greek *apostellō* means to send out with a commission: in this case, the commission to represent the Prophet Jesus). The task will not be easy; they are sent like lambs among wolves. They are given specific instructions about their travel; or rather, they are given strict instructions NOT to carry purse or bag, NOT to greet anyone on the road, and to accept whatever food and accommodation is offered to them. They are to offer peace but if that peace is not accepted, it will come back to them. All of these convey a sense both of urgency in the mission ('do not stop to greet anyone on the road'), and of the utmost importance in relying only on God and the hospitality of those to whom they proclaim Good News. They are not to rely on their own resources, because God will provide. Later, in the Passion Narrative Jesus will change the instruction. Whereas they had lacked nothing when sent out on this present mission, after Jesus' return to the Father disciples will need to use their own initiative as they move further and further afield in the spread of the gospel message (c.f. Luke 22:35-38). In the commission of the 72, the very real possibility is raised that there will be hostile and even violent opposition to the mission; this is to be acknowledged, and on the day of God's judgement, those who provide such opposition will rank along with those from the legendary evil city of Sodom: the Prophet has made a prophetic utterance against those who would reject his emissaries!
The edited lectionary passage we read this week has a break in the narrative, in that it omits Jesus' prophetic judgement pronounced against Chorazin, Bethsaida, Capernaum and Tyre and Sidon. Instead, the narrative goes on immediately to the return of the 72, who come back rejoicing that even devils submitted to them when they used Jesus' name. Jesus replies that he had watched Satan fall like lightning; the disciples have been given power over snakes and scorpions, which would have been understood in the biblical tradition as the agents of the Evil One: these, they can tread underfoot without incurring any harm from them, or even from the whole strength of the enemy! This in itself is however no reason for their rejoicing: rather, they should rejoice that their names are written in heaven! Yes, Jesus has destroyed the power of Satan. This has already been encountered in the Testing of the Prophet in Luke 4:1-13, and at the Last Supper, he will warn that Satan will sift all of them like wheat, but that he has prayed for them, and especially for Simon that his faith may not fail, and that when the power of Satan is finally destroyed in the *exodos* of the Prophet, Peter will once

again strengthen his brothers (c.f. Luke 22:31-32). Once more the Prophetic word will be fulfilled in the Acts of the Apostles, where Peter will be seen in the place of prominence among the community, especially in the early chapters.

Sunday 15, Year C. Luke 10:25-37
Questions to ponder

☐   Can you see any significance in Luke putting the formulation of the 2 great commandments of Deuteronomy 6:5 and Leviticus 19:18b on the lips of the questioning lawyer rather than on the lips of Jesus himself?

☐   Is this parable too far-fetched in stating that duty to a neighbour in need always takes precedence over everything else?

☐   Do you think the lawyer's disposition to Jesus is hostile from the start of the story, or does he grow in hostility?

The passages for this Sunday and the two which follow it are linked together in that they provide an unbroken sequence from Luke 10:25 through to 11:1-13. More importantly however, they all provide commentary and insight into the gospel summing up of the meaning of the entire Law: "You must love the Lord your God with all your heart, with all your soul, with all your strength, and with all your mind, and your neighbour as yourself" – or rather, the entire gospel sequence laid out over the next few weeks gives insight into the application of this great commandment. It will give practical applications first on the true meaning of neighbour, and then over the two Sundays which follow the remainder of the sequence will spell out some implications of what the love of God with all one's faculties should mean for us.

The sequence opens in this week's gospel with the information that a lawyer puts a question to Jesus, and we are told that the question is hostile in intent; the lawyer wants to disconcert Jesus, as the Jerusalem Bible has it; other English translations are more faithful to the Greek, which uses the word *peirazō*, which is the expression used when Jesus is put to the test by the devil in Luke 4:1-13. The lawyer's testing question is, "Master, what must I do to inherit eternal life? (Luke 10:25). Rather than give a direct answer - which of course he seldom does anyway - Jesus challenges the lawyer to provide his own answer from what he reads in the Law, and so the man says "You must love the Lord your God with all your heart, with all your soul, with all your strength, and with all your mind, and your neighbour as yourself". This is a conflation of the two principles from Torah, and is the only place in which, contrary to the common assumption that Jesus joins two commandments to make a single 'super commandment', two commandments are united in what appears to be a single statement. Even in this form however, it is clear that two separate entities are described. Not only is this the only gospel in which this happens; it is also the only place in which another (the lawyer in this case) and not Jesus who formulates the new commandment. Jesus is apparently pleased with the answer, because he replies, "You have answered right; do this and life is yours" (Luke 10:28). The issue however is not yet closed. The lawyer has a further question to ask, and he has a motive: he wants to justify himself. The question is, "and who is my neighbour?" The question has an answer in Leviticus 19:18, "You must not exact vengeance, nor must you bear a grudge against the children of your people. You must love your neighbour as yourself". The implication is that your neighbour is a member of your own people. Further on in Leviticus 19:33-34 the concept is widened to the stranger who comes to live among 'your people', "If a stranger lives with you in your land, do not molest him. You must count him as one of your own countrymen and love him as yourself - for you were once strangers yourselves in Egypt". So, a very narrow interpretation of neighbour is to be found in Leviticus, applying to fellow countrymen, and apparently relating to one's family as well. Why then, if the lawyer is hostile in intent, does he put the question to Jesus, when he already knows the answer? We can only speculate, but we are given something of a clue by the evangelist himself – the man asked the question because he was anxious to justify himself. There follows the famous parable, usually called the Good Samaritan parable, in which three different people have justification for acting in the way they do; only the third justifies his action in relation to a person in need.

The characters are, in typical Lukan fashion, well-developed. Two are respectable pillars of Jewish society: a priest, associated with Temple sacrifice, and a Levite, a lesser Temple functionary with responsibility for exercising liturgical functions. The third is a despised Samaritan, who emerges as the only one of the three to act as a neighbour. The issue is justification. The priest and the levite can justify themselves for not only not attending to the needs of a man who has been attacked and left for dead at the side of a notoriously dangerous road, but they can justify themselves for passing by on the other side, most likely from a range of plausible excuses. To begin with, there is personal danger. Those who attacked the man may still be around – or the man may be a decoy to lure unsuspecting travellers into a trap whereby they will be ambushed as they stop to examine the situation more fully. Furthermore, the man may already be dead, and if they touch a corpse, they would be ritually defiled, and thereby prevented from carrying out their religious duties. What they seem to have forgotten however, is the requirement for every Jew to provide decent burial for a fellow Jew. This obligation was so binding that even if the High Priest himself encountered an unburied corpse, if no one else was available, he had an obligation to carry out the burial personally: even if that would have prevented him from carrying out the most solemn of religious duties. The two characters in this story therefore justify themselves in walking past on the other side of the road.

Not so the Samaritan. He notices the situation, feels compassion for the man and attends to his needs. Compassion is a term which arises frequently in biblical texts. It has been described as the stage between recognising someone in need, and then responding to that need in a tangible way. The compassion of God is expressed to Moses in the episode of the burning bush when God says to Moses in effect; I have heard the cry of my people in their distress, I mean to act on their behalf. God has noticed their need; he is moved to the compassionate desire to want to respond; the last stage will be God's action in liberating his people. In this story, the Samaritan's compassion results for seeing the need of someone in great distress, a compassion which is transformed into action. The Samaritan translates his compassion into action resulting from the use of his own resources. He pours oil and wine into the man's wounds, bandages them up, puts him on the back of his own horse, takes him personally to the inn, parts with two *denarii* (very generous; one estimate states that the cost of a night's accommodation averaged at one twelfth of a *denarius*); this Samaritan pays up front for around three and a half weeks' accommodation: *and* promises to pay up on return from his journey should extra costs have been incurred.

Jesus concludes by asking the lawyer the question: which of the three in the story emerged as the true neighbour? The answer is obvious – neighbourliness is not bound by justification of self as to when the concept ceases to apply - for whatever reason! Rather, true neighbourliness is about responding to a person in need, regardless of circumstances. The lawyer wanted to justify himself in the sense that he wanted to identify the basic minimum requirement for his – or any other – to inherit, i.e. earn, eternal life, but eternal life is not earned: it is gifted by God. Those who seek eternal life as God's gift will then surely be so grateful for the gift that they will not seek to *earn* a place (which no one can do anyway) but *will* seek to communicate God's love for humanity through their concern for neighbours in need.

Sunday 16, Year C. Luke 10:38-42

Questions to ponder

☐　　In what way is Mary's chosen activity the 'better part'?
☐　　Why is Martha unnecessarily preoccupied, if hospitality is such an important theme in Middle Eastern etiquette?
☐　　What is the significance of Jesus being on his journey to Jerusalem for a correct understanding of this passage?
☐　　What is the significance of Jesus' portrayal as a prophet for this story?

If the parable of the Good Samaritan is a practical commentary on the commandment to love neighbour as self, it could be said that the episode in this week's gospel passage is a similar commentary on the application of the first commandment, and the love of God will all one's energy and powers. The story in today's gospel centres on Jesus' visit to the house of Martha and Mary, and the complaint of Martha that she is being left to do all the housework while Mary sits listening to her visitor.

The edited version of the passage provided for the liturgy begins with the information that "Jesus came to a village, and a woman named Martha welcomed him into her house". It is a pity that the passage does not begin with the full contextual information which the evangelist; that this happened 'in the course of their journey' (Jerusalem Bible translation), since the inclusion of this phrase would remind us of the constant background theme of gospel passages for almost all of the rest of this year: that Jesus is journeying to Jerusalem and the fulfilment of his destiny as the Son of Man, of whom it was ordained that he will suffer, die and rise again. In some way, everything that happens in the course of the Prophet Jesus' travels must relate in some way to the Prophet's destination. In this episode, the relevance of that background information will soon become apparent.

Martha welcomes Jesus into her house. She appears only here in Luke's gospel, although she, her sister Mary and brother Lazarus are found in John 11:1-39 and 12:2. Mary was such a frequently used name at the time and in this vicinity that it makes no sense to connect her with the Mary Magdalene named in Luke 8:2. In the present story, Mary is introduced as Martha's sister, and we are told that she "sat down at the Lord's feet and listened to him speaking" (Luke 10:39), literally, 'listening to his word'. A more literal translation than that offered in the Jerusalem Bible helps to remind us that the visitor to Martha and Mary's house is none other than the Prophet Jesus, the fulfilment of Moses' promise to the Israelites in Deuteronomy 18:15. 18: that the Lord would raise up a prophet like himself to whom they must listen. Mary, sitting at the feet of her visitor, is according him the attention he is due as prophet. Martha on the other hand, is preoccupied with the need to provide appropriate hospitality. She becomes overwhelmed by the enormity of the task she has set herself. She enlists Jesus' support of her cause, and asks if he is not concerned that her sister is leaving her to do all the work. At this point many readers feel more than a little sympathy for Martha, left as she is to carry the burden of providing hospitality; that great obligation to a guest that was and continues to be a hallmark of Middle Eastern etiquette. To her surprise, Martha receives no support from her visitor who tells her that she worries and frets "about so many things, and yet few are needed, indeed only one. It is Mary who has chosen the better part; it is not to be taken from her" (Luke 10:41-42). Martha has calculated wrongly: what she is doing is not of prime importance during Jesus' visit. The indications that she has seriously miscalculated are not difficult to understand. To begin with, there is the issue of the nature of the guest. Jesus is not just an important figure for whom preparations must be made; he is the Prophet who will pass this way but once. Mary on the other hand appreciates what Martha fails to recognise: the unique nature of this visit. There will never again be the same opportunity for Mary (or Martha, should she realise it) to listen to the Prophet – literally, to hear his word. So the question is, which is of the greater importance: to hear the words of God's prophet, long-awaited and now present, or to prepare a meal? There is of course no contest; listening to the word of the prophet must always rate more highly than preparing his meal. There is also a second issue relating to the rules governing hospitality toward guests. Martha has broken one of hospitality's most basic principles. She has involved a stranger, and honoured guest at that, in what is in effect a family dispute and she now asks Jesus to take sides. Later in this gospel, a man will shout out to Jesus from the crowd, "Master, tell my brother to give me a share of our inheritance", to which Jesus replies, "My friend, who appointed me your judge, or the arbitrator of your claims?" (Luke 12:13-14). Jesus has no desire in either case to become involved in domestic disputes.

There is a much larger issue at stake here. The Prophet Moses, who had promised a successor just like himself, had told the people that their most fundamental duty was to "love the LORD your God with all your heart, with all your soul, with all your strength" (Deuteronomy 6:5), which is precisely the first part of the commandment quoted by the lawyer in the gospel for last Sunday, who asks Jesus what he must do to inherit eternal life. This was of connected in the lawyer's answer to the commandment to "love your neighbour as yourself" (Leviticus 19:18). The parable of the Good Samaritan took on the form of a commentary on the exact meaning of loving one's neighbour as oneself. It was presented in the form of a lesson which cast the true neighbour in the mould of the one who provided for the needs of someone in trouble. In the story of Martha and Mary, the two sisters with very different and contrasting ideas of good manners, are set against each other to highlight which is the one who gives her whole attention to the love of the Lord God. In John's gospel, to love Jesus is to keep his commandments (c.f. John 14:15), and to listen to Jesus is to listen to the One who sent him; in Luke, to pay heed to the word of the Prophet is to pay heed to God himself. Mary has certainly chosen the better part, because she has focussed all her attention on what the prophet has to say –far more important than any domestic chore, display of hospitality or other frantic action. In next week's gospel, which is a direct follow on from today's passage, the lesson in the total commitment to God and his love is taken forward in a lesson on the way to pray.

Sunday 17, Year C. Luke 11:1-13

Questions to ponder

☐   What lessons do we really learn here from Jesus about prayer?

☐   Are sin and debt the same: or should a real distinction be maintained between the two words in this prayer?

☐   What does persistent prayer actually achieve: unshakeable confidence in God, or an expression of human will which forces a change of mind from God?

☐   What outcome can we ALWAYS anticipate from God's response to our prayers?

This passage takes us to a fresh chapter of Luke's gospel as well as an apparently new location, but there is strong continuity between this and the two passages we have read in the previous two weeks. The link is derived from the testing question posed to Jesus by the hostile lawyer in Luke 10:25-28 and in particular from the lawyer's own statement in v 28, "You must love the Lord your God with all your heart, with all your soul, with all your strength, and with all your mind, and your neighbour as yourself". The parable of the Good Samaritan which followed this brief conversation served as a commentary on the correct understanding of the concept of neighbourliness. The passage for the following week, set in the house of Martha and Mary, gave valuable insight into the concept of loving God with all one's resources. This became translated into listening to Jesus the Prophet, the one who speaks the Word of God on a singular and unique journey to Jerusalem. It was Mary who sat at the feet of Jesus as he spoke, while Martha remained preoccupied with the less than totally necessary serving at table. It was Mary who showed the greater appreciation of love of God. Today's passage adds another layer of understanding to the love and service of God in the teaching on prayer given by Jesus.

A characteristic of the gospel of Luke is that Jesus is found at prayer at significant moments. We have experienced examples of this at his baptism, at the call of the Twelve and the Transfiguration. Now, there appears to be no specific reason for Jesus' prayer. He is doing what he evidently had adopted as customary practice. His prayer here is private. He is not taking part in communal prayer with his disciples, but they are present and witness him at prayer, and this gives rise to their request: "Lord, teach us to pray, just as John taught his disciples" (Luke 11:1). The request was a reasonable one for disciples to make of their masters. It was accepted practice that rabbis would instruct their disciples in the art of prayer, and disciples might well choose rabbis on the basis of their teaching on prayer as well as of their teaching on the Law. John the Baptist had clearly given such instruction to his own disciples (remember that at least according to the tradition of St. John's gospel that at least some of Jesus' disciples had originally chosen John the Baptist as their master – c.f. John 1:35-37). Their request in Luke 11 gives rise to Luke's version of the Lord's Prayer. Three versions of this prayer are to be found in ancient documents – Luke's version; Matthew's longer version, and a final version in the Didache, which follows Matthew's very closely, but which adds the doxology, 'For Yours is the power and the glory for ever and ever. Amen' (Didache 8:10). This is followed by the instruction to pray these words three times every day. Luke's version is the shortest, and according to most commentators, probably the original. It consists of five statements (as opposed to Matthew's seven), and these statements have been described as a summary of this gospel's major themes. They are:

- <u>Father, may your name be holy</u>. This simple statement, which lacks the Matthean qualification that the Father is 'in heaven', means that from the outset the prayer that Jesus urges his followers to use is very similar to his own prayer (c.f. Luke 10:21). The statement recognises God's absolute difference from everything that is created.

- <u>May your kingdom come</u>. A prayer for God's reign to be effective in the world of humans. Luke does not add Matthew's additional qualification 'as it is in heaven'; here it is merely assumed.

- <u>Give us the bread we need</u>. This is the most difficult part of the prayer to render accurately. The difficulty lies in the meaning of the Greek word *epiousion*, which is not found anywhere else in Greek literature, so experts have had to try to deduce what it might mean. There are three most likely meanings: 1) 'daily' bread, 2) 'future' bread' or 3) 'necessary' bread. The third of these is possibly the most likely of all. Relating back to the Martha and Mary narrative, there is only one thing that is really necessary – expressed perhaps in this clause?

- <u>Forgive us our sins</u>. Luke uses the word for 'sins' (*hamartias*) in the first part; an expression retained for human transgressions, but he then goes on to link this to the human practice of releasing others from their 'debts' (*opheilonti* – lit. what is owing) to us.

Does this pave the way for the threefold example of comparing a parent's limited response to a child's request to God's response to human needs following the prayer? If we can release others from the debt of what they owe us, we can ask God to release us from the debt of our sins.

- <u>Do not lead us into testing</u>. Testing is a recurring theme in this gospel. Jesus was put to the test (*peirasmos*) in 4:1-13, and in 10:25-28, the lawyer puts Jesus to the test. The theme will recur at several points in the gospel narrative, and Jesus will frequently encourage disciples to pray not to be put to the test.

The prayer itself is followed by some lessons on prayer. The first is the parable of a friend who calls in the middle of the might to request food for unexpected guests who have just arrived. Even humans will respond to the basic law of hospitality and its obligations – out of persistence if not out of friendship! How much more then can God be relied upon to grant what is necessary? The man who appears at his neighbour's door and begs is 'shameless' in his action; another way to put this is to say that he is so confident that his wish will be granted that he can think of no reason why he should not make his request. The confidence of the one praying to God should be equally shameless. Thus, you may ask, search, or knock (just as the man in the very graphic parable has done) and a response will always be made. It is as if these three terms are simply other was of describing prayer – asking, searching, or knocking at the door. The one who trusts in God should never doubt that the response will be to the good of the one asking. Jesus uses a typically Semitic form of argument here, which goes from the small argument to the large (an argument known as *qal wehomer*): if parents, faulted and sinful as they may be, know how to give what is good to their children how much more can God be relied upon to give the Holy Spirit to those who ask him: no parent would trick a child by giving a stone that resembled bread, when the latter was sought, or a harmful snake instead of the requested fish, or indeed a dangerous scorpion which when curled up resembles a sought-for egg! In this light, persistent prayer is the expression of endless confidence in God to provide what is good and not harmful to his children, rather than a persistent trying to win God over, and to wear down God's apparent resistance. Prayer is never about a battle of wills, in which we try to change God's mind!

CHAPTER 8

The Jerusalem-bound Prophet challenges those he meets on the Journey

Sundays 18 - 26, Year C

Introduction:

As we saw at the very beginning of the previous chapter of these notes, the 'turning point' in the gospel of Luke occurs at 9:51 (Sunday 13, Year C). This is when Jesus set his face resolutely toward Jerusalem, since the time was drawing near for him to be taken up into heaven. It is the moment on which Jesus' fate turns, because it is the moment in which he embraces his destiny. This decision has several consequences. First, it means Jesus will leave the region of Galilee, never to return (at least as far as this gospel is concerned). Second, it means that Jesus will from now on be totally focussed on achieving his destiny. In Luke 12:49-53 (Sunday 20, Year C) Jesus says "There is a baptism I must still receive, and how great is my distress till it is over". This baptism (literally, this 'immersion') is his total preoccupation with his destiny, a destiny which he understood before he made the fateful decision to head for Jerusalem, which is that the Son of Man must "suffer grievously, to be rejected by the elders and chief priests and scribes and to be put to death, and to be raised up on the third day" (9:22). Third, this destiny is one which is somehow to be shared by any would-be disciple; "If anyone wants to be a follower of mine, let him renounce himself and take up his cross every day and follow me" (9:23). Fourth, the call to discipleship, or at least its acting out on the journey that Jesus is about to embark on, will not admit of any delay, higher priority or alternative agenda on the part of disciples is so uncompromising in its insistence that it requires as much commitment from disciples as it requires of Jesus himself. All of these features have been explored in the recent Sundays of Ordinary time this year; a very intense and concentrated series of gospel passages which leave us in no doubt as to the nature of Jesus' mission, and of the level of response expected of disciples. Then we can add to this the Transfiguration in 9:28-36

(2nd Sunday of Lent, Year C) in which the transformed Jesus discusses with Moses and Elijah his *exodos*, his passing which he was to accomplish in Jerusalem. The company of Moses and Elijah casts Jesus in the light of Prophet; the heavenly voice which identifies Jesus, "This is my Son, the Chosen One. Listen to him" (9:35). The command to 'Listen' to Jesus confirms this; Jesus is portrayed by Luke as the prophet promised by Moses; one like Moses himself, one from among themselves, to whom the children of Israel were to listen. (Deuteronomy 18:15.18).

It is not surprising, therefore, that Jesus spends much of his journey as the Prophet going to fulfil his destiny in teaching. Often his disciples are his audience, occasionally those gathered at dinner parties organised by one or more Pharisees, and sometimes the audience consists of the crowds who gather around him and grow ever larger. In such circumstances, as we will discover in the first example we encounter in this series, his teaching is prompted by a comment or a question from the crowd. Always, the content of the teaching can in some way be related back to that fateful decision to embrace his destiny that Jesus makes in Lk 9:51, and to its consequences for his disciples. Hence, in the passages we will consider in this series of notes, there will be a continual return to the theme of the correct use of material possessions and of the need to give alms. This should not be surprising, because the disciple is required to renounce self and take up the cross every day. This must be more than a theoretical principle: it has to take root in the reality of how to live in the material world.

Sunday 18, Year C. Luke 12:13-21
Questions to Ponder

☐ Why might the anonymous man from the crowd think that Jesus would be a suitable person to solve his inheritance dispute with his brother? What does his request suggest of his understanding of Jesus' mission?

☐ Why should avarice or greed be so contrary to the demands of Jesus' prophetic teaching?

☐ Where is the rich man in this parable at fault in making provision for his future?

The first person to make an appearance in this passage is an anonymous man who shouts out from the crowd, "Master, tell my brother to give me a share of our inheritance". This is the second time in the journey narrative that Jesus has been asked to intervene in a family dispute. The first time was by Martha against her sister Mary when Jesus visiting the two of them in their home early on in his journey (10:38-42; Sunday 16 Year C). In this case, Jesus is instantly dismissive of the very suggestion that he become involved. He has no intention of being judge or arbitrator in a question of claims, and challenges the man to identify the source of his assumption that Jesus could have been so appointed. Rather abruptly, the conversation with the man from the crowd is brought to an end. The brief episode does however allow Jesus to turn his attention to some serious teaching for those around him; presumably it is the crowd that he addresses. Having refused a legal role as judge or arbitrator, Jesus' actions remind us that his is the role of Prophet. He warns those who make up his audience to be on their guard against any kind of greed, since one's life cannot ever be made more secure by what one possesses, even if the person's possessions are considerable. This is a subject which will tend to dominate many of the gospel passages of the next nine or so weeks: crowds and disciples alike will be challenged to consider the cost of discipleship. Later, Jesus will compare the considerable costs of discipleship with the costs incurred by a man considering building a tower, and having to work out in detail whether or not he can afford to do so. If the cost of the tower is beyond him, the man will look foolish if he begins the task and has to leave it incomplete, much to his embarrassment and the comments of his neighbours! He also makes the comparison between a reasoned approach to discipleship and a king who is on the verge of going to war with another king. A serious calculation of his army's military capabilities is necessary before he can decide whether or not to go to war. If he is uncertain as to whether he can defeat his enemy, he had better pursue other means of resolving the dispute! This parable has of course very little to do with building projects and preparations for war – and it certainly does not advocate a military solution to diplomatic problems. Like all parables, Jesus used these as teaching aids – in this case, aids to prompting would be disciples to decide whether they can in fact make the necessary commitment. This is not the first time we have meth the question of the challenges of discipleship. As early as chapter 5, Peter (wrongly) considered he was excluded from discipleship because he saw himself as sinful because he had questioned Jesus' instruction to him to go back out to sea and cast the nets in the lake again after a particularly unsuccessful night! Peter had not realised that his recognition of his sinfulness was in fact an important opening o to his role as a disciple: only those who recognise they are sinful can realise the need to follow the master! Much later, when Jesus sets his face resolutely toward Jerusalem and begins the journey to that city which will end in his death and resurrection, he dismisses in almost cursory fashion three would-be disciples who appear to be eager to follow him, but who either have not through the commitment ("I will follow you wherever you go….foxes have holes…but the Son of Man has nowhere to lay his head"), or who will follow, but with qualifications.

In the episode we are considering today, Jesus prefaces his two parables on the cost of discipleship with a warning against avarice (greed) of any kind. If it is not immediately clear why avarice is a block to discipleship, then the uncompromising nature of the call to discipleship should make this clear: greed is the symbol of all that prevents a person making that commitment, because greed, avarice of any kind always involves the retention of something which should be given up for the sake of the kingdom. This will be a recurring theme in the remainder of the narrative of Jesus' journey to Jerusalem. Greed will be the motive which causes the separation of the Prodigal Son from his family, and will arguably also be the stumbling block in the relationship between the elder son and his father; an incompetent and fraudulent steward faced with dismissal is forced to consider what is truly important to him, and the greed of a rich man causes him to end up in eternal torment when the poor man who lay at his door is called to the bosom of Abraham. These passages, and particularly the last one cited here, are like commentaries on the first of the combined beatitudes and woes of the Sermon on the Plain; 'Blessed ('happy' in the Jerusalem Bible's inaccurate translation) are you poor, yours is the kingdom of God; woe to you who are rich, you are having your reward now'. This is precisely the issue that underlies the warning against greed, because no one's life can be evaluated solely on the value of anything material.

The teaching here concentrates on a parable about a rich man who begins to congratulate himself on his own cleverness and good fortune. He is the first of four characters in parables who think to, or talk to, themselves. The next one will be the prodigal son who 'comes to himself', i.e. wakens up to the reality of his situation. The third will be the unjust steward who debates with himself over what to do about his future. The final example will be the Pharisee at prayer in the parable involving himself and a tax-agent in the

Temple; instead of praying to God, the Pharisee talks to himself! The rich man in this parable is pathologically self-absorbed; his problem is that his harvest has been so good that he does not have enough space for his crops at harvest. Rather than dispose of them to those in need (this of course is not mentioned in the text, but should of course be a possibility when he finally decides what action to take), he decides he needs larger barns. When all his possessions are secure, he will relax and celebrate, happy in the knowledge that he has provided for himself for many years to come. So, he decides to 'eat, drink and have a good time'. This is an allusion to Old Testament texts which use the same phrase, but in somewhat different ways. Ecclesiastes 8:5 suggests that the only pleasure that exists to humans is eating and drinking; Tobit 7:10 suggests that eating and drinking is the epitome of a good evening, advice given to Tobias by Raguel whom Tobias has asked for his daughter Sarah's hand. Raguel, however, after recommending a celebration of eating and drinking does warn that seven times he has tried to find a husband for Sarah, and each time the poor husband died on his wedding night! Eating and drinking are therefore presented as activities of the moment, offering no lasting satisfaction. Isaiah 22:13 caricatures the attitude of those with no thoughts except for the present moment: "Let us eat and drink, for tomorrow we may be dead". Where Jesus' parable about the rich man and his barns makes passing reference to these passages, it is clear that it is to stress the folly of the rich man whose only thought is for present satisfaction from material belongings. This short-sightedness is soon shown in its fullest light; the man's life comes to an abrupt end that night, with the inescapable conclusion that the wealth he was so proud of is now of no use to him whatsoever. There is no suggestion or threat at this stage that the man will be denied eternal reward – that is a topic which will be discussed in the context of another parable, scheduled for Sunday 26 C, the parable of the rich man and Lazarus discussed at the end of this chapter, but the point is made that this particular rich man has been working so hard to amass his own treasure for his own pleasure that he can scarcely have had any time or opportunity to make himself rich in the sight of God!

So, how do we go about doing that? How do we become rich in the sight of God? This passage does not yet supply us with any information on this, but an inescapable conclusion must be that it is linked with Jesus' warning about the avoidance of avarice or greed, or possessiveness of any kind. In Luke's vision of the response to the call to become a disciple of Jesus, a first step must be a detachment from anything that is directed toward self. Greed, therefore, is the blindness to anything which involves anyone or anything other than oneself and the present moment; greed is the inability or the unwillingness to engage with not only the things of the future, but the things of the future which belong to the kingdom of God. This of course is nothing new; discipleship, we have already been told, involves renouncing self and taking up the cross each day. In the coming weeks, we will learn more of precisely how and where this detachment may be achieved.

Sunday 19, Year C. Luke 12:32-48
Questions to Ponder

☐ Why does Jesus insist that there is no need to be afraid? Why should the Father having given disciples the kingdom be reason for putting aside fear?

☐ How can hoarding material possessions be a form of fear?

☐ Why would the master wait on his servants if he finds them awake and ready for him to return, no matter which hour he arrives?

There is a gap of some ten verses between last week's and this week's gospel passages, and yet there is a clear connection between the two episodes. The omitted verses spell out the reasons why Jesus' disciples should not preoccupy themselves with possessions. He says that life is more than food, and the body more than clothing. The birds in the air don't sow seed, and they do not gather harvest or build barns (a clear follow-on from the parable about the man who built himself bigger barns and who got absolutely no use out of them). Anxiety cannot add a single cubit to a person's life, and the flowers in the field do not sow or spin, and yet they have a magnificent appearance that not even Solomon in all his glory could achieve.
At the end of last Sunday's gospel, Jesus concluded his remarks with the summary statement "So it is when a man stores up treasure for himself in place of making himself rich in the sight of God." This is now followed with Jesus turning to his disciples and urging them not to worry about what to eat or what to wear; what is the point of worrying about anything that cannot add to height or length of life! Therefore, people should set their hearts first on God's kingdom; all else will fall into place after that. From here, we arrive at the beginning of today's passage, "There is no need to be afraid, little flock,

for it has pleased your Father to give you the kingdom" (12:32). Notice the tone set here: Jesus calls his disciples 'little flock'; there is a gentleness here which paves the way for the instruction about not being afraid. It is also worth noticing that the kingdom has *already* been given to the disciples by the Father. This reinforces what we have already heard in the beatitudes/woes of Luke 6: "How happy (or better: 'blessed') are you who are poor: yours is the kingdom of heaven…but alas for you who are rich; you are having your consolation now". The statement that it has pleased the Father to give to his little flock the kingdom follows on perfectly from its immediately preceding verses, but then we are brought back to the subject of possessions: since the Father has been pleased to grant the kingdom, disciples should never need to fear disposing of their possessions, and setting their hearts on the true treasure which neither moth nor thief can destroy or steal. If the grass of the field which is destined to be thrown in the furnace is clothed with such care with God, how much more is God likely to look after the needs of those who are his own children? Another recurring theme in this gospel is that God will not fail to provide his children with what they need (as opposed to what they want!). Already in the lesson on prayer beginning with the Lord's prayer which we read a couple of weeks ago (Chapter 7; Sunday 17 C), Jesus had made the point that not even dysfunctional parents would be so cruel as to trick a child who asks for something by providing something that looks like what the child requested, but which turns out to be harmful instead; how much more than can God be relied upon!

So, having insisted that disciples have nothing to fear because the Father has given them the kingdom, the text now moves to a series of short parables, the exhortation in the lectionary gospel passage for this week now turns to readiness. Disciples are to be like servants ready and waiting for their master whenever he arrives, and at any hour even through the night. In a departure from what we might have expected, Jesus adds that if the master finds such ready servants on his return, it is he who will sit them down at table and serve them! This is best understood in the light of a later statement of Jesus at the Last Supper, when he declared "here am I among you as one who serves" (22:27). If we bear in mind that in the ancient world, it was unthinkable that a servant or slave would do anything other than serve the master; and under no circumstances could the master be made to wait on the slave! In this gospel, authority is frequently expressed in the language of table service: we might even be inclined to see in the English language term *'waiting* at table' a further illustration of the force of this parable. Another parable follows: the householder would not be caught unawares if he knew at what time the burglar was going to arrive! These two parables on the subject of readiness can also be traced back to Jesus' urging that disciples sell their possessions and focus on real treasures: those who are preoccupied with material things are distracted by them from the things which really matter, that is, the things pertaining to the kingdom of heaven; they are therefore much more prone to being caught out by the return of the Son of Man.

Peter asks a question: is this teaching directed only to disciples, or does it apply to everyone? Rather than answer directly, Jesus uses yet another parable. He returns to the theme of the household, but this time focuses on the image of the one put in charge of the household and the other servants (slaves is probably a better term). The *oikonomous*, the household manager would most probably also have been a slave, but one charged with responsibility for both the house and those who worked in it. Any such person who knows exactly what his master desires, but abuses his position in his master's absence by maltreating and beating the other slaves will, when caught, be given a very severe punishment: literally, he will be 'cut in two'. This is a figure of speech. It suggests that the person who has been given the advantage of knowing the master's wishes, but who lives a life of double standard by ignoring his master, will be given (figuratively speaking) a 'double existence' – cut in half! Again, what is stressed is that those to whom the kingdom has been given, and to whom some measure of authority has been given, are expected to exercise this in the service of others.

It is worth our while to return to the beginning of this passage, with its exhortation to dispose of possessions. Now it seems that those who fail to do so run a much higher risk of being distracted from the things of the kingdom which it has pleased the father to give the Jesus' little flock. We have perhaps the first motive behind Jesus' insistence on detachment from material things; there will be other insights given into this topic in the weeks ahead.

Sunday 20 C. Luke 12:48-53.

Questions to Ponder

☐ Why does Jesus refer to a baptism he has to undergo at this stage in his ministry when we was baptised at its inauguration?

☐ How can Jesus, who came to bring good news to the poor, also be the cause – or at least the occasion – of conflict?

☐   What is the real nature of Jesus' distress until his baptism is over? Is distress a useful word to describe his meaning?

Jesus' words are again addressed to the crowd, and he has no use for the language of compromise! He he has come to bring fire to the earth, and he wishes it was burning already. He is to receive a baptism, and how great is his distress until it is over. There are strange features to these stark utterances, and it is not immediately clear what Jesus means by them. For example, his ministry began with baptism, so how or why should he undergo it again? Fire has connotations of divine judgement: is this what he is now suggesting is imminent? John the Baptist went through the whole Jordan district, proclaiming a baptism of repentance for the forgiveness of sins (Luke 3:3). He was the one about whom 2nd Isaiah had written; a voice which cried out in the wilderness, "prepare a way for the Lord". Jesus was baptised by John, but why? We need some explanation if, a) this was directed to the forgiveness of sins and b) he now refers to another baptism.

We considered some of these points when we ended the Christmas season with the Feast of the Baptism of the Lord (c.f. Chapter 1. Advent and Christmas). We noted then that the word 'baptism' means 'immersion'. John was Isaiah's voice in the wilderness, preparing a way for the Lord, so that all should see the salvation of God. The Baptiser preaches repentance, for forgiveness of sins, but repentance and forgiveness of sins are not the same thing. New Testament repentance, *metanoia*, means a change of mind. If it is translated as change of heart, it is only in the sense of Hebrew usage where the heart is the organ responsible for thinking – precisely what today, following the model used by the ancient Greeks, we attribute to the mind. A sign of repentance that was accompanied by the complete immersion in water was therefore a powerful sign denoting that complete change of mind/heart was taking place. Total immersion (baptism) denotes total dedication. John, therefore, invites those who would repent to be baptised, or immersed, in the very concept that immersion represents. At the outset of his ministry, Jesus too can make this immersion as a symbol of whole-hearted acceptance of his fate. In baptism, Jesus repents in the sense that he sets his will totally toward obedience to that of his Father, who calls him 'Beloved Son', on whom rests God's favour.

In Luke 9:51, Jesus set his face resolutely toward Jerusalem. Here, the same dedication is implied, because he resolves to go where death will follow: it is fitting for the Prophet to die here. So, Baptism is an appropriate metaphor: Jesus has now 'steeped' himself in his destiny, a destiny in which he is now totally 'immersed'. The Jerusalem Bible says he is distressed until it is accomplished; perhaps determined, preoccupied or even obsessed would be better as the translation of *synekein* (as in Acts 18:5, where Paul is preoccupied/obsessed with preaching the gospel). This reading would also fit better with v. 49, which we will soon consider.

The other image, fire, also has roots in John the Baptist. Unlike baptism however, references to fire can be found throughout the Old Testament. The angel Gabriel said of John before his birth, "he will be filled with the Holy Spirit, and will bring back many sons of Israel to their God. With the spirit and power of Elijah, he will turn the hearts of fathers towards their children" (Luke 1:16-17). In Luke 9:54, we met allusions to Elijah and fire (1 Kings 18:38; 2 Kings 1:12). John foretold one who would come after him, baptising with the Holy Spirit and fire (Luke 3:16); in 3:17 John continues, "he will gather wheat into his barn; but chaff he will burn in a fire that never goes out". Acts also connects the Holy Spirit and Fire. At Pentecost, "something appeared to them that seemed like tongues of fire; these separated and came to rest on the head of each of them. They were all filled with the Holy Spirit" (Acts 2:3-4). In the other synoptic gospels, fire is a metaphor for judgment and divine retribution (c.f. Matthew 13:40, 18:8, 25:41). So, Jesus can draw on a strong tradition of fire as the instrument of divine judgement. He has come to bring fire on earth (as John had predicted), and wishes it were blazing already (because he is already immersed in a destiny yet to be fully accomplished, and which will only be accomplished in his death). John's ministry, announced by the angel of the Lord to Zechariah in the Temple, would be filled with the Holy Spirit, and with the spirit and power of Elijah about him, John would bring the hearts of children toward their fathers (c.f. Malachi 3:23-24).

Here however lies the problem. Jesus has apparently been using the image of fire in the Elijah/John tradition, but he is now about to depart from this, because he now predicts division rather than peace - the exact opposite of what John was to achieve. How, then, are we to resolve the contradictions that are emerging here? Jesus claims that anyone supposing he has come to bring peace is mistaken; he has come to bring division. Within a household of five, three will be divided against two, two against three; division will exist within families. At his birth however, Jesus was hailed as the one to bring peace on earth (2:14), and he will again be hailed as bringer of peace when he enters Jerusalem (19:38). Even in these opening chapters, though, Luke's gospel contains statements that counter the 'bringer of peace' theme. Soon after Jesus' birth, Simeon prophesied that this child would be a sign for the fall and the rise of many in Israel, 'destined to be a sign that is rejected, so that the secret thoughts of many may be laid bare' (Luke 2:34-35). This train of thought also has its origins in the Old Testament. Micah had bemoaned the fact that: "the devout have vanished from the land. For son insults father, daughter defies mother, daughter-in-law defies mother-in-law; a man's enemies are those of his own household" (Micah 7:2. 6).

All of this reminds us that much is paradoxical in the person and the ministry of Jesus. The gospels demonstrate that no single title can adequately sum up Jesus and his mission (c.f. Mark 8:27-33); likewise, no simple assessment of his ministry is possible. Certainly, he has come as the bringer of peace. He is not exactly the fiery reformer that the Baptist had foretold (Luke 3:16-17), but he will disturb any idea that seeks to equate peace with complacency. Ironically, Luke locates the birth of Jesus firmly within the reign of the Roman emperor Augustus, in an age famed for its peace. When Jesus proclaimed his peaceful message of Good News in the synagogue at Nazareth, both he and the message were rejected. The problem is: what the world considers to be peace tends to be at odds with what Jesus and his disciples proclaim as peace; Jesus' peace is a concept that the world will not accept. Inevitably the result is division, within households and families, a division that is rooted deep within the baptism that Jesus is determined to accomplish, that he is preoccupied with bringing about.

Sunday 21, Year C. Luke 13:22-30

Questions to ponder

☐　　What assumptions are we likely to make about our own right to salvation?

☐　　Do we consider that there is an elite group of those who merit entry to the kingdom of heaven more than others? Or do we consider there are those who are less deserving of the kingdom? Is there a difference between these two views?

☐　　Jesus presents the image of the need to shove through the way to entry at a narrow door. Does he envisage that this pushing might be to the detriment of other people?

As the Journey Narrative progresses, the evangelist reminds us again that Jesus and his companions are travelling. This is precisely what happens at the very start of today's passage, signalled with the straightforward comment, "Through towns and villages he went teaching, making his way to Jerusalem" (13:22). In a few words, we have a description of the journey (going through towns and villages), the activity (teaching; the Prophet at work) and the final purpose of the entire exercise (making his way to Jerusalem and to death and resurrection). So, our attention is brought to focus once more on the journey of the Prophet who goes to fulfil his destiny. Once more, someone from the crowd sets the scene for the forthcoming narrative. Someone said, "Sir, will there be only a few saved?" (13:23). There are a couple of points to note about the question and about the answer that Jesus gives. Like so many other English translations, the Jerusalem Bible sets the question as referring to the future, and yet a literal translation would take into account the Greek use of the present tense, which would suggest the question is rather "are there only a few being saved?" This would place the concept of being saved firmly within the scope of the ministry that Jesus is currently exercising. Either interpretation of the phrase – present or future - is possible. We will meet at least one other example of this use of the present tense in the story of Zacchaeus, Luke 19:8. Whether or not the question refers to the present or to the future, Jesus' response does not really answer the man's question. No indication is given as to numbers who are being/will be saved. Instead, the exhortation to listeners is to make a great effort to ensure that they are not excluded from salvation.

The question itself is perhaps best understood against the background of a debate on the subject which would have been prevalent in 1st Century Palestine. The issue concerned the relationship between what had been historical Judaism and the concept of the People of God. The question was: could a simple equation still be made between the Judaism which was historically focussed on the territory of ancient Israel when there were now so many people professing to be Jewish who were no longer resident in the former Promised Land? For the large number of Jews who belonged to the Diaspora, scattered throughout the nations surrounding the Mediterranean, the hope was that all Jewish people were included within the Chosen People of God. To the Essenes at Qumran, the authors of what we know today as the Dead Sea Scrolls, and other similar sectarian groups the Elect, the Chosen People consisted in a much smaller and highly exclusive remnant who had kept themselves pure according to the traditions of Israel. According to that narrow view, relatively speaking only a very small number would be saved. It would appear that such a view was not alien to the thinking of the Pharisees either. So, it is not terribly surprising that a question on the subject should be fired in Jesus' direction, especially given the insistence on repentance not only from the Prophet Jesus, but from John the Baptist who prepared the way before him with the proclamation of a baptism for repentance and the forgiveness of sins (3:3). Someone was bound to ask what the chances would be of a universally successful outcome to repentance!

The answer that Jesus gives does not of course address the numbers issue, but it does present a personal challenge to any individual who listens to his preaching. Each person is to make an effort for the sake of the kingdom if he or she is serious about entry. The phrase that Luke attributes to Jesus here involves 'struggle'; the word is from the same root as the 'struggle' or *agonia* that Jesus will later undergo on the Mount of Olives (Luke omits any reference to Gethsemane) before his arrest. *Agonia* is the supreme effort expended by wrestlers and similar athletes in their contests: the word has little similarity in meaning to the English word 'agony'. The *agonia* of any person desiring to be saved is an individual and personal struggle; it relates to the level of personal commitment that any one person will make to the teaching of Jesus the Prophet. The struggle is likened to squeezing and pushing in order to gain entry through a narrow door. Already, on Sunday 17C we heard the exhortation to knock, so that the door may be opened. Now, there is the warning that once the master (*kurie*- 'master' or 'Lord') has locked the door, there will be no possibility of entry, and at that point knocking will be futile. There is some subtlety in Luke's handling of the excuses offered by those outside: they claim to have had the master (Lord) teaching in their streets, and they have dined in his company! Notice that the only association the protesters can claim with the master is that they have been in physical proximity to him while he was teaching; but this is very different from them having engaged in any way with his teaching. There are instances in this gospel of Jesus dining with Pharisees by invitation, but there is certainly no 'meeting of minds' on these occasions. Likewise, as we shall see on Sunday 24C, the Pharisees and Scribes were complaining that Jesus habitually allowed tax-agents and sinners to seek out his company *because they wanted to hear him*, and that he customarily dined with them. It cannot be accidental that Luke homes in on this reality concerning those who would present only weak claims in their attempt to gain entry through the narrow door. The master's reply: "I do not know where you come from" is in effect a denial of any connection he may have had with those trying to gain entry once the door is locked, and makes clear that the master has nothing on common with these people who have in no way engaged with him as he exercised his teaching and prophetic ministry. As a result, they will find themselves locked outside where there will be 'weeping and grinding of teeth'. If, as was suggested earlier, the initial question from the anonymous man reflected a desire for people to know who constituted the Chosen People, we find that Jesus now addresses that very question: those who have not made the effort to enter by the narrow door, i.e. who have not responded with energy to the teaching of the Prophet will not only find themselves excluded, but they will find others, gathered from the north, south, east and west, that is from the ends of the earth, who will take their places along with Abraham, Isaac and Jacob; those pre-eminent figures of the Chosen People. Meanwhile, those who had assumed they had automatic right to entry to the kingdom will be reduced to watching the gathering from outside, unable to participate in the feast, and their places taken by none other than the outcasts and the marginalised who *did* respond to the teaching of the prophets in their streets, and who *did* seek his company at table. No wonder there will be weeping and gnashing of teeth: how devastating to find that an assumed right to entry was precisely that: and to realise too late that this was an assumption which was not backed up with adequate industry to ensure entry!

Sunday 22, Year C. Luke 14:1. 7-14

Questions to ponder

☐   We form the impression that the social conventions of the time were for Jesus a barrier to the gospel. What social conventions of today might run counter to the gospel?

☐   What is the equivalent today of vying for the best seats at dinner parties?

☐   Who are the marginalised of today who according to the dictates of this gospel deserve preferential consideration. What must we do about this if we are serious about implementing the gospel?

☐   The poor, crippled, lame and blind were considered beyond redemption in their own time. Can you identify any individual or class of people that you treat as being beyond redemption?

Following hard on the heels of last Sunday's exhortation to squeeze through the narrow door to gain entry to the kingdom of heaven, and the warning that insisting on being present when the Master taught, or being present at the same meal as him would not be enough to gain entry, we have a gospel episode in which Jesus actually dines with Pharisees! Or rather, he dines in the house of a leading Pharisee. A literal translation would be that Jesus went to dine at the house of one of the rulers (*archonton*) of the Pharisees. This is the only time in the New Testament the expression is used of a Pharisee, although Luke uses it to describe Zacchaeus and of the chief priests (plural) and the High Priest (singular). Jesus is being watched closely, and obviously in a way which is hostile in intent; it is also the Sabbath, so we have an explosive mix at dinner: Jesus, the Pharisees and the Sabbath. There's bound to be trouble before long!

The text jumps from verse 1 to verse 7, omitting the story of a cure by Jesus on the Sabbath, and moves on to a reflection on Jesus' own observations of what is going on at the meal: Jesus is not the only one being watched! Jesus has been observing how the guests had been choosing the places of honour (*prōtoklisias* literally, the first reclining positions). So Jesus 'speaks to them parabolically'. What follows is not a parable, but is an example of how Jesus sometimes teaches by giving examples of ideas to be taken together ('parable' means something like 'thrown together'). His first lesson is of a very practical nature, and is one which would have been acceptable according to the social norms of Greek culture and custom. He tells his fellow guests that they should begin by picking less rather than more important places for themselves at table, because if they go for the most prominent positions, they run the risk of being displaced to make room for a more distinguished guest, and then they will have to face the social embarrassment of being relegated to a humbler place. Therefore, the sensible thing to do is to take a humble place to begin with. Who knows, anyone doing so may well be asked to move to a more exalted position, because anyone who humbles himself will be exalted, but those who exalt themselves are sure to be humbled. Greek social conventions were every much based on status: it was important to be recognised, to have one's social standing acknowledged, but at all costs, one should avoid being humiliated on public occasions and formal dinners. Jesus' ideas go well beyond issues of social status, however. His words echo the sentiments we have already encountered in this gospel. In the Magnificat, Mary sings that the Lord "has pulled down princes from their thrones and exalted the lowly" (1:52); the beatitudes and woes in chapter 6 refer to many examples of the great reversal of fortunes which is a hallmark of this gospel. Jesus does not comment on social conventions: he speaks prophetically of the new order which will find its highest expression in the fullness of the kingdom of God, and which the Prophet provides more and more insights into as his journey to Jerusalem progresses.

Not only is Jesus unconcerned about social convention; in his very next teaching, he challenges those conventions by standing on its head one of the under-riding principles of these conventions. There was a great sense of reciprocity in social gatherings: people were inclined to invites guests in order to receive a return invitation; therefore, invitations were by and large confined to family, immediate and extended and to friends or rich neighbours. So if there was no real prospect of being invited to an event above one's social standing, neither was there any possibility of someone of lower social status being invited to anyone's dinner. Jesus advocates a radical departure from the norm in this regard. Instead of issuing invitations in the expectation of a return of the compliment, hosts should invite the poor, the crippled, the lame and the blind; the fact that they will be unable to repay the compliment of returning the invitation means that those who invited them in the first place will be repaid when the virtuous rise again. Once again we have a reference to the proper order of things existing not in this world, but in the world to come, where true values will be apparent.

The categories Jesus singles out for invitation are not chosen at random, and they are not of his invention. As far back as his inaugural address in the Nazareth Synagogue, Jesus had assumed the prophetic role in fulfilment of Isaiah in which he would "bring the good news to the poor, to proclaim liberty to captives and to the blind new sight, to set the downtrodden free, to proclaim the Lord's year of favour" (4:18-19). The poor, crippled, lame and blind were present when Jesus instructed John's disciples who had been sent by John to ask Jesus if he was the awaited one, or had they still to wait for another. Jesus cites his record so far. He has performed miracles of healing, here the blind receive their sight, the lame walk, lepers are cleansed, and the deaf hear, the dead are raised up, the poor have good news preached to them.

He adds that blessed are those who do not find this aspect of his ministry an obstacle – literally, a *scandalon*, a stumbling-block). These four groups of people listed by Jesus – the poor, the crippled, the lame and the blind were frequently those who were marginalized, even in the official expressions of religion; for example, according to Leviticus 21:17-21, the lame, the blind and the crippled were to be excluded from the priesthood. The poor is a generic term for all who are marginalised. The Essenes at Qumran extended their marginalisation even further: those disqualified from the priesthood on the grounds of disability were considered to be excluded from fighting in the great eschatological battle of the Holy War at the end of all things, and as a consequence would not be permitted to join the feast which would take place after the successful conclusion of the war. So, in his words it is once again those who are considered least in the eyes of the world who are to be singled out for preferential consideration in the ministry of Jesus; once again, the humble are to be exalted. Perhaps what is particularly noteworthy in this expression is that although material reward may be misplaced or even totally lacking in this world, on the world to come, when the dead rise again, proper reward, and total repayment will be made. This was a view not always to the fore in Jewish thought. As we learn from the gospels, the Pharisees professed a belief in a risen life after death; the Sadducees professed no such belief. Since the Sadducees party by and large consisted of the ruling classes of the Jewish religious system –the Chief Priests and the Elders, Jesus is doing himself no favours as he makes these points on his journey toward Jerusalem!

Sunday 23, Year C. Luke 14:25-33

Questions to ponder

☐　　　How could disciples possibly hate family and at the same time keep Jesus' commandment to love?

☐　　　How then could a lesser love for family etc. amount to renouncing self and taking up the cross?

☐　　　What is the relationship between the two parables of the tower builder and the king going to war, and discipleship that involves the renunciation of possessions?

Once again, Luke opens a passage with a reminder that Jesus is 'on his way'. The destination is not mentioned, but readers of the lectionary selection of

Sunday gospel passages will by now easily recall that it is Jerusalem. Great crowds accompany Jesus – another feature of Luke's description of Jesus' journey is the ever growing crowd, which will follow him all the way to Jerusalem – and as before, the introductory reminder about the journey makes way for further teaching from Jesus. In this example, Jesus' teaching looks both back and forward. It looks back, because it recalls Jesus' earlier instructions on the nature of discipleship: by both renouncing self and taking up the cross and by recognising the necessity of giving up possessions, and at the same time, it looks forward, because we have here additional ingredients which give further insight into why both of these conditions are inseparable from the notion of discipleship.

First, there is a reminder of the cross and renunciation of self. The latter is now extended to renunciation of family ties. Perhaps surprisingly Luke, who occasionally softens harsh Semitic phrases, chooses to retain the difficult phrase about anyone coming to Jesus without "hating his father, mother, wife, children" etc. Matthew opts for a softer version and demands that disciples 'love Jesus more' than family etc. Languages like Hebrew and Aramaic were limited in the way they could express preferences, and so to exercise a preference for one person over another is to love one and hate the other! Another feature of Semitic thinking and expression has to be taken into account here as well. For the most part, when Hebrew scripture (because of the nature of the Hebrew/Aramaic language) refers to love, it equates love with action rather than feeling. This has great significance for the meaning of what Jesus is actually saying in this passage. The question is not about whether hatred as an emotion is a necessary feature of Christian discipleship, but it is about the order of priority for giving service to Jesus relative to giving service to other human beings. In other words, what Jesus is demanding from disciples is that allegiance to him must take priority over allegiance to any relative, family member, and even to one's own life. Renunciation is not about giving up something (as in Lent, for example), but about placing one's own life lower in priority than the life of others, or in the case of discipleship, in the case of Jesus' life. In last week's gospel, we were reminded of the nature of Jesus' ministry as one of service to others, frequently expressed in this gospel by the example of table service, and of course taking on its ultimate expression in his death for the sake of humanity. If Jesus has placed greater value on the lives of sinful humans than he has on his own life (hence, as Paul says, Christ died for us while we were still sinners (Romans 6:8)), then it is to be expected that disciples will make a similar gesture in their response to Christ; hence they will renounce self, and all human relationships, in preference for Christ himself. It does not mean that they *think* any less of family, or any other humans who are close to them. Renunciation of self does not mean a denial of affection; it means a commitment to that practical love which means that Jesus has a higher call on our actions than even those close to us in affection can command. This explains also why discipleship requires us taking up the cross, 'on a daily basis' as Luke would have it – clearly not a physical possibility. If any disciple commits to Christ to the extent that he indicates, it means that total commitment to him that he made to his Father and to us by going to the cross , a commitment which can be expressed metaphorically in our taking up the cross each day. It is closely related to the concept of baptism which speaks of, which is not a baptism in water, but is a total commitment to his mission as the prophet who will be taken up into heaven in Jerusalem, i.e. at his crucifixion. This kind of baptism is the commitment, the immersion in discipleship, which Jesus is asking for here. This kind of commitment might also shed some light on Jesus' challenging statement to a would-be disciple at the beginning of his journey to Jerusalem, "leave the dead to bury their dead" (9:60).

Jesus reinforces his point with two mini parables, found only in Luke, inviting reflection on whether would-be disciples have understood both the personal cost involved in discipleship, and also whether they consider that they are able to pay that cost. The first mini parable is about a man who intends to build a tower. Before he begins the work, he must make two calculations. The first is to work out the cost, and the second is whether he is both able and willing to pay it. The implication is clear: how committed to the project is the would-be tower builder? If he begins the wok without realising the commitment required, and as a result begins what he cannot or will not finish, he runs the risk of ridicule from all who can see that his project has no realistic hope of completion. Alternatively a king going out to war against another king has to work out as realistically as possible his chances of winning a battle against the superior forces of his adversary. He has to make a good estimate at his chance of success before he commits his soldiers to a dangerous expedition: if the chances of victory are not great, then perhaps that king would be better advised to sue for peace (literally, ask for the things leading to peace); clearly a much more reasonable course of action!

These are not just theoretical considerations. In a very pointed conclusion to
this particular teaching session, Jesus relates these two parables and the
principles of discipleship that preceded them to those whom he is addressing:
that is, the crowds who have gathered. In his final statement, he relates his
ideas on discipleship to another principle outlined earlier on this journey – no
one can be his disciple without giving up (i.e. renouncing) possessions. We
have another insight here into why possessions are such a big issue for Jesus,
and therefore also for his disciples. We still need to learn more about the
subject, but it seems clear that renunciation of possessions is pretty much the
same as the renunciation of self. We have several strands emerging at work
here: we have had the challenge to renounce self and take the cross, the
challenge (to be returned to) of giving up possessions, and the identification
of the problem of renouncing self. Gradually a picture is building of the core
of discipleship: it is a total reliance on Jesus and his Father to provide what is
necessary for us, and not relying on our own resources – or worse, not trying
to justify ourselves. When Jesus sent out the 72 at the beginning of the
journey narrative, they were to avoid any sense of providing for their own
needs: they would be provided for by God and the hospitality of those whom
they visited. That in itself is a metaphor for true discipleship in Jesus' service.

Sunday 24, Year C. Luke 15:1-32

Questions to ponder

☐   What is the significance of the preamble to this story, outlining the
attitude of the Pharisees and scribes to the company kept by Jesus?

☐   Is the behaviour of the shepherd with the lost sheep and the woman
with the lost coin reasonable – or is their reaction 'over the top'? If so, what
does this tell us about God's attitude to those who have become lost to God?

☐   Is the elder son correct in thinking he knows better than his father how
to respond to the younger son's return?

☐   Do we harbour similar resentments to the forgiving God who might
welcome 'undesirables' back to the fold?

If last Sunday's gospel was unsettling as it related Jesus' words about
prospective disciples being required to hate father, mother, wife, children,
brothers, sisters etc., then there is some welcome assurance in the final tale of

the trio on offer this week where Jesus tells what is probably the finest
parable we have in the four gospels; the one we usually call the 'Prodigal
Son'. In this story, we have the tale of a man who is overjoyed at the return of
a son who has been lost to him, and his attempts to reach out to one who
stayed at home, but who unfortunately may be equally lost to his father.
There is a reassuring lack of hatred for family members from this particular
father!
The three parables in today's passage are again ones through which Jesus
reacts to a situation that has arisen. We have already encountered examples of
this on Sundays 18, 21 and 22, although the circumstances have been
different in each case. This week, we also encounter another of Luke's
techniques: when the subject matter of one passage is set against an echo of
another earlier one. Thus the agenda for today's passage brings back to mind
the gospel of two weeks ago when Jesus dined at the house of a leading
Pharisee, surrounded by guests who presumably included other Pharisees.
The trigger for recalling this episode is Luke's information that now the
Pharisees and scribes were complaining about Jesus' frequent habit including
tax agents and sinners among his dining companions, and that these were
now seeking his company and wanting to hear what he had to say. There are
two issues here: the Pharisees and scribes have become more and more cast
by Luke in the role of people who reject the teaching of Jesus, the Prophet
whom Moses had promised: they object that those they consider unworthy
are trying to have themselves included in the company of Jesus, and that they
seek him out to listen to him. So, Luke informs us that Jesus told this parable
– or more accurately, he tells three parables. Two of these are unique to Luke
(the lost coin and the lost son), and the other, the first in the sequence, is told
with a slightly different emphasis in Luke's version.

It is common for writers to point out the similarities in structure between the
first and second parables; in each case, the owner loses something of value –
the shepherd loses one sheep from his flock of 100, and the woman loses one
coin from her collection of 10. Both people who have experienced the loss go
to extraordinary lengths to find what they have lost: the shepherd leaves
(abandons?) the 99 in the wilderness (desert? – *erēmō*) until he finds it, i.e. he
will not rest until it is found; in Matthew's version, the shepherd searches,
and if he should happen to find it, he will carry it back rejoicing. Only in
Luke's version does the shepherd rejoice with friends and neighbours.

Likewise, the woman with the lost coin (drachma, a Greek coin worth about the same as the Roman *denarius*, and therefore worth about the basic daily wage of the time) from a collection of 10 coins spares no effort to find the missing coin. She lights a lamp on the off chance she will see the glint of the silver coin on the earthen floor of the house; she sweeps out the house on the off chance that she will hear the clink of the coin on the floor. When she finds it, she to gather her friends and neighbours to join with her and celebrate. Notice here the typically Lukan touch in placing together the male shepherd and the female owner of the coins. Both make every possible attempt to find what has been lost; and both not only celebrate the find, but they are irresponsible in their efforts and joy! The shepherd is foolhardy and downright irresponsible in leaving behind 99 sheep unattended in the desert; the woman may well spend more than the value of the coin is celebrating her joyous discovery! Both parables reveal to us the efforts of God to find whatever (or rather, whoever) had become lost, and God's utter delight and desire to share that delight with others when the lost have been rediscovered. The extravagance of these parables indicates that God's desire to search out, find, and bring back who has been lost knows no bounds. These two parables, as already indicated, form a complimentary pair, but the third parable (which is really almost a short story) has, at least initially, a similar structure even though the story is more fully developed, and the loss is of a son to his father. As with the first two parables, something (someone) has been lost to another (son to father). The father gives every indication of having no other interest apart from the return of his son (indicated by the father seeing the younger son while he was still a long way off), and rushes out to him. In his joy, he calls for a celebration on a huge scale because his son who was lost has been found; he was dead and has come back to life. So far, the focus of the stories we have explored is concentrated on the intent of God the Father to seek out and find at all costs whatever and whoever have become lost. There another agenda, however; one which compares the attitude with the Pharisees and the Scribes to the tax agents and sinners who seek Jesus' company and with whom he dines, with the desire of God to welcome back whoever. This third parable takes into account the concerns of those who feel they have legitimate complaints, and challenges the complainers to consider the full range of issues that they have, with perhaps surprising consequences.

The two sons who are depicted in the story are carefully described: we are invited in the telling of the parable to have serious difficulty in accepting the shocking behaviour of the younger son – he makes impatient demands for his share of the inheritance, not even having the decency to wait until his father has died. He loses little time is heading off to a distant land where his money soon disappear through 'dissipation', or foolishness, rather than debauchery as the Jerusalem Bible wrongly translates: the Greek word *diaskorpizōn* will appear again in next week's gospel about the incompetent steward who manages through carelessness to lose all his master's money. It is important to realise this point, because at the end of the story, the elder brother will attribute to his younger sibling's activities which are not provided in the text! Through a mixture of bad judgement and bad fortune the younger son is reduced to destitution; a famine means that he is lucky to find employment looking after pigs – utter degradation to a Jew, which we may suppose the young man to be. His humiliation is so total that he would willingly have eaten the food intended for the pigs, but none was available to him. No Jew could fall lower! We are still not expected to sympathise with him, because he is the same young man who has effectively treated his father as if he were dead already! Now he formulates a plan, and it is a cynical one too. His father's paid servants have all they need to eat, and here he is, starving. He will return and plead to his father, admitting his sin and asking for a place as a servant. This may sound impressive, but he is really ruling out a family relationship, because unlike family and even slaves, the paid servant (*misthios*) was the most casual of workers. Each was given a fixed wage for doing a fixed amount of work. Servants were under no further obligation to masters, and vice versa. We rightly think the idea of slavery to be utterly reprehensible, but in the ancient world, slavery was a fact of life. The reality was that slaves who were the property of owners, but the owner had obligations to feed and care for them. Odd as it may seem to us, there was some kind of relationship and even stability with the system. A slave (*doulos*) could even have a position of responsibility. The young man plans to return home, but still only with an eye open as to what might be in it for him. His father has a different idea, though. His son will be neither slave nor paid servant. While the young man is a long way off, he rushes out to meet him. He barely even hears the carefully constructed story; instead he orders a sumptuous feast by way of celebration, because his son was lost and is now found, was dead, and has come back to life. The connotations of the subsequent death and resurrection of Jesus himself cannot be lost here. Does the younger son return permanently to the family home? Is he a fully repentant character? We don't know. What we do know, however, is that he does respond to his father's overtures – as do the tax agents and sinners to whom, the Pharisees and scribes have been objecting.

The story is still not over, however. While the celebration is getting underway, we meet the second, elder son for the first time. He has been out working in the fields and when hears the noise, he asks what is going on. He is told that his father has killed the fatted calf in celebration, because he has got the other brother back safe and sound. The elder brother refuses to go in and join the celebration, so the father comes out to meet him too, to plead with him to welcome back his brother. This is where we learn of the frustration that has been building up for a long time in the elder brother, and his own alienation from his father emerges very strongly. He feels he has 'slaved' for his father all these years, and never once disobeyed his orders (literally, disobeyed his commandments – a claim that the Pharisees and scribes would claim was also true of them), and yet he has never received from his father so much as a kid to celebrate with his friends. Notice the direction of his argument here: he wanted to celebrate, but with his friends and not with his family. His resentment boils over when he refers to the returned young man, whom he cannot bring himself to address as anything other than "this son of yours" - despite the fact that the father calls him "your brother". He even resorts to adding details of the young man's misdeeds; he had swallowed up his father's property –'he and his women'. This is information which neither Jesus in the telling of the story, nor the young man himself had mentioned; it is detail the elder brother has added to heighten the crimes – real or supposed – of his younger sibling. Despite the father's assurance, the elder brother does not feel he shares all that his father owns. The image is of a dutiful son who nevertheless feels no connection with the one to whom he has always been obedient. Despite his compliance, he is every bit as estranged from his father as is his young brother was when he had gone missing. The question at the end of the parable which the reader is left to ponder is: which of the two sons is really lost? Two sons have become estranged from their father; by the end of the story, only one of them has been reconciled with the father, only one has formed a bond with the one who loves him so much, and wants to celebrate his return. As the story ends, we cannot but think of the Pharisees and the scribes in their righteous indignation at the beginning of the story. Like all parables, this one is it not about the people in the story; it is about those who read the story!

Questions to ponder

☐　What is the relationship between the story of the prodigal son and this story about an incompetent manager?

☐　What virtue is Jesus actually advocating in this parable?

☐　In what sense are money and possessions things which are never really ours, and what is meant by what we may be given as our own?

This week's parable is widely recognised as the most difficult to understand in all of the four gospels. There are several problems, but the major sticking point is in making sense of what appears to be Jesus' praise for the fraudulent action taken by the steward to save his skin, once he knows he has been found out! Other difficulties lie in trying to determine what the steward is actually doing: is he taking a cut in his own commission to which he would have been entitled as a result of carrying out these transactions? Or is he further depriving his master of what is rightfully his in the arrangements he makes with the latter's creditors? Does he hope that he can forge new friendships to assist his own prospects now that he has been dismissed from his position? It is now very difficult, if not impossible for us to understand what might have been current practice known to Jesus and/or Luke regarding such transactions, so we might never know precisely what the evangelist is describing in this particular parable. This however reminds us of the nature of the story; it is a parable, and parables were used by Jesus to provoke his hearers into a new way of thinking: they were not told to give accurate accounts of business practice, good or bad, in 1st century Palestine under Roman occupation!

One very important feature of this parable which is not often recognised is that it is really a companion piece to the parable of the two lost sons from the end of last week's gospel. Perhaps as a consequence of the chapter divisions we have become used to, we separate the two parables more than the evangelist would have intended: the 'two sons' brings chapter 15 to a close, and the parable we are about to consider opens chapter 16. A closer look at the beginning of today's passage shows, however, that there is continuity. Jesus had told the three lost and found parables from what we are used to calling chapter 15 to the Pharisees and scribes, but at the beginning of chapter 16, we are informed that after he had finished speaking to the Pharisees and scribes, "He also (*kai*) said to his disciples…" (16:1). This surely means that the evangelist wants to suggest continuity, and that the present parable is a further elaboration of the principle of rehabilitation of the wayward which was begun in the previous section. There are hints in the use of language that this is precisely what the evangelist intends. To begin with, the person at the centre of the story, is called steward in the Jerusalem Bible and several other English translations. More accurately, perhaps, the man could be called 'manager' or even an administrator, and in Greek, the expression is *oikonomous*. The term could be applied to one who managed someone's household. It could even refer to the 'City Administrator'; from the Greek title, the financial (economic) dimension of his area of responsibility is apparent. The person holding down the position could also be a slave; in this passage, there is no way of knowing if this is what the evangelist intended. The case of the manager is outlined briefly: he has been denounced to his rich master for being wasteful of the latter's property. The word used to describe his behaviour is the same as that which described the younger son's behaviour with the share of the inheritance that he had demanded be given to him by his father, *diaskortizo*. There is a suggestion of sheer carelessness, but not of dishonesty. The outcome is that the manager is dismissed from his position, and he has to give an account of his stewardship – perhaps a better contemporary phrase would be to say that he has to present his books for audit!

The ex-manager is now faced with a problem, whether he is a slave or a free person: once he had status and presumably a desirable and comfortable lifestyle. Now, he will have no influence, and will no longer be in a position to treat himself to the luxuries he once enjoyed as his master's administrator; even if he were a slave, he would probably have been able to avail himself of luxury in food and clothing, although not necessarily money. So, how is he to keep himself in the manner to which he has become accustomed? He does not fancy any of the options available to him: he is not strong enough to dig, and he would be too ashamed to beg. A third course however does suggests itself to him: if he will not be able to save his position when his master calls him in to audit his business affairs, he can at least ensure that he has a welcome extended to him by others who have reason to be grateful to him. Whether his means of doing this (reducing the debt owed by creditors to his master) is legal or otherwise is not really the issue: what is significant here is that, like the prodigal son in the previous parable, he takes action which he hopes will present him in a good light to other people in the near future. The Prodigal Son decided he would try to make himself popular with his father by preparing a speech in which he admits his unworthiness to be considered son any longer, but in which he intends to ask for a position as a paid servant. In this story, the manager tries to pave the way for a future position by doing a favour to creditors. In both cases, the characters who are in trouble show presence of mind in trying to arrange favours for themselves – after they have done something for others (coming back and presenting himself as contrite to his father in the case of the missing son, cancelling the debts of creditors to his master in the case of the disgraced manager). Both are trying to curry favour with those who may now be able to do them a favour.

So what moral is to be drawn from the parable? In telling two stories about people faced with an immediate and serious crisis, Jesus commends to his disciples that these singularly unpleasant people, far from being models to be emulated, do at least show great single-mindedness in seeking out what is important to them. Unfortunately, what is most important to them is saving their own skins! Now, as he addresses his disciples, Jesus rhetorically asks would it not be wonderful if 'the children of the light' showed the same determination in pursuing the kingdom of God? The shady characters in the parables are motivated when a crisis, that is, a time of decision arises in their lives. They are galvanised into action by a desire to preserve at all costs what is important to them – their luxury; but how galvanised into action are disciples, faced with a much more significant time of crisis – this time, the journey of the Prophet toward Jerusalem? How much are disciples prepared to respond to the call to follow the Prophet? Already, they have been told that they are to renounce themselves and to take up the cross each day and come after Jesus. They may be making the journey, but how committed are they to the Prophet's cause? Perhaps borrowing something from the example of the manager, Jesus exhorts his disciples to use money, tainted as it is, to win friends (to give alms), so that when it fails as it most certainly will (as the man with the great harvest and the large barns discovered in the parable), they may find they have made friends who 'will welcome them into the tents of eternity'.

The next statement is hard to follow, and the Jerusalem Bible phrase, "money, that tainted thing" does not help. Neither does the more accurate translation 'mammon of corruption'; it is possible that the phrase suggests idolatry; if so, according to Jesus love of money is a form of idolatry. It has been suggested that the word 'mammon' may mean 'something to be relied on'. If that is true, then reliance on money, i.e. 'mammon' is at odds with reliance on the word of the prophet, who alone can provide the true foundation for our lives (c.f. 6:46-49). The kingdom of God is eternal; money, earthly, is corruptible: hence those who cannot be trusted with what will not last will never be trusted with what is their own, i.e. a place in the kingdom of God. No one can serve two masters, the result will inevitably loving one and hating the other: the Prophet who calls to discipleship demands total allegiance. Will prospective disciples have the necessary level of commitment?

Sunday 26, Year C. Luke 16:19-31

Questions to ponder

☐   What is the real failure of the rich man in this story?
☐   What might be the significance of the rich man being unnamed, but the poor man being given the name Lazarus?
☐   Why is the rich man punished after death for the condition of a poor man he knew nothing about?
☐   How well does this passage explain for us Jesus' repeated insistence in this gospel about disciples renouncing possessions? What is the explanation?

There is a slight gap between the end of last Sunday's gospel and the beginning of today's passage. The gap consists mainly in three brief and apparently unrelated statements by Jesus, which bear little resemblance to the themes we have been considering for these past weeks. When today's gospel begins, it is with another well-known and uniquely Lukan parable. It is the story of the rich man and the poor man called Lazarus. This parable shows some similarities with two other parables we have read in recent weeks; it resembles the parable of the Good Samaritan in that the major characters in the narrative are carefully portrayed to draw from the original hearers' reactions based on the stereotypes of the day. Thus, there us a certain rich man and there is a certain poor man. It would have been likely that the hearers' sympathies would have lain with the rich man who is described in a most sympathetic way, whereas the poor man is depicted as the lowest of the low, and an object of derision to the Pharisees. The parable also resembles the Prodigal Son parable, not only because it is addressed to the Pharisees, but because like the earlier parable, it continues from what at first sight seems to be its ending (the punishment of the rich man and the exaltation of Lazarus), to a conclusion in which the implications of the parable are spelled out.

As we already noted, the portraits of the characters are carefully drawn: there was 1) a certain rich man who 2) was in the habit of dressing in purple and fine linen and who 3) feasted magnificently every day. The picture is of opulence which in a primitive Old Testament theology would have been taken as a sign of God's favour. This is presumably the view that the Pharisees, who in the synoptic gospels are noted for their ostentation, would have taken. No more really needs to be said about the rich man at this stage: he is the stereotypical 'good guy'. Attention turns to the other character, the poor man who, unlike his rich counterpart, is given a name: Lazarus. It is not clear why the poor man is named whereas the rich man is not. It may have something to do with Lazarus being the Greek version of the Hebrew name Eliezer, which means "My God helps". As the story unfolds, it becomes clear that Lazarus relies on God alone for help. This is just as well, since no one else comes to his help! On the other hand, the unnamed rich man is in his own mind self-sufficient (reminiscent of the rich man with the huge harvest and the bigger barns in 12:13-21), and does not need anyone's help. The poor man Lazarus' description is of a totally wretched human being in a horrible state: there is nothing in the telling of the parable that is designed to evoke anything other than horror at his condition; there is nothing sentimental in the description. The man is not only poor; he is a beggar, despised as coming from the lowest of the low of humanity. If he is seated outside the rich man's gate, it is not through choice; it is because he has been dumped there. The expression can mean two things. On one hand, it may simply mean that his circumstances controlled where he has, metaphorically speaking, 'landed' – that is, he has been brought low to this state; or it may mean that he has been physically dumped there, left by others to fend for himself by begging from those who entered and left the house. If this is the case, it might also suggest that he is crippled, and unable to move unaided. Lazarus longed to fill himself with whatever fell from the rich man's table. Again, we are reminded of the Prodigal Son parable, where the young man would willing have fed himself with the husks given as food to the pigs he had been reduced to shepherding. Lazarus is covered in sores which are licked by dogs; not a sentimental note, but a description of Lazarus' final degradation, since dogs and other animals were considered unclean. The characters could not be contrasted more fully.

Both men die, and meet totally different fates: "Now the poor man died and was carried away by the angels to the bosom of Abraham. The rich man also died and was buried. In his torment in Hades he looked up and saw Abraham a long way off with Lazarus in his bosom" (16:22-23). This latter idea is interesting. The phrase 'bosom of Abraham' occurs only here in the gospels and it may reflect the biblical expression of being gathered to one's people at death. So, Lazarus is gathered to his father Abraham. In contrast, the rich man addresses Abraham as "Father Abraham", but is in the place of torment and not with the one he calls "Father". As far back as the account of the preaching of John the Baptist, we read of John's warning to the crowds who came to him for baptism, "if you are repentant, produce the appropriate fruits, and do not think of telling yourselves, 'We have Abraham for our father' because, I tell you, God can raise children for Abraham from these stones" (3:8). The rich man's address to Abraham here is as hollow as John had suggested.

The arrogance of the rich man continues unabated even in torment. He asks Abraham to send Lazarus to dip the tip of his finger in water to cool his tongue; he is still dismissive of Lazarus, whose presence he acknowledges for the first time but only to have him provide some service. This arrogance provides the platform for the conclusion to the story: there is a divide between Lazarus and the rich man, which is in place because of their respective positions in life. The fortunes which the two men experienced in life are now reversed, and there is no way in which this reversal can be undone. The parable has now emerged as a commentary on the beatitudes and woes of the Sermon on the Plain, especially, "Blessed are you who are poor: yours is the kingdom of God. Blessed are you who are hungry now: you shall be satisfied" (6:20-21), and "woe to you who are rich: you are having your consolation now. Woe to you who have your fill now: you shall go hungry" (6:24-25). The parable illustrates the working out of the great promise of reversal of fortunes which is a frequent theme in this gospel, beginning with the Magnificat, "The hungry he has filled with good things, the rich sent empty away" (1:53).

Before the story concludes, however, there is one more disclosure to be made. When the rich man begs that Lazarus be sent to the rich man's brothers to warn them, so that they may avoid this place of torment, Abraham tells him that they have Moses and the prophets. Perhaps this recalls the repeated instruction of Moses to the Israelites to pay special heed to the widow, the stranger and the orphan when they take possession of the land that the Lord was to give to them (e.g. Deuteronomy 24:19-21). While feasting and ignoring the poor man at his door, the man and his five brothers have ignored the very words of Moses himself; they will not therefore be moved to repentance even should someone come back from the dead. These words have a strong prophetic ring: not only will Jesus come back from the dead: he will do so as the Risen Prophet whose coming Moses had prophesied! The rich man has been in serious dereliction of his duty under the Law of Moses; his duty was to keep open an eye for the most marginalized and vulnerable in his area. Not only do we have a reason here for the rich man's condemnation; we have perhaps the fullest explanation of the need for disciples to detach themselves from material possessions: they have a duty to use them for the benefit of those who cannot provide for themselves; renouncing self means putting the needs of others first. Jesus' ministry culminating in his death by which he is taken up to heaven, is one of renunciation of self, one of total service to others. Disciples are challenged to follow this example. Those who listen to the one who has risen from the dead, i.e. who listen to the constant message of this gospel, will know why this is so.

Chapter 9

The Prophet approaches Jerusalem, teaching through parables and in the Jerusalem Temple. The Son of Man, who came to seek out and saved what was lost, and who promises a repentant criminal a place in paradise.

Sundays 27 – Christ the King, Year C

Introduction:
A sub-heading for this collection of notes might be 'from somewhere between Samaria and Galilee to Jerusalem via Jericho'. It's not exactly attention grabbing, and it is geographically vague, but it does encompass the extent of Jesus' journey covered in these coming weeks. The starting point occurs, not on the first week of this selection, but on Sunday 28, where the

evangelist informs us that 'on his way to Jerusalem Jesus travelled between Samaria and Galilee'. It is a vague reference, and obviously not intended to convey geographical accuracy, but it could well have symbolic value. The evangelist suggests a journey somewhere between Samaria and Galilee. There is really no such place, since the two regions border each other, but the sense of neither one place nor the other is a good description of where we currently find ourselves in the journey narrative. Since Luke 9:51, we have systematically read examples of Jesus, the Prophet promised by Moses (Deuteronomy 18:15.18), teaching disciples, Pharisees and the crowd in general, answering questions raised by others on the journey, using parables and setting out challenging ideas. We have learned much on this journey so far but there are still matters things that are as yet unresolved, suggesting that we are at some indeterminate point on the journey – the spiritual equivalent of being somewhere between Samaria and Galilee! A good example of this 'unfinished business' is a theme that we have already encountered, and will continue to encounter, but which is not yet fully explained, and that is Jesus' repeated insistence that disciples are to give up their possessions! The physical journey being described in these coming weeks will move toward a very clearly defined destination for Jesus: Jerusalem. Likewise, our metaphorical journey will take on clearer definition as we near the destination of the end of this liturgical year, and issues like relinquishing possession will, hopefully, be more clearly understood as the full extent of the Lukan Jesus' teaching becomes clear to us.

Once more, the gospels for these weeks provide us with material unique to Luke. Every single Sunday from now until (and including) Christ the King will contain material not found in the other gospels. These will include the Parables of the widow and the unjust judge, the Tax Agent and the Pharisee at prayer, the stories of the ten lepers and Zacchaeus, and will culminate in Luke's own very singular account of the last words of Jesus on the cross. And for completeness, we may well find that it is Zacchaeus who best helps us understand the persistent command to relinquish possessions!

Sunday 27, Year C. Luke 17:5-10

Questions to Ponder

☐ What exactly, according to the Jesus of Luke's gospel, is the significance of the quantity of faith a person may possess?

☐   What do you think that Jesus means by the concept of faith itself?
☐   What is the gospel relationship between faith and action; and what kind of action should faith engender?

The question of faith is no stranger to the synoptic gospels, but once again Luke's treatment of the subject is particular to his own way of thinking. In the gospels of Matthew and Mark, the question of faith is raised in the context of other issues; for example, in Matthew the question arises as a consequence of disciples' inability to deal with a condition which may have been epilepsy, but which the evangelist (and presumably his contemporaries) considered a form of possession (Matthew 17:14-18). There, Jesus' disciples ask why they could not 'cast this out', and he replies that it is because they have so little faith (Matthew 17:19-20). In this passage from Luke, however, the disciples request more faith on their own initiative, and with apparently no context for the question. The request literally means: "add faith to us", which amounts to the 'increase our faith' of the Jerusalem Bible. Jesus uses the mustard seed as a standard of measurement of quantity of faith. In 13:19, the mustard seed had been chosen for its exemplary smallness in the parable illustrating the small beginnings of the kingdom, with the resulting vastness. In the present passage the mustard seed again symbolises smallness, but this time there is no growth to something greater; rather, it becomes clear that the disciples, patently unable to give commandments to mulberry trees that would result in them uprooting themselves and jumping into the sea, do not possess faith even so small as a mustard seed! This is an unusual way for arguments to be expressed in the gospels: we are more used to hearing Jesus argue that if 'a' is the case, then how much more will 'b' be so, or in other words a form of argument which is going from something small or trivial and arguing for something greater or more significant; a common form of Semitic teaching methodology. A good example of this was in the lessons on prayer we read on the 17th Sunday, when Jesus declared, "if you who are evil know how to give your children what is good, how much more will the heavenly Father give the holy Spirit to those who ask him!" In the current passage however, the argument proceeds in the opposite direction, effectively saying: 'if you had faith even the size of a mustard seed you would be able to move a mulberry tree with a word. You are not able to do this, therefore you don't even have faith the size of a mustard seed!'
This theme is not developed any further. There is no promise of a gift of

more faith, nor is there any suggestion as to how disciples might increase
their faith. Instead, using a parable Jesus gives his disciples an insight into
what faith actually is – or rather, how it is lived out. The parable uses a
household image quite common in the gospel of Luke – the relationship
between master and slave (the Jerusalem Bible translates the Greek word
doulos as 'servant', which is possible, but which perhaps weakens the gulf
that the parable hints at between master and slave. The parable capitalises on
the normal conditions in a household of the time. The master must be
absolutely confident that slaves will unquestioningly attend to his needs when
they return from their work in the fields: the slave's role is always to 'wait'
on or for the master; slaves attend to their own needs only after they have
attended to the master, and the master should never have to feel grateful to
slaves for their fidelity to the one to whom they have been assigned for
service.

It is not immediately apparent how this parable connects with the request
from the disciples for an increase in faith. They have been told in no
uncertain terms that their faith is smaller than the size of a mustard seed, and
the parabolic exhortation - it's scarcely a parable in the normal sense of the
term - which followed offered little prospect of any increase in faith being
handed out to them; if the parable has any relevance to the quantity of faith
and a request for more, it would surely be to make clear to those making the
request that they should be grateful for what they have: as slaves, they are not
entitled to make demands on their master!

There may however be another aspect to the 'parable' which is more
encouraging. Jesus has just told a parable about slaves being faithful to their
masters. Perhaps this is the first lesson in faith. Among its many aspects is
that of remaining faithful to the one in whose service they have committed
themselves. There will be many other lessons in faith before we end our
reflections on this gospel: we will hear of the relationship between faith and
salvation, of the need for prayer if faith is to be sustained, but perhaps before
any of these can be considered, Jesus lays out the most fundamental aspect of
faith: fidelity, constancy, commitment to the one they have been called to
follow and serve. In this, quantity of faith is not an issue: the disciples may
lack faith the size of a mustard seed, so they cannot uproot mulberry trees
with a word, but clearly they have sufficient faith to be faithful to the one
they follow on the journey to Jerusalem: this does not require faith which is
as small as even a mustard seed! Throughout the journey, indeed from its

very beginning, would-be disciples have been challenged to make serious commitment to follow the prophet: the son of man has no place to lay his head, the dead are to be left to bury their dead, and once the hand is laid on the plough, no one who turns back is fit for the kingdom (c.f. Luke 9:57-62); the commitment of the incompetent steward in securing his own future is praised (c.f. 16:8); it will never be enough for us to try to persuade Jesus of our commitment by saying, "you taught in our streets, we ate and drank in your company". Commitment to the Prophet is not an optional extra: it is fundamental to the call to discipleship, also defined as being prepared to renounce self and take up the cross every day (9:23). The faithfulness which Jesus requires of his disciples is nothing less than a fundamental commitment to the teaching which unfolds as the journey to Jerusalem heads toward its destination.

This passage may also serve as a reminder to us that from here until the end of the liturgical year, much, if not most of Jesus' teaching will both refer back to what has gone before in the gospel, and forward to what is yet to come.

Sunday 28, Year C. Luke 17:11-19

Questions to Ponder

☐   What could Luke possibly mean by placing Jesus 'somewhere between Samaria and Galilee' in this episode?

☐   What does it say about the level of faith of all ten lepers that they were prepared to carry out Jesus' instructions about going to the priest without first having any evidence of a cure?

☐   What is the real virtue of the Samaritan ex-leper in this story (on the assumption that it is about more than saying 'thank you')?

This is the passage which was referred to in the introduction as having only the vaguest geographical reference. The evangelist describes Jesus as on the way to Jerusalem (another reminder of the now always present destination of Jerusalem), and that he is travelling somewhere between Samaria and Galilee (and not 'on the border', as the Jerusalem Bible states). Also worth noting is the complete absence of any mention of disciples, or to the crowd that is now a regular feature of the journey narrative (which is a feature we have already encountered in Luke 10:38 where in the story of Jesus' visit to Martha and

Mary, there is no specific naming of the village, and the crowd and the disciples mysteriously disappear!). The passage is the unique Lukan story about the ten lepers cured by Jesus, one of whom is a Samaritan. Curiously, although this is found only in Luke, it has some similarities with the Markan account of the cure of one leper (Mark 1:40-45): both stories lack geographical precision; both lack reference to disciples, and for that matter both seem detached from the events that precede and succeed them.
In the Lukan passage, Jesus enters one of the villages (again, a vague reference), and ten lepers come out to meet him. In the Markan account Jesus reaches out and touches the leper who approaches him, but Luke, ever sensitive to the requirements of Jewish law makes sure that no such physical contact is even hinted at. Indeed, Luke's lepers are assiduous in observing the regulations that apply to them; they are to remain outside the encampment and to stay away from people (Numbers 5:2-3) and they are to warn those in danger of coming too close to them (Leviticus 13:43-46). In this episode, the ten keep their distance from Jesus and cry out to him, but they shout for help as well as giving the statutory warning. The lepers are the only people other than disciples to address Jesus as "master" (*epistratēs*), and they beg him to "have mercy". This is the same cry as the rich man made in appeal to Abraham in the parable about him and Lazarus. This cry will be uttered toward the end of the journey by a blind beggar outside Jericho (18:34-40). 'Mercy' (*eleos*) is a quality associated in this gospel with divine visitation (c.f. 1:50. 54 in Mary's song, the Magnificat, 1:58 to describe the reaction of the neighbours to God's mercy shown to Elizabeth on the birth of her son, and 1:72. 78 in Zechariah's song, the 'Benedictus').
Jesus' response to the lepers' cry for mercy is to command them to go and show themselves to the priest as Moses had prescribed – there is no question of rendering Jesus unclean through physical contact with the lepers that would cause problems under the terms of Jewish law; nor is there even a pronouncement that their request has been granted, or that a cure is being effected. This is a demonstration of the extent of Jesus' power: that a cure can be given without the need of either contact or word of command. The result is that we have an unexpected glimpse of the quite substantial faith of the ten lepers – they go off to see the priest as Jesus commands AND before they have been given any indication that their plea has been successful and their request granted. They depart from Jesus still as lepers, and it is only as they go on their way that they see they have been made clean! It is apparent

therefore that the Samaritan leper who returns to Jesus is NOT the only one to have faith; all of them have obeyed Jesus' instruction in hope and with faith. One of the lepers returns to Jesus because while he was on his way, he found himself cured. In returning, he did not (at least at this stage) go to the priest to hear the official declaration that he was now clean). This one came back, praising God (*dodazōn ton theou*) at the top of his voice, and threw himself at the feet of Jesus and thanked him. Luke informs us that the man was a Samaritan – the second time in this gospel that a person from that region so hated by the Jews becomes the hero in one of Luke's stories (the other being the Good Samaritan in 10: 28-37).

What then makes the Samaritan so notable among the ten, since all ten of them were, as Jesus himself acknowledged, made clean? The Samaritan thanks Jesus, but that is only part of the picture; there is much more to his actions. He praises God at the top of his voice, or at least that is how this is translated in the Jerusalem Bible. The word rendered 'praising' could equally be rendered 'giving glory to'. This is a much stronger biblical concept: to give glory to God is to respond to God's revelation, to acknowledge God's presence and action. The Old Testament expression "the glory of the Lord" was used to convey something of the closeness among his people of the God whom Israelites believed could not leave heaven, and yet of whom they had personal experience of closeness, presence and even involvement in their lives. When a Jewish person spoke of 'giving glory to God', it was an acknowledgement of the presence and action of God within that person's life. This means that when the Samaritan, along with thanking Jesus for his healing, actually does what the other nine are unable or unwilling to do, and that is to acknowledge the work of God, in the person of Jesus, in the events which have literally given him a new lease of life. That he recognises Jesus as the agent of God in all of this is demonstrated by the fact that he falls to his knees before Jesus – an action which is reserved solely for the recognition of the presence of the deity. In other words, the detested Samaritan is able to profess a faith which is not to be found in the nine other, presumably Jewish, lepers who have had the same experience as that Samaritan.

There is a final point that has to be noted for a full appreciation of this passage, as well as for a fuller appreciation of Jesus' ministry, and that is Jesus' response to the Samaritan, "Stand up and go on your way; your faith has saved you". 'Stand up' can also mean 'rise up', which has connotations of resurrection. This connects with "your faith has saved you", which may come as a surprise. We might expect "your faith has made you clean", even "your faith has made you well", but the outcome of the Samaritan's faith is salvation, promised since the earliest verses of this gospel. In 2:11, shepherds are told "today a Saviour has been born to you". Before that, the name of the child, the son of God to whom Mary will give birth is of course 'Jesus', the one who saves. What we learn here then is that salvation is not some theoretical concept relating to the future and the life beyond this: salvation is an enhancement of the quality of the life of those downtrodden by whatever afflicts them. Jesus the Saviour is the one who brings a new lease of life to all; the one who renounces his life so that the 'poor', that is the marginalized and afflicted, can become more alive. Again, this explains why Jesus is insistent that his disciples likewise place their resources, their own lives ultimately at the service of those who are more dead than alive. This is why so often those with possessions are urged to dispose of them and give the proceeds to the poor – clearly so that their experience of life may be enhanced, that they experience the salvation which is an increase in the quality of life.

Sunday 29 C. Luke 18:1-8

Questions to ponder

☐ Why might Luke be so insistent in telling the reader the purpose of some of Jesus' parables (and why then does he not do this for all parables)?
☐ What does it mean to 'pray continually'? Constantly say prayers? Something else?
☐ Why might the Son of Man fail to find any faith on his return?
☐ What does faith in this passage represent?

This week and next, we are faced with 'programmatic' parables, that is parables that Jesus told with a particular point in mind (this week, the point is about the need to pray always; next, it is for the benefit of those who take great pride in their own virtue, and who are contemptuous of others). Both of them belong to the large collection of uniquely Lukan parables. It may be worth pausing here for a moment to reflect on one aspect of the nature of parables – or at least of the parables attributed to Jesus that have come to us through the four canonical gospels. Parables are never designed to give single, clear cut answers to a question or to a problem: parables may be said to work best when they persuade us to ask questions, rather than to find answers, and every parable is capable of prompting the reader/hearer to a wide and legitimate range of meanings: in other words, there is no such thing as the correct answer to what a parable means! This point is worth stressing when we read Luke's parables, often introduced with the kind of formulaic introduction that 'Jesus spoke this parable with the point that…' or, 'for the benefit of those who…' and so on. The purpose of these parables may be clearly identified, but this does not mean that they have only one limited possible interpretation. Today's parable may be told to encourage disciples to continue to pray always, but it does not provide for us an answer as to how this is to be done in practice! The reader/hearer has to grapple with the parable time after time to determine how this might be achieved.

The next question we need to ponder is: what exactly is meant by 'pray continually'? The Greek is *pantote proseucheskai*, the two words meaning respectively 'always' and 'pray' (i.e., in the present tense). Is this the same as 'to pray continually'? The parable itself must be able to shed some light on this. In Jesus' telling, the attitude of praying always is somehow equated with the attitude of the widow who appeals for justice to a judge unworthy of the name. The story unfolds with typically Lukan expressions; literally, there was a judge in a certain town. In last week's gospel, we noted that Luke's geographical details were somewhat vague: in this parable, they are virtually non-existent. The characters and places are less important than the behaviour and circumstances they are employed to demonstrate; they are 'stock characters' of the kind we encounter for example in many types of jokes: 'there was this judge…in this town…and there was this widow…'

The first of these characters we encounter is the judge whom, we are told, has neither fear of God nor respect for humans; this man is not a nice person! These two qualities, totally absent in this judge, were considered characteristic of a virtuous person: Proverbs 1:7 stated that 'the fear of the Lord' is the beginning of wisdom, and frequently in the Psalms, the pious are described as those who 'fear the Lord'. In Acts, Luke uses the expression 'God fearers' for Gentiles who were attracted to Judaism (e.g. Acts 10:2, 22, 35; 13:16, 26). So, when the certain judge in a certain town is described as someone who has no fear of God, this is in effect the same as declaring he is not at all religious and is without scruples. Combine this with his lack of regard for people, and we have here a picture of a very unpleasant character: one who takes the concept of self-sufficiency to such extremes that he is in no need of anyone, human or divine.

One of Luke the evangelist's favourite literary devices is to tell stories of two contrasting, or complementary characters. His gospel opens with the contrast between Zechariah the priest who does not trust God's promises, and Mary, who does. Frequently a male character is followed by a female - for example, the short parable of the (male) shepherd who loses one of his 100 sheep is followed by and equally short one about a woman who loses 1 coin from her collection of 10. In today's gospel extract, the introduction of the male judge is followed by that of the female widow, and the two are contrasted, because just as the judge is a completely self-contained and cynically self-reliant individual, the widow is someone who has no voice of her own and who depends on other, male figures, for the provision of what she needs. In Israelite society, widows were considered to be among the most vulnerable and voiceless members of society, so much so that the Torah insists that special consideration must always be given to the widow, the orphan and the stranger. It is not difficult to see from where their vulnerability arises. Ancient Israel was a society in which the extended family was all important, and a patriarchal model was universal. In general, people could only find employment, support and aid from within the family unit; single women could only find support from their fathers: married women from their husbands. The other side of this was that those cut off from the support of the family were extremely vulnerable, and women without the support of father or husband were very much at risk; hence the inclusion of widows in the list of those most in need of special attention along with orphans and strangers. The Law of Moses repeatedly called for particular care to be taken of these three categories of people, widows, orphans and strangers when the people of Israel came to take possession of the land that God would give them; they were to exercise this watchful care for their well-being because Israel had known what it was to be dispossessed and marginalized during the time of slavery in Egypt. In particular, in justice (i.e. as executed by those with judicial powers) widows were to be protected (c.f. Deuteronomy 10:18; 14:29; 16:11. 14; 24:19-21; 26:12-13). Conversely, a curse was to be pronounced against anyone who 'prevents the justice due to the sojourner, the fatherless and the widow' (Deuteronomy 27:19).

The widow in this story appeals to the judge, demanding the justice against her enemy which has been denied her, although we are not told the precise nature of the case she brings to the judge. For a time (not specified), the judge refuses to respond, but then he reconsiders. Going over the matter in his own mind, the judge reminds himself (Luke's way of reminding the reader) that he has no fear of God nor respect for other human beings, but he reasons that if he does not grant the widow her request, she will persist in coming to him and (according to the Jerusalem Bible translation) will worry him to death. Here is another case in which a literal translation opens up further possible insights into the passage. Luke puts into the mouth of the judge a colloquial expression which literally means that the woman will come and 'strike him in (or under) the eye'. This seems to be an idiom for the woman 'wearing out' the judge with her persistence, but if we take the expression more literally, the judge might also be afraid of 'receiving one in the eye', that is, facing the public embarrassment of a black eye as a result of his refusal to grant this very persistent lady the justice that is due to her! This would serve the kind of argument that is so common in Luke's gospel and which we have already seen, where Jesus appeals to the fact that even the most unworthy characters can be persuaded to do the right thing, although perhaps for the wrong motives. How much more will God see justice done to his children who call to him (an earlier example of this was when Jesus posed the questions, 'what father would hand his son a stone when he asked for bread, or a snake when he asked for a fish, or a scorpion when he asked for an egg? (Luke 11:11-13)'. This, of course, is the point of the parable: the woman's persistence, her continual appeal to the judge for what she deep down believes will eventually come her way, is enough to break done the obstinacy of an unjust judge; how much more, says Jesus, should God's faithful children have confidence in God to answer them when they cry to him day and night, even if He appears to delay in responding to their need?

This final point is an echo of a recurring Old Testament theme, most famously encountered perhaps in the episode of Moses' encounter with God in the burning bush. A paraphrase of God's statement to Moses could run along the lines of 'I have heard the cry of my people in their distress; I mean to answer their cry' (c.f. Exodus 3:7. 9). Throughout the Old Testament, the faithful of God are those who are persistent in their prayer to God, confident that he will eventually respond to their cry off distress. It would seem that this is precisely the attitude that the Lukan Jesus is advocating among his faithful followers, a continuity in prayer which does not mean never ending, but which does mean an habitual attitude and experience of prayer. The widow was continually approaching the judge, not in the sense that she never went home until he request was granted, but because she repeatedly and determinedly came back to the judge with the same request. Her persistence was in never ceasing to believe that her demand would be answered in her favour. Jesus assures his disciples that they need never fear that Good will not listen to their cry, even if it appears as if he delays in doing so. So, it seems that persistent prayer is not about the supplicant trying to change God's mind (can you think of anything more impertinent for a human being to do than to try to change the mind of God?), but rather it is about expressing an unshakeable confidence that God will NEVER abandon his people when they are in need of him. Prayer is for the benefit of the human doing the praying: not for God. It is significant that at this point no indication is given as to what form this type of prayer is to take. The only example of what to pray in any of the four gospels is the one usually called the 'Lord's Prayer', in its longer form in Matthew 6:9-13, and its shorter form in Luke 11:2-4. Perhaps this is why Jesus ends with the question which concludes this passage for us "when the Son of Man comes, will he find any faith on earth?" (18:8). Faith here has little or nothing to do with theological statements or creedal content: the faith that is so important in this gospel is that faith which engenders trust in God, especially when the time of testing comes (remember the final phrase of the 'Lord's Prayer', "do not put us to the test" (11:4). If the Son of Man is to find any faith of this kind when he returns, it will be from disciples through the generations 'praying always'.

Sunday 30, Year C. Luke 18:9-14

Questions to ponder

☐ Could the Pharisees whom Jesus addresses have any justification for their self-righteousness?
☐ What is the significance of the tax collector's humility? Is he humble because he grovels before God, or is something else at work here?
☐ Why is the prayer of the virtuous Pharisee not heard?

Once again Luke takes us back to ideas that we have already encountered in the course of the narrative of Jesus' journey to Jerusalem. This week he returns to the theme of self-justification, which we already met in the attitude of the lawyer who, wishing to justify himself, asked Jesus the question 'and who is my neighbour?' (Lk 10:29). This, of course was the cue for Jesus to tell the parable of the Good Samaritan. That episode was followed by another instance of self-justification in the story of Martha, trying to justify her lack of attention to the prophet who visited her home, and trying to persuade Jesus to agree with her sense of being hard-done-to by her sister Mary (10:38-42; see notes on Sundays 15 and 16 C ; chapter 7 above). Now, as the journey narrative begins to draw to a conclusion, Luke quotes one of Jesus' parables that takes us back to the topic of self-justification, and in the process drawing out in a bit more detail what it consists of and how those who try to justify themselves are contrasted with those who seek only the justification that comes from God. This is the parable usually called the Pharisee and the tax-collector. Again, Luke employs the literary technique of setting side by side two very different characters, and he highlights the contrast between the two and in an unexpected (if you do not know the story, that is) twist at the end which ensures we identify the less likely of the two characters as the hero of the story.

Once more, Luke introduces the parable by informing us of Jesus' purpose in telling it. He does not explicitly state that it is about self-righteousness, but he tells his readers that "Jesus spoke the following parable to some people who prided themselves on being virtuous and despised everyone else" (18:9). The evangelist does not identify the people to whom the parable is addressed, but given his opening remarks, it is hard not to conclude that the Pharisees are at the receiving end! As noted already, a lawyer attempted to justify himself to Jesus in 10:29; Jesus explicitly accused Pharisees of seeking to justify themselves (passing themselves off as righteous in the Jerusalem Bible translation) in 16:15; that they were scornful of others, and especially they considered to be sinners is clear from e.g. 15:2. This attitude led to the parables of the lost sheep, the lost coin, and the lost son (or as was suggested in the notes for Sunday 24C, the two lost sons). As is so often the case in Luke, the attitude being described here (scorn for others) will take on a deeper significance later, as this is the expression used to describe Herod's contempt, expressed through mockery, for Jesus in 23:11. Of course, the story which Jesus is about to tell is not just about the Pharisees; it is also - and perhaps primarily - about the "everyone else" who are despised by them. The parable begins: "Two men went up to the Temple to pray, one a Pharisee, the other a tax collector" (18:10). The Temple is frequently identified as a place for prayer in Luke-Acts; the gospel narrative began in the setting of the temple where Zechariah is ministering, and a multitude of people are gathered outside in prayer (1:9-10); other references to the Temple and prayer are found in 19:46; 24:53 (where the gospel ends with the note that the disciples were continually in the Temple praising God); as well as Acts 2:46; 3:1; 22:17. The two men in this parable who go to the temple to pray are of course a Pharisee and a tax collector (more accurately, a tax agent; tax collectors as such had been abolished by the Romans in the time of the Emperor Augustus, who had died, according to Luke, some fifteen years before Jesus began his ministry (c.f. Luke 3:10). By this stage in the gospel, readers should be able to recognize Luke's literary tricks quite easily: we expect that there is going to be a comparison made between the two; we expect that the Pharisee, on paper the more impressive of the two men, will come out worst; and we expect that Luke's characteristic role reversal is about to happen again. Tax collectors and sinners are two groups of people frequently found in the gospel who sought the company of Jesus in order to hear what he had to say, and to whom Jesus responded positively. When John the Baptist was preaching, tax collectors asked him "Master, what must we do?" John's answer was; "exact no more than the appointed rate" (3:12-13). Tax collectors and sinners sought the company of Jesus in 15:1. They would not have known this, but they were therefore doing exactly what was commanded by the heavenly voice in the hearing of Peter, James and John at Jesus' transfiguration (9:35). By contrast, the Pharisees have been consistent in their refusal to listen to the one who is the prophet promised by Moses (Deuteronomy 18:15. 18). These two opposing attitudes to Jesus' words are now found in the prayer of the two men who visited the Temple.

The first one whom we hear at prayer is the Pharisee. This is to be expected: he is a member of that religious class renowned for its law-abiding lifestyle and total obedience to the Law. The Pharisee tells us as much himself, because he soon lists for us his virtuous practices. To begin with, he is not like other people whom he classes as adulterous, thieving, roguish: and above all he is not like the tax collector he sees beside him! We are obliged to take his words at face value for want of any evidence to the contrary. His exemplary observance of the law means that he avoids those sins that so many others fall into, and of which tax collectors were commonly supposed to be guilty. So much for what he doesn't do! On the positive side, he tells us that he fasts twice a week and he gives tithes of all that he possesses. Both of these practices are well above the required level for pious Jews. Fasting was extolled as a practice, but only the Day of Atonement was set aside as a day for compulsory fasting; tithing, giving a tenth of goods, was applicable only to certain goods that a person produced (hence Jesus' scathing remarks about the scrupulosity of Pharisees who measure out exactly one tenth of the very herbs they grow, c.f. Luke 11:420); this Pharisee pays tithes, not on designated produce, but on *everything* he possesses! This Pharisee does not go home at rights with God however, whereas the tax agent, to whom we will turn in a moment, does. So where does the Pharisee fail in his prayer? Luke gives us a possible clue in the opening description of the Pharisee's prayer, after he tells us that the man stands there and 'says this prayer to himself'. The expression could mean at least two things. One meaning might simply be that he does what is commonly expressed today as "saying your prayers into yourself', that is, praying silently, inaudibly. Somehow, this seems unlikely for a man who goes out of his way to stress the complete contrast between him and the tax agent (of course, he's absolutely correct on that one, although not for the reason he thinks). It is therefore more likely that the Pharisee is talking to himself in prayer. If this is the case (and it seems entirely likely) it explains why the Pharisee goes home after his prayer, not being at rights with God: in his prayer, he has just offered the most arrogant example of self-justification we will find anywhere in the gospel. His argument in his 'prayer' seems to be about convincing himself of his own virtue, his own spiritual and moral triumphs, and his own self-congratulation on his achievements. This is someone who takes all the credit for his own virtue; he has no need of God. He has defined his own parameters (which in fairness are impressive in their scope), and he apparently feels confident that his salvation is assured, thanks to his industry! We cannot help but think of the lawyer's trying to justify himself by seeking from Jesus a tight definition of who is his neighbour, so that he can 'keep himself right' and live within the boundaries of neighbourliness – or more to the point, of doing more than neighbourliness strictly demands! Nor can we forget Martha, who seeks to justify herself in the presence of Jesus for not following her sister's example in listening to the prophet who has come to their house, or even the man in the parable who justifies his celebration on the grounds that he has secured his future for many years to come, only to find that his life is destined to end that very night (12:16-21). All of these, and the Pharisee of the parable, have created for themselves self-contained worlds of which they are masters.

The prayer of the tax agent could not be in greater contrast to that of the Pharisee. To begin with, he stays some distance away, not even daring to raise his eyes to heaven. His prayer is simple "God, be merciful to me, a sinner", and he is the one who goes home at rights with God. It has to be stressed that the merit of his prayer is not in his assumed attitude of debasement: it is rather in his humble recognition of his need of God. Perhaps he is in dire need of God; perhaps his crimes are huge (the Pharisee certainly thought so!), but the important issue is that he alone of the two at prayer recognises that salvation (and the forgiveness he so desperately wants) comes from God alone. Unlike the Pharisee, the tax agent is aware that he is powerless to bring about his own salvation. It is precisely at this point that God is able to act to bring about the necessary forgiveness and to respond to his faith with the assurance of salvation (as Jesus had declared to the leper in last week's gospel, 17:19). The tax agent does not try to justify himself to anyone, least of all to God; he pleads that God will decide on his justification, that is, God will acquit him (c.f. Romans 8:33-34).

It is worth pondering for a moment on the true meaning of mercy as shown by God in the Bible, and especially in the Old Testament. A classic example of its meaning can be found in the episode where Moses encounters God at the burning bush. Mercy has been identified as that quality which occurs between the identification of the distress experienced by one person or a whole people, and the action which is taken in response. So, when God tells Moses that he has heard the cry of his people in their distress, and that he is going to relieve that distress, we recognise first that God is aware of the problem (He has heard the cry of his people in their distress), and then that God has decided the action He will take (freedom from slavery). God's mercy is the stage between hearing the cry and the action which results. Likewise, in the prayer of the tax agent God, we are told, has heard the prayer of the humble man (i.e. the one who cries to God from the distress of his sinfulness). God's mercy leads to His action on behalf of the one praying, an action which Jesus declares results in the tax collector going home at rights with God (18:14). The Pharisee did not go home at rights with God, because he expressed no need to God which would allow Him in His mercy to respond. That is why those who exalt themselves will be humbled, but the humble will be exalted, as Mary prophetically sang in the Magnificat (1:52).

Sunday 31, Year C. Luke 19:1-10

Questions to ponder

☐	Who are responsible for Zacchaeus being lost? Himself? The crowd? The society in which he lives? His fellow 'children of Abraham'? All of these?

☐	What form does salvation take for Zacchaeus?

☐	Is this a conversion story, or a call to discipleship?

☐	These notes suggest two possible readings of Zacchaeus' intentions; the traditional intention for future behaviour, and a more recent suggestion that Zacchaeus outlines habitual action. Which do you prefer?

Our readings from the travel narrative in Luke's gospel began on the 13th Ordinary Sunday this year, with Jesus setting his face resolutely toward Jerusalem. As the narrative has unfolded, it has become increasingly apparent just how focussed Jesus has become about reaching his destination; it's not at all so certain that as readers of the gospel during these weeks we can be as certain about our destination! This week, we read the final extract of the journey narrative, with Jesus going through the town of Jericho and meeting Zacchaeus; another famous gospel story found only in Luke's gospel. The first sentence sounds strange: Jesus enters Jericho and passes through! Presumably this odd statement is there to remind us for the last time that Jesus is on a journey. There are a few other details about this story which are not found anywhere else in the New Testament. One is the name Zacchaeus, although it is also found in 2 Maccabees 10:19; another is the title 'chief tax-agent' (*architelōnēs*). For a fuller explanation of the role, and the collection of taxes in the Roman Empire, see the EXCURSUS below.

EXCURSUS: Collection of taxes in the Roman Empire

First things first: the term 'tax-collector' which is so often found in English translations of the Gospel, including the Lectionary's Jerusalem Bible, is inaccurate. Strictly, speaking in Jesus' time, the correct term was toll-collector (or agent) and Zacchaeus would have been the chief toll-collector (or agent) for his area. Tax-collectors properly so-called were to be found in the period prior to 47 BC, when the collection of taxes was handled by a *societas publicanorum* (which explains where the translation 'publican' comes from in some of our older English translations, even although this is also inaccurate). Members of these societies were wealthy Roman citizens, whose activities exploited the people in the provinces, often to the point of near ruin. In 47 BC, Julius Caesar reformed the collection of taxes among the Jews, reducing them considerably, and making Jubilee years completely tax-free. Three years later, he introduced an entirely new system of taxation altogether. As a result, in areas under the control of prefects and procurators (Judaea, Samaria, Idumea), direct taxes were taken up by 'tax-collectors' employed directly by the Romans. The collection of the other taxes, such as tolls, tariffs, import taxes, customs etc. was auctioned off to the highest bidder, who then became the 'chief toll-collector', and this would have been Zacchaeus' position. The 'chief toll-collector' would then employ agents (toll-collectors) who would be responsible to the actual collection of the various tariffs. In Matthew 9:9, and Mark 2:14, we hear that Levi, or Matthew, was sitting by the customs-house at Capernaum in Galilee when Jesus calls him. Interestingly here, unlike in Jericho in Judaea, where Zacchaeus operated, Herod Antipas had more direct control over tax-collection. In both places, Jews were employed in the collection of both direct and indirect taxes. The chief toll-collector who had successfully bid for the franchise to collect, had to provide the revenue demanded by the authorities, therefore would have decided on the amount to collect to cover costs pay staff, and make a profit. Clearly, the popular perception was that these people were universally guilty of extortion, and it is easy to see how the system lent itself to abuse and dishonesty. No wonder that 'everyone' grumbles that Jesus goes to the house of a chief toll-collector!

In 18:18, Luke uses the title *archion* ('ruler') to describe the man who addresses Jesus; 'Good teacher, what must I do to inherit eternal life?' This story is not read in the Sunday liturgy, but it is well known as the tale of a wealthy (*plousios*) man who is unwilling to part with his wealth when challenged to do so by Jesus. It is likely that Luke wishes to create a comparison and a contrast between that rich ruler, and Zacchaeus, a 'ruler among tax agents' who is also wealthy; we have already had occasion to observe Luke's penchant for pairing characters in his stories who demonstrate contrasting responses to the Prophet with whom they come into contact. We are told more about Zacchaeus than the others in this story however. He was anxious to see who Jesus was, and sets out to achieve his objective; being rather short of stature (literally, short of maturity or age '*he was short for his age*' might be a contemporary equivalent) and unable to see for the crowd (the omnipresent crowd as a role yet again on this journey) he climbs a tree – usually translated 'sycamore' but which could also be a mulberry tree. There is irony at work here: Zacchaeus *seeks out* Jesus and find out about him, so he heads for the tree which he hopes will afford him a better sighting should Jesus passes that way; at the end of the story, Jesus will declare that his own mission is to *seek out* and find a certain class of people. Zacchaeus' guess was correct; Jesus did pass that way, and when he reached the spot he looked up, saw Zacchaeus and called him, "Zacchaeus, come down. Hurry, because I must stay at your house today". On one level, this is a very unremarkable statement, a request by Jesus for somewhere to stay; on another level, it is a statement which resounds with so many motifs from this gospel and the New Testament in general. To begin with, we see here the classic pattern found in all Jesus' calls to discipleship. In the synoptic gospels (perhaps also in John, although the pattern is often more complex), there is always a fourfold pattern: 1) Jesus is on the move, 2) he sees whoever he will choose to call, 3) he issues a verbal call, and 4) if the call is successful, the one called joins Jesus on the journey. All four of these are to be found in the Zacchaeus story: Jesus passes the tree that Zacchaeus has climbed; he sees Zacchaeus; he calls to him to come down and invite Jesus into his house, and of course Zacchaeus responds. There are other themes in this episode as well, characteristically Lukan in their expression, which recall earlier motifs in the gospel. Jesus announces that 'today' he must stay at Zacchaeus' house; and later Jesus will announce that 'salvation has come to this house'. We heard a reference to 'today' as early as in the account of Jesus' appearance in the synagogue at Nazareth, when he announced, 'Today this scripture has been fulfilled in your hearing' (4:21; RSV translation), and following various displays of faith which have led to people's cures of ailments, Jesus often proclaims that the recipients of his healing have been 'saved' (e.g. the Samaritan leper, 17:19).

Zacchaeus is responding to the visitation of the Prophet Jesus to his town, and now Jesus wishes to enter his house. Zacchaeus greets him with warmth. Not surprisingly in a Lukan story, not everyone responds to the Prophet with the same enthusiasm as Zacchaeus! An undefined 'they' all grumbled when they saw what was happening. The word (*diagonguzō*), given as 'complained' in the Jerusalem Bible, recalls the attitude of the Israelites when in the desert; they grumbled against Moses during the forty years in the desert, they also grumbled against God, at the lack of food, and at the lack of water. In each case, God addressed their complaint, but the grumbling continued. In John 6, the 'Jews' grumble as Jesus makes claims with overtones of divinity about him being the bread of life. Often in Luke, it is the scribes and Pharisees who are responsible for a fair bit of grumbling (c.f. 5:30; 7:24. 39; 15:2), and here 'they' are grumbling at Jesus giving time and attention to Zacchaeus; "He has gone to stay at a sinner's house". We are given no indication as to who 'they' are; presumably this refers to the crowd who have been accompanying Jesus on his journey to Jerusalem and who have been growing in number, but it probably also refers to Jesus' disciples. If this is so, the effect is to link Jesus' own disciples and the accompanying crowd with the Pharisees and scribes, who earlier had complained in 15:2 that Jesus 'welcomes sinners and eats with them'. Zacchaeus stands his ground in the face of complaints. His defiant statement is well known; it concerns the question of Zacchaeus giving half his property to the poor and making a four-fold restitution if he discovers that someone has been cheated. The Torah defined the amount of restitution to be offered in the case of fraudulent behaviour. A four-fold restitution is to be made for a stolen sheep according to Exodus 22:1, and Leviticus 6:5 and Numbers 5:6-7 demand that full restitution 'plus one fifth' is demanded for stolen goods. Zacchaeus is therefore offering very generous terms of recompense, well above anything demanded by the Law. As a matter of course, he disposes of half of what he owns.

There is an important question arising here: does Zacchaeus promise to do something in the future, in response to Jesus' teaching? Or is he making a declaration of what is his customary practice? The Jerusalem Bible translates the Greek in such a way that Zacchaeus is outlining a pledge of future behaviour, but the Greek text is written in the present tense. Now this can still indicate a promise for the future, but equally, it might mean that Zacchaeus is describing what is and has been his customary practice: 'I habitually give half of my property to the poor, and if I find that I have defrauded someone, I pay back four times the amount'. Commentators are divided as to which is the more appropriate reading here, and this is reflected in the various English translations. The Jerusalem Bible renders Zacchaeus' speech as a statement of intent for future behaviour, but the RSV makes it a statement of current practice on the chef tax agent's part. Michael Mullins, in his commentary on Luke's gospel, offers an intriguing suggestion. When John the Baptist was preaching and baptising (which he did in remarkably close proximity to Jericho), tax agents asked him, "Teacher, what shall we do?" and John replied, "Collect no more than the amount prescribed for you" (c.f. 3:12-13). Mullins poses the question: could Zacchaeus have been one of those who listened to, and heeded John? Is he now protesting to Jesus that he has already undergone a change of heart?

Whether or not the interpretation suggested here is accurate or not does not actually affect the import of Jesus' response to Zacchaeus. Whether Zacchaeus' repentance is very recent (i.e. only arose at the time of Jesus' arrival in Jericho), or whether it began some time earlier, Jesus responds not only to Zacchaeus but also to those who complain and who have decided, probably with no evidence whatsoever, that Zacchaeus is a sinner. Jesus' response is: "Today salvation has come to this house, because this man too is a son of Abraham" (19:9). Now, there is no dispute about the tense: Jesus refers to an on-going situation: Zacchaeus is, always was and always will be a son of Abraham, although the crowd members would apparently prefer to ignore the fact. The word 'today' is significant for the second time in this passage. Now it definitely has overtones of the arrival of salvation, 'today, salvation has come to this house'. This happens 'today' because the Prophet, the Saviour who has been born for us (2:11), has brought salvation to the house of Zacchaeus, because the Son of Man has come to seek out and save what was lost (19:10). This is the ironic turn of events alluded to earlier in these notes: the story began with Zacchaeus seeking out Jesus to see what he was like: now Jesus is the one who seeks out and saves Zacchaeus, and all who had become lost; and it's at least a possibility that Zacchaeus is lost, not as a result of immoral and unethical behaviour, but because he has been deemed lost by those he should have been able to consider brothers and sisters: children of Abraham together.

To conclude, we might well take another look at Zacchaeus' call to discipleship. Earlier in these notes, we explored the four-fold call to discipleship, but one part of the process was not explored, and that is Zacchaeus' following the precedent set by disciples like Peter, Andrew, James, John, and Matthew the tax-agent. All of these left behind some aspect of their previous lives: nets, boats, counting tables. Zacchaeus renounces half of his property in favour of the poor. In the gospel of Luke, Jesus issues a repeated call that all who would be his disciples are first to dispose of their possessions and give the money to the poor. It is not always clear why this should be, but now, in Zacchaeus' example, we have a strong clue; disciples are by definition required to follow the example of their Lord, who placed all of his resources (his life) at the disposal of broken humanity; the commitment of disciples can be seen in their resolve to place their resources at the disposal of those in need. At the beginning of the notes on this passage, reference was made to the rich leader who was challenged to give his possessions to the poor and then follow Jesus, but who was unwilling to part with his considerable wealth. Now Zacchaeus, another leader and a rich one, is prepared to give away half of what he owns as a sign of his commitment to the poor, that is, those in need. Zacchaeus is a powerful symbol of those who are open to the salvation brought to their houses by the Prophet journeying toward Jerusalem.

Sunday 32, Year C. Luke 20:27-38

Questions to ponder

☐   Does this passage give us any insight into Jesus' thoughts on marriage?

☐   What does the concept of 'the God of the living' mean to you?

☐   How much of the Sadducees' rejection of resurrection do you think depends on their outlook on material wealth?

Before we consider this week's passage in detail, it is important first to put it into context. Not only is the journey narrative which we have been following now for many weeks drawing to an end, but there are significant Lukan episodes which are located between the end of the story of Zacchaeus from last week, and the present passage. These include the parable of the pounds, Luke's version of what in Matthew is the parable of the talents. In Luke, this takes on the added significance of pointing to judgement on those who rejected the Prophet (cast as the King in the parable), and who now face a reckoning since the Prophet has reached Jerusalem, where his destiny is fulfilled. Following the parable is the entry of the prophet to Jerusalem (the Palm Sunday processional Gospel), which is itself followed by Jesus' lament over Jerusalem and its impending destruction. Once in Jerusalem, Jesus the Prophet cleanses the temple and is promptly challenged by scribes and chief priests to declare on whose authority he did this. Jesus challenges them in return on their take on the authority with which John the Baptist taught. They fail to give an adequate response to Jesus, and are afraid of the crowd who hold Jesus in high regard, so they send agents (spies) to try to trap Jesus on their behalf: their ploy is to ask whether it is lawful to pay tax to the Romans. We take up the narrative when the next group of leaders try their hand at catching Jesus out. We might do well to recall the final story in Luke's Infancy Narrative, where the twelve year old Jesus is to be found in the Temple, listening to and questioning the elders, who are amazed at his wisdom. This early episode was a prophetic announcement of what lay in store in the final stages of the ministry of the adult Jesus, whose wisdom was such that even his greatest opponents could not better him in argument.

The Sadducees become the next group to try to trap Jesus into making some incriminating statement. Sadducee and Pharisee are titles which are often assumed to belong to different orders of religious leadership, but they should more accurately be thought of as the names of political parties. See the Excursus below for more details.

EXCURSUS: SADDUCEES (and PHARISEES)

The origins of the name Sadducee are thought to be traceable back to the priest Zadok, from the time of King David. According to the Jewish historian Josephus, around the time of Jesus or just after, there were to be found among the Jews three sects: the Essenes, the Pharisees and the Sadducees. It is interesting that there is no mention of the Essenes anywhere in the Bible. However, we do have mention of Pharisees in all four gospels and Acts, and of Sadducees in the Synoptic gospels and Acts, but not in John. It may be more useful to think of the Pharisees and Sadducees as 'political' parties, rather than as sects. The Sadducees, according to Josephus, had the rich members of the nations in their membership. At the risk of some over-simplification, it is probably true to say that the richer chief priests tended towards the party of the Sadducees, rather than that of the Pharisees. The danger with this kind of over-simplification is that we can reduce real people to caricatures – a bit like making the assertion that all members of the aristocracy in a country belong to one party, whereas all working class people belong to another. What is certainly true is that there were theological differences between the two factions. Sadducees accepted religious tradition only from the written word of God, and for that matter only accepted the books of Genesis, Exodus, Numbers, Leviticus and Deuteronomy as scripture. Pharisees accepted non-written traditions. This is part explains why Sadducees could reject angels, spirits and resurrection; these are not included in the five books they accepted as authoritative. Pharisees, then, were theologically more liberal (despite the impression the gospels may give of them).

There were political differences too. Pharisees derived their name from their aim to keep pure the Jewish traditions. They were opposed, therefore, to any form of collaboration with occupying powers (the Romans being the obvious example). Sadducees, on the other hand, were in favour of co-operation with the Romans – which explains firstly why they occupied the senior positions in religious government: Caiaphas the High Priest and his Father in law Annas would undoubtedly have been Sadducees: no Pharisee would have curried favour with the Romans sufficiently to stay in power as high Priest throughout Pontius Pilate's time in office.

One final point should be noted. The gospels make out that the Pharisees were the implacable opponents of Jesus. This was probably not the case. Pharisees only came to prominence once the Temple was destroyed by the Romans in 70 AD, and there was therefore no more Temple sacrifice, and no more need for priests, chief or otherwise. Also, the Sadducees would have lost their influence with the Romans when they destroyed Jerusalem. Synagogues then became the places of importance and Pharisees took charge as rabbis. Historically, we know that there was great tension between early Christians and Pharisees who were responsible for their expulsion from synagogues. Without access to accurate historical fact, gospel writers seem to have assumed that since the Pharisees were the enemies of Christians in their own tine, the same must have been true in Jesus' time. However, the oldest parts of the gospels, the Passion Narratives, scarcely mention the Pharisees at all; here, the Sadducees, in the form of Chief Priests, are the architects of Jesus' death.

In this passage, the Sadducees resort to an old argument to refute Jesus' teaching on the resurrection of the dead and thus to discredit him as a teacher of the Law. It may come as a surprise to today's readers of the gospel to find that the highest ranking officials in the Temple priesthood did not profess a belief in the resurrection, but in fact the concept only came late to Jewish belief; it is not recorded at all in the biblical literature until the books of Daniel and Maccabees, that is, from the time of Antiochus Epiphanes and the Maccabean revolt of c. 165 AD, specifically in passages such as Daniel 2:2-3; 2 Maccabees 7:9, 11, 14, 23. The book of Daniel claims to describe events during the time of the Babylonian exile, but is today widely accepted as having been written during the much later time of the Maccabees – probably to boost the confidence of Jews who were again suffering persecution, by providing them with uplifting tales of the courage of their ancestors in exile. The concept of bodily resurrection is also found in the non-biblical texts of 1 Enoch 91;10, and 2 Baruch 49-52; and belief in the resurrection was firmly held by the Pharisees (as attested in Josephus, Jewish War 2:163), and was held to some extent by the Essenes at Qumran, but was not held by the Sadducees. Strange as it may seem to Christian gospel readers of today the Sadducees', in their rejection of the doctrine of resurrection, could claim to be holding the more traditional position, since they cited more ancient sources in their arguments against this new doctrine, as the Excursus above demonstrates. The conflict between Sadducees and Pharisees on this topic is exploited fully by Paul, himself Pharisee-trained, in Acts 223:7-10, where the Sadducees open their argument by appealing to Moses, whose authority alone they accepted.

In the passage we are currently exploring, they argue (very loosely) from Deuteronomy 25:5, which is concerned with what came to be known as the 'levirate' marriage, the word levirate being derived from the Latin for brother-in-law. The Deuteronomy text runs: "If brothers live together and one of them dies childless, the dead man's wife must not marry a stranger outside the family. Her husband's brother must come to her and, exercising his levirate, make her his wife". The loose quote from the Sadducees adds from Genesis 38:8, "…and raise up offspring for your brother", and is part of Judah's instruction to Onan. The Sadducees exaggerate the argument with their absurd tale of the woman married to seven brothers in turn, each one of whom dies childless. The woman herself dies, so to which of these will she be married in the resurrection? They really want to say 'the supposed' resurrection!

Luke's version of the story along with Jesus' reply to the Sadducees' nonsensical argument, follows that of Mark's gospel fairly closely, except for some minor additions by Luke. Most notable perhaps is Luke's addition to Jesus' reply of the words "they are the same as the angels", which possibly points ahead to the scene for Paul's trial where Pharisees and Sadducees are both present, and where the existence of angels is drawn into the dispute (Acts 23:8-9). Both Mark and Luke (from different angles) set out to demonstrate the vast difference in the perspective of the Sadducees compared with that of Jesus. The argument of the Sadducees concerning the 'marriage anomaly' which they think renders impossible any realistic prospect of a resurrection is diametrically opposed to Jesus' insistence that God is of the living, and not of the dead. In fairness, Jesus' argument is one that probably leaves the contemporary reader/hearer of the gospel rather cold, but it is one which his Jewish hearers would in all probability have found convincing. It runs as follows: when Moses encountered God at the burning bush, God said, "I am the God of your ancestors,' he said, 'the God of Abraham, the God of Isaac and the God of Jacob" (Exodus 3:6). Jesus argues that God speaks of generations of patriarchs in the present tense, although by Moses' time they are all dead. For God to speak thus means that to God, therefore, they are alive. The argument put forward by the Sadducees is by contrast firmly rooted in a view of unalterable death once this life is concluded.

Perhaps if we are to understand this argument more fully, we need to be aware of the conventions attached to marriage in New Testament times and even before. Marriage contracts were largely matters of family business. Marriage was usually arranged, and almost always within the extended family. A major factor in these arrangements was to ensure that family property and money remained always within the family – the only institution of social support available in ancient culture. Employment was found within the family, support in illness or times of hardship was only to be found within the family, and of course marriage and the procreation of offspring was directed toward the continuation of the family. Hence the 'levirate' law which required an unmarried man to assume the marital duties of his deceased brother, if the latter died childless. It is highly probable that the conventions of marriage thus understood would probably have had even greater significance for the Sadducees. At the risk of reducing them to mere caricatures Sadducees, who were the affluent members of Jewish society, may have tended to be preoccupied with property and wealth and therefore more likely to be directed to material things. They may therefore have been less likely to develop a theological interest in a world beyond this one; hence their reluctance to move from the old, traditional view that there is no resurrection of the dead. If this argument is correct, then the 'levirate marriage' question would be of great significance to them: if a wife was widowed and childless, it was of the utmost importance to the Sadducees and other senior religious figures who were likely to be the heads of families, to make sure the widow remarried within the family to ensure that all property and money was retained. Furthermore, if they argued that there was no resurrection, then it was also important to ensure that there were future generations to retain the memory of ancestors, since this was the only

possible way they could imagine anyone 'living on' after death.
Jesus' argument does not aim to 'unpick' the Sadducees' position; instead, he approaches the question from a totally different angle. If God is God of the living, and not of the dead, and if all people are alive to God – and further, although Jesus does not elaborate the point here, if Jesus has come so that all may have life and have it to the full (c.f. John 10:10), then the fullness of life is never to be equated with what a person owns, inherits, or possesses! We saw this clearly on Sunday 18 this year, where Jesus states explicitly, "for a man's life is not made more secure by what he owns, even when someone has more than he needs" (12:15). When we read this dispute between Jesus and the Sadducees in the wider context of Luke's gospel, it is difficult to avoid the memory of Jesus' repeated injunction to disciples and others during the Journey Narrative, 'no one can be my disciple unless he gives up all his possessions.' For Luke, the key to the Sadducees' inability to embrace the concept of resurrection seems to lie in their unwillingness to detach themselves form material possessions, and perhaps more crucially, from a world order whose success or failure is measured according to the possession and acquisition of wealth!

Sunday 33, Year C. Luke 21:5-19

Questions to ponder

☐   What do the destruction of the Temple and stories of persecution of early Christians tell us about the challenges of discipleship today?

☐   What form might the test take today that we are to pray to be able to survive?

☐   Endurance will win disciples' lives. Today, what kind of endurance will win us our lives?

The setting this week is still Jerusalem, but Jesus has now left the Temple area, having dealt decisively with the leaders who tried to find flaws in his teaching. Now, he is surrounded by people – presumably his own disciples – spellbound by the splendour of the Temple. It is not surprising that people from the agricultural and fishing background of Galilee would be so overwhelmed by what Luke describes as the 'beautiful stonework and votive offerings'. The latter were memorials paid for by wealthy Jews to adorn the Temple and of course to preserve their own memory after they had died.

Interestingly, the Greek word for these is *anathēma*, literally 'what is set up', and a term that came to be used in pronouncements from Church Councils against those who were condemned for unorthodox views.

The disciples' amazement provides a platform for Jesus to make another series of prophetic utterances, all of which are known to have been fulfilled. These, as we shall see, are all related to the destruction of the Temple, and the sufferings which disciples will face after Jesus has gone. Earliest readers of the gospel would have known that these things had indeed all come to pass, and that some of them are fulfilled in the pages of the Acts of the Apostles, the second volume of Luke's two-volume work. This is an important point to note, since it is too easy to assume that the sayings of Jesus in this passage refer to a future, fierce-sounding series of events relating to the end times and the return of the Son of Man. These words are very firmly related to events which are now long past. The passage reinforces Luke's favourite identification of Jesus as the prophet whom Moses had foretold, a prophet like Moses himself, raised from the Israelites' own stock. Throughout the Old Testament there is the conviction that a true prophet can only be recognised as such once his prophecy is fulfilled. Jesus is the genuine Prophet then because his prophetic utterances have been fulfilled before this gospel came to be written.

The disciples' reference to the magnificence of the Temple is where Jesus begins his prophetic statements. The very splendour they so admire will be entirely destroyed: not a single stone will be left standing on another. The disciples, horrified at his words, ask 'Master, when will this happen, and what sign will there be that this is about to take place?' It is to be taken for granted by now that Jesus will most likely refuse a direct answer to a question about times and signs. However, his response is more directed than usual, and more time conditioned than normal. He warns his listeners to take care, because many will come using his name and saying "I am he", and, "The time is near at hand." They are to refuse to join them. Further, they will hear of wars and revolutions. They are not to be afraid, because these things will of necessity take place (and of course still do), but these are not signs that the end is soon. Jesus' next prophecy, or rather collection of prophecies, are ones that we see being fulfilled all too often today; nation will fight against nation, and kingdom against kingdom. There will be earthquakes and plagues and famines here and there; there will be fearful sights and great signs from heaven. The past year, like each year before it has given us all of these – we could also add floods and volcanic eruptions and ash that for primitive peoples in the past could easily have understood as some portent or other coming from heaven! Readers of the gospel would remember all too clearly that this is precisely what they have already experienced – wars and natural disasters they shared in common with our own generation. They would have had a very graphic memory of the fulfilment of Jesus' prediction about the Temple's destruction, and not one stone standing on another; the first people to read this gospel probably did so within 10 years of the event itself, which took place during September/October 70 AD. They would read these words, conscious of how accurate were the prophecies of the 'Prophet like Moses' (although today we should also take into account the contribution of the evangelist in editing the words of Jesus in a way that sharpens the accuracy of his prophecy). This is only one aspect of the prophetic utterances however. In this narrative, Jesus insists that before the destruction of the Temple, wars, earthquakes and sundry disasters occur, other things will happen first. Disciples will be seized, persecuted and handed over to synagogues and governors because of his name; they will be betrayed even by parents and family and friends, and some will even be put to death. The reader who is familiar with the story will be aware that much of this prophecy is fulfilled also in the Passion Narrative in which Jesus is betrayed by one of the Twelve, handed over to both the governor (Pilate) and the 'king' (Herod; technically the tetrarch, and not the king) and put to death. Fulfilment of this prophecy will be found in Acts, where James is put to death, Paul and various other disciples are dragged before governors, Kings and Sanhedrins.

The accuracy of Jesus' prophecies is already well known, but the purpose of this passage is not simply to recall and validate the utterances of Jesus. He makes yet other predictions; they need not worry about what to say when these things happen, because it is Jesus himself who will give them words to speak (literally, give them a mouth). He assures them that although they will be hated by all men, not a hair of their heads will be lost. Their endurance will win them their lives. The direction of the evangelist's argument is not difficult to follow: if Jesus' prophetic statements about the Temple, and about persecution and betrayal have been so spectacularly accurate, then disciples should have total confidence in his predictions about their own future: and it will be their endurance in the midst of all the trials which he has predicted will come their way which will win every generation of disciples their lives. On several occasions throughout this gospel, Jesus made statements which may not have made too much sense at the time, but whose meanings become clearer later. The prophecies in this passage may help make sense of Jesus' earlier enigmatic statements about prayer and faith with which disciples must prepare themselves to face the test. For example, when teaching the disciples how to pray, Jesus urges them to include the clause, 'do not put us to the test' (11:4). In the present passage, we have a clearer idea of what that test may involve; persecution, betrayal, even death. Constant prayer, and especially the prayer that we may not be put to the test, is the way to achieve the endurance which Jesus now promises will win disciples their lives. Will disciples heed the command to constant prayer? Will they ask not to be put to the test? Is this why, at the end of the parable about the wicked judge and the persistent widow, Jesus posed the question, "when the son of man comes, will he find any faith on earth?" (Lk 18:8; Sunday 29).

Christ the King, Year C. Luke 23:35-43

Questions to ponder

☐   What do you understand by the concept of 'salvation'?
☐   The crowd who watch Jesus die are silent. Can we conclude anything of their attitude to his death in their silence?
☐   Why might Jesus have promised paradise, and not heaven to the criminal who requests that Jesus remember him in his kingdom? Is there a difference between the two terms?

In recent Sundays of this liturgical year (Sundays 28 and 32 in particular), the subject of salvation has featured – one of the major themes in the gospel of Luke. In fact, salvation is never far from the surface in this gospel: in the Infancy Narratives Jesus' birth is announced with the words "today a Saviour has been born to you" (2:11). In the notes for Sunday 28, there is an exploration of the width of the concept of salvation in Luke, a concept that seems to embrace the entire human existence, in this life as well as in the next.

On the final Sunday of this liturgical year, the Solemnity of Jesus Christ, Universal King, the gospel is concerned with the concept of salvation. The setting is the crucifixion of Jesus, and in common with the other two synoptic gospels, Luke examines the reactions of different groups of people who witness Jesus' death. These are 'the people' who stayed there watching; the 'leaders', that is, the chief priests and the elders, and Jesus' two 'co-crucified'. Briefly, the behaviour of these groups is recorded as they respond to the sight of the crucified Jesus. The first of these groups is dealt with differently by Luke in comparison with Mark who describes relentless human opposition to and rejection of Jesus right up to his death. Luke, on the other hand, is at great pains to separate the attitude of the crowd from that of its leaders. The crowd has been growing throughout the journey narrative, but has not really done anything except be present. Occasionally, someone from the crowd would shout out or ask a question, but for the most part the crowd is silent. At the foot of the cross, the Lukan crowd watches. In verse 48, beyond the extent of today's passage, and after Jesus has died, we are told that the crowd who have been watching and who had gathered simply to watch the spectacle (Roman crucifixions were very public affairs) go home, beating their breasts, a traditional sign of penitence.

If the crowds watched silently, the same cannot be said of the leaders who taunt Jesus on his apparent lack of ability to do for himself what he has done for others, "He saved others; let him save himself if he is the Christ of God, the Chosen One". Luke here gathers many of the important motifs which have been at the centre of Jesus' ministry and particularly his teaching throughout the gospel, and all of which are now firmly rejected by the leaders. Jesus is persuaded to save himself; as far back as his appearance in the Nazareth synagogue, however, he had said, rather prophetically, "No doubt you will quote me the saying, 'Physician, heal yourself'" (4:23). Despite everything that Jesus has said and done throughout the whole of his ministry, a similar jibe is thrown at him at the end of his life. Interestingly, the leaders do not appear to have a problem with the idea that Jesus saved others (examples are to be found in Luke 7:50; 8:48; 17:19; 18:24); they have however missed two important points. First, those whom Jesus has saved invariably become so as a result of their faith. Second, before he began his journey to Jerusalem, Jesus explicitly stated, "Anyone who wants to *save* his life will lose it; but anyone who loses his life for my sake, that man will *save* it" (9:24). The jibes go beyond this however, questioning whether Jesus can be the Christ of God, the Chosen One. They will not believe that this can be the case unless Jesus 'saves' himself, which of course they equate with self-preservation. However, Peter, who had identified Jesus as the Christ of God (9:20) - exactly the words used by the elders – had also heard, along with

James and John, a heavenly voice say at Jesus' transfiguration "this is my Son, the Chosen One", immediately followed by the instruction, "Listen to him" (9:35). Right up until Jesus' death, the leaders of the people are still refusing to listen to God's chosen one.

The soldiers also join in the abuse of the condemned Jesus, taunting him using the charge under which he has been (wrongly) condemned (remember that Pilate declared three times that he could find no charge to bring against Jesus, and no crime which was punishable by crucifixion, 23:4.14.22).

The final 'group' among those present at Jesus' death are two criminals hanging there: notice that Luke does not call them robbers, and does not explicitly state that they are crucified; he simply says that they were hanging there, although it is safe to assume they are being crucified. The explicit identification of them both as crucified and as thieves comes from Matthew 27:44. In Luke, the two criminals make another classic pair of contrasting figures; the first joins in the chorus of elders, taunting Jesus: "are you not the Christ? Save yourself", but he adds an additional comment, motivated by self-preservation right to the end of his life, "and us as well!" (23:39). Here again is the assumption that the only type of salvation is the preservation of one's own skin. By now, however, we know that the story can never end like this in Luke's gospel. The other criminal rebukes the first, "Have you no fear of God at all?" (23:40). Fear of the Lord is the classic attribute of the pious in the Bible. In the Psalms, special regard is given to those who 'fear the Lord', and the expression was used to describe the character of the unjust judge in 18:2 (Sunday 29 C), only in that case he was described as someone with no fear of God nor, for that matter respect for human beings! This criminal is clearly of the same mentality as the judge in the parable; neither is prepared to listen to the word of God, so his companion points out to him the facts of the situation: all three, Jesus and the two criminals, have had the same sentence passed on them; a sentence of death by crucifixion; but there is an ironic further meaning to that sentence. This is indeed God's judgement: in Jesus' case, it will mean God conferring on him the glory with which he was seen at the transfiguration. In the criminal who wants Jesus to save himself and him as well, it will mean the judgement that will be dealt to those who refuse to listen to the Christ, the Chosen One. To the other criminal, the outcome of God's judgement will soon be disclosed, and it will rest on the next words which he speaks.

The second criminal, having acknowledged that he and his companion were being punished for what they had done (notice that there was no mention of this from his 'friend') states that Jesus, on the other hand, was completely innocent, having done nothing wrong (this recalls 1 Peter 2:21-24; '…Christ suffered for you, leaving you an example for you to follow in His steps, who committed no sin, nor was any deceit found in His mouth; and while being reviled, He did not revile in return; while suffering, He uttered no threats, but kept entrusting Himself to Him who judges righteously…'). The man then famously turns to Jesus and says "Jesus, remember me when you come into your kingdom" (23:42). He is the only human being in the gospel who addresses Jesus by his name, which of course means 'saviour'. One condemned criminal frantically demands that Jesus save himself and the other condemned men too: the other turns to the one whom he can in faith call the Saviour. Making this recognition, he has no need to utter near-hysterical demands for release from his fate. Instead, he can make a humble, faith-inspired request. The result is that his faith, his hope, his request to be remembered is assured; Jesus, the Prophet who is able to pronounce God's judgement, replies with great solemnity, "Indeed, I promise you, today you will be with me in paradise" (23:43). No one in the gospel makes a more profound profession of faith and trust in the Saviour; no one is given such a direct and immediate assurance of salvation as a result of faith than this criminal. Jesus' initial prophetic utterance had been to promise Good News to the poor, liberty to captives etc. His last words are to announce the fulfilment of those words to the man beside him, and to make that further prophecy; today you will be with me in Paradise.

FEASTS ETC.

Easter is over, but there are two more Sunday Feasts to be celebrated before we return to the Ordinary Sundays of Year C. These are the Solemnities of the Most Holy Trinity, and the Solemnity of the Body and Blood of Christ. Neither is ever celebrated within the context of Easter, but both display characteristics that were associated this year with Easter.

Notes for these are given under Feasts, at the end of the nots for Sundays of Ordinary Time

The Solemnity of the Most Holy Trinity, Year C. John 16:12-15

Questions to Ponder

☐　　How can it be possible that the Paraclete, the Spirit, will add anything to the Truth already revealed by Jesus, since Jesus has already said he IS the Truth?

☐　　In what sense will the Spirit teach disciples about "the things yet to come"?

☐　　What is the role of the Spirit in 'bringing back to God' those who are drawn into the Truth of the Father which is revealed in the Son, through which the Son is revealed in the Spirit (or to put this another way: how does the Spirit complete the Progression of Father and Son toward humanity by bringing humanity back to God)?

The Mystery of the Blessed Trinity is that notoriously difficult topic for preachers and those who have to listen to them! The Good News is that Trinity Sunday is an occasion to celebrate rather than to understand the Trinity. In this context, the impenetrable mystery of the Trinity makes way for the much more accessible idea that the one God who is Father, Son and Holy Spirit is a God who has not only chosen to reveal God's self to humans, but to be present to humans. The highpoint in God's revealing to us what God is like was reached when the Son, the One whom the Father had sent, came into our world as Word made Flesh and who was raised up to give glory to God – i.e. to make God's intentions for humanity crystal clear: God loved the world so much that he gave his son so that through him the world might be saved (c.f. John 3:16-17). So, the Son of Man raised up is God, in human form, giving to humanity all that God has – God's life! After Jesus, the Spirit continues to make God known (give glory to God) to all future generations. So, today and every day, since normally in the liturgy we address our prayers to the Father, through the Son and by the power of the Holy Spirit, we celebrate the God who as Father, Son and Holy Spirit, enters and remains in our lives. The gospel for today explores these ideas in depth.
At first sight, this passage is just another from the Last Supper Discourse in

John's gospel about the Holy Spirit – we did read quite a few of these in the last few weeks of Easter this year, so the obvious question to ask is whether the liturgy of the word for Trinity Sunday is any more than a repeat of the themes we have already considered? In one sense this is a fair comment, but on closer examination we might just find that what we are being presented with in this gospel passage will provide an insight into the Trinity from the perspective of the action of the Holy Spirit, and that in fact what the liturgy brings us to this year is a realisation that we can only develop even the slightest insight into the life of the Trinity through the perspective of the Holy Spirit. In short, the Spirit's role is to keep before us what he has taken from the One whom the Father has sent: Jesus, the one who is the Word of God made flesh.

The tone is set in the very first verse of today's gospel passage. Jesus says, "I still have many things to say to you but they would be too much for you now" (John 16:12). The passage and indeed the entire liturgy for today is about the on-going task of the Revelation of God: that is, God's disclosure of self to humanity. Throughout this gospel, Jesus has been presented as the One whom the Father has sent, and therefore the One who gives glory to God and who is himself glorified. To put it another way: Jesus is the One in whom God is revealed as well as being the One who is thereby revealed as God. This is why Jesus has already described himself in this discourse as the Truth (along with the Way and the Life, c.f. John 14:6). Later when on trial before Pilate, Jesus will define his role as to bear witness to the Truth and he will add that those who are on the side of Truth listen to his voice, his words (John 18:37). During his ministry, Jesus challenged his hostile hearers to believe him on the strength of his works, even if they would not believe his words (e.g. John 10:38, "even if you refuse to believe in me, at least believe in the work I do; then you will know for sure that the Father is in me and I am in the Father").

The 'many things' that Jesus has still to say to his disciples are bound up in the notion of truth. The divine truth is and always will be too much for disciples to grasp, whether it be those present during the Last Supper discourse, and at the Hour of Jesus which the discourse introduces, or those who are disciples in any age of human history. Divine Truth is the Revelation of God, and therefore will always be too much for those limited by this world. Divine Truth is Divine consistency, that is, the complete harmony and total agreement that exists among Father, Son and Spirit – the three persons of the Trinity. It is the role of the Holy Spirit, the one called the Paraclete (the Comforter, the Advocate), the one whom the Father will send in Jesus' name, the one whom Jesus will ask the Father to send will lead the disciples to all truth. Perhaps what this means is that the Spirit will direct those whom the Father has given Jesus toward the very heart of truth, i.e. divine consistency; complete divine harmony. The Spirit therefore will glorify Jesus: that is, make Jesus known in the world, because all that the Spirit tells disciples of all generations will be taken from what Jesus himself has.

We begin now to be drawn into Trinitarian themes. Even though the gospel for today does not present a fully worked out Trinitarian theology (this would not appear until some considerable time after the period of the New Testament writings, and therefore should not be sought in even the gospel of John), we do see the emergence of a progression, a dynamic. The Spirit 'speaks' not as of himself but will only speak of what he has learned: what the Spirit has learned is what he has taken from the Son, and what the Son has is everything that the Father has. The Spirit, since he takes what he has learned from Jesus, glorifies Jesus: he makes Jesus known, he reveals the Son. The progression is therefore (in reverse order, as it were) that the Spirit, now active in the world because he has been asked for by the Son and sent by the Father, is the one who reveals the Son in the post-Resurrection (and Ascension) world. The Son was/is the One whom the Father sent into the world and who had made the Father known in the world (gave glory to the Father, revealed the Father).

As was noted at the beginning of this reflection, the mystery of the Trinity is never going to be an easy concept to master or on which to preach. Perhaps the best way we can make any sense of it is to use today's gospel to help us draw together the various strands and lines of thought that we have considered over the past few weeks from earlier sections in John's gospel and - following the image of this week's gospel - to allow the Holy Spirit to lead us further into the complete truth. In this way, we may recall the process which begins with the very first verse of John's gospel: that the Word existed from the beginning, the Word was God and the Word was with God. Nothing came into being except through or by the Word. This is of course an expression both of the act of creation and the will of God in creating: In the beginning, God spoke the Word and the Word acted in creation, and all that came to be had life in Him. In time (literally) the Word became flesh and dwelt among humanity; to all who accepted the Word, he gave the power to become children of God. God's purpose is unfolding in this. In his conversation with Nicodemus, Jesus says "God loved the world so much that he gave his only Son, so that everyone who believes in him may not be lost but may have eternal life. For God sent his Son into the world, not to condemn the world, but so that through him the world might be saved" (John 3:17-18). The sending of the Son is not a command or an order: it is the will of the Father, shared by the Son, expressed in the Incarnation, resulting in the life of the world. But the dynamic here is one way: it is God reaching out, giving life to the world. Without the role of the Holy Spirit, the dynamic would remain one way, because it would not be possible for humanity to reach back to God: but the Spirit will teach disciples all they need to know, will remind them of all that Jesus has taught, and will bring humanity back to the God who reached out to humanity with life: this is because the Spirit is the one who leads disciples to the complete truth: that is, to God!

The Body and Blood of Christ, Year C. Luke 9:11-17

Questions to Ponder

☐　　In the other accounts of this miracle, crowds find Jesus and he responds to their needs either by teaching or healing. In this account the Prophet Jesus welcomes his people. What do you think is the significance of this for the miraculous feeding of 5,000?

☐　　In a rather artificial way, Luke suggests a very formal arrangement of the 5,000 in groups of fifty, reclining on the grass and being served as if at table. How much of this is supposed to suggest Eucharist, and in what way?

☐　　Why were twelve baskets of food left over? What is the significance of this for us, in today's climate of ecological concern for what would seem like unnecessary waste?

☐　　How important is the role of the Twelve in this account of the feeding miracle?

Only in Year C does the gospel for the Body and Blood of Christ give us the Feeding of the 5000 from Luke's gospel. On other years, the gospels are form the Bread of Life Discourse in John chapter 6 (Year A) and Mark's account of the Last Supper (Year C). This miracle is the only one which is told in all four gospels, and it is told with remarkable consistency. There are however

significant –even if relatively small - differences in the narratives across the
four versions, as we shall see.

In Luke's version, Jesus welcomes the crowd and gathers the people to him.
Jesus the Prophet is gathering his people around him – Luke again presents
Jesus as the Prophet promised by Moses. Jesus engages in healing and
teaching the crowd (only Luke has Jesus both teaching and healing - the dual
work of prophetic figures like Elijah and Elisha); Mark tells us that Jesus
taught the crowd (but does not disclose the content of his teaching) and
Matthew says he healed their sick and that the disciples point out that it is
getting late and they are in a lonely place. They therefore urge Jesus to send
the people away to neighbouring villages to buy food, although we might
conclude that it can't be that much of a lonely place if it's surrounded by
villages! Luke subtly changes the order in which specific details of the story
are disclosed. First, he mentions at the beginning of the story rather than at
the end that there were about 5,000 men. Second, he quotes the disciples as
saying the people will have to be sent away, unless the disciples themselves
are supposed to go and buy food for them all. Third and perhaps most
significantly, in Luke Jesus instructs the disciples to place the people in a
very specific order. In Mark, we are told that the instruction was to get the
5,000 to sit down, but NOT in fifties and hundreds as in the Jerusalem Bible
translation. The expression Mark uses is *symposia symposia*, group by group,
or as some have suggested, drinking party by drinking party! The implication
is that the arrangement of the people was very informal, with everyone
sitting, or lying back on the grass, and in a relaxed manner. Luke uses the
same verb for the way the people are arranged on the ground (*klinas*), but
does so in a way that suggests that the people are made to recline, or are
instructed to do so, in much the same way as a waiter will ask diners to be
seated. The formality of this arrangement, incongruous as it would have
seemed at an outside gathering, is further suggested by the image of the
Twelve, once Jesus has pronounced the customary thanksgiving over the food
prior to eating, serving each of the groups of fifty: the verb Luke uses is
paratithēmi, which literally means to set beside, or in front of, with the
implied meaning of setting food before diners, or serving. Like Matthew and
Mark, Luke adds that everyone is satisfied, but the words have added
significance in this gospel because twice already in this gospel Luke has
given us references to the hungry being satisfied and the rich sent away
empty: c.f. Luke 1:53; "The hungry he has filled with good things, the rich

sent empty away", and even more explicitly, Luke 6:21, "Happy you who are hungry now: you shall be satisfied".

Finally, whereas Matthew and Mark stress the large size of the crowd at the very end of the narrative Luke, as already noted, places the reference to the 5,000 at the very beginning of the narrative. This means that the final emphasis here is not on the number of people involved, but in the great abundance that remains at the end of the meal – a huge crowd has been fed and twelve baskets of food have been gathered. There is clearly a link as well between the number of those appointed by Jesus to provide service for the crowd, and the number of baskets. Twelve was the number of tribes on which the people of God Israel was established, an Israel which has failed in its commission to feed the people of God. Especially in Luke, the ministry of the Prophet Jesus is to re-constitute the true Israel, now built on the foundation of the Twelve he has called to the special service of the people of God.

Luke's version of the feeding of the 5,000 shares with the other gospels its depiction of Jesus as the one who performs the work of God by feeding his people in desert (lonely) places, just as God had fed the Israelites with manna in the desert (Exodus 16). In Luke's version, however, another role is stressed, not only for Jesus but also for the Twelve, and that is the role of service. At the Last supper, Jesus will say to those reclining at table with him: "here am I among you as one who serves" (Luke 22:27). Some three chapters after the feeding of the 5,000, after Jesus has told a parable about preparing for the return of the Son of Man, Peter asks, "Lord, do you mean this parable for us, or for everyone?" (Luke 12:41). In his reply, Jesus compares the Twelve to stewards: those who know their master's wishes, but who don't carry out those wishes will carry more responsibility for their failures than those who did not know what their responsibilities were (c.f. Luke 12:47-48). In the Acts of the Apostles, the ministry of service to those 'at table' will become very important (c.f. Acts 4:35, where the apostles were responsible for the distribution of money to those who needed it; and Acts 6:1-2, were steps were taken to resolve the problem of uneven distribution of bread to widows. Deacons were appointed to oversee this very task).

These observations lead us to the realisation that in Luke's account the feeding of the 5,000 gives us insight into the nature of the Eucharist we celebrate and share. The following conclusions can be drawn. 1) Eucharist is the initiative, the gift of Jesus; 2) it is inseparably caught up in Jesus' dual role of teacher and healer (hence the inseparable nature of Word and

Eucharist in our celebration of the liturgy; 3) the nourishment provided by the Eucharist is in greater abundance than the need of those being nourished: there will always be more than enough for everyone, and finally 4) the distribution of the Eucharist (as well as its continued provision in the name of Jesus) is the responsibility of the Church which is given stewardship of the Eucharist; responsibility in the sense that it is the Church's obligation to provide that nourishment for those who would be fed, taught and healed by the Lord.

2 February

Feast of the Presentation of the Lord. Luke 2:22-40

The gospel for this feast is the same as is read on the Feast of the Holy Family Year B. Notes for that day are reproduced here.

Questions to ponder:

☐   Can we read the gospel texts offered for this feast without descending into a sentimental and totally unreal version of family life which the gospel does NOT describe for Jesus, Mary and Joseph?

☐   Conversely, how do we apply the various elements of prophetic utterance in word and action of this particular narrative as a genuine model for family life in contemporary society?

☐   The issues surrounding the Holy Family of Jesus, Mary and Joseph have a contemporary ring about them (see the first sentence below). What does this Feast say to us about these problems facing our own society?

Far from the sentimental – often sickeningly so – picture that can be conjured up when we consider the Holy Family of Jesus Mary and Joseph in their various surroundings at Nazareth, the hill-country of Judea, Bethlehem, not to mention Egypt, we have in fact in the narratives that cover their lives a rather extensive list of problems of a dysfunctional family, problems that are all too common in our own culture. To name but a few, we have a teenage unmarried mother, homelessness, a father presumably unemployed when the child is born, a child seriously at risk, albeit from the government of the day, the speedy flight to another land, and the resultant question of refugee status, asylum seeking, and underlying all of that there is the level of poverty that makes it necessary for a lesser form of ritual to be carried out in the aftermath of the child's birth. A model for family life? Proceed carefully on that one!

In Year C of the three-year liturgical cycle, it is again the prophecy and fulfilment theme that seems to work best for this particular celebration. The mood is set out early in the passage. Luke briefly describes two religious observances, but as was the case in his account if the Census his attention to detail is again somewhat lacking. One is the Rite of Purification for a mother after childbirth (and not the purification of both parents, as Luke seems to indicate), and the other what the Jerusalem Bible refers to as the consecration of the first-born to the Lord. This is taken from Exodus 13:2, "Consecrate all the first-born to me, the first issue of every womb, among the sons of Israel. Whether man or beast, this is mine." These two verses make it clear that Jesus was from the earliest brought up according to the precepts of the Jewish Law, and here his parents are cast in the role of pious and poor Jewish people. According to Leviticus 12:6, a mother was to bring to the temple an offering of a year-old lamb and either a turtle-dove or a pigeon for her purification after childbirth; however, if the mother cannot afford this offering, she can make the one indicated here by Luke: a pair of turtledoves or two young pigeons, as laid down by Leviticus 5:7 as the offering of the poor. To return to the consecration of the firstborn, other translations (e.g. the RSV) express the Exodus passage and its citation in Luke 2:23 as "Every male that opens the womb shall be called holy to the Lord". There is little difference in the meaning, but this latter reading helps us to remember the angel's prophecy at the Annunciation; the child would be holy, and called the son of God (c.f. Luke 1:35). Yet another prophecy about this child is fulfilled.

This leads us nicely to the two prophetic figures in the Temple, Simeon and Anna. Simeon is mentioned first. He, like the other characters in Luke's infancy narrative, is righteous and pious (even Zechariah comes into that category). Simeon is 'in waiting', expecting, looking forward to a 'comforting', or consolation of Israel (Luke 2:25). This provides an echo for the opening of the Book of Consolation in Isaiah 40:1, "'Console my people, console them' says your God". Consolation will be mentioned again in Luke, in 6:24, among the woes that parallel the Lukan Beatitudes: "…alas for you who are rich: you are having your consolation now", and in 16:25, in the story of the rich man and Lazarus: "My son," Abraham replied "remember that during your life good things came your way, just as bad things came the way of Lazarus. Now he is being comforted (consoled) here while you are in agony". Luke says that the Holy Spirit rested on Simeon, a Spirit of prophecy, that is, as has already been the role of the Spirit for John the Baptist in Luke 1:15, "Even from his mother's womb he will be filled with the Holy Spirit [i.e. will prophesy]"; 1:17, "With the spirit and power of Elijah…"; with Mary, in 1:47, "my spirit exults in God my Saviour"; and with Zechariah, now able to carry out his prophetic/priestly role, having finally accepted and carried out God's will in 1:67; "His father Zechariah was filled with the Holy Spirit and spoke this prophecy". In Simeon's case, the role of the Spirit is unmistakably prophetic, because the Spirit has revealed to Simeon, that he will "not see death until he had set eyes on the Christ of the Lord", and that "Prompted by the Spirit he came to the Temple" (Luke 2:26-27), an expression reminiscent of that in Matthew 2:12. 22 concerning Joseph's dreams. This prophesies, or foreshadows, the appearance of Jesus in the synagogue at Nazareth, described in similar language in Luke 4:1, 14.

The episode takes place in the Temple grounds, and not the sanctuary, which Simeon, Jesus, Mary and Joseph would have been unable to enter. Luke uses the Greek word *hieron* for this, whereas in the passage in which the angel appears to Zechariah, the word he uses for Temple is *naon*. The former refers to the whole Temple complex (mostly open courts), and the latter to the sanctuary that only priests could enter. (These two words for 'temple' were the basis for the play on words in the account of Jesus cleansing the Temple in John 2:19-21). As a woman, Mary would have been able to proceed only as far as the Temple outer courts, presumably taking a lead from Leviticus 12:6 on the way a woman was to bring an offering to the priest, "she is to bring to the priest at the entrance to the Tent of Meeting a lamb one year old for a holocaust, and a young pigeon or turtledove as a sacrifice for sin". Luke says that the parents of Jesus brought him "to do for him what the law required"; other translations describe their actions as doing what is customary according to the law.

Simeon sees in the child, whom he now holds in his arms, the fulfilment of all the promises he had been given. Fulfilment now having taken place, Simeon can say that now is the time for him to be released from this life, for his eyes have seen the salvation which God has prepared for all nations, just as God had said he would. The 'now' is emphatic: the time has come. We might think here of Jesus' announcement at the beginning of his ministry in Matthew and Mark that the time has come; the kingdom of God is at hand, and indeed of the 'hour' in John. Here, the Messiah's birth brings peace to Simeon, the first of those who are the fulfilment of the angels greeting at Jesus birth: Peace on earth to people of good will. Simeon has already been described as upright and devout, therefore Simeon is of good will. Simeon has seen the salvation prepared for all nations to see. Salvation will become a dominant theme in this gospel throughout Jesus' ministry: for example, the solitary leper of the ten made clean who returns to Jesus is told his faith has 'saved' him (Luke 17:19), likewise the blind beggar outside Jericho is told "Receive your sight. Your faith has saved you" (Luke 18:42) and in the last episode before his entry into Jerusalem, Jesus will say of Zacchaeus, that salvation has reached his house because the Son of Man came "to seek out and save what was lost" (Luke 19:10). Remember: the name Jesus is from a Hebrew root that means "Yahweh saves".

Simeon's prophecy is not all comfort, of course. His prophetic utterance now turns to the destiny of the child who is the salvation that God has promised. The child is destined to be the cause of the rise and fall of many. There are echoes here of Mary's Magnificat, "He has pulled down princes from their thrones and exalted the lowly.

The hungry he has filled with good things, the rich sent empty away" (Luke 1:52-53). The child is also to be a sign that is rejected (or a sign that is spoken against). The image may refer to Isaiah 8:14-15, and its image of God as the stumbling stone, "It is Yahweh Sabaoth, whom you must hold in veneration, him you must fear, him you must dread. He is the sanctuary and the stumbling-stone and the rock that brings down the two Houses of Israel; a trap and a snare for the inhabitants of Jerusalem. By it many will be brought down, many fail and be broken, be trapped and made captive". A sword will pierce the soul of his other also, so that the secret thoughts (or calculations) of many may be laid bare. The Greek for this is *dialogismos*, meaning the hidden thoughts of those who actively oppose Jesus.

Finally, Anna, the 'silent prophetess', appears. Her history of widowhood is told, although it is not exactly clear for how long she has been widowed: she had been married for seven years, and the various translations say she had been a widow for eighty four years, or that she was now eighty four years old, or indeed that she was a widow until she was eighty four! She is the type of character often found in Luke, a female introduced as a foil to a male who is already part of the narrative. The statement that she never left the temple should not be taken literally; it may well be a figure of speech similar to one we often use today – 'he/she is never out the chapel!' Anna has an additional important though often forgotten function. In Jewish law, two witnesses were necessary to sustain a charge, or a claim. Simeon's claim that the child who has been brought to the temple is the promised messiah will go unheeded without another witness: that is the function that Anna fulfils without saying a single word; her presence corroborates Simeon's prophetic utterance. And although she says nothing here, we are told that she spoke of the child to all who looked forward to the deliverance of Jerusalem. Once again, the theme of salvation is aired.

As a final footnote, we are informed that "the child grew to maturity, and he was filled with wisdom; and God's favour was with him" (Luke 2:40). This mirrors what had been said of John the Baptist earlier (c.f. Luke 1:18). The description of John's growing paves the way for his later appearance in the Judean wilderness and his preaching; the statement about Jesus paves the way for the remaining episode of the infancy narrative – the so-called finding in the Temple – which follows on.

<h1 align="center">29 June</h1>

<h2 align="center">Saints Peter and Paul. John 21:15-19 (vigil)/Matthew 16:13-19 (day)</h2>

(The gospel for this Solemnity is also the gospel for Sunday 21 A, covered in chapter 8 above, for convenience, the notes are repeated here).

Questions to ponder:

☐   What connection can we make between Peter as rock in this gospel, and Jesus; insistence that his words are like rock foundations for a house?

☐   This is the feast of both Peter and Paul. What do we need to learn from St. Paul for a fuller experience of the life of the Church?

The story of the double question at Caesarea Philippi ('who do people say the Son of Man is' and 'who do you say I am'), is found in all three synoptic gospels, but with some differences. The differences are most noticeable in Matthew's version. Many commentaries make the point that this episode takes place on the very frontier of ancient Israel. Several reasons for this have been suggested, including the observation that Jesus chooses as distant a place as possible from the heart of the religious system. This suggestion perhaps rests on the theory that Matthew, Jesus never left the confines of ancient Israel during his ministry, but now has reached one of the outermost limits of that ancient territory. So, why did he not pose this question when he was in the perhaps equally remote territory of the Decapolis region? However, another suggestion has been put forward. This one is based on a feature of Matthew's gospel which has not yet been mentioned, and that is the way in which Matthew draws from not only the canonical scriptures of the Old Testament, but also from Hebrew religious writings that are not considered part of the canon of scripture, but which are important in their own right. The book of Jubilees provides background for some of Matthew's themes, and here, it is more than possible that when he thinks of the incident at Caesarea Philippi (and especially that additional part of the narrative which only Matthew among the evangelists has recorded), he was thinking of an episode in 1 Enoch 12 – 16. In this source, Enoch is the recipient of divine revelation in exactly the same area, once known as Dan, but renamed Caesarea Philippi in honour of the Roman Emperor Tiberius by Philip the Tetrarch (hence the Philippi component in the name); "And I went off and sat down at the waters of Dan, in the land of Dan, to the south of the west of Hermon: I read their petition till I fell asleep. And behold a dream came to me, and visions fell down upon me..." 1 Enoch 13:7-8. Notice here the motif that occurs in Matthew, of dreams as vehicles of divine revelation, a motif that is frequent in Old Testament, e.g. Genesis, and the stories of Abraham and Joseph, to name but two. As we shall see, Matthew particularly stresses that what Peter is able to utter at Caesarea Philippi/Dan is the result of nothing other than divine revelation.

Once the geography is set, the narrative begins with Jesus; first question, "Who do people say the Son of Man is?" Matthew's list of the various replies is for the most part taken from Mark 8:28, but with the addition of Jeremiah. At first, the list seems like a catalogue of nonsense responses – a mixture of long dead figures, legendary characters, rumours of John the Baptist back from the dead. But there is some modicum of sense among the otherwise apparently superstitious collection of responses to Jesus' ministry. Certainly, equating Jesus with Elijah made sense in terms of the belief that Elijah, whose departure from earth was mysterious, would return. As far as the prophets go, Moses had promised that the Lord would send a prophet like himself. John the Baptist is harder to explain – this response does sound as though it is based more on superstition, the suggestion that there was something supernatural about John that meant he could not be put to death. The addition of Jeremiah, a purely Matthean touch, might suggest that Matthew, who draws heavily on the parallels between Jeremiah and Jesus in regard to the latter's passion, may want to indicate that the crowd had managed to penetrate something of Jesus' identity, and saw in a connection with Jeremiah a sort of undeveloped sense that Jesus' ministry was bound up in the need to suffer.

Then comes the second question: "'But you,' he said 'who do you say I am?'" (Matthew 16:15). Notice the shift to the personal. In his first question, Jesus asks who people think the Son of Man is, but now, in a more direct question, requiring a personal response, he changes to "who do you say I am?" In all three gospel accounts, Peter answers, but in all three versions, he gives a different answer: "the Christ" in Mark 8:29; "the Christ of God" in Luke 9:20, and now, "the Christ, the Son of the living God" in Matthew 16:16". Are the answers substantially different? Perhaps all Matthew wants to do here with his extended response from Peter is to make clear that Peter does not only equate Jesus as a military or political figure when he calls him 'Christ' or 'Messiah'. According to Matthew, Jesus acknowledges this aspect of Peter's reply. In Mark and Luke, there is no acknowledgement by Jesus, merely strict instructions not to tell anyone about this. Earlier in this gospel, Jesus has been called Messiah - the very first line, for instance, "A genealogy of Jesus Christ", (Matthew 1:1; repeated in v. 18). He has also been called the Son of God – at his baptism, a voice from heaven proclaims, "This is my Son, the Beloved" (Matthew 3:17), and even demoniacs recognize his identity, "What do you want with us, Son of God?" (Matthew 8:29). This is the first time, however, that Jesus has been so addressed by one of his disciples. Jesus' response to Peter's confession is to acknowledge that what Peter has said could not have been the result of human calculation; it could only have been an instance of divine revelation.

Peter is addressed as 'blessed', the only person who is singled out for such an accolade by Jesus. He is blessed because the Father has chosen to reveal to Peter Jesus' true identity. When we read this passage again in its proper context the overall gospel, it will be possible to think back to the remarkable statement of Jesus in chapter 11, where he exclaims, "I bless you, Father, Lord of heaven and of earth, for hiding these things from the learned and the clever and revealing them to mere children" (Matthew 11:25). Peter is the proof of the truth of what Jesus had held to be the case in the earlier chapter.

Let's pause for a minute here before going any further. The sequence we are considering here can be divided up into 3 sections, thus:

- Peter bestows a title on Jesus
- Jesus bestows a title on Jesus
- Jesus gives Peter authority

Or to put it another way, we have a movement in three stages of time;

- Peter says who Jesus has been up until now in his ministry (i.e. he has read correctly the signs that Jesus so far has worked) – the Christ, the Son of the living God.
- Jesus says who Peter now is – the Rock
- Finally, Jesus tells Peter what Peter will be in the future – the bearer of the keys of the kingdom of heaven.

The expanded material about Peter is of course the uniquely Matthean contribution to the Caesarea Philippi episode. Matthew alone records Jesus' 'beatitude' to Peter (bearing similarities to the beatitudes of chapter 5), Peter is blessed because it was not flesh and blood, but the Father who has revealed Peter's insight into Jesus' true identity. This 'blessedness' results in Peter's renaming, a feature that is found in significant places in the Old Testament: Abraham and Jacob are two examples that come instantly to mind. Here, Peter is called "Rock", involving a play on words that is most apparent in Aramaic, which presumably was the language in which the original words were spoken. The play involves the word kepha, rock. Some commentators suggest that Jesus here uses a nickname by which Peter was already known, perhaps because of his physical characteristics: Daniel Harrington SJ suggests that this was a bit like calling Peter 'Rocky' because of his stature. The problem with that seems to be that nowhere else is there any record of anyone else being called by that name. There is but one Kephas in the New Testament, and other literature. So, a better suggestion seems to be that Jesus, in keeping with divine practice in the Old Testament, bestows a new name on Peter, the Rock, because he, Peter, has been chosen to provide the foundation, the rock on which Jesus will build his Church. This immediately reminds us of the gospel for Sunday 9A, with which this session of these noted opened, "everyone who listens to these words of mine and acts on them will be like a sensible man who built his house on rock" (Matthew 7:24). Some argue that Simon was already known as Peter, for example, when the first four fishermen were called, and when the 12 apostles were selected, but surely that means no more than that Matthew was adding the name Peter to the disciple's earlier name of Simon to clarify identification (remember that there was another Simon in the apostolic list, so clarification was needed as to which was which).

This conversation between Jesus and Peter may be unique to Matthew, but that does not mean that it is without parallel in New Testament writing. We have already seen that Jesus regards his words as the rock foundation of disciples' lives. Luke writes of a house builder digging deep and placing foundations on rock. The early Christians were clearly moved by Psalm 117(118):22, and its reference to the stone rejected by the builders which has become the keystone (or cornerstone), and saw this as fulfilled in the crucified and risen Lord, but that is not the same as making Peter the rock foundation. Nowhere is Jesus referred to as the rock foundation of the Church. Ephesians does refer to the foundation of the Church; this foundation is the apostles (and prophets), and the letter adds that Christ is the cornerstone: "you are no longer aliens or foreign visitors: you are citizens like all the saints, and part of God's household. You are part of a building that has the apostles and prophets for its foundations, and Christ Jesus himself for its main cornerstone" (Ephesians 2:19-20). So we can say that the Matthean text has its parallels in New Testament theology.

Peter is the rock, but there is more that Peter is to become. He will be given the keys to the kingdom of heaven with power to bind and loose (a power which is given to the entire apostolic community in chapter 18, but without the reference to the keys). Underlying the promise of the keys to the kingdom is the passage in Isaiah where the prophecy states that the chief steward of the Royal Household, Shebna, is to be replaced by another, Eliakim, who is to have full control over entry and exit to the royal palace (Isaiah 22:22). This is now what it being offered to Peter. He is to have the keys to the household of the kingdom of heaven rather than the kingdom of David. Peter, as key bearer has control over who enters and leaves: hence the power to bind and loose; but who does Peter supplant as key-bearer? Various suggestions at analogy for Peter's role have been offered: Peter as Prime Minster, Peter as major-domo. What is more important, perhaps, is the recognition of Peter's power. He has been delegated the authority of the Messiah, the Son of the Living God, to determine passage to and from the kingdom of God. The terms binding and loosing were used in rabbinic writings to cover a variety of authoritative actions and functions. Most relevant to the present passage would be the authority to impose and to life excommunications, since Peter is handed the power to bind and loose in conjunction with his appointment as the key-bearer. Just as in Isaiah 22, Shebna had his authority as key bearer taken from him and given to Eliakim, so in Matthew, the rabbis have their authority taken from them and given to Peter.

This combined imagery of binding/loosing and holding the keys ties in with some themes we have already met in Matthew, and with some which are still to come. As we saw earlier, Peter the rock is clearly closely related to the rock foundation of those whose lives are built on Jesus' words. The rabbis claimed (especially after the destruction of the Temple, 70 AD) to be the authentic interpreters of the Law. Jesus has presented himself as the true fulfilment of the Law (c.f. Matthew 5:17), and now appoints Peter as his Regent, who will guarantee continuity with Jesus' teaching. Already, we have had reference to entering doors. The audience to the Sermon on the Mount were urged to enter by the narrow door (Matthew 7:13-14). Later, the parable of the bridesmaids will tell that those who had not made sufficient preparation for the bridegroom's arrival will find the door shut to them (Matthew 25:1-12). Other references are to those cast outside for not having made adequate attempts to prepare for the wedding banquet (c.f. Matthew 22:13). Now, we find that it is Peter who holds the key (literally and metaphorically!) to the door of the kingdom that is described as the wedding banquet.

Peter's role as Regent for the kingdom as laid out in Matthew is, then, clearly supported by internal connections throughout the gospel. What about the succession to Peter in this role? Most commentators agree that Peter was given a role of prominence by Jesus, but there has, of course, been much disagreement as to whether there is any indication that this authority should have been handed on. This is neither the time nor the place to examine the argument, except perhaps to note that the question of apostolic succession is very much in evidence in the New Testament. The very first post-Ascension action of the apostles in the election of Matthias as a replacement for Judas is the most obvious example (Acts 1:15-26), and in his introduction to the process, Peter himself cites scriptural precedent (Acts 1:20; quoting Psalm 109:8). So, there is clear precedence for a succession of apostolic power. The argument is often put forward that Peter's case was unique – but then again, so – thankfully - was that of Judas!

6 August

The Transfiguration of the Lord. Mark 9:2-10

(The gospel for this Solemnity is also the gospel for the Second Sunday of

Questions to ponder

☐ What is the significance of Jesus at prayer as a prelude to the Transfiguration?

☐ This is the only gospel version of the Transfiguration in which the actual content of Moses' and Elijah's conversation is recorded. This is coupled with the voice from heaven. How do the various voices help us understand Jesus' identity?

☐ The Transfiguration is often presented as an event which was designed to prepare Peter James and John for the Passion. If so, did it work? If not, what do you think its purpose is?

Just like the first Sunday of Lent each year, the second Sunday always carries the same theme: the Transfiguration of Jesus. Matthew, Mark and Luke tell substantially the same story – Jesus, accompanied by Peter, James and John, is on a high mountain somewhere in Galilee (there is no gospel evidence for the tradition that this mountain is Mt Tabor). There, in the presence of Moses and Elijah, Jesus is transformed, his clothing changes appearance and a voice from heaven, speaking for the benefit of the three disciples, identifies Jesus: "This is my Son, the Chosen One. Listen to him" (Luke 9:35). Peter wants to set up three tents, and on the way down from the mountain and beyond the disciples remain silent on what has happened. In each gospel version of the story, the transfiguration takes place after both Peter's confession at Caesarea Philippi and Jesus' first passion prediction. So much for the similarities; the differences between the gospel accounts are often significant, and nowhere more so than here. Luke includes many of his major themes in this strange episode which takes place near the end of Jesus' Galilean ministry: Jesus is at prayer before the experience begins; that he is cast as the Prophet is reinforced by the company of the prophetic figures from the past, Moses and Elijah. This is developed in a uniquely Lukan way; Jerusalem is the focus for what will soon begin, Jesus' 'passing' (*exodos*; and finally, Peter is treated more sympathetically than in Mark or Matthew: Luke makes no mention of his fear.

In Luke there is a clear separation between this episode and what has immediately preceded; this is about all that can be concluded from Luke's assertion that eight days had passed (Mark says that it was six days), so this episode is not closely linked to what has gone before (which for the record was the outline of the conditions attached to following the Christ). Luke stresses the importance of this episode by stressing that the transfiguration happened as Jesus was praying. This is always an important *motif* in Luke: Zechariah was at prayer in the Temple when the angel appeared; Jesus was praying after his baptism when the heavens opened, the heavenly voice spoke and the Spirit descended in bodily form. Likewise, Jesus prayed before he called the Twelve. Luke avoids stating that Jesus was transfigured, or transformed as Mark chooses to describe his change, and restricts himself to stating only that the *appearance* of his face was altered. In Exodus 24:17, the Israelites saw the glory of the Lord *appear* like a devouring fire before Moses; at Jesus' baptism, the Holy Spirit *appeared* (*eidos*) in bodily shape. Now, Jesus' face *appeared* to be altered, and his clothes were white and dazzling. This also recalls the *appearance* of the Ancient of Days in Daniel 7:9, who had garments as white as snow, and paves the way for the 'men in dazzling clothes' at the Resurrection (Luke 24:4) and the 'men in white garments' (angels?) at Jesus' Ascension (Acts 1:10).

In all three synoptic accounts, Moses and Elijah are with Jesus, but only in Luke is the content of the conversation recorded. Here, they also *appear* in their glory, and are discussing Jesus' 'passing' (*exodos*) which he was to accomplish in Jerusalem. These two unique details provide a link between the Transfiguration and Jesus' passion (surprisingly, the only direct reference to this on any of the Sundays of Lent in Year C with the obvious exception of Palm Sunday's Passion Narrative), and also to Jesus' prophecy about the Son of Man in 'his glory' which is found two verses before this passage begins (Luke 9:26), even though, as was discussed earlier, the evangelist sets out to create a separation between the two passages. The discussion about Jesus' 'passing', his '*exodos*', provides a clear link between him and Moses who led the 'passing' of Israel from Egypt to the promised land. Before his own departure from this life and prior to the entry to the promised land, Moses told the Israelites that "God will raise up for you a prophet like myself, from among yourselves, from your own brothers; to him you must listen" (Deuteronomy 18:15). A significant aspect of Luke's portrayal of Jesus is as the Prophet whom Moses had promised. This Prophet, Jesus, is now about to begin his own 'passing' which will involve not only a physical journey (which will be dealt with extensively in Luke 9:51- 19:27), but with his passing through death to resurrection. This passing is itself 'fulfilment' – an activity very much associated with prophets and prophecy.

Meanwhile, Peter and the other two were heavy with sleep (as they will be in the garden of Gethsemane, Luke 22:45-46). The Jerusalem Bible translation is strange here, suggesting that they struggled to stay awake, but the text seems to suggest that as they woke, or became fully awake, they saw Moses and Elijah in their glory; apparently they did not however hear the conversation. Perhaps Peter is impressed by the sight of glory, because he wants to construct three tents ('shrine' would be an acceptable translation here): one each for Jesus, Moses and Elijah, thereby preserving the image he has just witnessed. Luke gives no indication of fear on the part of the three at this point: that comes later!

The fear of the three comes as the scene changes. Moses and Elijah depart from the mountain and a cloud appears – another reference to the Exodus where the cloud signified the present of the Lord as the Israelites travelled through the desert; "Yahweh went before them, by day in the form of a pillar of cloud to show them the way, and by night in the form of a pillar of fire to give them light: thus they could continue their march by day and by night" (Exodus 13:21). The cloud was a frequent symbol for the presence of the Lord among the people while on their desert journey. While teaching in the Temple at the end of his ministry, Jesus will predict "the Son of Man coming in a cloud with power and great glory" (Luke 21:27). Now, a voice comes from the cloud, repeating almost exactly the words heard at Jesus' baptism. This time, however the voice says, "This is my Son, the Chosen One. Listen to him" (Luke 9:35). There are two features here. One is explicit; the voice addresses Peter, James and John, whereas after Jesus' baptism, he was the one addressed. Here the three disciples are commanded to listen to Jesus, which is an implicit reference to the command of Moses when he told the Israelites that God would raise up for them a prophet just like himself. They were to listen to that prophet. Here, the command is repeated, but from an authority higher than Moses! Now the disciples are afraid, and not without cause! Finding themselves once more alone with Jesus, they descend the mountain in silence, which they maintain.

Of course, it is one thing to piece together the component parts of the story; it is another to see its relevance for us today, and especially for our Lenten journey. Luke stresses the prophetic connection. This is one theme that we could preach about and link to the 'testings' of the previous Sunday's gospel:

the Prophetic Beloved Son, having shown his loyalty to the kingdom of his Father is the one qualified to teach us; we need to take seriously the heavenly command to listen to him. Listening will be particularly important over the next three weeks of this season as Jesus, the Chosen Son, tells us about the Father he knows so well. Jesus is moreover the Prophet whose passing is from death to resurrection, and who challenges his followers to take up the cross and renounce themselves in imitation of him. Finally, Peter's suggestion of building three tents (shrines) to preserve the memory of the image was inappropriate, because his challenge was, with the other two, to come down from that mountain and get on with the business of following the Prophet Jesus – almost immediately, because in a few verses he will embark on that (literally) fateful journey to Jerusalem. Our own Lenten challenge is therefore about us taking our religious experiences and insights and making sure they are not retained only as memories, but are lived out in our own journey of discipleship.

<h1 align="center">15 August</h1>

<h2 align="center">The Assumption of the Blessed Virgin Mary. Luke 11:27-28 (vigil)/Luke 1:39-56 (day)</h2>

Questions to ponder:

☐   What, apart from a domestic scene, is really depicted in this story of the meeting between Elizabeth and Mary?

☐   In what way does Mary's 'Magnificat' inform us about the dogma of the Assumption?

It is to be expected that the gospel for any feast or solemnity of the Blessed Virgin Mary will be taken from the Infancy Narratives in Luke, since there is little or no other material available anywhere else in the four gospels; Matthew's Infancy Narratives provide next to nothing in the way of Marian material, and even within Luke, there is a scarcity of suitable passages for liturgical use on Marian celebrations. Passages for these feasts are limited to the Annunciation (1:26-38), the Visitation (1:39-45), the Magnificat (1:46-56) and the immediate aftermath of Jesus' birth (2:16-21). For today's gospel, the chosen passage is a combination of the Visitation and the Magnificat, and the combined texts in many ways not only sum up the major themes opened up in the Infancy Narratives (which in any case contain in miniature the major themes of this gospel) but they manage to pinpoint much of what is central to the theology of the gospel of Luke – in particular, the 'reversal of fortune'. This theme is first flagged up by the adult Jesus in the 'mission statement' delivered in the Nazareth synagogue. With it, Jesus pledges to fulfil Isaiah's prophecy that he has been anointed and sent 'to bring the good news to the poor, to proclaim liberty to captives and to the blind new sight, to set the downtrodden free, to proclaim the Lord's year of favour' (4:18-18). The theme carries through to the beatitudes and woes of 6:20-26; the parable of the rich man and Lazarus and Jesus' teaching about inviting to meals not the influential relatives, friends and neighbours who will be able to return the favour, but the poor, the crippled, the blind and the lame who will be unable to return the compliment (14:7-14). We could say that the visitation narrative illustrates the attitude of the 'poor of the Lord' to whom the reversal of fortune will apply, embodied in both Mary's and her elder relative Elizabeth's fidelity to God's promises, and which is then sung in Mary's famous Magnificat. We have a gospel therefore which does not tell the story of the Assumption of Mary (which is of course is not described in any scriptural passage), nor does it explicitly prophesy the Assumption, but we do have a summary of the gospel attitudes expected of a disciple, found in the person of Mary and finding the expression of their fulfilment in the doctrine of her Assumption body and soul into heaven. Further, as Mother of God and Mother of the Church as proto-disciple, she is that prophetic figure who demonstrates the fulfilment of disciples' hopes to experience that gospel 'reversal of fortune' which is such a prominent feature in Luke.

The combined Visitation/Magnificat narrative is not without drama, and yet there is very little action taking place. We are told that Mary is in Zechariah's house, but there is no mention of Zechariah. This cannot be accidental; prior to this, we read the story of Zechariah the priest's unbelieving encounter with the angel Gabriel, which resulted in Zechariah's inability to speak until later in the narrative. Hence, this flawed representative of the religious system is excluded from the present story, which is the encounter of two faithful women, whose roles are about to turn them into the most prominent figures in the infolding of God's plans: one becomes the mother of the prophet who will prepare the way before the Lord; the other will become the mother of the Lord himself. Both roles have already been announced on the highest heavenly authority. Elizabeth and Mary both make theologically substantial statements about God's plans.

Mary's visit to Elizabeth has been compared to the Old Testament story of the Ark of the Covenant, that potent symbol of the presence of God among the Israelites, up to Jerusalem. Mary, travelling to the outskirts of Jerusalem, bears the reality of the presence of God among humanity; those bearing the Ark of the Covenant carried the stone tablet that embodied God's word (Law) to Moses; Mary, bearing the Holy One of God, carries the one who will be called in the Fourth Gospel the Word Made Flesh. Hence the welcome extended to Mary not only by Elizabeth, but by the child in her womb, the one who is to go before the Lord to make known his way before him (1:76). Elizabeth asks, "Why should I be honoured with a visit from the mother of my Lord?" (1:43). Mary's song, her Magnificat, addresses that very question in a series of verses which apply to both her and Elizabeth:

- The Lord has looked upon his lowly handmaid.
- Holy is his name, and his mercy reaches from age to age for those who fear him.
- He has shown the power of his arm, he has routed the proud of heart.
- He has pulled down princes from their thrones and exalted the lowly.
- The hungry he has filled with good things, the rich sent empty away.

From now on, all generations will call Mary 'blessed'. There are many occasions in this gospel where people are called blessed. This is the third, all of which apply to Mary, in contrast to the mighty, the powerful the rich, the proud of heart, who are to be cast down one way or another.

EXCURSUS: *The relationship between ancient Israel and Mary: some notes on Apocalypse 11:19; 12:1-6.10*

Since Patristic times, many have seen a connection between the Apocalypse text used for the 1ˢᵗ Reading on the Solemnity of the Assumption, with its reference to the woman and her new born child, and the Blessed Virgin Mary herself. It is however almost certainly true that the author of the Apocalypse had another connection in mind here, and that is the connection between the woman and her child and ancient Israel, sometimes known as 'son of God' in the Old Testament. That is not to say that the Marian connections are not valid, since references to ancient Israel as expounded in this text can be seen to refer to Mary by implication. These notes, a departure from normal practice of providing exegetical reflections only for gospel passages, are added to try to shed additional light both on the New Testament book most likely to be considered difficult to grasp, and the Solemnity of the Assumption as well.

The woman depicted in this passage is first seen in a setting of splendour, but she is also close to delivering her child. We are reminded of Eve's birth pains (Genesis 3:16), but they are perhaps much more pointedly the birth pangs of Israel heading for exile: "Writhe, cry out, daughter of Zion, like a woman in labour, for now you have to leave the city and live in the open country. To Babylon you must go and there you will be rescued; there Yahweh will ransom you out of the power of your enemies" (Micah 4:10). Most probably the author of the Apocalypse sees the woman as Israel which, in its travail (in the desert, in exile), brings forth a new, Messianic male child: Israel is then also a 'type' of the mother of God.

The other figure in this vision is of course the red dragon with seven heads and ten horns, a symbol drawing from Babylonian and Canaanite mythology in which either a great dragon with seven heads or a sea-serpent symbolize of chaos. The author of the Apocalypse links this mythological figure to the serpent of Genesis 3. Understanding the symbolism of the Apocalypse is of course so important, and it is essential to appreciate all Old Testament references. In Apocalypse 12:4, the great red dragon sweeps away 'a third of the stars'; according to Daniel 8:10, stars represent pagan powers, so the Apocalypse passage suggests that the great dragon is more powerful than the pagan nations. Contrary to popular misconception, this passage has nothing to do with the fall of angels from heaven, which is in any case recorded nowhere in Biblical literature, deriving from the non-Biblical 1 Enoch 6-13.

The conflict, as prophetically indicated in Genesis 3, is between the dragon or serpent, and the woman's male child which he wishes to devour. The next verse is a direct quotation from Psalm 2:9, a psalm with Messianic overtones connected with the coronation of kings of Judah, the point at which they were called 'sons of God': "the son who was to rule all the nations with an iron sceptre", and this child was immediately taken up into the safety of heaven – a reference to the death, resurrection and ascension of Jesus: in Johannine terms, his glorification! We can see overtones here of John 14:30, when Jesus declares, "the prince of this world is on his way. He has no power over me". The passage is an 'updating' of the role of the woman (Israel) giving birth to a male child (Messiah); this is fulfilled in the New Testament theology of the New Israel established by Jesus, whereby it is now the Church through whom the Messiah is made present to the world; therefore the woman ten becomes mother of the son of God, and also mother of the Church – i.e. a fulfilment of the woman who gives birth to a male child who is to be son of God, a title first attributed to Israel. For purposes of the celebration of the Assumption, the imagery of the first reading, the Apocalypse text, is pointing to a celebration of Mary, Mother of God and Mother of the Church, who being 'Assumed into heaven' paves the way for the fulfilment, the completion of the imagery that this passage, potent with symbolism, offers to us.

14 September.

Triumph of the Cross. John 3:13-17

The Son of Man Lifted Up and exalted

Questions to ponder:

☐   How does the Son of Man raised up reveal God to humanity?

☐   How can such a painful and humiliating fate as crucifixion possibly be equated with exaltation, as well as with physical raising up?

☐   How can we reconcile God's loving plan for humanity expressed in the Son of Man being raised up with the concept of judgment of people, brought upon themselves by their refusal to believe?

By the time we reach these verses in John Chapter 3, Jesus and Nicodemus have already had a significant discussion about the necessity of being born again. Nicodemus has of course had trouble understanding how a grown human being can be born again. Jesus challenges him although he is a teacher of Israel, he cannot understand the things of the Spirit. How then, can Nicodemus ever understand Jesus when he speaks of the things of heaven, because he, the Son of Man has alone come from heaven: no human being has ever gone up to heaven except the Son of Man who came from heaven? The implication is that the Son of Man alone can speak of the things of God, the things of heaven, the things of the Spirit. This is of course a working out in more detail of the contents of the Prologue to the Fourth Gospel: "the Word was made flesh and dwelt among us" (John 1:14).

The narrative now turns to the content of the revelation that the Son of Man brings. Verse 13 tells us that the Son of Man, Jesus, is the one who comes from heaven to reveal the things of God. Now, the next verse tells us *how* God's revelation will be made: in the Son of Man being lifted up. The narrative draws on a biblical image to make this clearer. During Israel's 40 years in the desert, the people were set upon by a plague of poisonous serpents. In a response which seems bizarre to us today, and the origins of which we cannot now really determine, Moses made a cast of a bronze serpent, stuck it on a pole, and raised it up. Anyone who had been bitten by a serpent was saved by looking on the bronze serpent raised up by Moses. It all smacks a bit too much of superstition for our eyes and ears, and it is difficult to know what is meant by the bronze serpent: it's probably now not possible to get to the origins of this tale. For the purposes of the 4th Gospel, however, there are clear features of the story that Jesus now makes use of. First, the image was to be raised up, and all would be able to look at it – just as Jesus himself was to be raised up in full gaze of all while on the cross. Second, the image that saves is also an image of what had killed in the first place – the serpents in the desert. Likewise, the sight of Jesus on the cross to save all who gaze on him is also the sight of one dying by being raised on the cross (not only dying, but cursed, if we take into account Deuteronomy 21:23, that "one who has been hanged is accursed of God").

The description of the Son of Man being lifted up uses a word with a double meaning. It refers first and foremost to the physical act of lifting up, that is, raising him above ground level, which will be done when Jesus is nailed to the cross, but it also has the additional meaning of 'being exalted'.

We have had the assertion that the Son of Man who has come down from heaven, is the revelation of God. Now, we are told precisely how this revelation is to take place – when the Son of Man is lifted up/exalted. It is also the fine detail missing in the narrative of the cleansing of the Temple, and the explanation of what Jesus means when he says: "Destroy this sanctuary, and in three days I will raise it up" (John 2:19). There is however an extraordinary element which will need further developing, and which is indicated here. This is the all-important question: how can the raising of someone on a cross be the revelation of God? The answer becomes clear in v. 16, where God's intention is made clear, "God loved the world so much that he gave his only Son". It is in the Son of Man being raised up on the cross that God's love is revealed at its greatest. God's intention is not that the word be condemned, but that through his Son, "the world might be saved" (v. 17). Salvation and condemnation are not decreed, because "God sent his Son into the world not to condemn the world, but so that through him the world might be saved" (v. 17).

Background to the other readings for today

1st Reading; Numbers 21:4-9
This episode tells of the final occasion when the Israelites complained about their food and yearned for all the delicacies (real or imagined) which they had enjoyed in Egypt. They complain about the manna, unsatisfying food (or better, worthless), forgetting that for them it was literally the bread which kept them alive. This behaviour provokes God's anger, which takes the form of 'fiery snakes' whose bite was lethal. Presumably the fiery designation came about as a result of the inflammation caused by the snake bites. Moses is instructed to apply an antidote to the lethal bites. He is to make a bronze (copper) snake and mount it on a stick. It is not at all clear where this idea may have come from, but its use has some parallels with those of purification and atonement. Certain characteristics of Hebrew ritual illustrate the connection. First, in sacrificial ritual, blood is important. Contact with blood polluted humans, yet sacrificed blood sanctified and purified people and objects. Second, the colour red is important, for example the blood of sacrificed animals, the red heifer of Numbers chapter 19, and the

scarlet material thrown into the fire which burns the heifer to add to the ashes of the heifer which themselves are used for adding to the water of purification. Both of these elements may be present in the copper serpent. Here, the snake fashioned from which heals counters the fiery snakes which kill; copper is as near to red as any metal can be. Third, the person offering an animal in sacrifice had to make contact (touch) the animal. Clearly it was not going to be possible for afflicted people to touch the snake which had bitten them, but they are to make *eye* contact with the copper snake lifted up by Moses. These three aspects may help explain why in John's gospel Jesus speaks of the Son of Man lifted up (on the cross, with the shedding of his blood) for all to see (eye contact). Perhaps we can conclude this line of thought with the reminder in John Chapter 9 of the play on the ideas of physical sight and the sight of faith. It is those who see and believe the Son of Man lifted up who have life.

2nd Reading; Philippians 2:6-11

The dominant theme from this hymn for the purposes of this feast is that of Jesus lifted up on high (exalted) and given 'a name which is above all other names' (Philippians 2:9). In this hymn, Jesus' exaltation comes about because he underwent death on a cross in obedience to his Father; in the gospel of John, Jesus is glorified *through* being lifted up on a cross (e.g. John 12:23-24). This passage from Philippians has been the subject of a huge debate on what exactly might be meant by the phrase that Jesus was 'in the form of God' (the translation given in many English translation, and much preferable to the Jerusalem Bible's 'his state was divine). Does the phrase mean, as the Jerusalem Bible suggests, that Jesus was equal to God, or does it recall Genesis 1:27, which states that humanity was created in the image and likeness of God? In a sense, both readings of the passage are relevant in the context of this feast. The question of Jesus leaving aside equality with God (as in the Jerusalem Bible translation) to embrace the cross, and through it to be raised on high has clear implications for the feast of the Triumph of the cross. So too has the idea deriving from Genesis in a way which is not always appreciated. As noted, Genesis 1:27 states that God created make and female in his own image; Philippians says in similar language that Jesus was in the 'form' (*morphē*) of God. The first humans 'grasped' at the suggestion that they should become 'like God' (c.f. Genesis 3:5). Jesus, on the other hand did not cling to his equality with God (Philippians 2:6, RSV: did not count equality with God a thing to be grasped). The ultimate expression of Jesus' lack of grasping at being like God (in contrast to Adam) is of course in accepting the cross and renouncing self (c.f. Mark 8:34; 9:35). It is precisely because of his lack of grasping at equality with God that Jesus is ultimately raised in high and given the name above all other names.

1 November

All Saints. Matthew 5:1-12

Those to whom the kingdom of heaven belongs; who are the 'poor in spirit'

Questions to ponder:
- [ ] Which version of the first beatitude do you prefer – Matthew's or Luke's - and why?
- [ ] How might the other beatitudes in Matthew's version relate to the first?
- [ ] How might we tie together the beatitudes in Matthew 5 and the parable of the last judgement, Matthew 25:31-36?

No gospel passage on offer in our lectionary is used for so many diverse purposes, and on as many occasions as the Matthean beatitudes. Their nearest rival is Matthew 11:28-30 (or more usually, only verses 25-30). When we also consider the number of weddings and funerals for which the Matthean beatitudes are chosen, it is clear that it must rank as the all-time favourite gospel passage for big occasions. There are no doubt several reasons for the popularity of the beatitudes as a gospel choice, and there are doubtless several related reasons why some preachers may consider it their least favourite passage! One possible way to approach this or any other passage which the risks liturgical over-exposure might be to look at it from a range of different perspectives on different occasions. In a sense this is something that has already been done in these notes. When Matthew 5:1-12 is considered for the 4$^\text{th}$ Sunday, Year A, it is placed within the context of the five discourses of this gospel which portray Jesus as the ultimate Teacher of the Law and its true meaning. Matthew's beatitudes can be cast against a whole host of Old Testament texts, which the evangelist understands are fulfilled in and by Jesus, the teacher who comes, not to abolish the law, but to fulfil it (Matthew 5:17).

Our reading of the passage on this occasion is however set against a different backdrop – the Solemnity of All Saints. The teaching ministry of Jesus is still relevant to our present celebration, but it may be more useful for the present to concentrate on the first (and last) and the emphasis on "theirs is the kingdom of heaven" - for obvious reasons. It will also, I think, be useful to compare the first beatitude in both Matthew's and Luke's version, and to see if there is something to be gained for the purposes of preaching on this feast by taking a close look at the 'core set' of beatitudes from both gospels. We'll begin with this latter aspect.

Some number crunching first. Matthew's beatitudes number eight which are written in the third person plural (Blessed are *those...*) and a final one which is in the second person (Blessed are *you...*). This means that the first eight are addressed to a general audience, no doubt including those present, but also addressed to anyone else who fits the categories described. The last one is directed toward those whom Jesus directly speaks: these are his disciples, which we can deduce because verse 2 indicates that he is teaching his disciples in the manner of a rabbi teaching his pupils. This does not, however, exclude the crowd which has gathered and who have already been noticed by Jesus. Luke gives four beatitudes, all of which are written in the second person, and which therefore apply to disciples; we know this because Luke tells us that Jesus first 'lifts up his eyes' (RSV translation) on them. In both sets of beatitudes, the first and the last refer to the possession of the kingdom of heaven (kingdom of God in Luke). Finally, four of Matthew's beatitudes are essentially the same as Luke's set of four. This has led commentators to call those four which the two gospels share the core set of Jesus' beatitudes, with Matthew adding others from a separate tradition to which he has access.

Working with those four core beatitudes, we can see pairings of themes. The first and last beatitudes both point to future heavenly reward: the kingdom of heaven (or God) for the poor (or poor in spirit) as well as for the abused, persecuted and 'calumnised'; whereas the other two point toward future earthly reward; inheriting the earth, and having hunger satisfied. On closer inspection, however, even the inner ones have a heavenly or eschatological dimension. The book of the Apocalypse has a vision of a new heaven and a new earth, and Isaiah prophesied a banquet on God's holy mountain (Isaiah 25:6), and the feeding miracles in the synoptic gospels (Matthew 14:13-21; 15:32-39; Mark 6:30-44; 8:1-10; Luke 9:10-17), as well as the parables about the heavenly banquet, or wedding feast (Matthew 22:1-14; 25:1-13; Luke 14:15-24), with their fulfilment in the future as prophesied by Jesus at the last supper (Matthew 26:29; Mark 14:25; Luke 22:15-16). So in fact all four core beatitudes point to a reality beyond this world. It has been said that the beatitudes are not entry requirements into the kingdom of heaven; rather, they are a summary of what awaits those who currently live according to the values of the kingdom. Much later, the parables in Matthew 24:45 – 25:46 exhort a watchful and awake diligence to what is required in this life: otherwise, the promised reward may be forfeited. These parables demand attitudes and actions in the present.

We can say even more about the pairings of beatitudes. There is a link between the first and the fourth, which explains why their respective rewards are the same. The link is between the poor, or in Matthew, the poor in spirit, and those who suffer abuse, persecution and all kinds of calumny spoken against them in Jesus' name. It is not perhaps immediately apparent why the two groups should be linked, until we explore further what tends to be meant by the poor in the Bible literature. Originally the physically poor, the term came to be used for all who were oppressed, marginalized, ostracised or persecuted. In time, it became a religious term for 'the poor of the Lord', the *ănāwîm* in Hebrew. Another factor is the word for 'poor', which is used by both Matthew and Luke in their versions of the first beatitude: *ptōchos*, the Greek word which also denotes a beggar. It is here that the link becomes apparent. The abused, persecuted, those against whom calumny is spoken are the marginalized, the outcasts who are dependent on the assistance of others if they are to survive, because to be marginalized, to be cast out in ancient society was to be without any means of support from family, culture, even religion. To be this marginalized is to be the same as the beggar, one who is equally dependent on the assistance of others since there are no social services or benefits on which beggars can rely. So the poor are the chronically dependant. In Luke's gospel, Jesus twice courts trouble by proclaiming good news to the poor. The first occasion is in the Nazareth synagogue, where he quotes Isaiah to announce his own ministry: "The spirit of the Lord has been given to me, for he has anointed me. He has sent me to bring the good news to the poor, to proclaim liberty to captives and to the blind new sight, to set the downtrodden free, to proclaim the Lord's year of favour" (Luke 4:18-19). The thought of reaching out to the marginalized provokes the congregation to such an extent that they chase Jesus out of the synagogue, intending to throw him over a cliff. The second is when the imprisoned John the Baptist sends his disciples to ask Jesus, "Are you the one who is to come or have we to wait for someone else?" (Luke 7:20). Jesus' answer is, "Go back and tell John what you have seen and heard: the blind see again, the lame walk, lepers are cleansed, and the deaf hear, the dead are raised to life, the Good News is proclaimed to the poor" (Luke 7:22). But then he adds the strange verse 'and blessed is anyone if he is not scandalised in me' (a more literal translation than the Jerusalem Bible gives, Luke 7:23). A '*skandalon*' was a large piece of masonry, an obstruction to passers-by, something they might trip over. Jesus is a *skandalon*, an obstacle, to those who will not accept good news to the poor, the marginalized. In Luke, Jesus speaks directly to his disciples, and calls them 'the poor'; in Matthew, he speaks to his disciples, but addresses 'the poor' in general. He calls them the 'poor in spirit', perhaps to make clear he is not referring only to physical poverty. His disciples are poor in the sense that they have already shown, in accepting his call to follow him, that they are dependent on God; they have left aside their means of self-sufficiency – nets and boats for Peter, Andrew, James and John, the counting house for Matthew the tax-agent. So, the poor in spirit, the abused, the persecuted, those against whom calumny is committed on account of Jesus' name – that is, those who are in need of Jesus – are those who already possess the kingdom of heaven, and will be greatly rewarded when they reach heaven. These are the numberless and nameless people we honour on All Saints' Day.

2 November

Commemoration of the Faithful Departed. Luke 7:11-17

The readings for this commemoration can be taken from any of those found in the Lectionary Vol. III, Masses for the Dead, from p. 849 onwards. However, the Lectionary Vol. 1, p. 1002-1005 offers a selection of readings for this occasion, and I have used the gospel of this selection for these notes. The suggested gospel for Year C is Luke 7:11-17; the raising of the widow's son. The notes below are the same as those for Sunday 10, Year C. An appropriate focus for the Commemoration of all the Faithful departs may include a thought on Jesus restoring to life in a figurative way the woman whose son is restored to us. As we pray for our departed brothers and sisters, we express our hope that those whose deaths have diminished something of our life will rise with Christ, and that this realisation will enhance our own experience of life through the Risen Christ who reaches out to us in our bereavement.

☐ Prophecy and its fulfilment in Jesus was clearly an important theme to Luke, and presumably to his initial readers. How important is it to you that Jesus fulfils the prophets from of old, or that his own ministry is prophetic?

❑   In what way should the prophetic action of Jesus shape the prophetic role of the Church today? In other words, what does it mean to say that the Church must be prophetic (hint: this has nothing to do with predicting the future!)?

❑   How are Jesus' prophetic acts fulfilled today in your life?

It's a pity that the lectionary version of this passage omits the phrase which the gospel text itself uses to open the story. Had this been included, it would have made clear that this text is to be read in in conjunction with the previous episode, read in last week's gospel text. The phrase, when translated literally, gives us that famous biblical link expression which is well known to us from the King James translation: 'and it came to pass…' This is followed by 'the day after…'. In contemporary translations this is usually expressed as something like 'soon afterwards…', or even 'the next day'. It is clear therefore that Luke intends to link this episode with the one immediately preceding, and that's why it is unfortunate that the lectionary does not make the connection explicit: not least because the passages follow one after the other in the sequence of Sundays. Perhaps the omission was due to the realisation that there are times when one or other of these Sundays may be omitted from the Sunday lectionary due to the Easter season or the Solemnities that follow Easter. So, if Sunday 9 is missing, it makes no sense to begin the reading of Sunday 10's gospel with the phrase 'soon afterwards', since this would then relate to nothing we have already heard. Nevertheless, it is important for us to be aware of the link between these two passages. The story at the heart of today's gospel is unparalleled in any other gospel text: Jesus restores to life and returns to his mother the only son of a widow. It is not unparalleled in biblical literature, however. In 1 Kings 17:20-24, Elijah raises a dead man to life, returning him to his widowed mother. The details of the Elijah story are replicated in Luke's gospel to such an extent that we must assume the evangelist intends us to see Jesus' miracle as a prophetic action which mirrors and fulfils Elijah's deed in history long past. It may also be helpful at this stage to recall that although the Lukan story set in the town of Nain is not found in any other gospel, stories of Jesus raising the dead to life occur in all four canonical gospels. In Matthew and Mark (as well as in Luke) Jesus raises Jairus' 12 year old dead daughter to life. In John chapter 12, he famously calls the dead Lazarus from his tomb. Raising the dead to life is the ultimate act that Jesus performs as an illustration of the scope of the kingdom of God which he proclaims. It is the ultimate expression of the Good News Jesus announces – until his own resurrection, that is.

The text we are now considering shows every sign of having been carefully edited, along with the previous story of the cure of the centurion's seriously ill servant, in order to present Jesus as the ultimate prophet foretold by Moses: "Moses said to the people: "The Lord your God will raise up for you a prophet like myself, from among yourselves, from your own brothers; to him you must listen. I will raise up a prophet like yourself for them from their own brothers; I will put my words into his mouth and he shall tell them all I command him" (Deuteronomy 18:15.18). Luke introduces Jesus' first declaration of his prophetic ministry in the Nazareth synagogue, quoting a combination of texts from Isaiah (c.f. Sundays 3, 4C) and stating that "this text is being fulfilled today even as you listen" (Luke 4:21; Sunday 3C). From that point until now, Jesus' words and actions, substantially covered in the Ordinary Sundays of this year, have revealed him as the one who speaks and acts prophetically while at the same time fulfils prophecies of old. The gospels for last week and this show Jesus fulfilling the legendary prophets of old: Elijah and his disciple Elisha. Luke arranges his material in a deliberate way to highlight the connections between these two and Jesus. This does not mean, however, that Luke actually created the story. There are several features of the story, even in Luke's highly edited form, which point to it being historically rooted, and we will consider these before examining the lessons which the evangelist proposes for us in the narrative.

First, we are told that Jesus is accompanied by his disciples and a large number of people. The two groups are distinct. The crowd has a complex function in Luke. It grows as Jesus' ministry unfolds. It is normally silent, but on occasion, a member of the crowd will ask a question, or make some demand on Jesus or simply shout out (c.f. Luke 10:25; 12:13; 11:27). The crowd has particular function as Jesus moves to Jerusalem from 9:51 onwards, since it will provide the witnesses cited at Jesus' trial before the Jewish authorities about what he said and did in the open, and not in secret. Finally, this large crowd which continues at all times to grow demonstrates that Jesus is not merely an itinerant preacher who would occasionally attract the attention of passers-by. This is the leader of a new and expanding movement.

Second, Luke's description of the place makes it all the more probable that he is reporting the facts. There are episodes where Luke's geography is vague; for example, when he says that Jesus was in the house of Martha and Mary, he omits any reference to the house's location and also omits any references to the disciple's and crowds present on either side of that story (Luke 10:38-24). Luke places the story alongside its predecessor and links the two (we will consider this in greater detail on Sundays 15 and 16 of this year) by removing any difficult location identifiers. Second, in the story of the dead young man raised to life, Luke is explicit that Jesus was nearing a town called Nain (a town which has been identified), and that as he was nearing the gate, a funeral was taking place. Nain's gate has not so far been discovered by archaeologists, but burial grounds outside the town have been found. Likewise, Jewish funeral practices are indicated: the man is being carried on a bier and not in a closed coffin. This suggests Jewish practice rather than Roman custom. Third, Luke does not say that Jesus touched the body of the dead man: had Jesus done so it would have made him ritually unclean. Luke does say that Jesus touched the bier. This may have caused some ritual difficulty, but its purpose was clearly to stop the funeral procession. These and other details therefore point to an historically accurate account, edited in such a way as to highlight the prophetic significance of Jesus' action.

It has already been noted that all four gospels give accounts of one kind or another where Jesus raises the dead to life. The remarkable feature in each of these stories is that little attention is given to the person who is raised: not one of them speaks, and each of them is only mobile enough to prove that they are no longer dead. In this present story, we are made to focus on the mother of the dead man, and not on the man himself – just as in John's account of the raising of Lazarus, there is more focus on his sisters Martha and Mary than there is on Lazarus, and when Jairus' daughter is raised, the father has a more prominent role than his little girl. In the case of this young man, we are told that when Jesus saw the mother, he was filled with compassion for her. This word is used to translate a Greek expression which conveys the sense of an inner feeling that leads to an action for the good of the person who elicited a compassionate response. In this case, Jesus' compassion for the mother leads to him raising the dead son. The reason is not hard to understand when we consider the social climate of the time. In a highly patriarchal society, it was practically impossible for any woman to support herself without male assistance. Until she was married, a woman had to rely entirely on the support of her father. Once married, her husband took on that responsibility. A widow would have to look to her sons for the necessities of life. So, the tragedy of this story is that here is a woman with no husband and no son. It is not impossible that she might starve to death with no male to provide for her (the assumption seems to be that her own father will either be dead or in need of support from others). The widow is almost as dead as her only son – or could become so very soon! Hence Jesus' compassion.

For the first time in this gospel, the evangelist explicitly calls Jesus "the Lord" although the title has been used by others. It is a hint that something prophetic is about to happen. The Lord touches the bier, and the bearers stop. With a word (a prophetic word at that), Jesus, who has not touched the dead man at all, says "young man, I tell you to get up". And the young man sat up and began to walk. When Jesus raised Jairus' daughter, he said "Little girl, I tell you to get up" (Mark 5:41), and when he has instructed them to remove the stone from Lazarus' tomb, Jesus calls to the dead man, "Lazarus, come out". In each case, a prophetic word effects the raising to life. The prophetic word of God is also the creative word of God; therefore when The Lord gives the command, the word becomes deed. Also significant is the wording used for both Jairus' daughter and the young man at Nain: Jesus tells both to 'arise'. This is the word (*egeirō*) which is used of Jesus' own resurrection in the synoptic gospels. It is also the verb used when Jesus cures the paralysed man in 5:23-24, and when he heals the man with the withered hand in 6:8. There is one other example here of Luke using an expression found elsewhere. When he says that Jesus gave the young man back to his mother, he uses exactly the same words as are used in the Greek Septuagint (LXX) version of 1 Kings 17:23 (*edōken auton tę mētri autou*). The observant bystander may well have heard these words and remembered the Elijah story (or not as the case may be) but at least Luke uses the expression to lead into the reaction of the crowds: "a great prophet has appeared among us" is the Jerusalem rendition; the phrase should say that a great prophet has *been raised*, since the verb is once more *egeirō*.

This is an acknowledgement of an earlier prophecy in Luke's gospel. When John the Baptist's father Zechariah regained his speech, he proclaimed in the song we call the Benedictus, that the Lord has "raised up for us" a power for salvation – again, *egeirō*.

On a final note, this passage also looks to the next episode in Luke's gospel, although this is unfortunately not read on the Sundays of Ordinary time. It is the story of John sending two of his own disciples as messengers to Jesus to ask, "Are you the one who is to come, or must we wait for someone else?" (Luke 7:19). John does this, because reports of Jesus raising the dead man to life had gone out all through the countryside and Judea (Luke 7:17). Jesus sends the messengers back to tell John what they had seen and heard: "the blind see again, the lame walk, lepers are cleansed and the deaf hear, the dead are raised to life, the Good News is proclaimed to the poor" (Luke 7:22). With these words we are reminded of the way Jesus inaugurated his ministry: by proclaiming Good News to the poor, giving new sight to the blind etc. He insisted that these words were being fulfilled as the congregation in the synagogue at Nazareth listened, and he cited the example of two legendary prophets Elisha and Elijah who brought healing and resuscitation. Now, we have reached that part in Luke's ordered account of the things that Jesus said and did where he has fulfilled even the mighty deeds of those two prophets. Over the next two Sundays, Jesus, the prophet will demonstrate his prophetic gifts further. He does this first by reading the thoughts of both Simon the Pharisee, who doubts Jesus 'prophetic status on the basis of his association with a woman who had a 'bad reputation' in the town. Jesus demonstrates his powers by reading the thoughts (heart) of both Simon, and the woman whom he pronounces forgiven for her many sins. Next, when he asks who the crowds say he is, the disciples say that they state 'John the Baptist (a prophet); Elijah (the most famous of all ancient prophets – perhaps because he raised the dead to life); or any of the ancient prophets come back to life'. These may sound far-fetched, but the crowd have perceived the prophetic nature of Jesus' work. Following these two episodes, we will read that the prophet has concluded his Galilean ministry, and will head to Jerusalem: the rightful place for a prophet to die.

9 November

Dedication of the Lateran Basilica. John 2:13-22

Questions to ponder:

☐ The disciples, in response to Jesus' cleansing of the Temple, remembered the scripture, "zeal for your house will devour me (Psalm 69:9). What form should zeal for the house of God take for us today?

☐ Can concern for bricks and mortar blind us to the true meaning of 'the sanctuary' in our own time?

☐ It is difficult for us to relate the concept of sacrifice to our contemporary world: how do we recapture a sense of sacrifice in our worship of God 'in spirit and in truth' (c.f. John 4:23)?

When the Feast of the Dedication of the Lateran Basilica falls on a Sunday, we find that the themes of its gospel are not so far from those of the Sundays from this time of Year A. The confrontations between Jesus and the leadership of Judaism as well as the parables about the end-times and the judgement all fit in with today's gospel. The gospel setting today is John's account of Jesus cleansing the Temple, an episode recorded in all four gospels. Of course, this is not to say that all four gospels handle the incident in the same way; the synoptics set it at the end of Jesus' ministry, whereas John places it at the beginning. A moment's reflection on Jesus' relation with the religious customs and leadership of his time would suggest that it was not unlikely that sooner or later, Jesus would tackle head on that centre of the religious and national identity of the Palestine that he belonged to: the trouble is that the gospels have Jesus take the action he does in the Temple both sooner *and* later! So, the question arises, which account of the cleansing of the Temple is more likely to be historically accurate – the synoptic account, or the Johannine account? Could Jesus have cleansed the Temple on two different occasions? Does it matter? On balance, it could be argued that the Johannine account is the most accurate historically. John describes three separate Passover celebrations during Jesus' ministry and several other visits to Jerusalem and the Temple during that time. A cleansing at the beginning of his ministry could explain the origins of the mounting hostility that the authorities show Jesus in the gospel. The synoptics on the other hand have Jesus' ministry condensed into a single year (or at least not spanning more than one Passover). Since this means that Jesus makes only one trip to Jerusalem in his ministry (and takes a long time to do so in Luke: 9:51-19:27 is devoted to Jesus' decisive journey to Jerusalem), then inevitably that must be the trip at the end of his life since his crucifixion took place outside the city of Jerusalem walls. That being the case, the cleansing of the temple must be located within those few days in Jerusalem prior to his death. For the synoptics, the cleansing of the Temple is related to the Messiah taking possession of his Temple, and one way or another (we need not go into the details here), has to do with the false charges made against Jesus before the Sanhedrin. This smacks of an editorial arrangement of material to fit the single-year span of Jesus' ministry, rather than as an exact historical record of Jesus' controversial activity in the Temple. That having been said, the timing of this event is less important than is its theological significance. The three synoptics give varying degrees of detail about Jesus' action here, but all say that the cleansing was done against the background of both Is 56:7, "my house will be called a house of prayer for all the peoples", and Jeremiah 7:11, "Do you take this Temple that bears my name for a robbers' den?"

John uses these elements, but he adds particular significance in a very well developed theology centred on this action. In this account, John relies heavily on irony, so that conversations take place on different levels for different people. There is a play on words, there is a demand for a sign when a perfectly clear sign has been given, and there are themes which will be returned to later in the gospel. But first there is attention to detail. The first detail we notice is evidently the one that caught Jesus' attention too; the trade that was taking place in connection with the Temple cult. There are people selling cattle, sheep and pigeons; the animals connected with Temple sacrifice. There are also money-changers on hand, to allow the exchange of the Roman coinage which bore the imprint of the Roman emperor. Since graven images were not allowed according to the Jewish religion, they would be especially abhorrent in the Temple context; therefore, 'bureaux de change' were set up in the temple area to provide a service for those needing to change their coinage into the acceptable, i.e. imageless Tyrian coinage. None of these practices constituted something intrinsically evil, it has to be said, but Jesus evidently finds in their presence on the temple something repugnant. It should, of course, be remembered that what is commonly referred to as the Temple was in fact a large complex, consisting mostly of open courts. Whereas the authorities would no doubt justify these practices on the grounds that their presence was restricted to certain courts, Jesus is incensed that they are allowed to take place anywhere within the temple perimeter: if they are necessary, that necessity should be dealt with outside the temple walls. He makes a whip of cord, drives out the traders and the animals and scatters the money-changers' coins and knocks over their tables.

Perhaps it should be stressed at this point that it does nothing to the passage to read this as an expression of 'righteous anger' on Jesus' part, as we have all heard done in the past. Jesus' anger cannot have been very severe, if he vents it using a whip made out of string! How much damage is he going to inflict with that? Rather, the entire serious of actions that Jesus stages are more in the nature of a carefully acted out prophetic gesture than a fit of anger, and this is backed up by the way John tells the story. During his 'outburst', Jesus says nothing, but every verb that is used in describing the action applies to Jesus, i.e. it is Jesus who takes the (silent) initiative here: he _makes_ a whip out of cord, _drives_ trades and their animals from the Temple, _scatters_ the coins and _knocks over_ the money changers' tables. When Jesus speaks, it is to address the pigeon sellers: "Take all this out of here and stop turning my Father's house into a market" (John 2:17). There is a play on words here: literally, Jesus is saying, 'stop turning my Father's house into a house of trading' (_oikon emporiou_). We might ask why he addresses the pigeon sellers and not the others. A very practical suggestion has been made for this – Jesus can chase away sheep and cattle; he cannot chase pigeons in cages, so he demands their removal! The disciples are first to react to Jesus' prophetic gesture when they remember words of scripture, "Zeal for your house will devour me".

'The Jews', in response to his actions, have the temerity to ask, "What sign can you show us to justify what you have done?" (John 2:18). What more sign can they need? It is here that we come to the heart of the matter. The Temple was the house of God, the house of prayer even (c.f. Isaiah 56:7), but the Jews have turned it into a market (not a robber's den, as the synoptics have it). The house of God (c.f. 2 Samuel 7:1-17) is now re-designate by Jesus as 'his Father's house' (John 2:16). Jesus will say in the following chapter, "No one has gone up to heaven except the one who came down from heaven, the Son of Man who is in heaven", and the Son of Man is the one who reveals the Father, particularly when he is lifted up, so that all who believe in him might have eternal life. It is the Son of Man, raised up, who can reveal that God so loved the world that he sent his only Son, not to condemn the world, but so that through him the world might be saved (c.f. John 3:13-17). Jesus' complaint against his Jewish contemporaries is that they have turned his Father's house into a market (not a den of thieves as in the synoptics). Still later, he will predict, while in conversation with the Samaritan woman, that the hour will come, in fact it has by then arrived, when true worshippers will worship in spirit and in truth. The crux of the matter is that the Jewish institutions, while ostensibly serving the God of Israel, have ceased to function in a legitimate fashion. Jesus will replace these with himself as the true access to the God of Israel, because the God of Israel is the one he calls Father, because he is the only one to have come down from heaven. The one whom the Baptist described as the Lamb of God who takes away the sins of the world (John 1:29) has replaced the sacrifice of sheep and cattle, and the offerings of pigeons.

Interpreting correctly the demand for a sign depends on the realisation that there is here a play on words that unfortunately does not work too well in English, although the Jerusalem Bible does make an attempt to reproduce the effect of the Greek. The play depends on two different words being used for 'temple'. The first, which clearly refers to the physical temple within which Jesus performed his prophetic gesture, is _hieron_, but when Jesus speaks about the temple, which the narrator explains refers to his body, he uses another word for temple, _naos_. Now, this can equally refer to the 'bricks and mortar' temple, so the Jewish audience do not see the significance of Jesus; choice of words. The Jerusalem Bible tries to respect the difference by having Jesus talk of the destruction of this sanctuary' which is his body, rather than the temple, which is the edifice. But the confusion over the two meanings of the one word _naos_ only serves the evangelist's purpose in showing up the obtuseness of Jesus; audience, who fail to grasp his revelation. To those who have the eyes of faith to understand Jesus' revelation (he will emerge in later chapters as the One the Father has sent), Jesus speaks of his body, which will be destroyed, only to rise on the third day. As Jesus predicts, and as we have already seen, that revelation will come when the Son of Man is raised up. And as the narrator explains, it was when Jesus rose that the disciples remembered and believed the scripture and what he had said (John 2:22).

That, of course, will be the ultimate sign, the Hour when the Son of Man is glorified, and in him God is glorified (c.f. John 13:31). But if they will not understand the sign of the cleansing of the temple, by the one who can speak of the house of his Father, if this sign causes division for or against Jesus, how much more will the sign of the Son of Man lifted up be a sign that causes division for or against Jesus, because God sent his son, not to condemn the world, but so that through him the world might be saved, but, "whoever refuses to believe is condemned already, because he has refused to believe in the name of God's only Son" (John 3:18).